Lecture Notes in Computer Science 1926

Edited by G. Goos, J. Hartmanis and J. van Leeuwen

T0223567

Springer

Berlin
Heidelberg
New York
Barcelona
Hong Kong
London
Milan
Paris
Singapore
Tokyo

Mathai Joseph (Ed.)

Formal Techniques
in Real-Time and
Fault-Tolerant Systems

6th International Symposium, FTRTFT 2000
Pune, India, September 20-22, 2000
Proceedings

 Springer

Series Editors

Gerhard Goos, Karlsruhe University, Germany
Juris Hartmanis, Cornell University, NY, USA
Jan van Leeuwen, Utrecht University, The Netherlands

Volume Editor

Mathai Joseph
Tata Research Development and Design Centre
54B, Hadapsar Industrial Estate, Pune 411013, India
E-mail: mathai@pune.tcs.co.in

Cataloging-in-Publication Data applied for

Die Deutsche Bibliothek - CIP-Einheitsaufnahme

Formal techniques in real time and fault tolerant systems : 6th
international symposium ; proceedings / FTRTFT 200, Pune, India,
September 20 - 22, 2000. Mathai Joseph (ed.). - Berlin ; Heidelberg ;
New York ; Barcelona ; Hong Kong ; London ; Milan ; Paris ; Singapore; Tokyo :
Springer, 2000
    (Lecture Notes in Computer Science ; 1926)
    ISBN 3-540-41055-4

CR Subject Classification (1998): D.3.1, F.3.1, C.1.m, C.3, B.3.4, B.1.3

ISSN 0302-9743
ISBN 3-540-41055-4 Springer-Verlag Berlin Heidelberg New York

Springer-Verlag Berlin Heidelberg New York
a member of BertelsmannSpringer Science+Business Media GmbH
© Springer-Verlag Berlin Heidelberg 2000
Printed in Germany

Typesetting: Camera-ready by author
Printed on acid-free paper   SPIN 10722874   06/3142   5 4 3 2 1 0

Preface

The six Schools and Symposia on Formal Techniques in Real Time and Fault Tolerant Systems (FTRTFT) have seen the field develop from tentative explorations to a far higher degree of maturity, and from being under the scrutiny of a few interested software designers and academics to becoming a well-established area of inquiry. A number of new topics, such as hybrid systems, have been germinated at these meetings and cross-links explored with related subjects such as scheduling theory. There has certainly been progress during these 12 years, but it is sobering to see how far and how fast practice has moved ahead in the same time, and how much more work remains to be done before the design of a mission-critical system can be based entirely on sound engineering principles underpinned by solid scientific theory.

The Sixth School and Symposium were organized by the Tata Research Development and Design Centre in Pune, India. The lectures at the School were given by Ian Hayes (U. of Queensland), Paritosh Pandya (Tata Institute of Fundamental Research), Willem-Paul de Roever (Christian Albrechts U.) and Joseph Sifakis (VERIMAG). There were three invited lectures at the Symposium, by Werner Damm (U. of Oldenburg), Nicholas Halbwachs (VERIMAG) and Yoram Moses (Technion).

A sizable number of submissions were received for the Symposium from authors representing 16 different countries. The papers were reviewed by the Programme Committee, who along with other specialists made up a panel of 50 reviewers. After electronic discussion by the Programme Committee, 21 papers were selected for presentation.

The School and Symposium were organized by a committee consisting of Aditya Nori, Purandar Bhaduri and R. Venkatesh. They were assisted in no small measure by Sandeep Bodas, Kalyanmoy Dihingia, Adi Irani, Dinaz Irani, Shirish Lele, Nitin Purandare, Jyotsna Ravishankar and Parag S. Vazare, who all deserve particular thanks for all their help.

The School and Symposium were supported most generously by Tata Consultancy Services and our thanks go to S. Ramadorai, the Chief Executive Officer.

Finally, having survived the anxieties of organizing the first FTRTFT meeting in Warwick in 1988, it has given me great pleasure to participate in the organization of FTRTFT 2000 in Pune, which marks the first time that the meeting has been held outside Europe.

September 2000   Mathai Joseph

Program Committee

R. Alur (Univ. of Pennsylvania)
A. Arora (Univ. of Ohio)
H. Hannson (Mälardalen Univ.)
I. Hayes (Univ. of Queensland)
L. Huimin (IOS, Beijing)
H. Jifeng (IIST Macau)
M. Joseph (chair) (TRDDC)
Z. Liu (Univ. of Leicester)
A. Mok (Univ. of Texas)
K.V. Nori (TRDDC)
P. Pandya (TIFR)
A. Pnueli (Weizmann Inst)
K. Ramamritham (IIT Mumbai)
S. Ramesh (IIT Mumbai)
A. Ravn (Aalborg Univ.)
H. Rischel (TU Denmark)
W.-P. de Roever (CAU Kiel)
N. Shankar (SRI)
J. Vytopil (KU Nijmegen)
S. Yovine (VERIMAG Grenoble)

Steering Committee

M. Joseph (TRDDC)
A. Pnueli (Weizmann Inst)
W.-P. de Roever (CAU Kiel)
J. Vytopil (KU Nijmegen)

Organizing Committee

P. Bhaduri
A. V. Nori
R. Venkatesh

Referees

Tamarah Arons
Parosh Aziz Abdulla
Rana Barua
Purandar Bhaduri
Ahmed Bouajjani
Alan Burns
A. Cerone
Supratik Chakrabarty
Jing Chen
Bruno Dutertre
Kai Engelhardt
Colin Fidge
Felix C. Gartner
Dimitar Guelev
Nicolas Halbwachs
Anna Ingolfsdottir
Henrik Ejersbo Jensen

Josva Kleist
Kaare Kristoffersen
Vinay Kulkarni
Guangyun Li
Xiaoshan Li
Xuandong Li
Kamal Lodaya
Gavin Lowe
Richard Moore
Madhavan Mukund
Kedar Namjoshi
K. Narayan Kumar
R. Narayanan
S. Parthasarathy
Sasi Punnekkat
Zongyan Qiu
Xu Qiwen

John Rushby
Partha S. Roop
Manoranjan Satpathy
Steve Schneider
R.K. Shyamasundar
G. Sivakumar
Graeme Smith
A. Sowmya
Ashok Sreenivas
Henrik Thane
Dang Van Hung
R. Venkatesh
Thomas Wilke
Wang Yi
Naijun Zhan

Sponsor

Tata Consultancy Services and
Tata Research Development and Design Centre
54-B, Hadapsar Industrial Estate
Pune-411013
INDIA

Table of Contents

Validation

Refinement

Verification

Logic and Automata

Author Index

Stability of Discrete Sampled Systems

N. Halbwachs[1], J.-F. Héry[2], J.-C. Laleuf[2], and X. Nicollin[1]

[1] Vérimag, Grenoble - France
{Nicolas.Halbwachs,Xavier.Nicollin}@imag.fr
[2] EDF/DER, Clamart - France
{Jean-Francois.Hery,Jean-Claude.Laleuf}@der.edfgdf.fr

Abstract. We consider the wide class of real-time systems that periodically sample their inputs. A desirable property of such systems is that
their outputs should be, in some sense, more precise when the sampling
period gets shorter. An approximation of this property consists in requiring that, whenever the inputs don't change, the outputs stabilize after
a finite number of steps. We present a set of heuristics to check this stability property, in the case of purely Boolean systems. These heuristics
have been experimented on a nuclear plant control software, and have
been shown to dramatically reduce the cost of stability analysis.

1 Introduction

Many real-time embedded systems, appearing in industrial control (e.g., plant
supervision, flight control, ...), are *periodic sampled systems*. The global behavior of such systems is quite simple: it consists in a periodic loop, sampling inputs
— from sensors or, more generally, from a shared memory — computing the corresponding outputs, and updating the local memory for the next step. Generally
speaking, this periodic behavior is a discrete approximation of an ideal, analog,
behavior, which would instantly compute a continuous result from continuous
inputs, and instantly react to any relevant discrete change of the inputs. With
this intuitive intention in mind, one would naturally expect that the shorter
is the period, the more accurate is the approximation. If we restrict ourselves
to *discrete* control systems, shortening the period should only involve a more
precise perception of input events — i.e., detecting transient changes, suitably
ordering events that was previously considered simultaneous, ... — and a faster
reaction to these events. Let us call *monotonicity* this intuitive property.

Now, in actual discrete systems, it happens that, in some situations, some
Boolean outputs of the system oscillate permanently while the inputs don't
change. This behavior obviously violates our intuitive notion of monotonicity,
since shortening the period would only speed up the oscillation (see Fig. 1).

Such a phenomenon is generally considered as an error, and appears to be
very difficult to detect statically, since it can happen only in very specific states of
the system. A system where it cannot happen is called *stable*: in a stable system,
whenever the inputs remain unchanged, the outputs reach stable values after a

M. Joseph (Ed.): FTRTFT 2000, LNCS 1926, pp. 1–11, 2000.
© Springer-Verlag Berlin Heidelberg 2000

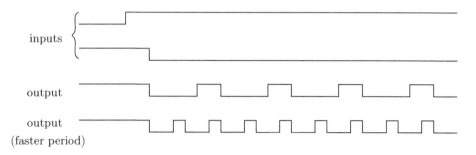

inputs

(faster period)

Fig. 1. Output oscillation

finite number of periods. Deciding system stability may require the knowledge of its whole state graph.

Notice that stability is also an important concern in other domains, like in the *superstep* semantics of statecharts [HN96], or in sequential function charts [IEC93]. The problem of stability is also closely related to *causality* is synchronous languages and to the analysis of combinational loops in circuits [Mal93,SBT96,HM95,NK99].

The goal of this paper is to propose some heuristic techniques allowing, in most practical cases,

– either to ensure the system stability without building its state graph;
– or to focus the problem to some small parts of the system, corresponding to small parts of the state graph, which can be efficiently built.

We restrict ourselves to discrete sampled systems: they are formalized in Section 2, as standard *Mealy machines*, which can classically be represented as *operator networks* (sequential circuits), made of combinational Boolean gates and Boolean memories. In Section 3, we formally define the notion of stability, and the little stronger property that will be actually analyzed: it requires that whenever the inputs stay stable, the outputs *and the state* (i.e., the memories) stabilize after a finite number of steps. In Section 4, we show that each strongly connected component (SCC) of the operator network can be analyzed in turn, and that the stability of some simple SCCs, containing only one memory, can be shown. In Section 5, we use local necessary conditions of instability, called *local cycle conditions*, the unfeasibility of which is often easy to show. In Section 6, we broaden these cycle conditions, using approximate values of the involved stable variables.

2   Definitions and Notations

Throughout the paper, we will assimilate discrete systems with standard Mealy machines. Let $\mathbb{B} = \{0,1\}$ be the set of Boolean values, and let us note the disjunction additively, the conjunction multiplicatively, and the negation by the "*bar*" notation ($\overline{f} = \neg f$). A *Mealy machine* with n state variables, m input variables and p output variables, is a pair (τ, δ) where

- τ is a total function from $\mathbb{B}^{m+n}$ to $\mathbb{B}^n$ (transition function) given as a vector $[\tau_k]_{k=1...n}$ of n functions from $\mathbb{B}^{m+n}$ to $\mathbb{B}$. If $s \in \mathbb{B}^n$ (state), $\iota \in \mathbb{B}^m$ (input), $\tau(\iota, s)$ denotes the vector $[\tau_k(\iota, s)]_{k=1...n} \in \mathbb{B}^n$ (next state from s for ι).
- δ is a total function from $\mathbb{B}^{m+n}$ to $\mathbb{B}^p$ (output function), also given as a vector $[\delta_\ell]_{\ell=1...p}$ of p functions from $\mathbb{B}^{m+n}$ to $\mathbb{B}$. $\delta(\iota, s)$ is the output in s for ι.

An *input sequence* to the machine is an infinite sequence $\mathcal{I} = (\iota_0, \iota_1, \ldots, \iota_i, \ldots)$ of vectors of $\mathbb{B}^m$. The *run* and the *image* of the machine on such an input sequence $\mathcal{I}$ are, respectively, the sequence $\mathcal{S} = (s_0, s_1, \ldots, s_i, \ldots)$ of elements of $\mathbb{B}^n$ (states), and the sequence $\mathcal{O} = (\omega_0, \omega_1, \ldots, \omega_i, \ldots)$ of elements of $\mathbb{B}^p$ (outputs), defined by

$$s_0 = 0^n \text{ (initial state}^1) \text{ and } \forall i \geq 0, \quad s_{i+1} = \tau(\iota_i, s_i), \quad \omega_i = \delta(\iota_i, s_i)$$

More concretely, we will name input, output, and state variables by identifiers, and define the transition functions using the "*prime*" notation (read x' as *next* x).

Example 1: For instance, the system of Boolean equations:

$$x' = \overline{b}\,(a + x) \quad y' = \overline{z} + y.\overline{x} \quad z' = \overline{y}\,(\overline{x} + z) \quad u = y + z$$

is a convenient way of describing a machine with 2 input variables (a, b), 3 state variables (x, y, z), and 1 output variable (u), with

$$\tau_1(\iota, s) = \neg\iota[2] \wedge (\iota[1] \vee s[1]) \qquad \tau_2(\iota, s) = \neg s[3] \vee (s[2] \wedge \neg s[1])$$
$$\tau_3(\iota, s) = \neg s[2] \wedge (\neg s[1] \vee s[3]) \qquad \delta(\iota, s) = s[2] \vee s[3]$$

Another classical way of describing a Mealy machine is by an **operator network**. Boolean functions are described by their gate networks, and state variables correspond to memories. Fig. 2 shows a network corresponding to the above machine.

An operator network can be viewed as a directed graph, the nodes of which are the operators and memories of the network, and the edges of which are the "wires" oriented according to the direction of data circulation. In such a graph, we will use the standard notion of "strongly connected components[2]" (SCC for short): In Fig. 2, the two SCCs of the network are shown in dashed boxes. Let us recall that SCCs can be determined in linear time [Tar72].

---

[1] We could have let the initial state be a parameter of the machine. The choice of 0^n is for simplicity.

[2] i.e., a subset of operators, each pair of which is connected by a directed path.

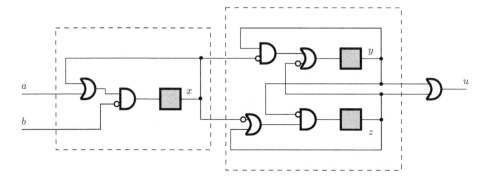

Fig. 2. a Mealy machine as an operator network

Finally, we will make an extensive use of the following representation of memories by two-state automata: let x be a state variable, whose evolution is defined by the equation "$x' = f_x$". Let us consider the Shannon expansion of the Boolean function f_x according to x: $f_x = \overline{x}.f_x^0 + x.f_x^1$, where f_x^0 and f_x^1 are independent of x. Then f_x^0 (resp., $\overline{f_x^1}$) is the condition that sets the memory x from 0 to 1 (resp., that resets it from 1 to 0); we will note it set_x (resp. $reset_x$). As a consequence, each memory x has a canonical representation as the opposite two-state automaton.

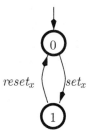

For instance, in Example 1, the state variable z is defined by the equation $z' = \overline{y}(\overline{x} + z)$. Its Shannon expansion according to z is $z' = \overline{z}\,\overline{y}\,\overline{x} + z\overline{y}$, so $set_z = \overline{y}\,\overline{x}$ and $reset_z = y$.

3 Stability

We formalize, now, the notion of stability we want to analyze: an infinite sequence $\mathcal{I} = (\iota_0, \iota_1, \ldots, \iota_i, \ldots)$ is said to be *ultimately stable* if it is constant from some term, i.e., if

$$\exists i \in \mathbb{N} \text{ such that } \forall j \geq i, \iota_j = \iota_i$$

A machine is said to be *weakly stable* if and only if, on every ultimately stable input sequence, its image (sequence of outputs) is ultimately stable.

First notice that this property is neither trivial to specify, nor to verify. As a temporal logic formula [Pnu77], it would be written like

$$\Box\left(\Box(\iota \equiv \bigcirc\iota) \Rightarrow \Diamond\Box(\omega \equiv \bigcirc\omega)\right)$$

and verifying it by model-checking [VW86] is likely to be very expensive.

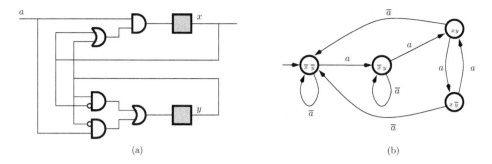

(a)   (b)

Fig. 3. A simple machine and its state graph

Weak stability is the property we are interested in, in view of the arguments given in the Introduction. In fact, we will consider a stronger property, because it is easier to check, and because experience shows that, on actual applications, it is generally very close to the wanted property. This stronger property states that, in presence of ultimately stable inputs, the *state* stabilizes in a finite number of steps:

A machine is said to be *strongly stable* (or simply *stable*) if and only if, on every ultimately stable input sequence, its run (sequence of states) is ultimately stable. Obviously, strong stability implies weak stability.

Example 2: Fig. 3.a shows the network of a machine with 1 input a, 2 state variables x, y, and one output x, defined by the system of equations

$$x' = a(x + y) \qquad y' = a\overline{y} + \overline{x}\,y$$

Fig. 3.b shows the graph of reachable states of the machine. Possible unstabilities appear on this graph as circuits: apart from self-loops (which cannot correspond to unstabilities), the graph contains 3 elementary circuits:

$$(1)\ (\overline{x}\,\overline{y})\xrightarrow{a}(\overline{x}\,y)\xrightarrow{a}(xy)\xrightarrow{\overline{a}}(\overline{x}\,\overline{y})$$
$$(2)\ (\overline{x}\,\overline{y})\xrightarrow{a}(\overline{x}\,y)\xrightarrow{a}(xy)\xrightarrow{a}(x\,\overline{y})\xrightarrow{\overline{a}}(\overline{x}\,\overline{y})$$
$$(3)\ (xy)\xrightarrow{a}(x\,\overline{y})\xrightarrow{a}(xy)$$

Circuits (1) and (2) don't correspond to unstabilities, since their traversal involves input changes. Now, circuit (3) corresponds to an oscillation when the input a remains true. This oscillation does not change the output x but makes the state variable y oscillate. As a consequence, the machine is weakly stable, but not strongly stable.

This example shows that both weak and strong stability can be checked on the state graph of a machine, by examining its elementary circuits. Now, this method is clearly expensive, and unfeasible for complex systems. This is why we investigate, now, heuristic methods to avoid the construction of the state graph.

In the current state of our research, these heuristics only apply to strong stability. Let us stress out that, in the rest of the paper, we will never consider state graphs and their circuits, but only the operators networks and their strongly connected components!

4   Strongly Connected Components

A very first (obvious) remark is that a memory cannot oscillate if its input is stable; so, a memory can only *cause* an unstability if it appears in a loop of the network. An important consequence is that we can consider each strongly connected component of the network separately:

– An SCC of the network is *stable*, if, considered alone, it represents a stable machine. A sufficient condition for a machine to be stable is that all the SCCs of its network be stable.
– A memory that doesn't belong to an SCC cannot introduce unstability.

Another simple case concerns SCCs that contain only one memory: let this memory be associated with a state variable x, defined by the equation "$x' = f_x(x, y_1, \ldots, y_k)$", where the y_i are either inputs or state variables from other SCCs. The function f_x is said to be *monotonic* in x, if, for each valuation of $y_1, \ldots, y_k$, the implication $f_x(0, y_1, \ldots, y_k) \Rightarrow f_x(1, y_1, \ldots, y_k)$ holds.

Condition 1: If an SCC contains only one memory x, and if f_x is monotonic, the considered SCC is stable.

For instance, in our Example 1 (Fig. 2), the network has two SCCs: the former contains only the memory x, and the latter contains both y and z. Then, since the function defining x, $\overline{b}(a + x)$, is monotonic in x, the former SCC is stable, and we only have to analyze the second SCC, considering x as its only input.

5   Local Cycle Conditions

Our second criterion looks very weak at first glance, but provides surprising good results [HL97]: for a memory x to oscillate, it must be able to change in both directions with the same values for input variables. More formally, there should exist two instants t_1 and t_2 at which the inputs are the same, and such that set_x holds at t_1 and $reset_x$ holds at t_2. If ι (resp. s) represents the vector of input (resp., state) variables, if s_1 and s_2 represent the values of state variables at t_1 and t_2, respectively, this condition can be written

$$\exists \iota, s_1, s_2, \; set_x(\iota, s_1).reset_x(\iota, s_2) = 1$$

Moreover, state variables that have already been found stable can be considered (as inputs) to have the same values in s_1 and s_2. So, in general, we will have a set σ of stable variables (including inputs) and a set ξ of remaining variables, and, for each $x \in \xi$, the considered condition will be

$$\exists \sigma, \xi_1, \xi_2, \ set_x(\sigma, \xi_1).reset_x(\sigma, \xi_2) = 1$$

Let us note $\mathcal{U}_x^\sigma$ the condition $\quad \exists \xi_1, \xi_2, \ set_x(\sigma, \xi_1).reset_x(\sigma, \xi_2) \quad$ and call it the *local cycle condition* for x in σ.

Condition 2: If σ is a set of inputs or stable variables, the unsatisfiability of $\mathcal{U}_x^\sigma$ is a sufficient condition for x to be stable[3].

This provides us with an algorithm to analyze an SCC of the network: let ι and s be, respectively, the set of input and of state variables of the SCC. The following algorithm returns in σ (resp., in ξ) the set of memories that have been found stable (resp., the stability of which is not guaranteed):

> *Algorithm 1:*   start with $\sigma = \iota$; $\xi = s$;
>   while $\exists x \in \xi$ such that $\mathcal{U}_x^\sigma \equiv 0$ do
> $\xi := \xi \setminus \{x\}$; $\sigma := \sigma \cup \{x\}$;
>   end while

Example 3: Let us consider an SCC with 2 inputs a and b, and two state variables x and y, defined by $\quad x' = \overline{y} + \overline{a} \qquad y' = \overline{b}(x + y)$
We have $\quad set_x = \overline{y} + \overline{a} \quad , \quad reset_x = y.a \quad , \quad set_y = x.\overline{b} \quad , \quad reset_y = b$
Starting the algorithm with $\sigma = \{a, b\}, \xi = \{x, y\}$, we get

$$\begin{aligned} \mathcal{U}_x^\sigma &= \exists y_1, y_2, \ set_x(a, b, y_1).reset_x(a, b, y_2) \\ &= \exists y_1, y_2, \ (\overline{y_1} + \overline{a})(y_2.a) \\ &= \exists y_1, y_2, \ \overline{y_1}.y_2.a \\ &= a \\ &\not\equiv 0 \quad \text{(so, nothing can be concluded for } x) \\ \mathcal{U}_y^\sigma &= \exists x_1, x_2 \ set_y(a, b, x_1).reset_y(a, b, x_2) \\ &= \exists x_1, x_2 \ (x_1.\overline{b}).b \\ &= 0 \end{aligned}$$

So, y is stable, and we iterate with $\sigma = \{a, b, y\}$ and $\xi = \{x\}$. For this new σ, we get

$$\begin{aligned} \mathcal{U}_x^\sigma &= set_x(a, b, y).reset_x(a, b, y) \\ &= (\overline{y} + \overline{a}).(y.a) \\ &= 0 \end{aligned}$$

and x is found stable too.

A more precise condition can be found, by considering *pairs* of depending state variables in the same SCC. Let $\mathcal{D}(x)$ be the set of state variables that belong to the same SCC as x, and appear either in set_x or in $reset_x$. Assume the previous algorithm failed to show the stability of two variables x, y, with $y \in \mathcal{D}(x)$. We already know that, when $\mathcal{U}_y^\sigma$ is false, y is stable. So we can split the definition of $\mathcal{U}_x^\sigma$ into two cases:

---

[3] Notice that Condition 1 is only a special case of Condition 2.

- the case where $\mathcal{U}_y^\sigma$ holds
- the case where $\mathcal{U}_y^\sigma = 0$, in which case the value of y can be assumed to be stable (i.e., $y_1 = y_2$).

This leads to a stronger condition of unstability for x:

$$\mathcal{U}_{x,y}^\sigma = \exists \boldsymbol{\xi_1}, \boldsymbol{\xi_2}, \ (\mathcal{U}_y^\sigma.set_x(\boldsymbol{\sigma}, \boldsymbol{\xi_1}).reset_x(\boldsymbol{\sigma}, \boldsymbol{\xi_2})) \\ + (\overline{\mathcal{U}_y^\sigma}.set_x(\boldsymbol{\sigma}, \boldsymbol{\xi_1}).reset_x(\boldsymbol{\sigma}, \boldsymbol{\xi_2}).(y_1 = y_2))$$

Condition 3: If σ is a set of inputs or stable variables, if $y \in \mathcal{D}(x)$, the unsatisfiability of $\mathcal{U}_{x,y}^\sigma$ is a sufficient condition for x to be stable.

Obviously, this condition is more likely to succeed for x and y satisfying $\mathcal{U}_x^\sigma.\mathcal{U}_y^\sigma = 0$.

When Algorithm 1 fails to show that all memories of an SCC are stable (i.e., returns $\xi \neq \emptyset$), we can apply the following one:

Algorithm 2:   while $\exists x \in \xi$ such that $\exists y \in \mathcal{D}(x)$ such that $\mathcal{U}_{x,y}^\sigma \equiv 0$ do
$\qquad\qquad\qquad \xi := \xi \setminus \{x\}; \ \sigma := \sigma \cup \{x\};$
$\qquad\quad$ end while

Of course, this approach could be continued with 3 variables and more, but would become more and more expensive.

Example: Let's come back to Example 1. In Section 4, we showed that the first SCC of the network — reduced to the state variable x —, is stable. Now, if we apply Algorithm 1 to the second SCC, we get:

$$\sigma = \{x\}, \ \xi = \{y, z\}$$
$$\mathcal{U}_y^\sigma = \exists z_1, z_2, \ x.\overline{z1}.z2 = x$$
$$\mathcal{U}_z^\sigma = \exists y_1, y_2, \ \overline{x}.\overline{y_1}.y_2 = \overline{x}$$

So, nothing can be deduced about the stability of y and z. Now, algorithm 2 provides:

$$\mathcal{U}_{y,z}^\sigma = \overline{x}.x + x.(\exists z, \ x.\overline{z}.z) = 0$$
$$\mathcal{U}_{z,y}^\sigma = x.\overline{x} + \overline{x}.(\exists y, \ \overline{x}.\overline{y}.y) = 0$$

from which we can conclude that y and z are stable.

6 Approximation of Stable Values

When the previous heuristics fail to show the stability of an SCC, the SCC contains variables with feasible cycle conditions $\mathcal{U}$: these are formulas involving input and state variables, some of which are already found stable. We can try to show that no *stable* values of the stable state variables can make the cycle condition feasible. Now, we don't know the possible stable values of state variables. Here, we propose [HL97] to use an approximation of these values: as a matter of fact, for each state variable x, we have the following information about its stable values:

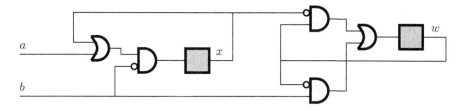

Fig. 4. The network of Example 4

When x stabilizes to 1, surely $reset_x$ is false

When x stabilizes to 0, surely set_x is false

In other words, the stable values $\hat{x}$ of x satisfy: $set_x \Rightarrow \hat{x} \Rightarrow \overline{reset_x}$

So, if, in a cycle condition $\mathcal{U}$, we replace each occurrence of x (resp., of $\overline{x}$) by $\overline{reset_x}$ (resp., by $\overline{set_x}$) we get a new condition $\mathcal{U}'$ which is weaker than $\mathcal{U}$ $(\mathcal{U} \Rightarrow \mathcal{U}')$. If $\mathcal{U}'$ happens to be identically false, so is $\mathcal{U}$, and the considered cycle cannot introduce unstability. Of course, this can be tried with all state variables appearing in $\mathcal{U}$, or with combinations of these variables.

Example 4: Let us consider the system represented in Fig. 4, whose system of equations is: $x' = \overline{b}(a + x)$, $w' = b.\overline{w} + \overline{x}.w$.

There are two SCCs, one containing x and the other containing w. The first one is found stable, as in Section 4. In the second SCC, none of our previous heuristics works:

- $f_w = b.\overline{w} + \overline{x}.w$ is not monotonic in w
- $\mathcal{U}_w^{\{a,b,x\}} = b.x \not\equiv 0$
- $\mathcal{D}(w) = \emptyset$

Now the local cycle condition for w in $\{a, b, x\}$ is $\mathcal{U}_w^{\{a,b,x\}} = b.x$. Since $reset_x = b$, we get $\mathcal{U}' = b.\overline{b}$, which is identically false. This shows that w is stable.

7   Application and Future Work

From an industrial point of view, stability is by no means a theoretical problem.

The first reason is that oscillating Booleans are frequently observed in nuclear power plants. This may result from various causes, including hysteresis phenomena concerning analog signals, or other physical or technological reasons; but there has been evidence of such oscillations due to the functional specification level itself. In these cases, formal analysis would have detected the problem before it actually occured.

The second implication of instability concerns distributed command: as many industrial systems are implemented on several processors (and this is obviously the case in power plants), stability often appears as a necessary condition for the global validity of the command system. Therefore, it may be useful to predict both stability itself, and the maximum delay within which it is reached.

Being aware of these reasons amongst others, the French nuclear safety authority (IPSN) is keeping a close look on formal methods, even if it has not *formally* recommended them up to now. Anticipating the recommendation, the French utility Electricité de France (EDF) has already undertaken an R&D program on the subject; it is interesting to point out that Boolean stability was the first item to be studied.

The techniques proposed in this paper have been experimented on actual systems (control software for nuclear plants). All the presented examples come from this actual software, and were considered to be problematic before being analyzed. These experiments show that the proposed heuristics give precise results, in practice: almost all the cases which were not found stable presented actual unstability problems. These experiments were performed by hand, but the feasibility of such a manual application shows that its cost has nothing to do with that of exact verification, a point which is highly confirmed by the first experiments with the implemented prototype.

These results are so encouraging that an actual industrial tool for checking stability is under implementation. The tool takes system descriptions written in LUSTRE [HCRP91], or by means of "logical functional diagrams" used at EDF. All the Boolean conditions are dealt with using BDDs [Ake78,Bry86].

Stability should be a very interesting concept in synchronous programming [Hal93]. In fact, the stable state graph is an abstraction very similar — on a macroscopic level — to the synchronous abstraction, that considers as atomic all the "micro-steps" performed in the same reaction. From this point of view, stability is the macroscopic counterpart of the "causality" [SBT96,HM95,NK99] property, considered in synchronous programs. An interesting perspective would be to adapt the techniques proposed here to obtain a cheap causality checker for synchronous programs and circuits.

The notion of stability can also be very fruitful in verification. For the kind of systems we consider, critical properties are very likely to be required to hold only in stable states. In this case, only the reduced graph of stable states has to be examined, and this can dramatically reduce the cost of verification by model-checking. For instance, in a machine with n inputs, if all the inputs are sampled in a memory before being used, the number of states is multiplied by 2^n with respect to the number of stable states.

References

Ake78.   S. B. Akers. Binary decision diagrams. *IEEE Transactions on Computers*, C-27(6), 1978.

Bry86.   R. E. Bryant. Graph-based algorithms for boolean function manipulation. *IEEE Transactions on Computers*, C-35(8):677–692, 1986.

Hal93.   N. Halbwachs. *Synchronous programming of reactive systems*. Kluwer Academic Pub., 1993.

HCRP91. N. Halbwachs, P. Caspi, P. Raymond, and D. Pilaud. The synchronous dataflow programming language LUSTRE. *Proceedings of the IEEE*, 79(9):1305–1320, September 1991.

HL97.   J.-F. Héry and J.-C. Laleuf. Stabilité de la réalisation des DFL. Technical Report Electricité de France, 1997.

HM95.   N. Halbwachs and F. Maraninchi. On the symbolic analysis of combinational loops in circuits and synchronous programs. In *Euromicro'95*, Como (Italy), September 1995.

HN96.   D. Harel and A. Naamad. The Statemate semantics of Statecharts. *ACM Transactions on Software Engineering and Methodology*, 5(4), October 1996.

IEC93.   IEC. International standard for programmable controllers: Programming languages. Technical report iec1131, part 3, International Electrotecnical Commission, 1993.

Mal93.   S. Malik. Analysis of cyclic combinational circuits. In *ICCAD'93*, Santa Clara (Ca), 1993.

NK99.   K. S. Namjoshi and R. P. Kurshan. Efficient analysis of cyclic definitions. In *11th International Conference on Computer Aided Verification, CAV'99*, Trento (Italy), July 1999.

Pnu77.   A. Pnueli. The temporal logic of programs. In *18th Symp. on the Foundations of Computer Science*, Providence R.I., 1977. IEEE.

SBT96.   T. R. Shiple, G. Berry, and H. Touati. Constructive analysis of cyclic circuits. In *International Design and Testing Conference IDTC'96*, Paris, France, 1996.

Tar72.   R. E. Tarjan. Depth-first search and linear graph algorithms. *SIAM Journal on Computing*, 1:146–160, 1972.

VW86.   M. Y. Vardi and P. Wolper. An automata-theoretic approach to automatic program verification. In *Symposium on Logic in Computer Science*, June 1986.

Issues in the Refinement of
Distributed Programs
(Invited Talk)

Yoram Moses

Department of Electrical Engineering
Technion—Israel Institute of Technology
Haifa, 32000 Israel
moses@ee.technion.ac.il

Developing correct computer programs is a notoriously difficult task, which has attracted a significant intellectual effort over the past decades. One attractive methodology that has been proposed to tackle this problem consists of systems for *program refinement*, in which a calculus is given for transforming, often in a top-down manner, the specification of a computational task into a program implementing this specification (excellent introductions to refinement are Back and von Wright 1998 and Morgan 1994). Calculi for the refinement of sequential programs are by now a mature and well-established field. In this abstract, I wish to discuss some issues that arise when we try to develop a refinement calculus for distributed programs. This discussion is based on a joint project with Ron van der Meyden and Kai Engelhardt of the University of New South Wales, Sydney, Australia. Some insight into the technical aspects of the approach we are pursuing can be found in Engelhardt et al. 1998 and 2000 and in van der Meyden and Moses 2000.[1] An obvious point to start a discussion of refinement for distributed programs is the sequential case. The subtlety and inherent complexity of distributed systems make the task of refinement for distributed programs much harder. The purpose of this abstract is to discuss, in an informal fashion, some of the distinctive issues that seem to play a role in this effort. The hope is that a discussion of these issues may contribute to other work on formal and algorithmic approaches to distributed computation.

On sequential refinement: We have described the goal of a refinement calculus as being the transformation of a specification into an implementation. Roughly speaking, then, we start out with an object of one type—*specification*—and end up with an object of another type—an *executable program*. In the process of transforming the former to the latter we may have "intermediate" objects that do not qualify as being pure specifications nor as being executable programs. To overcome this disparity, it is common to define a larger class of programs that will contain specifications and executable programs, as well as all of the intermediate-form programs that can arise in the course of the refinement process. A natural question, then, is what this space should consist of. For sequential programs,

---

[1] Insights described here have been obtained as part of this joint work; any mistakes or misrepresentations are my own doing.

M. Joseph (Ed.): FTRTFT 2000, LNCS 1926, pp. 12–17, 2000.

the picture is simplified by the fact that the model and goals are clear and well-defined. A sequential program starts at an initial state and, if it ever halts, ends at a final state. Moreover, its input is provided in the initial state, and its output is given in the final state. Notice that a nonterminating execution of a such a program is considered useless. Typically all that we care about is the possibly partial input/output relation that this program instantiates. We can therefore identify programs with input/output relations. Specifications of a program can be described in terms of a desirable input/output relation, and concrete program commands can also be given semantics in this fashion. A more general view is to consider a program as a *predicate transformer*, following Dijkstra 1976: In this case, we identify a program with the change it brings about to the truth of predicates on the program's state. This space is larger, it has very elegant logical properties, and it has proven a very useful basis for the refinement of sequential programs.

What should the program space be for distributed programs? The distributed settings adds complexity in a number of different ways. First, we believe that the notion of the state of a distributed computation is much less obvious than in the sequential case. Second, the concurrency of the computation adds a whole layer of complexity. Third, there are many models in which distributed computations are carried out, and a refinement calculus need not fully commit to a particular model at the outset. Finally, in a distributed system there can be many tasks that are reactive and ongoing. As a result, nonterminating programs are often desirable or even necessary. We now consider some of these issues in greater detail.

Distributed States—transition vs. composition: The *state* plays two important roles in the context of a sequential computation. One is to be the object that actions performed by the program modify. Thus, for example, an action such as setting the variable x to 1 can be thought of as being applied to the state, resulting in a new state that differs from the first only in that the value of x is 1. With every program action we can thus associate a transition function on the states. A second role the state plays is being the start and end point of programs: A program will start at a well-defined state (its *initial state*), and if it terminates will end at a state (its *final state*). When we compose two programs p and Q by running P followed by Q, the final state of program P will be the initial state of Q. Moreover, whatever properties the output of P is guaranteed to have can be used as valid assumptions about the input of Q in this case. We thus view the state as playing a role in the *transition* caused by actions, and a role as the location at which control is passed from one program to the next in sequential *composition* of programs. The reader is fully justified in doubting the value of what has just been said. The distinction drawn between the two "roles" of the sequential state might not be all that convincing. After all, we can associate a transition function with a terminating program as well, and view a such a program as a slightly generalized action. This distinction will hopefully be more vividly drawn out when we consider the distributed case.

What does the notion of a state become when we move to a distributed model? Perhaps the most popular answer taken in the literature is the state of a distributed system amounts to an instantaneous "snapshot" of the system. This is sometimes called the *global state* of the system, and sometimes it is called the *configuration* of the system (cf. Lynch Lynch 1996, Attiya and Welch 1998). Typically it will consist of local states for the different active processes in the system, as well as states for inactive elements such as communication channels, shared variables and the like. Clearly, the effect of actions performed by the processes in a distributed system depend on the global state. The actions indeed transform the global state and we would argue that the global state is the analogue of a sequential state for the purpose of transition.

The analysis of distributed algorithms and distributed programs in general is often performed for each specific task in isolation. It is typically carried out in essentially the same terms as we have described for the sequential case: Such a program will start in an initial (global) state and end in a final state that results when all participating processes have completed carrying out their individual tasks in the program. While this is adequate for the analysis of a given task in isolation, it is sometimes less so when solutions are to be composed. Let us consider an example of a refinement of a distributed task that breaks it into smaller subtasks. Suppose our goal is to perform a vote among the processes in a distributed system. Consider a refinement of this task into three parts: (a) Compute a minimum spanning tree (MST) of the network; (b) elect a leader using the MST; and (c) coordinate the vote through the leader. Clearly, these operations should be performed in sequence: Each of them relies on the completion of the previous ones.

How should we compose the solutions? Solutions to each of the subtasks are typically assumed to start operating at a well-defined initial global state. But solutions to the MST problem or to leader election are not guaranteed to terminate at a well-defined global state (see, e.g., Gallagher et al. 1983). The fact that the last process to perform an action on behalf of one of these tasks has completed doing so does not immediately become known to all of them. It is possible to overcome this problem by performing a synchronization step at the end of the intermediate steps, say in the form of termination detection (Francez 1980). The cost of synchronizing the processes in the network can be high, however, and should be incurred only if needed. In our particular example this should not be necessary.

Extending the intuitions underlying the work on communication-closed layers (Elrad and Francez 1982, Chou and Gafni 1988, Stomp and de Roever 1994, Zwiers and Janssen 1994), we prefer to view distributed programs as operating between *cuts*, where a cut specifies an instant on the time-line of each of the processes. Intuitively this means that, as far as sequential composition is concerned, cuts constitute a distributed analogue of states of a sequential computation. With this view, it is possible to sequentially compose terminating programs such as those in our voting example.

The seemingly small move of viewing distributed programs as operating between cuts has considerable repercussions. For example, we now need to consider much more carefully what assumptions must be made about the *initial cut* of a given program, to ensure the program behaves in the desirable fashion. In some cases, the initial cut needs to be fairly tightly synchronized, perhaps a global state or something very close to it (a consistent cut or a communication-closed cut). In other cases, we can make do with much less. For example, in many cases it suffices that a message that is sent by process i in the course of executing its portion of the distributed program P and is received by j before j crosses the initial cut of P, will be presented again to j after j starts executing its portion of P. Properly formalized, such a condition is all that is needed to solve our voting example in a reliable asynchronous model, without needing to perform costly synchronization between the three layers of the computation. We believe that the issues of synchronization between distributed activities raised by this form of refinement of distributed tasks deserve more attention than they have received in the past.

High-level programs: It is possible to extend the discussion on properties and assumptions on initial cuts one step further. Informally, let us define a *cut formula* to be a formula that is interpreted over cuts. For every cut formula φ there will be a set of pairs r, c where r is a run and c is a cut, at which φ will be considered true, and false for all other pairs. Cut formulas can be treated just like state formulas in a sequential computation. In fact, we can now define branching and iteration at the level of distributed programs. If P and Q are distributed programs and φ is a cut formula, we can define

$$\textbf{if } \varphi \textbf{ then } P \textbf{ else } Q \qquad \text{and} \qquad \textbf{while } \varphi \textbf{ do } P$$

as *high-level* distributed programs. High-level programs of this nature resemble structured programs in sequential computing. But there is an important difference between the two. Whereas in the sequential case the tests in **if** and **while** statements are usually executable and can be accepted by the compiler as such, the corresponding tests on cut formulas are not expected to be executable. Nevertheless, such high-level constructs of distributed programming can serve as rigorous *descriptions* of the desired behavior. This, in turn, can be helpful in the process of designing a distributed program, when the designer wishes to transform a specification of a desired program into a concrete implementation. For example, we might decide to implement a program for computing the MST of a network in an incremental fashion by repeatedly adding an MST edge to the forest under construction. This will correspond to executing a loop of the form **while** φ **do** P, where φ is the cut formula stating that the MST is not completed yet, and P is a distributed program that adds one edge to the MST. We shall return to this point when we discuss refinement below.

Termination: We have argued that considering programs as operating between cuts provides us with an improved facility for handling sequential composition of distributed programs. We need to assume, of course, that each participant in a distributed program ultimately terminates its participation in the program, before it can go on to performing the next program. This is taken for granted when dealing with sequential programs, where a nonterminating computation amounts to an outright failure and is usually totally undesirable. When we deal with distributed programs, however, there are common settings in which it is provable that interesting distributed programs cannot guarantee termination. For example, the work of Koo and Toueg 1988 shows that in a setting in which messages may be lost but communication channels are *fair*, every protocol that requires the successful delivery of at least one message in each run, must have executions in which one or more of the processes cannot terminate. This appears to be an issue if we are after sequential composition of programs in this model.

An example of a nonterminating program in this context is the standard protocol for sending a single bit between a sender S and a receiver R. The sender's program is to send the bit repeatedly until it receives an acknowledgement. The receiver, in turn, sends one acknowledgement for each message it receives. A close analysis shows that the receiver must forever be ready to send one more acknowledgement in case it receives another copy of the bit. This example indicates that while the receiver cannot safely reach a terminating state with respect to the bit transmission program, the situation is not similar to the divergence of a sequential program. Despite not reaching a terminating state, the receiver should not be expected to abstain from taking part in further activities, provided that the receipt of a new copy of the bit will prompt the sending of an additional acknowledgement.

Inspired by the work of Havelund and Larsen 1993, we subscribe to an approach by which part of the activity of a process can be considered as taking place "in the background." This activity need not terminate, and if it does, its termination need not cause another activity to start. We call a program that operates in the background a *forked* program, and have an explicit **fork**(P) operator in our framework. In the bit transmission problem, for example, we can view the receiver having a *top-level* or "foreground" activity consisting of waiting for the sender's message, and consuming it, or making use of the information therein once it arrives. The "background" activity, which the receiver would happily delegate to an assistant or, say, the mail system, involves sending the acknowledgements. Once the message is obtained by the receiver, the receiver can proceed to its next task. A similar approach is readily applicable to a variety of well-known protocols and problems.

A separation of concerns between foreground and background activities makes sequential composition of programs possible again even in models or for problems where termination is not a simple matter. It also facilitates modelling various delicate aspects of concurrency in a natural fashion.

In summary, this abstract has covered only a few of the issues that arise when we attempt to develop a refinement calculus for distributed programs. We believe that the concerns raised by such a top-down view of distributed programming should receive more attention than they have in the past, and could give rise to new problems and techniques in the fields of distributed algorithms and program refinement.

References

Attiya, C., Welch, J.L.: *Distributed Computing: Fundamentals, Simulations and Advanced Topics.* McGraw-Hill (1998)

Back, R. J., von Wright, J.: *Refinement Calculus: A Systematic Introduction.* Springer Verlag Graduate Texts in Comp. Sci. (1998)

Chou, C., Gafni, E.: Understanding and verifying distributed algorithms using stratified decomposition. Proc. 7th ACM PODC (1988) 44–65

Dijkstra, E.W.: *A Discipline of Programming.* Prentice Hall (1976)

Engelhardt, K., van der Meyden, R., and Moses, Y.: Knowledge and the logic of local propositions, Proc. 7th Conf. on Theor. Aspects of Reasoning about Knowledge (TARK), Gilboa, T. Ed., Morgan Kaufmann (1998) 29–42

Engelhardt, K., van der Meyden, R., and Moses, Y.: A program refinement framework supporting reasoning about knowledge an time. *Foundations of Software Science and Computations Structures,* Tjuryn J. Ed., Springer Verlag (2000) 114–129

Francez, N.: Distributed Termination. ACM Trans. Prog. Lang. and Syst., **2**(1) (1980) 42–55

Gallager, R., Humblet, P., Spira, P.: A distributed algorithm for minimum-weight spanning trees. ACM Trans. on Prog. Lang. and Syst., **5**(1) (1983) 66–77

Elrad, T., Francez, N.: Decomposition of distributed programs into communication-closed layers. Sci. Comp. Prog., **2**(3) (1982) 155-173

Havelund, K., Larsen, K.G.: The fork calculus. Proc. 20th ICALP, LNCS **700** (1993) 544–557

Koo, R., Toueg, S.: Effects of message loss on termination of distributed protocols. Inf. Proc, Letters, **27** (1988) 181–188

Lynch, N.A.: *Distributed Algorithms,* Morgan Kaufmann Publishers (1996)

van der Meyden, R., Moses, Y.: On refinement and temporal annotations, *this volume.*

Morgan, C.: *Programming from Specifications - 2nd ed.* Prentice Hall (1994)

Stomp, F., de Roever, W.P.: A principle for sequential reasoning about distributed systems. Form. Asp. Comp., **6**(6) (1994) 716–737

Zweirs, J., Janssen, W.: Partial-order based design of concurrent systems. Proc. REX Symp. " A decade of concurrency", J. de Bakker, W. P. de Roever, G. Rozenberg eds., LNCS **803** (1994) 622-684

Challenges in the Verification of Electronic Control Units

Werner Damm

OFFIS, University of Oldenburg
Werner.Damm@Informatik.Uni-Oldenburg.DE

Electronic Control Units control our cars, airplanes, trains, and other safety critical systems. The key motivation to maintain high safety standards in the light of increasing complexity as well as the need to reduce development costs, in particular time spent in testing, have been driving forces in promoting the use of formal techniques in software requirement specifications as well as during design and validation of software. As a result of this drive and the growing maturity of the employed verification tools, formal techniques have found their way into industrial design flows, such as the use of the B- method in Matra-Transport, and the use of the Sternol Verification Environment based on Prover at Adtranz Signaling Sweden. We see an increased pressure on the design process for on-board control software to move towards a formally based process, a central prerequisite being the introduction of a model-based development process. This in itself constitutes already a significant shift. The step to model-based design processes has to a somewhat larger extent already been taken in both avionics and automotive, where tools like STATEMATE[1], Mathworks[2], MatrixX[3], Scade[4], ASCET[5] are routinely used at different stages in the development process for control software. E.g. Aerospatial uses the Scade tool to generate airborne software and the induced cost benefits. The same concern about safety has caused companies like Boeing and British Aerospace to also asses the use of formal verification methods. Similarly, in automotive, the incentive to reduce development costs by letting model-checking catch errors early on in the development process, or the use of model-checking to create a golden reference model in the manufacturer-supplier chain, has been a major motivation to investigate the use of model-checking based verification techniques.

The talk surveys the state of the art in employing verification techniques in the above application domains, stressing the role of such techniques in a model based design process. The technical focus of the talk will be on recent advances in model-checking, allowing to integrate a limited degree of first- order reasoning into symbolic model-checking. The talk will also present evaluation results on using SAT based methods in connection with bounded model checking on representative industrial designs.

---

[1] a registered trademark of I-Logix Inc.

[2] a registered trademark of TheMathworks, Inc

[3] a registered trademark of ISI Inc

[4] a registered trademark of Verilog SA

[5] a registered trademark of ETAS GmbH

Scaling up Uppaal

Automatic Verification of Real-Time Systems using Compositionality and Abstraction

Henrik Ejersbo Jensen, Kim Guldstrand Larsen, and Arne Skou

BRICS**, Aalborg University, Denmark
{ejersbo,kgl,ask}@cs.auc.dk

Abstract. To combat the state-explosion problem in automatic verification, we present a method for scaling up the real-time verification tool UPPAAL by complementing it with methods for abstraction and compositionality. We identify a notion of timed ready simulation which we show is a sound condition for preservation of safety properties between real-time systems, and in addition is a precongruence with respect to parallel composition. Thus, it supports both abstraction and compositionality. We furthermore present a method for automatically testing for the existence of a timed ready simulation between real-time systems using the UPPAAL tool.

1 Introduction

Since the basic results by Alur, Courcoubetis and Dill [2] on decidability of model-checking for timed automata, a number of tools for automatic verification of hybrid and real-time systems have emerged [19,9,6]. These tools have by now reached a state, where they are mature enough for application on industrial development of real-time systems as witnessed by a number of already carried out case-studies [10,16,13,15,7]. Despite this success, the state-explosion problem is a reality[1] which prevents the tools from ever[2] being able to provide fully automatic verification of arbitrarily large and complex systems. Thus, to truely scale up, the automatic verification offered by the tools should be complemented by other methods.

One such method is that of *abstraction*. Assume that SYS is a model of some considered real-time system, and assume that we want some property φ to be established, i.e. SYS $\models \varphi$. Now, the model, SYS, may be too complex for our tools to settle this verification problem automatically. The goal of abstraction is to replace the problem with another, hopefully tractable problem ABS $\models \varphi$, where ABS is an abstraction of SYS being smaller in size and less complex. This

---

** BRICS – Basic Research in Computer Science – is a basic research centre funded by the Danish government at Aarhus and Aalborg University
[1] Model-checking is either EXPTIME- or PSPACE-complete depending on the expressiveness of the logic considered.
[2] unless we succeed in showing P=PSPACE

M. Joseph (Ed.): FTRTFT 2000, LNCS 1926, pp. 19–30, 2000.

method requires the user not only to supply the abstraction but also to argue that the abstraction is *safe* in the sense that all relevant properties established for ABS also hold for SYS; i.e. it should be established that SYS $\leq$ ABS, for some property-preserving relationship $\leq$ between models[3]. Unfortunately, this brings the problem of state-explosion right back in the picture because establishing SYS $\leq$ ABS may be as computationally difficult as the original verification problem SYS $\models \varphi$.

To alleviate the above problem, the method of abstraction may be combined with that of *compositionality*. Here, compositionality refers to principles allowing properties of composite systems to be inferred from properties of their components. In particular we want to establish the safe abstraction condition, SYS $\leq$ ABS, in a compositional way, that is, assuming that SYS is a composite system of the form SYS$_1$ $\parallel$ SYS$_2$, we may hope to find simple abstractions ABS$_1$ and ABS$_2$ such that:

$$\mathrm{SYS}_1 \leq \mathrm{ABS}_1 \quad \text{and} \quad \mathrm{SYS}_2 \leq \mathrm{ABS}_2 \tag{1}$$

Provided the relation $\leq$ is a precongruence with respect to the composition operator $\parallel$, we may now complete the proof of the safe abstraction condition by establishing:

$$\mathrm{ABS}_1 \parallel \mathrm{ABS}_2 \leq \mathrm{ABS} \tag{2}$$

This approach nicely factors the original problem SYS $\leq$ ABS into the smaller problems of (1) and (2), and may be applied recursively until problems small enough to be handled by automatic means are reached.

The method of abstraction and compositionality is an old-fashion recipe with roots going back to the original, foundational work on concurrency theory. For a nice survey on the history of compositional proof systems see [11]. Due to the reality of the state-explosion problem in automatic verification, there has recently been a renewed interest in applying the principles of abstraction and compositionality in combination with automatic model-checking [5,21,20,8,14]

The purpose of this paper is to present a tool-supported method for verifying properties of real-time systems using abstraction and compositionality. The tool we apply is the real-time verification tool UPPAAL [19] developed jointly by BRICS at Aalborg University and Department of Computing Systems at Uppsala University. UPPAAL provides support for automatic verification of safety properties of systems modelled as networks of timed automata communicating over (urgent) channels and shared integer variables. A fundamental relationship between timed automata preserving safety properties — and hence useful in establishing safe abstraction properties — is that of timed simulation. However, in the presence of urgent communication and shared variables, this relationship fails to be a precongruence, and hence does not support compositionality. A

---

[3] i.e. $A \leq B$ and $B \models \phi$ should imply that $A \models \phi$.

main contribution of this paper is to identify a notion of timed ready simulation supporting both abstraction and compositionality.

Having identified the notion of timed ready simulation as the fundamental condition for property preservation between timed automata, there still remains the problem of how to establish such a relation in practice. In this paper, we provide a method for automatically *testing* for the existence of a timed ready simulation between timed automata using reachability analysis. Thus UPPAAL may be applied for such tests. Assume that $\leq$ is the simulation relation and that we want to check if SYS $\leq$ ABS. Our testing method then prescribes (1) the construction of a test automaton T_{ABS} for ABS and (2) a check of whether a certain *reject* node can be reached in the composition SYS $\parallel T_{\text{ABS}}$. If a reject node can be reached, SYS $\not\leq$ ABS; otherwise SYS $\leq$ ABS. The automaton T_{ABS} will continuously monitor for compliance with ABS and may be seen as a generalization of the early complement construction for deterministic timed automata [4,3] to take into account urgent channels and shared variables.

In Section 2 we present the timed automaton model and the fundamental notions of timed simulation and timed reachability. Section 3 presents our notion of timed ready simulation, which is shown to be a precongruence with respect to parallel composition. Section 4 presents our method for testing for the existence of a timed ready simulation, and Section 5 concludes.

2 Timed Automata

Semantically we model shared variable real-time systems using a standard labelled transition system model extended with capabilities for describing real-time behavior and communication via shared multi-reader/multi-writer variables. Our transition system model has two types of labels: atomic actions and delays, representing discrete and continuous changes of real-time systems. We will assume that $\mathcal{A}$ is a universal set of actions used for synchronization between transition systems and $\mathcal{A}_u \subseteq \mathcal{A}$ is a special subset of *urgent actions* used to enforce immediate synchronization among transition systems. We use a to range over $\mathcal{A}$. We assume that $\mathcal{A}$ is equipped with a mapping $\bar{\cdot} : \mathcal{A} \to \mathcal{A}$ such that $\bar{\bar{a}} = a$ for every $a \in \mathcal{A}$. Moreover, we assume that for any $a \in \mathcal{A}_u$, $\bar{a} \in \mathcal{A}_u$ as well. We also assume the existence of a special internal action τ distinct from any action in $\mathcal{A}$. We write $\mathcal{A}_\tau$ to denote $\mathcal{A} \cup \{\tau\}$ and we use μ range over $\mathcal{A}_\tau$. We use $\mathcal{D}$ to denote the set of delay actions $\{\epsilon(d) \mid d \in \mathcal{R}_{\geq 0}\}$ where $\mathcal{R}_{\geq 0}$ denotes the set of non-negative real numbers.

We consider transition systems capable of communicating over a universal set V of shared integer variables. A transition system comes equipped with a *signature* Σ which is a tuple (R, W, IW) of subsets of V. The signature describes sets of shared variables that are *readable* (R), *writable* (W), and *internally writable* (IW) by the transition system. We do not require sets R and W to be disjoint. Set IW is a subset of W consisting of variables writable only by the system itself but readable by all systems.

We assume that any state s of a transition system at least provides a value for each integer variable $v \in V$.[4] By slight misuse of function notation we denote this value by $s(v)$. We extend this notation in the obvious way to subsets X of V. We define $s[X] = s'[X]$ iff $s(v) = s'(v)$ for all $v \in X$.

In order to represent the effect of an environment upon an "open" transition system, we use a special set of environment actions $\mathcal{E} = \{\varepsilon(X) \mid X \subseteq V\}$. An action $\varepsilon(X)$ represents the environment updating the variables in X. We let ν range over $\mathcal{A}_\tau \cup \mathcal{E}$. We now define our notion of *timed transition system* as follows.

Definition 1. *A timed transition system (TTS) is a tuple* $\mathcal{T} = \langle S, s_0, \Sigma, \longrightarrow \rangle$ *where S is a set of states, $s_0 \in S$ is the initial state, $\Sigma = (R, W, IW)$ is a signature, and* $\longrightarrow \subseteq S \times (\mathcal{A}_\tau \cup \mathcal{E} \cup \mathcal{D}) \times S$ *is a transition relation.*

For any state s of a TTS we write $s \xrightarrow{\nu}$ iff there exists a state s' such that $s \xrightarrow{\nu} s'$. We require $\longrightarrow$ to satisfy the well-known time properties of (1) time determinism, (2) time additivity and (3) zero-delay [1]. Also, the environment should have the freedom to update any variable outside IW. Thus, (4) for all $X \subseteq V \backslash IW : s \xrightarrow{\varepsilon(X)} s'$ iff $s'[\overline{X}] = s[\overline{X}]$, and (5) if $X \cap IW \neq \emptyset$ then $s \xnrightarrow{\varepsilon(X)}$.

In UPPAAL, timed transition systems are described syntactically by timed automata [4,19]. A timed automaton is a standard automaton extended with finite collections of real-valued clocks and integer-valued data variables. We consider automata where actions are taken from the infinite set $\mathcal{A}_\tau$ and data variables are integer variables in the global set V. The automaton model considered here is a slight variation of the one supported by UPPAAL. All results of this paper however do generalize to the model of UPPAAL.

Each automaton has a local set C of clock variables. For any subset $R \subseteq V$, we use $G(C, R)$ to stand for the set of *guards* g generated as a conjunction of logical constraints g_c over clock variables in C and g_v over data variables in R.[5] To manipulate clock and data variables we use *reset sets*. We denote by $R(C)$ the set of all resets of clocks. For any subsets $W, R \subseteq V$, we denote by $R(W, R)$ the set of all assignments $w := e$ where $w \in W$ and e is an expression only depending on variables in R. We let $R(C, W, R) = R(C) \cup R(W, R)$.

Definition 2. *A timed automaton A is a tuple* $\langle N, l_0, C, I, \Sigma, E \rangle$, *where N is a finite set of locations, $l_0 \in N$ is the initial location, C is a finite set of real-valued clocks, I is an invariant function assigning a C predicate $I(l)$ to each location l, $\Sigma = (R, W, IW)$ is a signature, and $E \subseteq N \times G(C, R) \times \mathcal{A}_\tau \times 2^{R(C,W,R)} \times N$ is a set of edges.*

We write $l \xrightarrow{g,\mu,r}_A l'$, or simply $l \xrightarrow{g,\mu,r} l'$ when A is clear from the context, to denote that $\langle l, g, \mu, r, l' \rangle$ is an edge of A.

A state of an automaton A is a pair $\langle (l, w), v \rangle$ where l is a node of A, w is a clock assignment for A, and v is a data variable assignment. The initial

---

[4] State s could yield other interesting information such as program location etc.

[5] We leave the syntactic restrictions of g_c and g_v unspecified since they are not important here.

state of A is $\langle (l_0, w_0), v_0 \rangle$, where l_0 is the initial node of A, w_0 is the initial clock assignment mapping all clock variables to 0, and v_0 is the initial data assignment that maps all variables in V to 0.

Definition 3. *The operational semantics of a timed automaton A is given by the TTS, $\mathcal{T}_A = \langle S, s_0, \Sigma, \longrightarrow \rangle$, where S is the set of states of A, s_0 is the initial state of A, $\Sigma = (R, W, IW)$ is the signature of A, and $\longrightarrow$ is the transition relation defined as follows:*

- $\langle (l, w), v \rangle \xrightarrow{\mu} \langle (l', w'), v' \rangle$ *iff* $\exists r, g.\ l \xrightarrow{g, \mu, r} l' \wedge g_c(w) \wedge g_v(v) \wedge$
$$w' = r_c(w) \wedge v' = r_v(v)$$

- $\langle (l, w), v \rangle \xrightarrow{\epsilon(X)} \langle (l', w'), v' \rangle$ *iff* $l' = l \wedge w' = w \wedge X \cap IW = \emptyset \wedge$
$$v'[\overline{X}] = v[\overline{X}]$$

- $\langle (l, w), v \rangle \xrightarrow{\epsilon(d)} \langle (l', w'), v' \rangle$ *iff* $l' = l \wedge w' = w + d \wedge w' \models I(l) \wedge$
$$v' = v$$

UPPAAL supports verification of simple reachability properties of timed automata, in particular whether certain locations and constraints on clock and data variables are reachable from an initial state. UPPAAL only allows for reachability analysis of *closed* transition systems. A system $\mathcal{T}$ with internally writable variables IW is closed, if all variables in V are internal, i.e. $IW = V$, and if the environment cannot synchronize with $\mathcal{T}$, i.e. $\mathcal{T} = \mathcal{T} \backslash \mathcal{A}$ where $\backslash$ is the standard action restriction operator.

For any states s and s' of a TTS, we write $s \xrightarrow{\epsilon(d)} s'$ iff there exists a finite transition sequence $s = s_0 \xrightarrow{\alpha_1} s_1 \xrightarrow{\alpha_2} \cdots \xrightarrow{\alpha_n} s_n = s'$ such that for all $i \in \{1, \ldots, n\}$, $\alpha_i = \tau$ or $\alpha_i \in \mathcal{D}$, and $d = \sum \{d_i \mid \alpha_i = \epsilon(d_i)\}$.

Definition 4. *Let $\mathcal{T}$ be a TTS. We say that a state s of $\mathcal{T}$ is reachable in time d, written $\mathcal{T} \xrightarrow{\epsilon(d)} s$, iff $s_0 \xRightarrow{\epsilon(d)} s$, where s_0 is the initial state of $\mathcal{T}$.*

For A a timed automaton, we say that state s is reachable in time d, written $A \xrightarrow{\epsilon(d)} s$, if $\mathcal{T}_A \xrightarrow{\epsilon(d)} s$.

We now want to define a condition between two timed automata that preserves timed reachability from one system to the other. Let $\xrightarrow{\tau}{}^*$ denote the reflexive and transitive closure of $\xrightarrow{\tau}$. For any states s and s' of a TTS, we write $s \xRightarrow{\mu} s'$ iff there exists s'', s''' such that $s \xrightarrow{\tau}{}^* s'' \xrightarrow{\mu} s''' \xrightarrow{\tau}{}^* s'$. Also, let $\hat{\mu} = \epsilon(0)$ if $\mu = \tau$ and $\hat{\mu} = \mu$, otherwise.[6]

In the following let $\mathcal{T}_1$ and $\mathcal{T}_2$ be any two TTS's with signatures $\Sigma_1 = (R_1, W_1, IW_1)$ and $\Sigma_2 = (R_2, W_2, IW_2)$, respectively. We let $V_1 = R_1 \cup W_1$ and $V_2 = R_2 \cup W_2$. We write $sta(\mathcal{T}_1)$ and $sta(\mathcal{T}_2)$ to denote the set of states of $\mathcal{T}_1$ and $\mathcal{T}_2$, respectively. Let s_0 and t_0 denote the initial states of $\mathcal{T}_1$ and $\mathcal{T}_2$, respectively.

---

[6] For any state s, $s \xrightarrow{\epsilon(0)} s$ (zero-delay property).

Definition 5. *Let R be a relation from $sta(\mathcal{T}_1)$ to $sta(\mathcal{T}_2)$. We say that R is a timed simulation from $\mathcal{T}_1$ to $\mathcal{T}_2$, written $\mathcal{T}_1 \leq \mathcal{T}_2$ via R, provided $(s_0, t_0) \in R$ and for all $(s, t) \in R$, $s[V_2] = t[V_2]$ and*

$$- \ s \xrightarrow{\tau} s' \ \Rightarrow \ \exists t'. \ t \xRightarrow{\hat{\tau}} t' \ \wedge \ (s', t') \in R$$
$$- \ s \xrightarrow{\epsilon(d)} s' \ \Rightarrow \ \exists t'. \ t \xRightarrow{\epsilon(d)} t' \ \wedge \ (s', t') \in R$$

Timed simulation is a sound condition for preservation of timed reachability in the following sense.

Theorem 1. *If $\mathcal{T}_1 \leq \mathcal{T}_2$ and $\mathcal{T}_1 \overset{\epsilon(d)}{\rightsquigarrow} s$, then there exists t such that $\mathcal{T}_2 \overset{\epsilon(d)}{\rightsquigarrow} t$ and $s[V_2] = t[V_2]$.*

Thus, any invariance property of $\mathcal{T}_1$ only referring to variables in V_2 may be immediate concluded provided the same invariance property holds in the more abstract system $\mathcal{T}_2$.

3   Timed Ready Simulation

In order to be of practical use, any verification methodology must be able to support compositional reasoning. In our setting this means that we want timed simulation to be a precongruence with respect to parallel composition of timed automata. As we will see in this section, the timed simulation relation from Definition 5 is not a precongruence. In this section we strengthen the notion of timed simulation to a new kind of simulation called *timed ready simulation* and we show that this relation is indeed a precongruence. Our compositionality principle is, to the best of our knowledge, the first to allow compositional verification of real-time systems with urgency and with shared multi-reader/multi-writer variables. We begin this section by defining the notion parallel composition. We will say that two TTS's are *compatible* provided that none of them can write into variables that are declared as internally writable by the other part. In the following let $\mathcal{T}_1$ and $\mathcal{T}_2$ be TTS's with signatures $\Sigma_1 = (R_1, W_1, IW_1)$ and $\Sigma_2 = (R_2, W_2, IW_2)$, respectively. Also, let $V_1 = R_1 \cup W_1$ and $V_2 = R_2 \cup W_2$.

Definition 6. *We say that Σ_1 and Σ_2 are compatible iff $IW_1 \cap W_2 = IW_2 \cap W_1 = \emptyset$. Moreover, $\mathcal{T}_1$ and $\mathcal{T}_2$ are compatible iff Σ_1 and Σ_2 are compatible.*

When composing two TTS's we are allowed to "hide" some variables, i.e. to make them internally writable. We define a signature composition as follows.

Definition 7. *A signature $\Sigma = (R, W, IW)$ is said to be a composition of Σ_1 and Σ_2 iff $R = R_1 \cup R_2$, $W = W_1 \cup W_2$, and $IW \supseteq IW_1 \cup IW_2$.*

We can now define the notion of parallel composition. Let s be any state of a TTS. We can then consider s as a pair $\langle p, v \rangle$ where v is the projection of s onto variables of the global set V and p is the projection onto elements not in V. For simplicity, we will use this presentation style in the following. Let s_0 and t_0 be the initial states of $\mathcal{T}_1$ and $\mathcal{T}_2$, respectively. We let $p_{1,0}$ and $p_{2,0}$ denote the projections of s_0 and t_0, respectively, onto elements not in V. Also, let v_0 denote the assignment mapping all elements of V to 0.

Definition 8. *Assume that T_1 and T_2 are compatible and let $\Sigma = (R, W, IW)$ be a composition of Σ_1 and Σ_2. The parallel composition $T_1 \parallel T_2$ with signature Σ is the TTS, $\langle S, s_0, \longrightarrow \rangle$, where,*

- $S = \{\langle (p_1, p_2), v \rangle \mid \langle p_1, v \rangle \in sta\,(T_1) \wedge \langle p_2, v \rangle \in sta\,(T_2)\}$,
- $s_0 = \langle (p_{1,0}, p_{2,0}), v_0 \rangle$, *and*
- $\longrightarrow$ *is defined by the rules in Figure 1.*

$$(1) \quad \frac{}{\langle (p_1, p_2), v \rangle \xrightarrow{\epsilon(X)} \langle (p_1, p_2), v' \rangle} \quad X \cap IW = \emptyset \wedge v'[\overline{X}] = v[\overline{X}]$$

$$(2) \quad \frac{\langle p_1, v \rangle \xrightarrow{\mu} \langle p_1', v' \rangle}{\langle (p_1, p_2), v \rangle \xrightarrow{\mu} \langle (p_1', p_2), v' \rangle} \qquad (3) \quad \frac{\langle p_2, v \rangle \xrightarrow{\mu} \langle p_2', v' \rangle}{\langle (p_1, p_2), v \rangle \xrightarrow{\mu} \langle (p_1, p_2'), v' \rangle}$$

$$(4) \quad \frac{\langle p_1, v \rangle \xrightarrow{a} \langle p_1', v' \rangle \quad \langle p_2, v \rangle \xrightarrow{\overline{a}} \langle p_2', v'' \rangle}{\langle (p_1, p_2), v \rangle \xrightarrow{\tau} \langle (p_1', p_2'), v^* \rangle} \quad v'[W_1 \cap W_2] = v''[W_1 \cap W_2]$$

$$\text{where,} \quad v^*[X] = \begin{cases} v'[X] & \text{if } X = W_1 \\ v''[X] & \text{if } X = W_2 \\ v[X] & \text{otherwise} \end{cases}$$

$$(5) \quad \frac{\langle p_1, v \rangle \xrightarrow{\epsilon(d)} \langle p_1', v \rangle \quad \langle p_2, v \rangle \xrightarrow{\epsilon(d)} \langle p_2', v \rangle}{\langle (p_1, p_2), v \rangle \xrightarrow{\epsilon(d)} \langle (p_1', p_2'), v \rangle} \quad \begin{array}{l} \forall t \in [0, d[,\ a \in \mathcal{A}_u,\ s_1, s_2 : \\ \neg(\langle p_1, v \rangle \xrightarrow{\epsilon(t)} s_1 \xrightarrow{a} \wedge \\ \langle p_2, v \rangle \xrightarrow{\epsilon(t)} s_2 \xrightarrow{\overline{a}}) \end{array}$$

Fig. 1. Rules defining the transition relation $\longrightarrow$ in $T_1 \parallel T_2$

Assume that A and B are timed automata. We say that A and B are compatible iff T_A and T_B are compatible, and we define $A \parallel B$ as the TTS $T_A \parallel T_B$. We extend the above notions inductively to hold for compositions of automata.

We now consider how the notion of timed simulation needs to be strengthened in order to be guaranteed a precongruence. First of all, the existing definition of timed simulation does not take into account the synchronization capabilities of the related systems. Second, the definition does not take into account the possible effects of an environment on the related systems. And third, urgent actions can have some effect on the delay properties of a composition that need to be taken into account. Figure 2 shows an example illustrating the above mentioned problems.

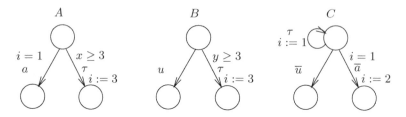

Fig. 2. Example illustrating that $\leq$ is not a precongruence. Here $A \leq B$ but $A \parallel C \not\leq$ $B \parallel C$ due to the following problems: (1) A and B do not react in the same way to effects of their environment C. When automaton C sets data variable i to 1 it enables an a action in A but not in B. Thus, $A \parallel C$ can synchronize on a and $\bar{a}$ thereby set $i = 2$; whereas $B \parallel C$ cannot synchronize. (2): Urgent action u of B can preempt delaying in $B \parallel C$ but not in $A \parallel C$. In $A \parallel C$ a delay of more than 3 time units is possible, thereby enabling a transition setting $i = 3$. In $B \parallel C$ urgent synchronization on u and $\bar{u}$ preempts the possibility of an initial delay and thus the possibility of setting $i = 3$.

We now strengthen the definition of timed simulation in order to remedy the above mentioned problems. We will say that T_2 is a *valid abstraction* for T_1 provided $R_2 \subseteq R_1$, $W_2 \subseteq W_1$, and $IW_2 \subseteq IW_1$. If T_2 is a valid abstraction for T_1 then for any $X \subseteq V$ such that $X \cap IW_1 = \emptyset$, we also have $X \cap IW_2 = \emptyset$. Thus, any environment "valid" for T_1 is also "valid" for T_2.

Definition 9. *Assume that T_2 is a valid abstraction for T_1. Let R be a relation from $sta(T_1)$ to $sta(T_2)$. We say that R is a timed ready simulation from T_1 to T_2, written $T_1 \preceq T_2$ via R, provided $(s_0, t_0) \in R$ and for all $(s, t) \in R$, $s[V_2] = t[V_2]$ and*

$$- s \xrightarrow{\mu} s' \Rightarrow \exists t'. t \xRightarrow{\hat{\mu}} t' \wedge (s', t') \in R$$
$$- s \xrightarrow{\epsilon(d)} s' \Rightarrow \exists t'. t \xRightarrow{\epsilon(d)} t' \wedge (s', t') \in R$$
$$- s \xrightarrow{\varepsilon(X)} s' \wedge t \xrightarrow{\varepsilon(X)} t' \wedge s'[X] = t'[X] \Rightarrow (s', t') \in R$$
$$- t \xrightarrow{a} \wedge a \in \mathcal{A}_u \Rightarrow s \xrightarrow{a}$$

We lift the notion of timed ready simulation to timed automata just as we did for timed simulation. We now state our wanted theorem saying that $\preceq$ is indeed a precongruence and hence supports compositional reasoning.

Theorem 2. *Let $A \parallel C$ and $B \parallel D$ be timed automata compositions such that $IW_{B \parallel D} \subseteq IW_{A \parallel C}$. Also, assume that B and D are both τ-free. If,*

1. *$A \preceq B$ and $C \preceq D$, and*
2. *$V_A \cap V_D \subseteq V_B$ and $V_C \cap V_B \subseteq V_D$,*

then $A \parallel C \preceq B \parallel D$

Condition 2 says that variables visible for D (and hence C) cannot be removed by the abstraction from A to B. Analogously, variables visible by B (and hence A) cannot be removed by the abstraction from C to D.

4   Testing for Timed Ready Simulation

In this section we show that the problem of checking whether $A \preceq B$, for timed automata A and B, is equivalent to that of testing whether a special *reject* node of the composition $A \| T_B$ is reachable. Where T_B is a special construction called the *test automaton* for B. Hence, we can use UPPAAL to automatically check whether $A \preceq B$. We begin by introducing our general notion of *testing* a timed automaton. This notion follows closely the one presented in [1]

Definition 10. *A test automaton is a tuple* $T = \langle N, N_T, l_0, C, I, \Sigma, E \rangle$ *where* N, l_0, C, I, Σ, *and* E *are as in Definition 2, and* $N_T \subseteq N$, *is the set of reject nodes.*

Intuitively, a test automaton T interacts with a tested system, represented by a composition of timed automata, by communicating with it. The dynamics of the interaction between the tester and the tested system is described by the parallel composition of the automaton composition that is being tested and of T. We now define failure and success of a test as follows. For A an automaton composition and l a location of A, we write $A \rightsquigarrow l$ if there exists a state s of A with location component l, and a delay d such that $A \overset{\epsilon(d)}{\rightsquigarrow} s$.

Definition 11. *Let A be an automaton composition with set of reject nodes N_T and let T be a test automaton. We say that A fails the T-test iff $A \| T \rightsquigarrow l$ for some $l \in N_T$. Otherwise, we say that A passes the T-test.*

The following theorem shows that it is possible to check for the existence of a timed ready simulation between two automata compositions, using the notion of testing introduced above. We will say that a timed automaton B is *deterministic* provided that for any states s, s', s'' of T_B, if $s \overset{\nu}{\longrightarrow} s'$ and $s \overset{\nu}{\longrightarrow} s''$ then $s' = s''$.

Theorem 3. *Let A be a timed automata composition, and let B be a τ-free and deterministic timed automaton. Then there exists a test automaton T_B such that $A \preceq B$ iff A passes the T_B-test.*

In Figure 3 we have shown how the test automaton T_B of Theorem 3 is constructed node-wise by considering each node l of B. For any data variable $i \in V_B$ we assume that $\bar{i}$ is a fresh variable in V_{T_B}. Guards and reset operations in T_B are identical to the ones in B except for substitution of $\bar{i}$ for any data variable i. For simplicity we have shown the test construction for special case where all variables of V_B are internally writable. The construction easily generalizes to the case where some variables are not internally writable.

5   Conclusion

In this paper we have presented a tool-supported method for verifying properties of real-time systems using abstraction and compositionality. In order to support both abstraction and compositionality, we have identified a notion of timed ready

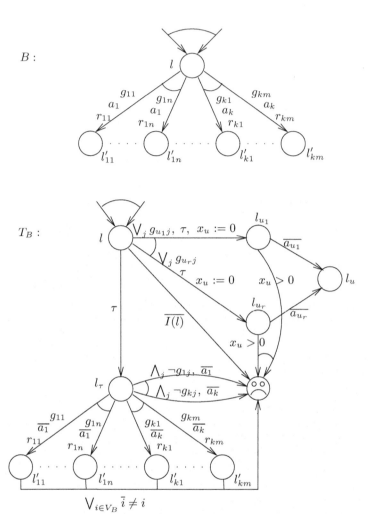

Fig. 3. Automaton B and its test automaton T_B. Actions $\{a_{u_1}, \ldots, a_{u_r}\}$ are assumed to form the urgent subset of $\{a_1, \ldots, a_k\}$. The subgraph of T_B induced by nodes l, $l_{u_1}, \ldots l_{u_r}$, l_u is used to test for the backwards-match requirement of urgent actions in the $\preceq$ definition. If urgent action a_{u_i} of B is enabled in l, T_B enables the action $\overline{a_{u_i}}$ and resets clock x_u. Now, if the automaton that B is supposed to simulate does not have an a_{u_i} action immediately enabled, time can pass and thereby allow T_B to enter the reject node (sad face). The subgraph induced by the reject node and node l tests that the automaton that B must simulate cannot delay beyond the node invariant $I(l)$ of l. The transitions with guard $\bigvee_{i \in V_B} \overline{i} \neq i$ test that corresponding states in the simulation relation agree on variables of V_B. The remaining part of T_B test for the forwards-match of all actions. The τ-transition from node l to node l_τ is required to allow time to pass in node l in the presence of urgent actions.

simulation between timed automata. We have shown that timed ready simulation is a precongruence and hence does support compositional reasoning. To the best of our knowledge, this is the first compositionality principle for timed automata with both urgent channels and shared multi-reader/multi-writer variables. Based on the work of Larsen [17,18] on *context-dependent bisimulation*, we are currently extending our notion of timed ready simulation to a *context-dependent timed ready simulation*, which is an extension of the timed ready simulation parameterized with an assumption about environments. This extension will allow for *assume-guarantee* style reasoning.

We have further provided a method for automatically testing for the existence of a timed ready simulation between timed automata using reachability analysis. The reachability analysis can be automatically performed by the real-time verification tool UPPAAL.

The results of this paper have been applied by us in the verification of a large industrial design - the Bang & Olufsen (B&O) audio/video power controller. This system is supposed to reside in an audio/video component and control links to neighbor audio/video components such as TV, VCR and remote–control. In particular, the system is responsible for the powering up and down of the components in between the arrival of data, and in order to do so, it is essential that no link interrupts are lost. In an earlier work [12] we successfully verified a scaled–down version of the full protocol. However, the size of the full protocol model is so large that UPPAAL immediately encounters the state-explosion problem in a direct verification (on a 1 GByte SUN computer). By application of our developed compositionality and testing results we are able to carry through a verification of the full protocol model within a few seconds.

References

1. Luca Aceto, Augusto Burgueno, and Kim G. Larsen. Model checking via reachability testing for timed automata. In Bernhard Steffen, editor, *Proc. 4th Int. Conference on Tools and Algorithms for the Construction and Analysis of Systems (TACAS'98)*, volume 1384 of *Lecture Notes in Computer Science*, pages 263–280. Springer, 1998.
2. R. Alur, C. Courcoubetis, and D. Dill. Model-checking for Real-Time Systems. In *Proc. of Logic in Computer Science*, pages 414–425. IEEE Computer Society Press, 1990.
3. R. Alur and D. Dill. Automata for Modelling Real-Time Systems. In *Proc. of ICALP'90*, volume 443, 1990.
4. R. Alur and D. Dill. A theory of timed automata. *Theoretical Computer Science*, 126:183–236, 1994.
5. R. Alur, T. A. Henzinger, F. Y. C. Mang, S. Qadeer, S. K. Rajamani, and S. Tasiran. MOCHA Modularity in Model Checking. In *Computer Aided Verification, Proc. 10th Int. Conference*, volume 1427 of *Lecture Notes in Computer Science*, pages 521–525. Springer Verlag, 1998.
6. R. Alur, T.A. Henzinger, and P.-H. Ho. Automatic symbolic verification of embedded systems. *IEEE Transactions on Software Engineering*, pages 22:181–201, 1996.

7. Johan Bengtsson, David Griffioen, Kåre Kristoffersen, Kim G. Larsen, Fredrik Larsson, Paul Pettersson, and Wang Yi. Verification of an Audio Protocol with Bus Collision Using UPPAAL. In *Proceedings of CAV'96*, volume 1102 of *Lecture Notes in Computer Science*. Springer Verlag, 1996.

8. D. Dams. *Abstract Interpretation and Partition Refinement for Model Checking*. PhD thesis, Eindhoven University of Technology, 1996.

9. C. Daws, A. Olivero, S. Tripakis, and S. Yovine. The tool KRONOS. In *Hybrid Systems III, Verification and Control*, volume 1066 of *Lecture Notes in Computer Science*. Spinger Verlag, 1996.

10. C. Daws and S. Yovine. Two examples of verification of multirate timed automata with KRONOS. In *Proc. of the 16th IEEE Real-Time Systems Symposium*, pages 66–75, December 1995.

11. Willem-Paul de Roever. The need for compositional proof systems: A survey. In Willem-Paul de Roever, Hans Langmaack, and Amir Pnueli, editors, *Compositionality: The Significant Difference, International Symposium, COMPOS'97*, volume 1536 of *Lecture Notes in Computer Science*, pages 1–22. Springer-Verlag, 1997.

12. K. Havelund, K. Larsen, and A. Skou. Formal Verification of a Power Controller Using the Real-Time Model Checker UPPAAL. In Joost-Pieter Katoen, editor, *Formal Methods for Real-Time and Probabilistic Systems, 5th International AMAST Workshop, ARTS'99*, volume 1601 of *Lecture Notes in Computer Science*, pages 277–298. Springer Verlag, 1999.

13. Pei-Hsin Ho and Howard Wong-Toi. Automated Analysis of an Audio Control Protocol. In *Proc. of CAV'95*, volume 939 of *Lecture Notes in Computer Science*. Springer Verlag, 1995.

14. Henrik Ejersbo Jensen. *Abstraction-Based Verification of Distributed Systems*. PhD thesis, Aalborg University, Institute for Computer Science, Aalborg, Denmark, 1999.

15. Henrik Ejersbo Jensen, Kim G. Larsen, and Arne Skou. Modelling and Analysis of a Collision Avoidance Protocol Using SPIN and UPAAL. In J-C. Gregoire, G.J. Holzmann, and D.A. Peled, editors, *Proceedings Second Workshop on the SPIN Verification System*, American Mathematical Society, DIMACS/39, 1996.

16. Kåre Jelling Kristoffersen. *Compositional Verification of Concurrent Systems*. PhD thesis, Aalborg University, Department of Computer Science, Institute for Electronic Systems, Aalborg, Denmark, August 1998.

17. K.G. Larsen. *Context-Dependent Bisimulation Between Processes*. PhD thesis, University of Edinburgh, Mayfield Road, Edinburgh, Scotland, 1986.

18. K.G. Larsen. A context dependent bisimulation between processes. *Theoretical Computer Science*, 49, 1987.

19. Kim G. Larsen, Paul Pettersson, and Wang Yi. UPPAAL in a Nutshell. *Int. Journal on Software Tools for Technology Transfer*, 1(1–2):134–152, October 1997.

20. C. Loiseaux, S. Graf, J. Sifakis, A. Bouajjani, and S. Bensalem. Property Preserving Abstractions for the Verification of Concurrent Systems. *Formal Methods in System Design*, pages 6:11–44, 1995.

21. K. L. McMillan. Verification of an Implementation of Tomasulo's Algorithm by Compositional Model Checking. In *Computer Aided Verification, Proc. 10th Int. Conference*, volume 1427 of *Lecture Notes in Computer Science*, pages 110–121. Springer Verlag, 1998.

Decidable Model Checking of Probabilistic Hybrid Automata

Jeremy Sproston*

School of Computer Science, University of Birmingham,
Birmingham B15 2TT, United Kingdom. J.Sproston@cs.bham.ac.uk

Abstract. Hybrid automata offer a framework for the description of systems with both discrete and continuous components, such as digital technology embedded in an analogue environment. Traditional uses of hybrid automata express choice of transitions purely in terms of non-determinism, abstracting potentially significant information concerning the relative likelihood of certain behaviours. To model such probabilistic information, we present a variant of hybrid automata augmented with discrete probability distributions. We concentrate on restricted subclasses of the model in order to obtain decidable model checking algorithms for properties expressed in probabilistic temporal logics.

1 Introduction

Many systems, such as embedded controllers, can be modelled in terms of interaction between discrete and continuous components. Examples of such *hybrid systems* include robots, medical equipment and manufacturing processes. Traditionally, formal techniques for the description of hybrid systems express the system model purely in terms of nondeterminism. However, it may be desirable to express the relative likelihood of the system exhibiting certain behaviour. This notion is particularly important when considering fault-tolerant systems, in which the occurrence of the discrete event *malfunction* is less likely than the event *correct_action*. Furthermore, it may be appropriate to model the likelihood of an event changing with respect to the continuous behaviour of the environment; for example, *malfunction* may become more likely if the system is operating at extreme temperatures or at high speeds. We may also wish to have a model checking algorithm for verifying automatically such hybrid systems against temporal logic properties referring explicitly to likelihoods. The feasibility of such verification methods is suggested by the successful development of model checking algorithms and tools both in the domain of hybrid systems [11] and that of discrete, finite-state probabilistic-nondeterministic systems [8].

Therefore, we extend the model of *hybrid automata* [1], a framework for the description of hybrid systems, with *discrete probability distributions*. This approach is inspired by the work of [16], which presents firstly a model of timed automata (a highly restricted subclass of hybrid automata) extended with such

---

* Supported in part by the EPSRC grant GR/N22960.

M. Joseph (Ed.): FTRTFT 2000, LNCS 1926, pp. 31–45, 2000.

distributions, and secondly a decidable algorithm for verifying instances of this model against formulae of a probabilistic temporal logic. Our new model, *probabilistic hybrid automata*, differs from traditional hybrid automata in that the edge relation of the graph representing the system's discrete component is both nondeterministic and probabilistic in nature. More precisely, instead of making a purely nondeterministic choice over the set of currently enabled edges, we nondeterministically choose amongst the set of *enabled discrete probability distributions*, each of which is defined over a set of edges. Then, a probabilistic choice as to which edge to take according to the selected distribution is performed. Although probability is defined to affect directly only the *discrete* dynamics of the model, the proposed model would nevertheless be useful for the analysis of many systems, such as embedded technology operating according to randomised algorithms, or the aforementioned fault-tolerant systems, for which an appropriate probabilistic hybrid automaton may be obtained given appropriate failure specifications of the system's components.

A substantial body of work has been devoted to exploring notions of *decidability* of *non-probabilistic* hybrid automata, particularly with regard to problems which underly model checking procedures. These problems are usually addressed by utilising refinement relations such as simulation and bisimulation in order to introduce notions of equivalence and abstraction on the infinite state space of a hybrid automaton. It follows that model checking can then be performed not on the original, infinite state space, but on a quotient induced by an equivalence relation; therefore, if the number of equivalence classes for a given hybrid automaton is finite, then model checking is decidable. However, such finitary quotients exist only for certain classes of model [12,18]. In particular, the *rectangular automata* of [12] feature differential inequalities which describe the continuous evolution of system variables taking place within piecewise-linear, convex envelopes, and can be used to state, for example, that a system variable increases between 1 and 3 units per second. Another such class is that of *o-minimal hybrid automata* [18], which permit expressive (albeit deterministic) continuous behaviour, and feature restricted discrete transitions. The remit of this paper is to extend these classes with discrete probability distributions, and to explore the way in which established model checking techniques for probabilistic-nondeterministic systems [7,6] may be used to verify such models against probabilistic temporal logic specifications. This provides us with a means to verify probabilistic extensions of rectangular or o-minimal automata against properties such as 'soft deadlines' (for example, a response to a request will be granted within 5 seconds with probability at least 0.95), or those which refer to the probability of malfunction or component failure (such as, with probability 0.999 or greater, less than 1 litre of coolant leaks from the nuclear reactor before an alarm is sounded).

The paper proceeds by first introducing probabilistic hybrid automata in Section 2. Section 3 explains how their semantics can be presented in terms of infinite-state, nondeterministic-probabilistic transition systems. Strategies for model checking probabilistic rectangular automata and probabilistic o-minimal automata are presented in Section 4.

2 Probabilistic Hybrid Automata

The purpose of this section is to present a model for probabilistic hybrid systems using the framework of hybrid automata, based on the probabilistic timed automata of [16]. For a set Y, a (discrete probability) *distribution* on Y is a function $\mu : Y \to [0,1]$ such that $\mu(y) > 0$ for at most countably many $y \in Y$ and $\sum_{y \in Y} \mu(y) = 1$. We use $\mathsf{Dist}(Y)$ to denote the set of all distributions on Y. Given a distribution μ on a set Y, let $\mathsf{support}(\mu)$ be the support of μ; that is, the set of elements y of Y such that $\mu(y) > 0$. If Y contains one element, then a distribution over Y is called a *Dirac distribution*, and is denoted $\mathcal{D}(y)$ where $Y = \{y\}$. Next, let $\mathcal{X} = \{x_1, ..., x_n\}$ be a set of real-valued variables. We write $\mathbf{a} \in \mathbb{R}^n$ for a vector of length n which assigns a *valuation* $\mathbf{a}_i \in \mathbb{R}$ to each variable $x_i \in \mathcal{X}$. We fix a finite set AP of atomic propositions.

A *probabilistic hybrid automaton* $H = (\mathcal{X}, V, L, init, inv, flow, prob, \langle pre_v \rangle_{v \in V})$ comprises of the following components:

Variables. $\mathcal{X}$ is a finite set of real-valued variables.

Control modes. V is a finite set of *control modes*.

Labelling function. The function $L : V \to 2^{AP}$ assigns a set of atomic propositions to each control mode.

Initial set. The function $init : V \to 2^{\mathbb{R}^n}$ maps every control mode to an *initial set* in $\mathbb{R}^n$.

Invariant set. The function $inv : V \to 2^{\mathbb{R}^n}$ maps every control mode to an *invariant set* in $\mathbb{R}^n$.

Flow inclusion. The partial function $flow : V \times \mathbb{R}^n \to 2^{\mathbb{R}^n}$ maps control modes and valuations to a *flow inclusion* in $\mathbb{R}^n$, and is such that, for each $v \in V$ and $\mathbf{a} \in inv(v)$, the set $flow(v, \mathbf{a})$ is defined.

Probability distributions. The function $prob : V \to \mathcal{P}_{fn}(\mathsf{Dist}(V \times 2^{\mathbb{R}^n} \times 2^{\mathcal{X}}))$ maps every control mode to a finite, non-empty set of distributions over the set of control modes, and the powersets of both $\mathbb{R}^n$ and $\mathcal{X}$. Therefore, each control mode $v \in V$ will be associated with a set of distributions denoted by $prob(v) = \{\mu_v^1, ..., \mu_v^m\}$ for some finite $m \geq 1$.

Pre-condition sets. For each $v \in V$, the function $pre_v : prob(v) \to 2^{\mathbb{R}^n}$ maps every probability distribution associated with a control mode to a *pre-condition set* in $\mathbb{R}^n$.

For simplicity, and without loss of generality, we assume that the initial point is unique; that is, for a control mode $v_0 \in V$, the initial condition $init(v_0)$ is a singleton in $\mathbb{R}^n$, and $init(v') = \emptyset$ for all other $v' \in V \setminus \{v_0\}$. Therefore, control of the model commences in a mode v_0 with the variable valuation given by $init(v_0)$. When control of a probabilistic rectangular automaton is in a given mode $v \in V$, the values of the real-valued variables in $\mathcal{X}$ change continuously with respect to time. Such continuous evolution is determined by the mode's flow inclusion $flow$; that is, $flow(v, \mathbf{a})$ gives the set of values that the first derivative with respect to time $\frac{dx_i}{dt}$ of each variable $x_i \in \mathcal{X}$ may take in the control mode v when the current value of the variables is given by $\mathbf{a}$. A discrete transition, henceforth called a *control switch*, from v to another mode, may take place if the

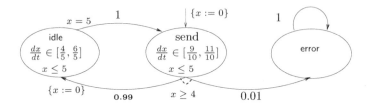

Fig. 1. The probabilistic hybrid automaton H_1.

pre-condition $pre_v(\mu)$ of a distribution $\mu \in prob(v)$ is satisfied by the current values of the variables. In such a case, we say that μ is *enabled*. Conversely, such a control switch *must* take place if the passage of some time would result in the current variable values leaving the invariant set $inv(v)$. For simplicity, the invariant and pre-condition sets are subject to the assumption that, if allowing any amount of time to elapse would result in the departure of the set $inv(v)$, then the current point in the continuous state space must be in the pre-condition set of at least one distribution in $prob(v)$.

Given that it has been decided to make a control switch via a particular enabled distribution $\mu \in prob(v)$, then a probabilistic choice as to the target mode of the switch, and to the discrete changes to the continuous variables, is performed. More precisely, with probability $\mu(w, post, X)$, a transition is made to mode $w \in V$ with the valuation $\mathbf{b}$, such that $\mathbf{b}$ is in the set $post \subseteq \mathbb{R}^n$ and $\mathbf{b}_i = \mathbf{a}_i$ for every variable $x_i \in \mathcal{X} \setminus X$. Sets such as $post$ are referred to as *post-conditions*, and variable sets such as X are referred to as *reset sets*. Together, post-conditions and reset sets determine the effects that a probabilistic hybrid automaton's control switches have on its continuous variables. These sets are subject to the following simplifying assumption: for each $v \in V$, each $\mu \in prob(v)$, and each $(w, post, X) \in \mathsf{support}(\mu)$, we have $post \subseteq inv(w)$.

An example of a probabilistic hybrid automaton is given in Figure 1. A number of standard conventions concerning the diagrammatic representation of hybrid automata are used here (see, for example, [1]). The probabilistic hybrid automaton H_1 models a process in which data packets are repeatedly sent from a sender to a receiver. We explain only the action of a fragment of the model. The process measures time according to a drifting clock, which is represented by the variable x. When the process is ready to send a packet (control is in the mode send), the clock progresses at any rate between $\frac{9}{10}$ and $\frac{11}{10}$ units per millisecond, and when it is idle (control is in the mode idle), the clock progresses at between $\frac{4}{5}$ and $\frac{6}{5}$ units per millisecond. In the former case, the process waits until its clock is equal to or greater than 4 before transmitting data, and must transmit before the clock exceeds 5. However, when transmission takes place, there is a 1% chance of the occurrence of an unrecoverable error (control passes to the mode error), as represented by a distribution over the edges from send to idle, and from send to error. More precisely, the distribution $\mu \in prob(\mathsf{send})$ is such that $\mu(\mathsf{idle}, [0,0], \{x\}) = 0.99$, $\mu(\mathsf{error}, \mathbb{R}, \emptyset) = 0.01$ and $pre_{\mathsf{send}}(\mu) = [4, \infty)$.

Subclasses of probabilistic hybrid automata. A *rectangular inequality* over $\mathcal{X}$ is of the form $x_i \sim k$, where $x_i \in \mathcal{X}$, $\sim \in \{<, \leq, =, \geq, >\}$ and $k \in \mathbb{Q}$. A *rectangular predicate* over $\mathcal{X}$ is a conjunction of rectangular inequalities over $\mathcal{X}$. For any rectangular predicate P, the set of valuations for which P is true when each $x_i \in \mathcal{X}$ is replaced by its corresponding valuation $\mathbf{a}_i$ is denoted by $[\![P]\!]$ (intuitively, $[\![P]\!]$ is the set of points in $\mathbb{R}^n$ that satisfy P). Furthermore, we call $[\![P]\!]$ a *rectangle*, and occasionally refer to such a set as *rectangular*. A closed and bounded rectangle is described as being *compact*. The set of rectangles over $\mathcal{X}$ is obtained from the set of rectangular inequalities over $\mathcal{X}$, and is denoted $Rect(\mathcal{X})$. The projection of the rectangle Z onto the axis of x_i is denoted by Z_i.

We now introduce a probabilistic extension of rectangular automata [12]. A *probabilistic rectangular automaton* R is a probabilistic hybrid automaton such that, for every $v \in V$, the sets $inv(v)$ and $flow(v, \cdot)$ are rectangles, for every $\mu \in prob(v)$, the set $pre_v(\mu)$ is a rectangle, and, for every $(w, post, X) \in \mathsf{support}(\mu)$, the set *post* is a rectangle. The probabilistic rectangular automaton R is *initialised* if, for every pair of modes $v, w \in V$, and every $x_i \in \mathcal{X}$ for which $flow(v, \cdot)_i \neq flow(w, \cdot)_i$, then if there exists a distribution $\mu \in prob(v)$ and a tuple $(w, post, X) \in \mathsf{support}(\mu)$, we have $x_i \in X$. Intuitively, if the execution of a control switch results in a variable x_i changing the condition on its continuous evolution, then the value of x_i must be reinitialised. The probabilistic rectangular automaton R has *deterministic jumps* if for every $v, w \in V$, $\mu \in prob(v)$, and $(w, post, X) \in \mathsf{support}(\mu)$, then the set $post_i$ is a singleton for every $x_i \in X$. Intuitively, this requirement states that, for every control switch, each variable either remains unchanged or is deterministically reset to a new value. A *probabilistic multisingular automaton* M is an initialised probabilistic rectangular automaton with deterministic jumps such that, for each $v \in V$ and for each $x_i \in \mathcal{X}$, we have $flow(v, \cdot)_i = k$ for some $k \in \mathbb{N}$. [1]

Next, the o-minimal hybrid automata of [18] are extended to the probabilistic context. The definition is as in Theorem 5.7 of [3], except for the following alterations: naturally, we dispense with the notion of edges connecting control modes, and replace them with a set of distributions; also, for every $v \in V$ and all $\mu \in prob(v)$, the sets $inv(v)$ and $pre_v(\mu)$ are semi-algebraic with rational coefficients, and, for every $(w, post, X) \in \mathsf{support}(\mu)$, the set *post* is semi-algebraic with rational coefficients and $X = \mathcal{X}$. Finally, to obtain *probabilistic o-minimal hybrid automata*, we assume that the initial point of the model is unique.

3 Semantics of Probabilistic Hybrid Automata

3.1 Concurrent Probabilistic Systems

The underlying transition system of a probabilistic hybrid automaton will take the form of a *concurrent probabilistic system* [6]. These systems are based on

---

[1] Observe that a *probabilistic timed automaton* [16] is a probabilistic multisingular automaton such that $flow(v, \cdot)_i = 1$ for each $v \in V$ and for each $x_i \in \mathcal{X}$.

Markov decision processes, and are a state-labelled variant of the "simple probabilistic automata" of [21]. Formally, a *concurrent probabilistic system* S is a tuple $(Q, q^0, \mathcal{L}, \Sigma, Steps)$, where Q is a (possibly infinite) set of *states*, $q^0 \in Q$ is the *initial state*, $\mathcal{L} : Q \to 2^{AP}$ is a function assigning a finite set of atomic propositions to each state, Σ is a set of *events*, and $Steps \subseteq \Sigma \times \mathsf{Dist}(Q)$ is a function which assigns to each state a non-empty set $Steps(q)$ of pairs comprising of an event σ and a distribution ν on Q.

A *transition* of S from state q comprises of a nondeterministic choice of an event-distribution pair $(\sigma, \nu) \in Steps(q)$, followed by a probabilistic choice of a next-state q' according to ν such that $\nu(q') > 0$, and is denoted by $q \xrightarrow{\sigma, \nu} q'$. A *path* of S is a non-empty finite or infinite sequence of transitions of the form $\omega = q_0 \xrightarrow{\sigma_0, \nu_0} q_1 \xrightarrow{\sigma_1, \nu_1} q_2 \xrightarrow{\sigma_2, \nu_2} \cdots$. The special case $\omega = q$, for some $q \in Q$, is also a path. The following notation is employed when reasoning about paths. For a path ω, the first state of ω is denoted by $first(\omega)$, and, if ω is finite, the last state of ω is denoted by $last(\omega)$. If ω is infinite, then $step(\omega, i)$ is the event-distribution pair associated with the i-th transition for each $i \in \mathbb{N}$. We denote by $Path_{ful}$ the set of infinite paths, and by $Path_{ful}(q)$ the set of paths ω in $Path_{ful}$ such that $first(\omega) = q$.

An *adversary* of a concurrent probabilistic system S is a function A mapping every finite path ω of S to an event-distribution pair (σ, ν) such that $(\sigma, \nu) \in Steps(last(\omega))$. Intuitively, an adversary resolves all of the nondeterministic choices of S. For an adversary A of S, we define $Path_{ful}^A$ to be the set of paths in $Path_{ful}$ such that $step(\omega, i) = A(\omega^{(i)})$ for all $i \in \mathbb{N}$. Furthermore, $Path_{ful}^A(q)$ is defined to be the set of paths of $Path_{ful}^A$ such that $first(\omega) = q$ for all $\omega \in Path_{ful}$. For each adversary, we can define a probability measure $Prob^A$ on infinite paths in the standard manner (see, for example, [6]).

We introduce two state relations for concurrent probabilistic systems, namely *probabilistic bisimulation and simulation*. In the standard manner, the concept of weight functions [15] is used to provide the basis of the definition of simulation, and bisimulation is defined as a symmetric simulation [21]. Let $\mathcal{R} \subseteq Q_1 \times Q_2$ be a relation between the two sets Q_1, Q_2, and ν_1, ν_2 distributions such that $\nu_1 \in \mathsf{Dist}(Q_1)$ and $\nu_2 \in \mathsf{Dist}(Q_2)$. A *weight function* for (ν_1, ν_2) with respect to $\mathcal{R}$ is a function $w : Q_1 \times Q_2 \to [0, 1]$ such that, for all $q_1 \in Q_1$, $q_2 \in Q_2$:

1. if $w(q_1, q_2) > 0$, then $(q_1, q_2) \in \mathcal{R}$, and
2. $\sum_{q' \in Q_2} w(q_1, q') = \nu_1(q_1)$, and $\sum_{q' \in Q_1} w(q', q_2) = \nu_2(q_2)$.

We write $\nu_1 \mathcal{R} \nu_2$ if there exists a weight function for (ν_1, ν_2) with respect to $\mathcal{R}$. For example, if $Q_1 = \{q_1, q_1'\}$, $Q_2 = \{q_2, q_2'\}$, $\nu_1(q_1) = \nu_1(q_1') = \frac{1}{2}$, $\nu_2(q_2) = \frac{1}{3}$, $\nu_2(q_2') = \frac{2}{3}$, and $\mathcal{R} = \{(q_1, q_2), (q_1, q_2'), (q_1', q_2')\}$, then a weight function w for (ν_1, ν_2) with respect to $\mathcal{R}$ is $w(q_1, q_2) = \frac{1}{3}$, $w(q_1, q_2') = \frac{1}{6}$, $w(q_1', q_2') = \frac{1}{2}$.

The following definitions, which follow immediately from the probabilistic simulations and bisimulations of [15,21], are with respect to the concurrent probabilistic system $S = (Q, q^0, \mathcal{L}, \Sigma, Steps)$. We write $q \xrightarrow{\sigma, \nu}$ if there exists a transition $q \xrightarrow{\sigma, \nu} q'$ for some $q' \in Q$. A *simulation of* S is a relation $\mathcal{R} \subseteq Q \times Q$ such that, for each $(q_1, q_2) \in \mathcal{R}$:

1. $\mathcal{L}(q_1) = \mathcal{L}(q_2)$, and
2. if $q_1 \xrightarrow{\sigma, \nu_1}$, then $q_2 \xrightarrow{\sigma, \nu_2}$ for some distribution ν_2 such that $\nu_1 \mathcal{R} \nu_2$.

We say that q_2 *simulates* q_1, denoted by $q_1 \preceq q_2$, iff there exists a simulation which contains (q_1, q_2). A *bisimulation of* S is a simulation of S which is symmetric. Two states q_1, q_2 are called *bisimilar*, denoted by $q_1 \simeq q_2$, iff there exists a bisimulation which contains (q_1, q_2). As any simulation is a preorder, a bismulation is an equivalence relation. We can define simulation and bisimulation with respect to the composition of concurrent probabilistic systems in the standard manner [19,5] in order to obtain a notion of relation between two such systems.

If an equivalence relation $\mathcal{R}$ on (a finite- or infinite-state) concurrent probabilistic system S contains a finite number of classes, we can define a finite-state *quotient concurrent probabilistic system* S_{fin}, the states of which are the equivalence classes of $\mathcal{R}$, and the transitions of which are derived from those of S, such that the initial state of S is related to the initial state of S_{fin} by $\mathcal{R}$. We omit details for reasons of space.

3.2 Probabilistic Temporal Logic

We now present a probabilistic temporal logic which can be used to specify properties of probabilistic hybrid automata. In brief, PBTL (Probabilistic Branching Time Logic) [6] is an extension of the temporal logic CTL in which the until operator includes a bound on probability. For example, the property of Section 1 regarding component failure is represented by the PBTL formula $[(coolant) \forall \mathcal{U} (alarm)]_{\geq 0.999}$, where *coolant* and *alarm* are atomic propositions labelling the appropriate states. Note that PBTL is essentially identical to the logics PCTL and pCTL presented in [9] and [4,7] respectively, and that PBTL model checking of finite-state concurrent probabilistic systems may be performed using the algorithms of [7,6]. The syntax of PBTL is defined as follows:

$$\Phi ::= \texttt{true} \mid a \mid \Phi \wedge \Phi \mid \neg \Phi \mid [\Phi \exists \mathcal{U} \Phi]_{\sqsupseteq \lambda} \mid [\Phi \forall \mathcal{U} \Phi]_{\sqsupseteq \lambda}$$

where $a \in \text{AP}$, $\lambda \in [0, 1]$, and $\sqsupseteq \in \{\geq, >\}$. The satisfaction relation for $\texttt{true}$, $a \in \text{AP}$, $\wedge$ and $\neg$ are standard for temporal logic. In the following definition of the semantics of the probabilistic operators $[\Phi_1 \exists \mathcal{U} \Phi_2]_{\sqsupseteq \lambda}$ and $[\Phi_1 \forall \mathcal{U} \Phi_2]_{\sqsupseteq \lambda}$ we make use of the 'path formula' $\Phi_1 \mathcal{U} \Phi_2$, the interpretation of which is also standard; that is, $\Phi_1 \mathcal{U} \Phi_2$ is true of a path ω if and only if Φ_2 is true at some point along ω, and Φ_1 is satisfied at all preceding points (for a formal description, see, e.g., [6]). For a concurrent probabilistic system S, a set $\mathcal{A}$ of adversaries on S, and a state q of S, the satisfaction relation for $q \models_{\mathcal{A}} [\Phi_1 \exists \mathcal{U} \Phi_2]_{\sqsupseteq \lambda}$ is as follows:

$$q \models_{\mathcal{A}} [\Phi_1 \exists \mathcal{U} \Phi_2]_{\sqsupseteq \lambda} \Leftrightarrow Prob^A(\{\omega \mid \omega \in Path_{ful}^A(q) \ \& \ \omega \models_{\mathcal{A}} \Phi_1 \mathcal{U} \Phi_2\}) \sqsupseteq \lambda$$
$$\text{for some adversary } A \in \mathcal{A}.$$

The semantics for $[\Phi_1 \forall \mathcal{U} \Phi_2]_{\sqsupseteq \lambda}$ is obtained by substituting "all adversaries $A \in \mathcal{A}$" for "some adversary $A \in \mathcal{A}$" in the above equivalence. The concurrent probabilistic system $S = (Q, q^0, \mathcal{L}, \Sigma, Steps)$ satisfies the PBTL formula Φ iff $q^0 \models_{\mathcal{A}} \Phi$.

We now introduce ∀PBTL as a fragment of PBTL involving only *universal quantification over adversaries*.The syntax of ∀PBTL is defined as follows:

$$\Phi ::= \texttt{true} \mid \texttt{false} \mid a \mid \neg a \mid \Phi \wedge \Phi \mid \Phi \vee \Phi \mid [\Phi \, \forall \mathcal{U} \, \Phi]_{\sqsupseteq \lambda}$$

where a, λ and $\sqsupseteq$ are as in the definition of PBTL. The following theorem states that simulation and bisimulation preserve certain (∀)PBTL formulae, and is inspired by a conjecture in [5]. The proof follows from similar results of Segala [21], which are defined for an action-based, rather than a state-based logic such as PBTL, and of Aziz et al. [4], which concern fully probabilistic systems (that is, Markov chains, or, equivalently, concurrent probabilistic systems for which $|Steps(q)| = 1$ for all states $q \in Q$).

Theorem 1. *Let $\mathcal{S}$ be a concurrent probabilistic system, a set $\mathcal{A}$ of adversaries of $\mathcal{S}$, let $\Phi_\forall, \Phi$ be formulae of ∀PBTL and PBTL respectively, and let $q_1, q_2 \in Q$.*

- *If $q_1 \preceq q_2$, then $q_2 \models_{\mathcal{A}} \Phi_\forall$ implies $q_1 \models_{\mathcal{A}} \Phi_\forall$.*
- *If $q_1 \simeq q_2$, then $q_1 \models_{\mathcal{A}} \Phi$ iff $q_2 \models_{\mathcal{A}} \Phi$.*

Naturally, for the two concurrent probabilistic systems $\mathcal{S}_1 = (Q_1, q_1^0, \mathcal{L}_1, \Sigma_1, Steps_1)$ and $\mathcal{S}_2 = (Q_2, q_2^0, \mathcal{L}_2, \Sigma_2, Steps_2)$, if $q_1^0 \preceq q_2^0$, then $\mathcal{S}_2 \models_{\mathcal{A}} \Phi_\forall$ implies $\mathcal{S}_1 \models_{\mathcal{A}} \Phi_\forall$. Similarly, if $q_1^0 \simeq q_2^0$, then $\mathcal{S}_1 \models_{\mathcal{A}} \Phi$ if and only if $\mathcal{S}_2 \models_{\mathcal{A}} \Phi$. Observe that Theorem 1 implies a decidable PBTL model checking procedure for any infinite-state concurrent probabilistic system with a finitary bisimilarity relation via reduction to the quotient concurrent probabilistic system, which can then be verified using the techniques of [7,6].

3.3   Semantics of Probabilistic Hybrid Automata

The semantics of a given probabilistic hybrid automaton H can be represented in terms of a concurrent probabilistic system in the following way. The subsequent notation is used to reason about the target states of the probabilistic transitions of H. Let $\mathbf{a} \in \mathbb{R}^n$, $Z \in Rect(\mathcal{X})$ be a rectangle and $X \subseteq \mathcal{X}$. Then $\mathbf{a}[X := Z]$ denotes the set of valuations such that $\mathbf{a}' \in \mathbf{a}[X := Z]$ iff $\mathbf{a}' \in Z$ and $\mathbf{a}'_i = \mathbf{a}_i$ for all $x_i \in \mathcal{X} \setminus X$. Now, consider the valuation $\mathbf{a} \in \mathbb{R}^n$ and the m-vector $\langle \eta \rangle = [(Z^1, X^1), ..., (Z^m, X^m)]$, where, for each $j \in \{1, ..., m\}$, the set Z^j is a rectangle and $X^j \subseteq \mathcal{X}$ is a variable set. Then we generate the m-vector of valuations $\langle \mathbf{b} \rangle = [\mathbf{b}^1, ..., \mathbf{b}^m]$ in the following way: for each $j \in \{1, ..., m\}$, we choose a valuation $\mathbf{b}^j \in \mathbb{R}^n$ such that $\mathbf{b}^j \in \mathbf{a}[X^j := Z^j]$. Observe that, for any $i, j \in \{1, ..., m\}$ such that $i \neq j$, it may be the case that $\mathbf{a}[X^i := Z^i]$ and $\mathbf{a}[X^j := Z^j]$ have a non-empty intersection, and therefore it is possible that $\mathbf{b}^i = \mathbf{b}^j$. Let Combinations$(\mathbf{a}, \langle \eta \rangle)$ be the set of all such vectors $\langle \mathbf{b} \rangle$. In the sequel, we use exclusively vectors of the form of $\langle \eta \rangle$ which comprise of post-conditions and variable sets in the support of a distribution. For the distribution μ, we let the vector extract$(\mu) = [(post^1, X^1), ..., (post^m, X^m)]$ if support$(\mu) = \{(w^1, post^1, X^1), ..., (w^m, post^m, X^m)\}$.

The (time-abstract) *concurrent probabilistic system* $\mathcal{S}_H = (Q_H, q_H^0, \mathcal{L}_H, \Sigma_H, Steps_H)$ of the probabilistic hybrid automaton $H = (\mathcal{X}, V, L, init, inv, flow, prob, \langle pre \rangle_{v \in V})$ is defined as follows:

- $Q_H \subseteq V \times \mathbb{R}^n$ such that $(v, \mathbf{a}) \in Q_H$ iff $\mathbf{a} \in inv(v)$;
- $q_H^0 \in Q_H$ such that $q_H^0 = (v, init(v))$ for $v \in V$ such that $init(v) \neq \emptyset$;
- for each $(v, \mathbf{a}) \in Q_H$, we have $\mathcal{L}(v, \mathbf{a}) = L(v)$;
- $\Sigma_H = \{\theta, \tau\}$;
- for each $(v, \mathbf{a}) \in Q_H$, we have $Steps_H(v, \mathbf{a}) = Cts_H(v, \mathbf{a}) \cup Disc_H(v, \mathbf{a})$, where:
  - for each $\delta \in \mathbb{R}_{\geq 0}$, there exists the pair $(\tau, \mathcal{D}(v, \mathbf{b})) \in Cts_H(v, \mathbf{a})$ iff $\mathbf{b} \in inv(v)$, and there exists a differentiable function $f : [0, \delta] \to \mathbb{R}^n$ with $\dot{f} : (0, \delta) \to \mathbb{R}^n$ such that $f(0) = \mathbf{a}$, $f(\delta) = \mathbf{b}$, and $\dot{f} \in flow(q, f(\epsilon))$ and $f(\epsilon) \in inv(v)$ for all $\epsilon \in (0, \delta)$;
  - for each $\mu \in prob(v)$, if $\mathbf{a} \in pre_v(p)$, then there exists the pair $(\theta, \nu_{\langle \mathbf{b} \rangle}) \in Disc_H(v, \mathbf{a})$, for each $\langle \mathbf{b} \rangle \in \mathsf{Combinations}(\mathbf{a}, extract(\mu))$, iff there exists $\mu \in prob(v)$ such that:

$$\nu_{\langle \mathbf{b} \rangle}(w, \mathbf{c}) = \sum_{i \in \{1, \ldots, |\mathsf{support}(\mu)|\}\,\&\,\mathbf{c} = \mathbf{b}^i} \mu(w, post^i, X^i).$$

For a state $(v, \mathbf{a}) \in Q_H$, the definition of the continuous transitions in $Cts_H(v, \mathbf{a})$ is identical to the analogous definition for non-probabilistic hybrid automata, except that we require them to be made according to Dirac distributions (that is, with probability 1). The definition of the transitions in $Disc_H(v, \mathbf{a})$ reflects the intuition that H performs a control switch in the following manner: by (a) choosing an enabled distribution nondeterministically; (b) selecting a target mode and post-condition set probabilistically; and (c) choosing a successor state within the post-condition set nondeterministically. It is easy to verify that combining the two nondeterministic choices that comprise the first and third steps of the transition into a *single* nondeterministic selection, in the manner of the definition of $\mathcal{S}_H$, results in an equivalent transition. Naturally, if the post-condition set of at least one tuple in the support of a distribution μ is uncountable, then the set of vectors of the form $\langle \mathbf{b} \rangle$ associated with this set will also be uncountable, as will the set of transitions in $Disc_H(.)$ corresponding to μ. As a further note, observe that the definitions of (bi)simulation are applicable to concurrent probabilistic systems of probabilistic hybrid automata. Finally, a notion of *time divergence* can be associated with adversaries of the concurrent probabilistic systems of probabilistic hybrid automata; we omit details for reasons of space.

4   Model Checking Subclasses of Probabilistic Hybrid Automata

4.1   Probabilistic Multisingular and O-Minimal Hybrid Automata

The results of [1] and [18], which state the existence of finite bisimulation quotients of non-probabilistic multisingular and o-minimal hybrid automata respectively, can be extended to the probabilistic context in the following way. Firstly, the *region equivalence* of [2,1] can be used to subdivide the infinitary state space of a probabilistic multisingular automaton M into a finite number of equivalence classes. Without loss of generality (see [3]), let all endpoints of rectangles used in the description of M be non-negative integers, with the maximal such integer denoted by c. For any $t \in \mathbb{R}$, let $\lfloor t \rfloor$ denote its integral part and $frac(t)$ its fractional part. For a vector $\mathbf{a}$, let $\lfloor \mathbf{a} \rfloor$ denote the vector whose ith coordinate is $\lfloor \mathbf{a}_i \rfloor$, and $frac(\mathbf{a})$ the vector whose ith coordinate is $frac(\mathbf{a}_i)$. For each mode $v \in V$, let $\langle \zeta^v \rangle = [\zeta_1^v, ..., \zeta_n^v]$ be the n-vector such that the ith element of $\langle \zeta^v \rangle$ is $flow(v)_i$ if $flow(v)_i \neq 0$, and is 1 otherwise. Let $\equiv^{\zeta^v}$ be the equivalence relation on $\mathbb{R}^n$ such that $\mathbf{a} \equiv^{\zeta^v} \mathbf{b}$ iff, for each $x_i, x_j \in \mathcal{X}$, (1) $\lfloor \zeta_i^v \mathbf{a}_i \rfloor = \lfloor \zeta_i^v \mathbf{b}_i \rfloor$, (2) $frac(\zeta_i^v \mathbf{a}_i) = frac(\zeta_i^v \mathbf{b}_i)$, and (3) $frac(\zeta_i^v \mathbf{a}_i) = frac(\zeta_j^v \mathbf{a}_j)$ iff $frac(\zeta_i^v \mathbf{b}_i) = frac(\zeta_j^v \mathbf{b}_j)$. Two states $(v, \mathbf{a})$ and $(w, \mathbf{b})$ are *region equivalent*, written $(v, \mathbf{a}) \equiv^R (w, \mathbf{b})$, if (1) $v = w$, (2) for each $x_i \in \mathcal{X}$, either $\lfloor \mathbf{a}_i \rfloor = \lfloor \mathbf{b}_i \rfloor$, or both $\mathbf{a}_i > c$ and $\mathbf{b}_i > c$, and (3) $frac(\mathbf{a}) \equiv^{\zeta^v} frac(\mathbf{b})$ (our notation is adapted from [10]). Intuitively, for each control mode $v \in V$, region equivalence subdivides $\mathbb{R}^n$ into a finite grid of unit hypercubes, which are in turn subdivided according to the flow gradients $flow(v, \cdot)_i = k_i$ of each $x_i \in \mathcal{X}$.

Lemma 1. *Let M be a probabilistic multisingular automaton. Region equivalence $\equiv^R$ is a finite bisimulation of $\mathcal{S}_M$.*

Proof. Clearly $\equiv^R$ has a finite number of equivalence classes; therefore, it remains to show that $\equiv^R$ is a bisimulation. The case for the continuous transitions in the sets $Cts_M(.)$ is similar to that in the non-probabilistic context, and therefore we concentrate on the discrete transitions in $Disc_M(.)$.

Observe that the set of valuations in a given region equivalence class is either contained within any rectangle Z used in the description of M, or is disjoint from Z. In particular, all valuations within such a class must be in the same pre-condition sets of M, and therefore enable the same distributions for choice. That is, if two states $(v, \mathbf{a}), (v, \mathbf{b}) \in Q_M$ are such that $(v, \mathbf{a}) \equiv^R (v, \mathbf{b})$, then, for any $\mu \in prob(v)$, we have $\mathbf{a} \in pre_v(\mu)$ if and only if $\mathbf{b} \in pre_v(\mu)$. Therefore, there exists an event-distribution pair $(\theta, \nu^1) \in Steps_M(v, \mathbf{a})$ if and only if there exists $(\theta, \nu^2) \in Steps_M(v, \mathbf{b})$, such that both ν^1 and ν^2 are derived from μ. Now we show that $\nu^1 \equiv^R \nu^2$. A standard fact is that, given $(v, \mathbf{a}) \equiv^R (v, \mathbf{b})$, for any tuple $(w, post, X) \in V \times 2^{\mathbb{R}^n} \times 2^{\mathcal{X}}$ such that $post$ is a singleton, we have $(w, \mathbf{a}[X := post]) \equiv^R (w, \mathbf{b}[X := post])$. Furthermore, if the tuples $(w, post, X), (w, post', X') \in V \times 2^{\mathbb{R}^n} \times 2^{\mathcal{X}}$ are such that $(w, \mathbf{a}[X := post]) = (w, \mathbf{a}[X' := post'])$, then it must be the case that $(w, \mathbf{b}[X := post]) = (w, \mathbf{b}[X' := post'])$. The combination of these facts then gives us that, for $(w, \mathbf{c}), (w, \mathbf{d}) \in Q_M$ which are such that $(w, \mathbf{c}) \equiv^R (w, \mathbf{d})$:

$$\nu^1(w, \mathbf{c}) = \sum_{\substack{i \in \{1,...,k\} \\ \& \mathbf{c}=\mathbf{a}[X^i:=post^i]}} \mu(w, post^i, X^i) = \sum_{\substack{i \in \{1,...,k\} \\ \& \mathbf{d}=\mathbf{b}[X^i:=post^i]}} \mu(w, post^i, X^i) = \nu^2(w, \mathbf{d}),$$

where $k = |\mathsf{support}(\mu)|$. The fact that $\nu^1 \equiv^R \nu^2$ then follows. We can repeat this process for all region equivalence classes, and all distributions enabled in these classes, to conclude that $\equiv^R$ satisfies the properties of bisimulation. □

Secondly, we show that the model checking results for o-minimal hybrid automata of [18,3] transfer to the probabilistic context. Observe that the previous decidability results for this class necessitate the *decoupling* of discrete and continuous behaviour of the hybrid automata; more precisely, all variables are reset to a new value at every discrete transition. The result of [18] then shows that, for each control mode $v \in V$, the associated continuous state space of v has a finite bisimulation quotient. This quotient is obtained after an initial subdivision of the continuous space of v according to the invariant set of v, the pre-condition sets of all the outgoing discrete transitions of v, and the post-condition sets of all incoming discrete transitions of v. Similarly, in our context, we require that such an initial subdivision is made according to $pre_v(\mu)$, for all $\mu \in prob(v)$, in addition to $inv(v)$ and all post-condition sets *post* appearing in tuples of the form $(v, post, \mathcal{X}) \in \mathsf{support}(\mu')$, for all $\mu' \in prob(v')$ and $v' \in V$.

Consider the probabilistic o-minimal hybrid automaton O, and let $(v, \mathbf{a})$, $(v, \mathbf{b}) \in Q_O$ be two states such that $\mathbf{a}, \mathbf{b} \in pre_v(\mu)$ for some $\mu \in prob(v)$. Because the reset set for all tuples $(w, post, \mathcal{X}) \in \mathsf{support}(\mu)$ is the full variable set $\mathcal{X}$, it follows that $\mathsf{Combinations}(\mathbf{a}, \mathsf{extract}(\mu)) = \mathsf{Combinations}(\mathbf{b}, \mathsf{extract}(\mu))$. Intuitively, given that the distribution μ is enabled in $(v, \mathbf{a})$ and $(v, \mathbf{b})$, the distinction between the valuations $\mathbf{a}$ and $\mathbf{b}$ is lost after taking μ. Therefore, the sets of concurrent probabilistic system distributions corresponding to the choice of μ is the same for $(v, \mathbf{a})$ and $(v, \mathbf{b})$. Now consider the case in which $(v, \mathbf{a})$ and $(v, \mathbf{b})$ lie in the intersection of the pre-condition sets of multiple distributions $\mu_1, ..., \mu_l \in prob(v)$, where $l \in \{1, ..., |prob(v)|\}$. Then, extending our intuition from the single distribution μ to the set $\{\mu_1, ..., \mu_l\}$, we have the strong characteristic that $Disc_O(v, \mathbf{a}) = Disc_O(v, \mathbf{b})$. Such intersections of pre-conditions are further subdivided with respect to continuous transitions using the methodology of [18]. Given that $(v, \mathbf{a})$ and $(v, \mathbf{b})$ lie in the same portion of the state space according to this subdivision, we conclude that $(v, \mathbf{a})$ and $(v, \mathbf{b})$ are bisimilar.

Lemma 2. *Let O be a probabilistic o-minimal hybrid automata. O has a finite bisimulation quotient.*

Corollary 1. *The PBTL model checking problems for probabilistic multisingular automata and probabilistic o-minimal hybrid automata are decidable.*

4.2   Probabilistic Rectangular Automata

We now introduce a model checking strategy for initialised probabilistic rectangular automata, based on similar results in the non-probabilistic context of [20,12]. From an initialised probabilistic rectangular automaton R, we construct a probabilistic multisingular automaton M_R, such that M_R is a *sufficient abstraction* of R which can subsequently be verified. More precisely, each variable $x_i \in \mathcal{X}$ of R is represented by two variables $y_{l(i)}, y_{u(i)} \in \mathcal{Y}$ of M_R, with the intuition that $y_{l(i)}$ tracks the least possible value of x_i, whereas $y_{u(i)}$ tracks its greatest possible value. Therefore, singular flow conditions for $y_{l(i)}$ (respectively, $y_{u(i)}$) are derived from the minimal (respectively, maximal) slopes that x_i may take in R. Furthermore, the probabilistic edge relation of M_R updates $y_{l(i)}$ and $y_{u(i)}$ so that the interval $[y_{l(i)}, y_{u(i)}]$ represents the possible values of x_i. For example, consider Figure 2(a); say the current control mode is v, and that the flow

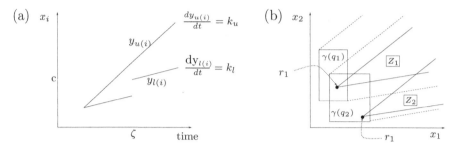

Fig. 2. (a) Updating the value of x_i. (b) M_R simulates R.

condition $flow(v)_i$ of the variable x_i is the rectangle $[k_l, k_u]$. As time passes, the possible values of x_i are contained within an envelope, the lower (respectively, upper) bound of which is represented by $y_{l(i)}$ (respectively, $y_{u(i)}$). If a control switch occurs, the values of $y_{l(i)}$ and $y_{u(i)}$ must continue to represent the possible values of x_i; this may involve resetting $y_{l(i)}$ or $y_{u(i)}$, or both, even if x_i is not reset by the corresponding control switch. In Figure 2(a), at time ζ a distribution μ is chosen, where $pre_v(\mu) = [c, \infty)$, and say a tuple $(w, post, X) \in \mathsf{support}(\mu)$ is probabilistically selected for which $x_i \notin X$. Then, for $y_{l(i)}$ to correctly represent the lower bound on x, it must be updated to c when emulating this control switch, as its value is below c when the distribution μ was selected. This reflects the standard intuition in the non-probabilistic case of [12].

Let $R = (\mathcal{X}, V, L, init^R, inv^R, flow^R, prob^R, \langle pre_v^R \rangle_{v \in V})$ be an initialised probabilistic rectangular automaton subject to the following simplifying assumptions. For all control modes $v \in V$, we have $inv^R(v) = \mathbb{R}^n$, and the rectangle $flow^R(v, \cdot)$ is compact; for all $\mu \in prob^R(v)$, the rectangle $pre_v^R(\mu)$ is compact, and for each $(w, post, X) \in \mathsf{support}(\mu)$, the rectangle $post$ is compact. [2] Then $M_R = (\mathcal{Y}, V, L, init^{M_R}, inv^{M_R}, flow^{M_R}, prob^{M_R}, \langle pre_v^{M_R} \rangle_{v \in V})$ is the probabilistic multisingular automaton constructed in the following way.

Variables $\mathcal{Y} = \{y_1, ..., y_{2n}\}$, where the $l(i)$-th variable $y_{l(i)}$ represents the lower bound on the i-th variable $x_i \in \mathcal{X}$ of R, the $u(i)$-th variable $y_{u(i)}$ represents the upper bound on $x_i \in \mathcal{X}$, and $l(i) = 2i - 1$, $u(i) = 2i$.

Initial and invariant sets. For each control mode $v \in V$ and each $x_i \in \mathcal{X}$, we have $init^{M_R}(v)_{l(i)} = init^{M_R}(v)_{u(i)} = init^R(v)_i$, and $inv^{M_R}(v) = \mathbb{R}^{2n}$.

Flow inclusion. For each control mode $v \in V$ and $x_i \in \mathcal{X}$, if $flow^R(v, \cdot)_i = [l, u]$ then $flow^{M_R}(v, \cdot)_{l(i)} = l$ and $flow^{M_R}(v, \cdot)_{u(i)} = u$.

Probability distributions. For each control mode $v \in V$ and $\mu^R \in prob^R(v)$, there exists a corresponding set $\{\mu_1^{M_R}, ..., \mu_4^{M_R}\} \subseteq prob^{M_R}(v)$, which takes the following form. For each tuple $(w, post^R, X) \in \mathsf{support}(\mu^R)$, and for all $j \in \{1, ..., 4\}$, a corresponding tuple $(w, post_j^{M_R}, Y_j) \in \mathsf{support}(\mu_j^{M_R})$ exists, such that $\mu_j^{M_R}(w, post_j^{M_R}, Y_j) = \mu^R(w, post_j^R, X)$. Let $[l_i, u_i] = pre_v^R(\mu^R)_i$

---

[2] Note that it follows from [12] that *all* of these assumptions may be dropped; however, in such a case, the construction of M_R requires significant book-work that is independent of probabilistic concerns.

and $[l'_i, u'_i] = (post^R)_i$ for each $i \in \{1, ..., n\}$. If $x_i \in X$, then $(post_j^{M_R})_{l(i)} = l'_i$, $(post_j^{M_R})_{u(i)} = u'_i$, and $y_{l(i)}, y_{u(i)} \in Y_j$ for each $j \in \{1, ..., 4\}$. However, if $x_i \notin X$, then $(post_j^{M_R})_{l(i)}$, $(post_j^{M_R})_{u(i)}$, and Y_j are defined as follows:

$$
\begin{aligned}
(post_1^{M_R})_{l(i)} = l_i, \quad &(post_1^{M_R})_{u(i)} = u'_i, \quad y_{l(i)} \in Y_1; \\
(post_2^{M_R})_{l(i)} = l_i, \quad &(post_2^{M_R})_{u(i)} = u_i, \quad y_{l(i)}, y_{u(i)} \in Y_2; \\
(post_3^{M_R})_{l(i)} = l'_i, \quad &(post_3^{M_R})_{u(i)} = u'_i; \quad \text{no requirement on } Y_3; \\
(post_4^{M_R})_{l(i)} = l'_i, \quad &(post_4^{M_R})_{u(i)} = u_i, \quad y_{u(i)} \in Y_4.
\end{aligned}
$$

Pre-condition sets. For every $v \in V$ and $\mu^R \in prob^R(v)$, we define the pre-condition sets for $\{\mu_1^{M_R}, ..., \mu_4^{M_R}\} \subseteq prob^{M_R}(v)$ in the following way. For every $i \in \{1, ..., n\}$, if $pre_v^R(\mu^R)_i = [l, u]$, let:

$$
\begin{aligned}
pre_v^{M_R}(\mu_1^{M_R})_{l(i)} &= (-\infty, l), \quad pre_v^{M_R}(\mu_1^{M_R})_{u(i)} = [l, u]; \\
pre_v^{M_R}(\mu_2^{M_R})_{l(i)} &= (-\infty, l), \quad pre_v^{M_R}(\mu_2^{M_R})_{u(i)} = (u, \infty); \\
pre_v^{M_R}(\mu_3^{M_R})_{l(i)} &= [l, u], \quad pre_v^{M_R}(\mu_3^{M_R})_{u(i)} = [l, u]; \\
pre_v^{M_R}(\mu_4^{M_R})_{l(i)} &= [l, u], \quad pre_v^{M_R}(\mu_4^{M_R})_{u(i)} = (u, \infty).
\end{aligned}
$$

The function $\gamma : Q_{M_R} \to 2^{Q_R}$ of [12], where $\gamma(v, \mathbf{a}) = \{v\} \times \Pi_{i=1}^n [\mathbf{a}_{l(i)}, \mathbf{a}_{u(i)}]$, can also be used in the probabilistic context to relate a set of states of R to a state of M_R. We now propose a strategy for model checking R via the construction of M_R. More precisely, R is simulated by M_R (that is, the initial state of R is simulated by the initial state of M_R), and, by Theorem 1, if a $\forall$PBTL formula Φ is satisfied by M_R, then this is sufficient for concluding that Φ is also satisfied by R. Observe that the simulation is obtained by viewing γ as a relation.

Lemma 3. *Let R be a probabilistic rectangular automaton, and M_R be the probabilistic multisingular automaton constructed from R. Let $q \in Q_{M_R}$ be a state of $\mathcal{S}_{M_R}$, and let $r \in \gamma(q)$ be a state of $\mathcal{S}_R$. Then $r \preceq q$.*

We omit the proof of Lemma 3 for reasons of space. An example of the way in which M_R forward simulates R is shown in Figure 2(b). Let the variable set of R contain two variables, x_1 and x_2. Consider a state $r \in Q_R$ of R, and a state $q \in Q_{M_R}$ of M_R which are such that $r \in \gamma(q)$. Say R nondeterministically selects an enabled distribution μ^R for choice, which, by construction of M_R, can be matched in q by one (and because the pre-conditions of each distribution are disjoint, only one) of the four distributions $\{\mu_1^{M_R}, ..., \mu_4^{M_R}\}$; let $\mu_j^{M_R}$ be this distribution, for some $j \in \{1, ..., 4\}$. Let $\mu^R(w, post_1^R, X_1) = \frac{1}{3}$, $\mu^R(w, post_2^R, X_2) = \frac{1}{6}$, and $\mu^R(w, post_3^R, X_3) = \frac{1}{2}$. From the construction of M_R, $\mu_j^{M_R}(w, post_{j,1}^{M_R}, Y_1) = \frac{1}{3}$, $\mu_j^{M_R}(w, post_{j,2}^{M_R}, Y_2) = \frac{1}{6}$, $\mu_j^{M_R}(w, post_{j,3}^{M_R}, Y_3) = \frac{1}{2}$. Say $post_2^R, X_2$ and $post_3^R, X_3$ are such that, when applied to r, they result in the same target sets of states. Then the maximal and minimal values of x_1, x_2 encoded in M_R will be the same for $post_2^R, X_2$ and $post_3^R, X_3$, and therefore the probability of M_R making a transition to the state q_2, which encodes these values, will be $\nu^{M_R}(q_2) = \mu_j^{M_R}(w, post_{j,2}^{M_R}, Y_2) + \mu_j^{M_R}(w, post_{j,3}^{M_R}, Y_3) = \frac{1}{6} + \frac{1}{2} = \frac{2}{3}$. We encode the maximal and minimal values reached by M_R from q after the probabilistic choice of $(w, post_{j,1}^{M_R}, Y_1)$ to be q_1; therefore, $\nu^{M_R}(q_1) = \mu_j^{M_R}(w, post_{j,1}^{M_R}, Y_1) = \frac{1}{3}$. Say the rectangular sets encoded by q_1 and q_2 via γ overlap (see Figure 2(b)). Consider the case in which, after probabilistically choosing either of the tuples $(w, post_1^R, X_1)$ and $(w, post_2^R, X_2)$, the *same* target state r_1 is selected by R, which, naturally, is in the intersection of the state sets defined by $\gamma(q_1)$ and $\gamma(q_2)$. We let the choice of target state after the probabilistic choice of $(w, post_3^R, X_3)$ to be r_2, which is in $\gamma(q_2)$ but not $\gamma(q_1)$. Then, from our view of γ as inducing the simulation, we have $r_1 \preceq q_1$ and $r_1, r_2 \preceq q_2$. Say ν^R is the distribution of $\mathcal{S}_R$ corresponding to the states r_1 and r_2; then $\nu^R(r_1) = \mu^R(w, post_1^R, X_1) + \mu^R(w, post_2^R, X_2) = \frac{1}{3} + \frac{1}{6} = \frac{1}{2}$, and $\nu^R(r_2) = \mu^R(w, post_3^R, X_3) = \frac{1}{2}$. To show that $\nu^R \preceq \nu^{M_R}$, the weight function w, which relates ν^R and ν^{M_R} via $\preceq$, is defined: let $w(r_1, q_1) = \frac{1}{3}, w(r_1, q_2) = \frac{1}{6}, w(r_2, q_2) = \frac{1}{2}$. Note that the weight function is obtained from the probabilities assigned by μ^R to tuples in its support; this fact can be used to derive a weight function for any probabilistic transition of R and M_R.

The argument that γ induces a simulation with regard to *continuous* transitions follows from the non-probabilistic precedent of [20,12]. In Figure 2(b), both q_1 and q_2 can simulate all of the transitions from any state lying in the intersection $\gamma(q_1) \cap \gamma(q_2)$, such as r_1. For example, the distribution with the precondition Z_1 is enabled in r_1, q_1 and q_2, after some time has elapsed. However, as r_2 is in $\gamma(q_2)$ but not $\gamma(q_1)$, the state q_2, but not q_1, can simulate the choice of the distribution with the pre-condition Z_2 by r_2.

Proposition 1. *Let R, M_R be defined as in Lemma 3. For any $\forall PBTL$ formula Φ, if $\mathcal{S}_{M_R} \models_\mathcal{A} \Phi$ then $\mathcal{S}_R \models_\mathcal{A} \Phi$.*

5   Conclusions

Model checking for hybrid systems is well known to be expensive, and the strategies presented in this paper are no exception. For multisingular automata, the size of the region quotient is exponential in the number of variables used and the magnitude of the upper bounds used in the description of the sets of the model. Furthermore, the verification algorithm for PBTL [7,6] is polynomial in the size of this quotient and linear in the size of the formula. Therefore, further work could address the inefficiencies of this method, for example exploiting model checking methods of [13] for rectangular automata. Formalisms which admit continuous probabilistic behaviour, such as stochastic hybrid systems [14], are also of interest, and could be subject to a variant of the model checking technique for timed automata with continuously distributed delays of [17].

References

1. R. Alur, C. Courcoubetis, N. Halbwachs, T. A. Henzinger, P.-H. Ho, X. Nicollin, A. Olivero, J. Sifakis, and S. Yovine. The algorithmic analysis of hybrid systems. *Theoretical Computer Science*, 138:3–34, 1995.

2. R. Alur and D. Dill. A theory of timed automata. *Theoretical Computer Science*, 126:183–235, 1994.
3. R. Alur, T. A. Henzinger, G. Lafferriere, and G. J. Pappas. Discrete abstractions of hybrid systems. To appear in *Proceedings of the IEEE*, 2000.
4. A. Aziz, V. Singhal, F. Balarin, R. Brayton, and A. Sangiovanni-Vincentelli. It usually works: the temporal logic of stochastic systems. In *Proc. 7th CAV*, volume 939 of *Lecture Notes in Computer Science*, pages 155–165. Springer-Verlag, 1995.
5. C. Baier. On algorithmic verification methods for probabilistic systems, 1998. Habilitation thesis, University of Mannheim.
6. C. Baier and M. Kwiatkowska. Model checking for a probabilistic branching time logic with fairness. *Distributed Computing*, 11:125–155, 1998.
7. A. Bianco and L. de Alfaro. Model checking of probabilistic and nondeterministic systems. In *Proc. FST&TCS'95*, volume 1026 of *LNCS*, pages 499–513. Springer-Verlag, 1995.
8. L. de Alfaro, M. Kwiatkowska, G. Norman, D. Parker, and R. Segala. Symbolic model checking of concurrent probabilistic processes using MTBDDs and the Kronecker representation. In *Proc. TACAS'00*, volume 1785 of *LNCS*, pages 395–410. Springer-Verlag, 2000.
9. H. Hansson and B. Jonsson. A logic for reasoning about time and reliability. *Formal Aspects of Computing*, 6(5):512–535, 1994.
10. T. A. Henzinger, B. Horowitz, and R. Majumdar. Rectangular hybrid games. In *Proc. CONCUR'99*, volume 1664 of *LNCS*, pages 320–335. Springer-Verlag, 1999.
11. T. A. Henzinger, B. Horowitz, R. Majumdar, and H. Wong-Toi. Beyond HyTech: hybrid systems analysis using interval numerical methods. In *Proc. HSCC'00*, volume 1790 of *LNCS*, pages 130–144. Springer-Verlag, 2000.
12. T. A. Henzinger, P. Kopke, A. Puri, and P. Varaiya. What's decidable about hybrid automata? *Journal of Computer and System Sciences*, 57(1):94–124, 1998.
13. T. A. Henzinger and R. Majumdar. Symbolic model checking for rectangular hybrid systems. In *Proc. TACAS'00*, volume 1785 of *LNCS*, pages 142–156. Springer-Verlag, 2000.
14. J. Hu, J. Lygeros, and S. Sastry. Towards a theory of stochastic hybrid systems. In *Proc. HSCC'00*, volume 1790 of *LNCS*. Springer-Verlag, 2000.
15. B. Jonsson and K. G. Larsen. Specification and refinement of probabilistic processes. In *Proc. 6th LICS*, pages 266–279. IEEE Computer Society Press, 1991.
16. M. Kwiatkowska, G. Norman, R. Segala, and J. Sproston. Automatic verification of real-time systems with discrete probability distributions. To appear in *Theoretical Computer Science*, special issue on *ARTS'99: Formal Methods for Real-time and Probabilistic Systems*, 2000.
17. M. Kwiatkowska, G. Norman, R. Segala, and J. Sproston. Verifying quantitative properties of continuous probabilistic timed automata. In *Proc. CONCUR'00*, *LNCS*. Springer-Verlag, 2000.
18. G. Lafferriere, G. Pappas, and S. Yovine. A new class of decidable hybrid systems. In *Proc. HSCC'99*, volume 1569 of *LNCS*, pages 137–151. Springer-Verlag, 1999.
19. R. Milner. *Communication and Concurrency*. International Series in Computer Science. Prentice Hall, 1989.
20. A. Olivero, J. Sifakis, and S. Yovine. Using abstractions for the verification of linear hybrid systems. In *Proc. 6th CAV*, volume 818 of *LNCS*, pages 81–94. Springer-Verlag, 1994.
21. R. Segala and N. Lynch. Probabilistic simulations for probabilistic processes. *Nordic Journal of Computing*, 2(2):250–273, 1995.

Invariant-Based Synthesis of Fault-Tolerant Systems

K. Lano[1], David Clark[2], K. Androutsopoulos[1], and P. Kan[1]

[1] Department of Computer Science,
King's College London, Strand, London WC2R 2LS
[2] Department of Computing, Imperial College, London SW7 2BZ

Abstract. Statecharts are a very widely used formalism for reactive system development, however there are problems in using them as a fully formal specification notation because of the conflicting variants of statechart semantics which exist. In this paper a modular subset of statechart notation is defined which has a simple semantics, and permits compositional development and verification. Techniques for decomposing specifications in this notation, design strategies for incorporating fault tolerance, and translation to the B formal language, are also described, and illustrated with extracts from a case study of a fault tolerant system.

1 Introduction

Finite state machines (FSMs) are highly recommended as a design method for safety-related systems of SIL levels 2 and above in the IEC 61508 standard [4]. Statecharts are based on state machines but add extra capabilities of modularization and expressiveness: grouping of states into superstates (OR composition) and grouping of OR states into concurrent collections (AND composition). However, in terms of their semantics, statecharts are much less transparent and more difficult to analyse than FSMs, a situation which is compounded by the conflicting variants of statechart semantics which exist. By taking advantage of the characteristic structures of reactive systems, a subset of classical statecharts may be selected as a modular specification notation for reactive systems, including real-time and fault-tolerant systems.

Section 2 defines SRS. Section 3 describes the overall development process and the translation from SRS to B AMN [9]. Section 4 illustrates the process on the case study.

2 Structured Reactive System (SRS) Statechart Notation

SRS is a modular subset of statecharts in which strong scoping on the parts of the statechart affected by a given event is imposed. An SRS statechart S is an AND composition of a set of *modules*: OR states which do not have AND states as direct or indirect substates. Modules are organised into a (client-server) hierarchy: a module transition may only send events to modules lower in the

M. Joseph (Ed.): FTRTFT 2000, LNCS 1926, pp. 46–57, 2000.
© Springer-Verlag Berlin Heidelberg 2000

hierarchy (the *receivers* of the module). Transitions in a SRS module M have labels of form $t : e[G]/e_1 \frown \ldots \frown e_n$ where t is an (optional) transition name, e the name of the event triggering t, G is a logical *guard condition*, and the e_i are the events generated by t. G is optional and defaults to *true*. The e_i are also optional. The e_i are events of modules in *receivers*(M), and only the states of modules in *receivers*(M) can be referred to in G.

Appendix A gives the formal definition of SRS and module systems. Typically modules in a module system represent sensors, controllers, subcontrollers, and actuators.

Figure 1 shows the typical arrangement of modules for a reactive system (LHS), and the associated hierarchy of modules under the *receivers* relation (RHS). *Subcontroller* 1 and *Subcontroller* 2 are the receivers of *Controller*, etc, *Actuator* 3 has transitions for $g1$ and $g2$. Each module is a separate OR state within an overall AND state representing the complete system.

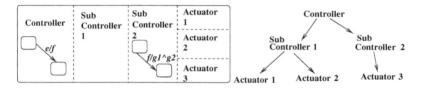

Fig. 1. Typical subsystem structure

3   Development Method

In our method, RSDS, reactive control systems are initially represented using data and control flow (DCFD) notation. Usually the behaviour of sensors, controllers and actuators will be specified using SRS modules in the notation of the appendix. Initially only sensors and actuators will have explicit state machine/module representations, and the specification of the mediating controller(s) will be implicit in a system invariant P in terms of sensor and actuator states. The form of P can be used to guide the decomposition of the controllers and to synthesise control actions, as described in [6]. Invariants of SRS modules are expressed in the following language. Let S consist of modules M_1, …, M_n where some of these modules describe the behaviour of sensors, others of controllers and others of actuators. For each module M a variable m_state is defined, of type $States_{flatten(M)}$, and formulae based on equalities $m\_state = s_1$ are used to express the current state of module M.

Except for the most trivial systems, it is necessary to modularise the specification of the control algorithm, in order to obtain analysable descriptions. There are several ways in which such a decomposition can be achieved:

1. *Hierarchical* composition of controllers: events e are dealt with first by an overseer controller S which handles certain interactions between components, and e (or derived events) are then sent to subordinate controllers responsible for managing the individual behaviour of subcomponents.

   This design can also be used to separate responsibility for dealing with certain aspects of a control problem (such as fault detection) from the calculation of control responses. For example in the steam boiler system of [1], detection and responses to inputs that indicate failure of components are handled in separate controllers to those which handle non-failed signals, using a "chain of responsibility" design pattern. A similar approach is used in the case study of Section 4.

2. *Horizontal* composition of controllers: events are copied to two separate control algorithms S_1 and S_2, which compute their reactions independently.

3. *Decomposition by control mode/phase:* A separate controller is specified for the control reactions to be carried out in each *mode* or *phase* of the system.

The first two are based on the *physical* decomposition of the actual system, whilst the third is based on *temporal decomposition*.

Invariants of controllers are decomposed into invariants of subcontrollers when the controller is structurally decomposed. A control algorithm is then synthesised for each of the controllers, based on their invariants [6].

Controller specifications expressed in a SRS module with invariants produce B machines whose set of operations correspond to the events which the controller responds to.

If the SRS description has a tree structured *receivers* relation, then the SRS structuring can be mapped directly to a corresponding structure in B: if module D is in *receivers*(C), then the machine C' for C INCLUDES the machine D'.

4   Case Study: Fault Tolerant Production Cell

This system [8] is one of a series of industrial case studies based on automated manufacturing requirements. It involves the processing of metal pieces which enter the system on a feed belt, are conveyed by robot arms to a press, processed in the press, and then conveyed by the robot to a deposit belt. The layout of this version differs from the simple production cell [7] in two ways: (i) there is no crane to make the whole process cyclical; (ii) there are two presses rather than one. Otherwise, the movements of the robot arms etc. are identical.

The specification makes no requirement of alternating the presses. Should one fail, then the other takes on all the blanks coming into the system, and once the faulty press is working properly, it is brought back online again.

The system is expected to conform to the three state safety model shown in Figure 2, with transitions between the normal operating and recoverable failure states, and transitions from these to the unrecoverable failure state. In the following section we prove this conformance by constructing abstraction morphisms from the full state space of the system to the 3 state model.

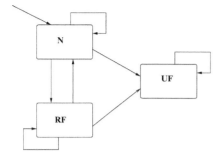

Fig. 2. Three State Failure Model for Production Cell

4.1 Statecharts and Abstraction

For each component of the cell, a series of abstractions and abstraction morphisms can be constructed. At the lowest level are the tuples of states of individual sensors and actuators within the component. For a press, for example,
the basic state is a tuple $(ok, lows, mids, ups, bs, ms, pts, stm, pval)$ where ok is a
boolean indicating if the press is failed or not, $lows$ is the lower position sensor,
etc, bs is the blank in press sensor, stm is a boolean indicating that the arm is
clear of the press, pts is the press timer state ($idle$, $active$ or $expired$), $pval$ is
the timer value (pul, plm, pmu reflecting the deadlines for movement from the
upper to the lower position, etc) and ms is the press motor state. For a single
press there are therefore $4 * 3^7$ basic component states (8748). By constructing
a suitable abstraction morphism to a simpler component model, we can create a
clearer and more easily verified specification, both at the requirements and SRS
level and in the B code.

In this case the high-level state ($pstate$) of a press is one of: (i) waiting to
receive ($w2r$): $ok = true$, ($bs = no$ or $stm = false$), $mids = yes$, $lows = no$,
$ups = no$, $ms = off$, $pts = idle$; (ii) processing: $ok = yes$, $bs = yes$, $lows = no$,
$ms = up$, $pts = active$, $stm = true$, $pval = pmu$, $ups = no$; (iii) completing: $ok =$
yes, $bs = yes$, $ms = down$, $lows = no$, $stm = true$, $pts = active$, $pval = pul$;
(iv) waiting to deliver ($w2d$): $ok = yes$, ($bs = yes$ or $stm = false$), $lows = yes$,
$mids = no$, $ups = no$, $ms = off$, $pts = idle$; (v): returning: $ok = yes$, $bs = no$,
$mids = no$, $ups = no$, $ms = up$, $stm = true$, $pts = active$, $pval = plm$; (vi):
failure: any state where $ok = false$. $ms = off$ will also be true in this state.

States where $bs = 0$ or $lows = 0$ or $mids = 0$ or $ups = 0$, where any
two of $lows$, $mids$ and ups are yes, or where $stm = false$ with $ms \neq off$, or
$pts = expired$ with $ms \neq off$ are excluded from (i) to (v): any event which leads
to any of these conditions triggers a transition to $failure$. There are transitions
to $failure$ from any of the other states (which can be grouped into a superstate
$normal$). Operational invariants of the system can then be simply defined using
the abstract state $pstate$, for example

$$pstate = w2r \land \bigcirc stm = true \land bs = yes \implies \bigcirc pstate = processing$$

The module defining the control algorithm derived from these invariants is shown in Figure 3. States are expressed in the form $(lows, mids, ups, bs, ms, pts, stm, pval)$, superstates indicated by letters C, R, etc.

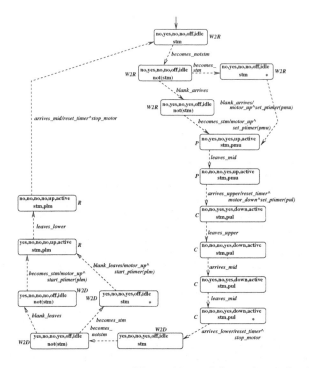

Fig. 3. Normal State Controller for Press

A further abstraction to a two state (normal/failure) model can then be made simply on the basis of the *ok* state value.

Each of the components of the production cell can likewise be abstracted to a basic safety/operational model consisting of two states, a normal and a failed state, and a transition from normal to failed and self-transitions on both states. The flattened product of these component models therefore has 256 states in the form of tuples: (feed belt, elevating rotating table, robot, robot arm 1, robot arm 2, press 1, press 2, deposit belt).

An abstraction morphism from this state machine to the three state global safety model for the cell is defined by:

1. All components *normal*: $\longmapsto$ N
2. One component failed, either press 1 or press 2 $\longmapsto$ RF
3. Both presses failed, or some other component failed $\longmapsto$ UF

Transitions are mapped correspondingly. This abstraction is an adequate refinement. A complete reachability analysis concerning failure modes can therefore be carried out on this model more effectively than on the fully flattened state machine model of the system (adequacy of $\sigma : C \rightarrow A$ implies that t is reachable from s in a concrete model C iff $\sigma(t)$ is reachable from $\sigma(s)$ in the abstraction A).

4.2 Controller Decomposition

Because of the relative independence of the control invariants for the separate sub-components of the cell, a hierarchical control structure can be used (Figure 4). Interaction between components is managed by supervisor controllers which send commands to the controllers of the individual components involved in a particular interaction. Detection of failures is handled by the FDC (Failure Detection Controller).

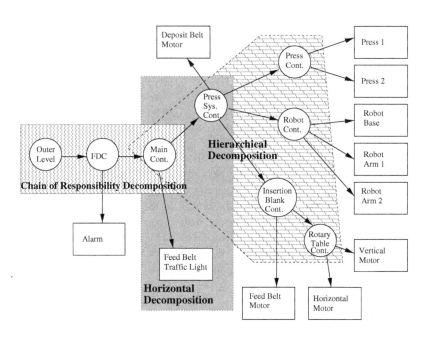

Fig. 4. Decomposition of Controllers

Failure detection is managed using the hierarchical *chain of responsibility* pattern described in [1] for fault-tolerance: at each cycle, the vector of sensor readings are checked for fault conditions, and failures notified to relevant components (if an unrecoverable failure occurs, a *shutdown* message is sent to the main controller, which then propagates it to individual controllers). Otherwise, the main controller is only sent events which do not represent failures.

4.3   Fault Detection

Checking for faults at the initial stage of sensor reading delivery to the system is essential if properties relating to individual polling cycles must be detected. For example, it could be regarded as a sign of sensor failure if both a *becomes_stm* (*stm* goes from *false* to *true*) event and a *blank_arrives* (*bs* goes from *no* to *yes*) event happen for a particular press within the same cycle (normally the arm delivering a blank would only start moving away once the blank had been confirmed to have arrived, or a timeout expired). This could not be detected at inner control levels as these know nothing of polling cycles.

Fault conditions are described by sets of invariants or control rules to be implemented by the FDC. Examples of these for a press are: (i) the arm moving into the vicinity of the press while the press is moving:

$$stm = false \land ms \neq off \ \Rightarrow \ ok = false$$

Or (ii) the blank falling off during a movement:

$$pstate = completing \land bs = yes \land \bigcirc bs = no \ \Rightarrow \ \bigcirc ok = false$$

For the feed belt we have rules: (i) If feed belt motor is on and S1 (blank sensor at start of belt) detects presence of blank, but state of S1 does not change in next cycle, then the motor has failed. (ii) If S2 (blank sensor at end of belt) changes from blank present to absent, and motor is off, then the motor has failed or blank has fallen off belt.

The system has no way of deducing the failure of the feed belt sensors if these both fail at the same time. Both the belt motor and traffic lights depend on the signal from S1. If S1 fails at *no* during an idle period of the belt, then the belt motor will not be triggered, and the traffic lights will remain green. In this situation, blanks can begin to pile up on top of each other at S1, which may eventually cause damage to the system. Only at this time will some sensor not included in the system specification as it stands detect the failure. For this reason, we assume that sensors give a 0 reading (distinct from *yes* and *no*) to indicate their failure.

Fault detection rules are implemented in the FDC, which is directly called by the outer controller. The outer controller has the form:

```
MACHINE OuterLevel
INCLUDES FailureDetectionController
VARIABLES
   fbok, fbtok, ...
INITIALISATION
   fbok := TRUE || fbtok := TRUE || ...
OPERATIONS
   cycle(curr_S1, curr_S2, ..., curr_S20, clockTick) =
      PRE curr_S1 : SENSOR_STATES ∧ ... ∧ curr_S20 : SENSOR_STATES ∧
          clockTick : TIME
      THEN
        / * call FDC : */
```

$$fbok \quad \longleftarrow \quad check\_feedbelt\_sensors(curr\_S1, curr\_S2) \quad ||$$
$$fbtok \quad \longleftarrow \quad check\_feedbelt\_rTable(curr\_S1, curr\_S2, curr\_S3, curr\_S6) \quad ||$$
$$\vdots$$

    END

END

The checking of failure conditions is split into checks for individual components (eg. the first *check* operation) and checks concerning the interaction of several components (the second operation). The *FailureDetectionController* has the form:

MACHINE *FailureDetectionController*
INCLUDES *MainController*
$\vdots$

OPERATIONS
    $res \quad \longleftarrow \quad check\_feedbelt\_sensors(cS1, cS2) \quad =$
        PRE $cS1, \; cS2 \; : \; SENSOR\_STATES$
        THEN
          IF $/ *$ *rule* (i) *for feedbelt* $* /$
          $(a1\_fbelt\_motor\_switch \; = \; on \; \wedge \; s1\_blankFB\_start \; = \; yes \; \wedge$
          $cS1 \; = \; yes) \; or$
          $/ *$ *rule* (ii) *for feedbelt* $* /$
          $(a1\_fbelt\_motor\_switch \; = \; off \; \wedge \; s1\_blankFB\_start \; = \; yes \; \wedge$
          $cS1 \; = \; no) \; or \; ...$
          THEN
            $res \; := \; FALSE$
          ELSE
            $res \; := \; TRUE$
          END
        END;

$\vdots$

END

5   Conclusion

This paper has defined improvements to statechart notation for use in safety related reactive systems, and demonstrated the use of this notation and associated refinement rules on a case study of a fault-tolerant production cell control system. Tools have been developed to assist in the construction of DCFD and statechart models of a reactive system, and in the construction of abstraction mappings between refined and abstract statechart models [2]. The benefits of the approach include a systematic approach to reactive system development, using mainly graphical rather than explicitly formal notations, without sacrificing rigor.

    The approach taken is an advance on previous work, since it incorporates a concept of refinement and safety into software tools for statecharts, which

Statemate and RSML do not. In addition, it provides a structured translation from statecharts into the B notation, instead of the translation to flat B modules given in [10].

A related approach to reactive system specification in B is that of [11]. Structuring is introduced as part of refinement in this approach, however, which may make it less simple to use for non-software engineers. In our approach the structure of specifications and implementations is identical as both are derived from the SRS specifications.

References

1. M. Ali, *B Specification of Steam Boiler*, MSc thesis, Dept. of Computing, Imperial College, 1998.
2. K. Androutsopoulos. *The Reactive System Design Tool*, ROOS Project report, Department of Computing, Imperial College, 1999.
3. I. Hayes, *A Survey of Data Refinement and Full Abstraction in VDM and Z*, Dept. of Computer Science, University of Queensland, 1991.
4. International Electrotechnical Commission, *IEC 61508: Functional Safety of Electrical/Electronic/Programmable Electronic Safety-Related Systems*, 1999.
5. K. Lano, J. Bicarregui, and A. Evans. *Structured Axiomatic Semantics for UML Models*, ROOM 2000 Proceedings, to appear in Electronic Workshops in Computer Science, Springer-Verlag, 2000.
6. K. Lano, K. Androutsopoulos, D. Clark, *Structuring and Design of Reactive Systems using RSDS and B*, FASE 2000, to appear in LNCS, Springer-Verlag, 2000.
7. C. Lewerentz, T. Lindner (eds.), *Formal Development of Reactive Systems*, LNCS Vol. 891, Springer-Verlag, 1995.
8. A. Lötzbeyer, R Mühlfeld, *Task Description of a Flexible Production Cell with Real Time Properties*, FZI, Karlsruhe, 1996.
9. F. Mejia, *Formalising Existing Safety-Critical Software*, FMERail Workshop No. 2, London, UK, 1998. http://www.ifad.dk/Projects/fmerail.htm.
10. E. Sekerinski. Graphical Design of Reactive Systems. *2nd International Conference on B*, Lecture Notes in Computer Science, Springer Verlag, pages 182–197, 1998.
11. H. Treharne, S. Schneider, *Using a Process Algebra to Control B Operations*, IFM '99, Springer-Verlag, 1999.

A   Formal Definition of SRS Statechart Notation

State machines Restricted statecharts are defined in terms of state machines. Formally, a *state machine* A consists of sets $States_A$ of states, $Events_A$ of events and $Trans_A$ of transitions. Each transition t of A has a source state $source_A(t) \in States_A$, a target state $target_A(t) \in States_A$, and an event $event_A(t) \in Events_A$ which denotes the event which may trigger the transition.

There is a designated initial state $init_A$. It is denoted as the target of a virtual transition arrow which has no source.

States will be classified as *safe* or *hazard* states (accidents are events which may occur from hazard states). Disjoint sets $Safe_A$, Haz_A denote the respective sets of safe and hazard states of A.

State machine abstraction morphisms and refinements Stepwise refinement of reactive systems involves the successive elaboration of controller responses and details of the equipment under control. A refinement C of a system A must be able to respond to all requests that A can, in a compatible way. This is formalised by the concept of an *abstraction morphism.*

A *state machine abstraction morphism* $\sigma : C \rightarrow A$ is a function from $States_C \cup Events_C \cup Trans_C$ to $States_A \cup Events_A \cup Trans_A$ which maps each state s of C to a state $\sigma(s)$ of A, each event α of C to an event $\sigma(\alpha)$ of A, and each transition t of C to a transition $\sigma(t)$ of A, such that:

1. If the event of t in C is α, then the event of $\sigma(t)$ in A is $\sigma(\alpha)$: $event_A(\sigma(t)) = \sigma(event_C(t))$.
2. $source_A(\sigma(t)) = \sigma(source_C(t))$ and $target_A(\sigma(t)) = \sigma(target_C(t))$.
3. $\sigma(init_C) = init_A$.

Such a morphism preserves the behaviour of a state machine in the sense that all transitions $t : s \rightarrow s'$ in C for a given event α must correspond to some abstract transition $\sigma(t) : \sigma(s) \rightarrow \sigma(s')$ in A for the same event. That is, no essentially new behaviour can be introduced for α.

C is a *refinement* of A via σ if σ is a state machine abstraction morphism which is an isomorphism on the set of events of C and A: no new events are introduced and no abstract events are deleted.

A refinement σ is *adequate* if every state s of A has some corresponding state of C:

$$\forall s : States_A \cdot \exists s' : States_C \cdot \sigma(s') = s$$

and if every event α which has an abstract transition from some s also has a corresponding concrete transition from each corresponding state:

$$\forall s : States_A; \ t : Trans_A \cdot$$
$$event_A(t) = \alpha \wedge source_A(t) = s \Rightarrow$$
$$(\forall s' : States_C \cdot \sigma(s') = s \Rightarrow$$
$$\exists t' : Trans_C \cdot \sigma(event_C(t')) = \alpha \ \wedge \ \sigma(t') = t \ \wedge \ source_C(t') = s')$$

This ensures that C can react to α in every situation that A can. By definition of refinement, the effect of this reaction is also consistent with that given in A. The adequacy condition is similar to the "preservation of precondition" requirement of Z refinement [3].

An abstraction morphism $\sigma : C \rightarrow A$ is *safety preserving* if $s \in Haz_C$ implies $\sigma(s) \in Haz_A$.

Such a σ is referred to as a *safety abstraction.* Likewise a safety refinement is defined as a refinement which additionally preserves safety.

OR and AND composition Statecharts are defined as for state machines, with the additions of the two constructions of nesting of statecharts within states (OR composition) and concurrent (AND) composition. In the SRS formalism, these constructs can be eliminated successively to reduce a statechart to a state machine (a statechart with only basic states) [5].

An OR state s of a statechart A has an enclosed statechart $smach_A(s)$ and otherwise has the same properties as a state machine state. $States_{smach_A(s)}$ are included in $States_A$

and similarly $Trans_{smach_A(s)}$ are included in $Trans_A$ and $Events_{smach_A(s)}$ in $Events_A$. The graphical notation for an OR state s is a state enclosing $smach_A(s)$.

An AND state s is a parallel (AND) composition $A \mid B$ of two OR states. The states of $A \mid B$ are effectively pairs (a, b) of states a of A and b of B. The graphical notation for $A \mid B$ consists of A and B separated by a dashed line. $States_{A \mid B} = States_A \cup States_B$ and similarly for $Trans_{A \mid B}$ and $Events_{A \mid B}$.

Modules and subsystems In SRS statecharts all systems are described in terms of *modules*: an OR state containing only basic and OR states. A system description S is specified by the AND composition $M_1 \mid \ldots \mid M_m$ of all the modules contained in it, $modules(S) = \{M_1, \ldots, M_m\}$. Such an S is termed a *module system*.

Each module M in S has a set $receivers_S(M)$ of modules in S, which are the only modules of S which it can test or send events to: transitions t of M may refer to the state of modules $M' \in receivers_S(M)$ via a guard condition $condition_M(t)$ built from logical combinations of formulae $in\ x$ or $not(in\ x)$ where x is a state of M', representing that M' is in state x or not, respectively. t may have a generation sequence $generations_M(t) : \text{seq}(\bigcup_{M' \in receivers_S(M)} Events_{M'})$.

The collection of all generated events of a statechart M is $Gen_M = \bigcup_{t : Trans_M} ran(generations_M(t))$.

$Gen_M \cap Events_M = \varnothing$ for a module M in S, and $Gen_M \subseteq \bigcup_{M' \in receivers_S(M)} Events_{M'}$.

$receivers_S$ is acyclic: $M \notin receivers_S^*[\{M\}]$ where $receivers_S^*$ is the transitive closure of $receivers_S$ considered as a relation. For each module, M, the set $receivers_S^*[\{M\}]$ is termed the *subsystem* S' defined by M. M is then the *outer module* of S'.

Additional constraints may be placed on the form of $receivers_S$, for example, requiring that it is a tree: no two modules have a common receiver. This corresponds to the purely hierarchical structure of subsystems within a B development [9].

The set of *external events* Ext_S of a module system S is the set $\bigcup_{M \in modules(S)} Events_M - \bigcup_{M \in modules(S)} Gen_M$. Normally these are the events of the sensor modules and the controller at the top of the controller hierarchy.

For module systems, the external events of the system must not change in a refinement. That is $Ext_S = Ext_{S'}$ where S' is the refinement of S.

Definition If s, s' are states of a statechart C, the notation $s \sqsubseteq_C s'$ denotes that $s = s'$ or s' is an OR state, $smach_C(s') = M$ and $s \in States_M$.

Definition For any state s of a statechart C, s_{init} denotes the initial state of s: $s_{init} = s$ if s is basic, $s_{init} = (s')_{init}$ if s is an OR state with initial state s', and $s_{init} = (s_{1\,init}, \ldots, s_{n\,init})$ if s is an AND state $s = s_1 \mid \ldots \mid s_n$. s_{init} is therefore always a basic state or tuple of basic states.

Definition If M contains only basic states, then $States_{flatten(M)} = States_M$. Otherwise $States_{flatten(M)} = \bigcup_{s : States_M} States^{M,s}$, where, if s is a state of a statechart M, then, if s is basic: $States^{M,s} = \{s\}$. If s is an OR state, $E = smach_M(s)$: $States^{M,s} = \bigcup_{s' : States_E} States^{E,s'}$. If s is an AND state, $s = s1 \mid s2$: $States^{M,s} = States^{M,s1} \times States^{M,s2}$.

Definition For a tree-structured module system S, $flatten(S)$, the flattened version of S, can be constructed by systematic removal of OR and AND states, with appropriate re-targeting of transitions [2,5]. It is a state machine.

Definition A (SRS) statechart abstraction morphism σ from a concrete statechart C to an abstract statechart A maps states of C to those of A, events of C to events of A and transitions of C to those of A such that:

1. Source, target and trigger of transitions are preserved:

$$source_A(\sigma(t)) = \sigma(source_C(t))$$
$$target_A(\sigma(t)) = \sigma(target_C(t))$$
$$event_A(\sigma(t)) = \sigma(event_C(t))$$

2. If s is an OR state of C then $\sigma(s)$ is an OR state or basic state of A, and initial states are preserved:

$$\sigma(s_{init}) \ = \ (\sigma(s))_{init}$$

3. σ preserves $\sqsubseteq$: $\quad s \sqsubseteq_C s' \ \Rightarrow \ \sigma(s) \sqsubseteq_A \sigma(s')$. This means that states within particular modules M of C remain in the abstraction $\sigma(M)$ of M in A.
4. The module structure of C is preserved, ie: $receivers_A(\sigma(M)) = \sigma[receivers_C(M)]$.
5. Conditions and generations are preserved:

$$condition_A(\sigma(t)) \ = \ \sigma(condition_C(t))$$
$$generations_A(\sigma(t)) \ \ll \ \sigma \circ generations_C(t)$$

where $s_1 \ll s_2$ denotes that s_1 is a (possibly non-contiguous) subsequence of s_2.

Further conditions are needed in order that $flatten(\sigma)$ can be defined:

1. σ is the union of separate morphisms $\sigma_i : MC_i \to MA_i$ between corresponding modules of C and A, $\sigma(MC_i) = MA_i$, with these morphisms being compatible on events:

$$\alpha \in Events_{MC_i} \wedge \beta \in Events_{MC_j} \ \Rightarrow \ (\sigma_i(\alpha) = \sigma_j(\beta) \ \Rightarrow \ \alpha = \beta)$$
$$\alpha \in Events_{MC_i} \cap Events_{MC_j} \ \Rightarrow \ \sigma_i(\alpha) = \sigma_j(\alpha)$$

where $i \neq j$.
2. Each of the σ_i are adequate, and every module of A must correspond to some module of C.
3. $x \models E$ in C (x satisfies E, where x is a state of C and E a transition condition) implies that $\sigma(x) \models \sigma(E)$, for each such condition.
   This is ensured in particular for *positive* E, ie, for E containing no occurrences of $\neg$ or $\Rightarrow$.

Given these constraints, if S and S' are tree-structured module systems, connected by $\sigma : S' \to S$, then there is an abstraction morphism $\tau = flatten(\sigma) : flatten(S') \to flatten(S)$ derived from σ. This is proved by structural induction on S'.

Similarly there are results showing that τ is also adequate under these constraints, provided that $\sigma(s_1) \sqsubseteq_A \sigma(s_2)$ implies $s_1 \sqsubseteq_C s_2$ for states of C, the receivers structure of C and A are identical except for new, complete, leaf modules in C, and there are no generations on initial transitions of C or A. In addition it can be shown that if σ is safety-preserving, so is τ.

Modeling Faults of Distributed, Reactive Systems[*]

Max Breitling

Institut für Informatik
Technische Universität München
D-80290 München, Germany
http://www.in.tum.de/~breitlin

Abstract. Formal methods can improve the development of systems with high quality requirements, since they usually offer a precise, non-ambiguous specification language and allow rigorous verification of system properties. Usually, these mainly abstract specifications are idealistic and do not reflect faults, so that faulty behavior – if treated at all – must be specified as part of the normal behavior, increasing the complexity of the system. It is more desirable to distinguish normal and faulty behavior, making it possible to reason about faults and their effects.

In this paper the notions of faults, errors, failures, error detection, error messages, error correcting components and fault tolerance are discussed, based on a formal model that represents systems as composition of interacting components that communicate asynchronously. The behavior of the components is described by black-box properties and state transition systems, with faults being modeled by modifications of the properties or transitions.

1 Introduction

One of the goals of software engineering is the development of *correct* software. Correctness needs to be defined, usually by a *specification* that describes the system to be constructed in a precise and unambiguous way. The most rigorous approach to establishing the correctness of the system under consideration are formal methods, which allow us to *prove* that the system indeed meets its specification.

Nevertheless, systems developed using formal methods can still fail: subcomponents can be unreliable, some (possibly undocumented) assumptions turn out to be invalid, or the underlying hardware simply fails. It can be argued that this was caused by mistakes introduced during the formal development, e.g. by making too idealistic assumptions about the environment. In this paper, we explore another approach: We embed the notion of a *fault* in the context of formal methods, targeting two major goals:

– Support for the development of *fault-tolerant systems*, requiring a precise definition of faults and errors.

[*] This work is supported by the DFG within the Sonderforschungsbereich 342/A6.

M. Joseph (Ed.): FTRTFT 2000, LNCS 1926, pp. 58–69, 2000.

– Reduction of the complexity of formal development by allowing a methodological separation of normal and faulty behavior. After the fault-free version of the system is developed, the possible faults and appropriate countermeasures can be integrated seamlessly in the system.

To model faults already at the level of specifications could sound contradictory, because the specification is intended to describe the *desired* behavior, and nobody wants faults! But in an early development phase it is normally unknown which faults can occur in a system, simply because it is even still unknown what components will be used and how they can fail. Nevertheless, certain kinds of faults can be anticipated already during system development in general, as e.g. by experience or for physical reasons: a transmission of a message can, for instance, always fail. If these faults can be treated already at an abstract level by a general fault handling mechanism, it is sensible to describe the faults already within the specification, and not postpone it to a later phase in the development process.

In this paper, we enrich the model of FOCUS with the notions of faults, errors, failures and fault-tolerance and discuss their connections and use. Since FOCUS offers methodological support for specifying and verifying reactive systems including a formal foundation, description techniques, a compositional refinement calculus and tool support, we expect benefits when FOCUS is combined with results from the area of fault-tolerance. While most other approaches are concerned mainly with foundations of fault tolerance, we try to keep an eye on the applicability for users that are not experts in formal methods. Therefore, our long-term target - not yet reached - are syntactic criteria for certain properties instead of logical characterizations, diagrams instead of formulas, and easy-to-use recipes how to modify systems to their fault-tolerant versions.

In the next section, we describe very briefly our system model of distributed, interacting, reactive components. In Section 3 we introduce faults as modifications of systems. Section 4 contains a discussion how the formal definitions can be used to describe fault assumptions, and detect, report and correct faults. In the last section we conclude and discuss future work.[1]

2   System Model

Our system model is a variant of the system model of FOCUS [5,6]. A system is modeled by defining its interface and its behavior. The system's interface is described by the (names of the) communication channels with the types of the messages that are sent on them. The (asynchronous) communication along all channels is modeled by (finite or infinite) message streams. The behavior of a system is characterized by a relation that contains all possible pairs of input and output streams. This relation can be described in (at least) two ways on different abstraction levels.

---

[1] Due to lack of space, all examples are omitted but can be found in an extended version of this paper on the author's homepage.

A *Black Box Specification* defines the behavior relation by a formula Φ with variables ranging over the input and output streams. The streams fulfilling these predicates describe the allowed black-box-behavior of a system. We can use several operators to formulate the predicates, as the prefix relation $\sqsubseteq$, the concatenation of streams $\frown$ and the expression $s.k$ for the k-th element of a stream s, to mention just a few [5].

A more operational *State-Based View* is offered by *State Transition Systems* (STS) that describe the behavior in a step-by-step manner: Depending on the current state, the system reads some messages from the input channels, and reacts by sending some output and establishing a successive state. A STS is defined by its internal variables with their types, an initial condition, a set T of transitions and T^ϵ of environment transitions, precisely formalized in [3]. The possible behaviors of a system are described by the set $\langle\langle S \rangle\rangle$ containing all executions ξ of the system. Executions are defined in the usual way as sequences of states α. A STS can be defined in a graphical or tabular notation.

Both views on systems can be formally connected: An infinite execution of a STS defines least upper bounds for the message streams that are assigned to the input/output channels, and therefore establishes a black-box relation. In [3,4] the language, semantics and proof techniques are investigated in detail.

FOCUS offers notions for *composition* and *refinement* supporting a top-down development of systems. The behavior of a composed system $S_1 \otimes S_2$ can be derived from the behavior of its components. The interface refinement $S_1 \overset{R_I \rhd R_O}{\leadsto} S_2$ states that the executions of S_2 are also executions of S_1 with modifications at the interface described by the relations R_I, R_O. Compositionality ensures that refining a system's component means refining the overall system.

3   Modifications and Faults

Intuitively, faults in a system are connected with some discrepancy between an intended system and an actual system. To be able to talk about faults, their effects and possible countermeasures, we need a clear definition of the term *fault*. We suggest to identify faults with the *modifications* needed to transform the correct system to its faulty version.

In this section, we define modifications of systems, both for the black-box and the operational view, and base the notions of fault, error and failure on these modifications.

3.1   Modifying a System

In the process of adapting a specified system to a more realistic setting containing faults, we have to be able to change both the interface and the behavior.

Interface modifications We allow the extension of a type of a channel and the introduction of new channels. The behavior stays unchanged if the specification is adjusted so that it ignores new messages on new input channels, while it may behave arbitrarily on new output channels. For development steps towards a fault-tolerant system it is normally expected that the behavior does not change in the case faults do not occur. Therefore we are interested in criteria for behavior maintenance that are easy to be checked. For interface modifications, these criteria can be defined syntactically according to the description technique used, as e.g. black-box formulas, tables or state machines. We do neither allow the removal of channels nor a type restriction for a channel, because this could easily lead to changes of the behavior. A change of the types for the channels follows the idea of *interface refinement*. Under certain conditions, these changes maintain (the properties of) the behavior. In this paper, we will not investigate this topic.

Behavior modifications A fault-affected system normally shows a different behavior than the idealistic system. Instead of describing the fault-affected system, we focus on the *difference* of both versions of the system and suggest a way to describe this difference for black-box views and state machines.

Having Φ as the black-box specification of the fault-free system, we need to be able to strengthen this predicate to express further restrictions, but also to weaken it to allow additional I/O-behaviors. We use a pair of formulas $\mathcal{M} = (\Phi_E, \Phi_F)$ and denote a modified system by

$$\Phi \triangle \mathcal{M} \quad \text{(read: } \Phi \text{ modified by } \mathcal{M})$$

whose black-box specification is defined by

$$(\Phi \wedge \Phi_E) \vee \Phi_F$$

The neutral modification is denoted by (true, false), and the modification towards an arbitrary Ψ is expressed by (false, Ψ).

For a state-based system description, we express modifications of the behavior by modifications of the transition set (as e.g in [1,9,12]). Obviously, we can add or remove transitions and define a behavior-modification $\mathcal{M}$ by a pair (E, F) of two sets of transitions. The set E contains transitions that are no longer allowed in an execution of the modified system. The set F contains additional transitions. The transitions in F can increase the nondeterminism in the system, since in states with both old and new transitions being enabled, the system has more choices how to behave. We can use F to model erroneous transitions the system can spontaneously take. The executions of a modified system are defined by

$$\langle\!\langle \mathcal{S} \triangle \mathcal{M} \rangle\!\rangle \stackrel{\text{df}}{=} \{\xi \mid (\xi.k, (\xi.k + 1)) \in (T \setminus E) \cup F \cup T^\epsilon\}$$

i.e. a non-environment transition has to be in F or in T but not in E. In this formalism, $(\varnothing, \varnothing)$ is the neutral modification, and choosing E to contain all transitions and F as arbitrary set of transitions shows that this formalism is again expressive enough.

It is an interesting but open question if and how both notions for modifications can be connected. If Φ is a property of a STS $\mathcal{S}$, and both are modified in a similar way, then $\Phi \triangle (\Phi_E, \Phi_F)$ should be the modified property of the modified system $\mathcal{S} \triangle (E, F)$. Similar approaches and partial results are discussed in [2,7,13].

3.2   Combining Modifications

To explore the effect of multiple modifications, we define the composition of modifications. For black-box specifications, the operator $+$ combines two modifications (Φ_E^i, Φ_F^i) of a system $(i = 1, 2)$, assuming $\Phi_F^1 \Rightarrow \Phi_E^2$ and $\Phi_F^2 \Rightarrow \Phi_E^1$, to one modification by

$$(\Phi_E^1, \Phi_F^1) + (\Phi_E^2, \Phi_F^2) \stackrel{\mathrm{df}}{=} (\Phi_E^1 \wedge \Phi_E^2, \Phi_F^1 \vee \Phi_F^2)$$

We reuse the operator $+$ for transition systems, and define for (E_i, F_i), assuming $E_1 \cap F_2 = \varnothing$ and $E_2 \cap F_1 = \varnothing$, the combination

$$(E_1, F_1) + (E_2, F_2) \stackrel{\mathrm{df}}{=} (E_1 \cup E_2, F_1 \cup F_2)$$

The assumptions avoid confusion about executions resp. transitions that are added by one modification but removed by the other, and asserts the following equalities, with S representing Φ resp. $\mathcal{S}$:

$$S \triangle (\mathcal{M}_1 + \mathcal{M}_2) \;=\; (S \triangle \mathcal{M}_1) \triangle \mathcal{M}_2 \;=\; (S \triangle \mathcal{M}_2) \triangle \mathcal{M}_1$$

We can use this operator to express combinations of faults for defining the notion of fault-tolerant systems.

For a composite system $S = S^1 \otimes S^2$ we can derive the modification of this system from the modifications of its constituents, and can calculate the impact of a fault of a component upon the overall system. For black-box specifications, we define the derived modification of the system by

$$\Phi_E = \Phi_E^1 \wedge \Phi_E^2 \qquad\qquad \Phi_F = (\Phi^1 \wedge \Phi_F^2) \vee (\Phi^2 \wedge \Phi_F^1) \vee (\Phi_F^1 \wedge \Phi_F^2)$$

For modifications of the transition sets of the components, we can define $\mathcal{M} = (E, F)$ with ($\overline{\wedge}$ denotes the pairwise conjunction of elements of both sets)

$$E \stackrel{\mathrm{df}}{=} E_1 \overline{\wedge} T_2^\epsilon \;\cup\; T_1^\epsilon \overline{\wedge} E_2 \quad\text{and}\quad F \stackrel{\mathrm{df}}{=} F_1 \overline{\wedge} T_2^\epsilon \;\cup\; T_1^\epsilon \overline{\wedge} F_2$$

With the same assumptions for the component's modifications as above, this results for both formalisms in

$$\mathcal{S} \triangle \mathcal{M} = (\mathcal{S}_1 \triangle \mathcal{M}_1) \otimes (\mathcal{S}_2 \triangle \mathcal{M}_2)$$

3.3   Faults, Errors and Failures

In the literature the meaning of the terms *fault*, *error* and *failure* is often described just informally (e.g. [10,11]). In our setting, we can define these notions more precisely.

The *faults* of a system are the *causes* for the discrepancy between an intended and actual system. Therefore, it makes sense to call the transitions of a modification $\mathcal{M}$ the faults of a system. What is called a fault of a system cannot be decided by looking at an existing system alone; this normally depends on the intended purpose of the system, on an accepted specification and even on the judgment of the user or developer. What one person judges as fault, the other calls a feature. The definition of modifications given in the previous sections is intended to offer a possibility to document that decision, and explicitly represent the faults in a modified system. Of course, the modified system could be described by one monolithic specification without reflecting the modifications explicitly, but it is exactly this distinction between "good" and "bad" transitions that allows our formal definitions.

A fault can lead to an erroneous state, if an existing faulty transition is taken during an execution of the system. We define a state α to be an *error* (state) if this state can only be reached by at least one faulty transition. The set of errors of a system $\mathcal{S}$ under the modifications $\mathcal{M} = (E, F)$ is defined as

$$ERROR(\mathcal{S}, \mathcal{M}) \overset{\text{df}}{=} \{\alpha \mid \forall k \in \mathbb{N}, \xi \in \langle\!\langle \mathcal{S} \triangle \mathcal{M} \rangle\!\rangle \bullet$$
$$\xi.k = \alpha \Rightarrow \exists l < k \bullet (\xi.l, \xi.(l+1)) \in F\}$$

Note that all unreachable states are error states, and the set E enlarges the set of unreachable states. The set of correct states can be defined as the set of valuations that can be reached by normal transitions (in T) only. As long as we do not require $F \cap T = \varnothing$, it is possible that states are both correct states and error states. We cannot sensibly define errors for the black-box view, since neither states nor internals do exist in that context.

A *failure* is often defined as a visible deviation of the system relative to some specification. Since we can distinguish the inside and outside of systems, we can also reflect different visibilities of errors. Our definition of a failure depends on the kind of specification: If we regard a black-box specification Φ as the specification of a system, a failure occurs in a state α if the property gets violated in that state. But we can also define a failure if the unmodified STS $\mathcal{S}$ is understood as specification, and $\mathcal{S} \triangle \mathcal{M}$ as faulty system. An error state α is additionally called a failure if all states with the same visible input/output behavior are error states:

$$FAILURE(\mathcal{S}, \mathcal{M}) \overset{\text{df}}{=} \{\alpha \mid \forall \beta \bullet \beta \overset{I \cup O}{=} \alpha \Rightarrow \beta \in ERROR(\mathcal{S}, \mathcal{M})\}$$

Two valuation α and β coincide on a set of variables V, if they assign the same value to all variables in V, i.e. $\alpha \overset{V}{=} \beta \Leftrightarrow \forall v \in V \bullet \alpha.v = \beta.v$.

3.4   Internal vs. External Faults

Up to this point, we focused on internal faults: The behavior deviation resp. the faulty transitions occurred *inside* the system. But a system can also suffer from faults taking place *outside* a system, i.e. in its environment. A discussion of failures of the environment requires explicit or implicit assumptions about its behavior. An explicit assumption can be formulated in the context of black-box views by a formula that describes the assumed properties of the input streams. If this assumption is not fulfilled, the system's behavior is usually understood to be not specified so that an arbitrary, chaotic behavior may occur. We think this situation relates to an external fault, and should be treated by a reasonable reaction of the system instead of undefined behavior. We need further methodological support offering notions of refinement for these cases: Given an assumption/guarantee specification A/G, we need to be able to weaken A and adapt G so that the original behavior stays untouched if no external faults occur, but a sensible reaction is defined if they do.

The type correctness of the input messages can be regarded as another explicit assumption about the environment. If the interface is changed so that new messages can be received, we have to refine the behavior of the system in an appropriate way.

If the system is specified by a STS, but no explicit environment assumptions are defined, we can nevertheless try to find implicit assumptions. If the system is in a certain state, it is normally expected that at least one of the transitions should be eventually enabled. It some cases, it can indeed be meant that a system gets stuck in certain situations, but normally a weak form of liveness is wanted: The inputs should finally be consumed, and a state where a system gets stuck is a kind of error state with invalidated liveness. We regard these questions and the distinction of internal and external faults as an interesting area for future research.

4 Dealing with Faults

Introducing a formal framework for formalizing faults needs to be accompanied with some methodological advice how the formalism can be used. In this section, we discuss how fault occurrences and dependencies between fault models can be expressed by virtual components, mention requirements for error detection and the introduction of error messages and define fault-tolerance.

4.1 Refined Fault Models

To describe a system with certain faults, we can modify a system accordingly by adding fault transitions. In specific cases, these modifications could change the behavior too much, since these transitions can be taken whenever they are enabled. Sometimes, we want to express certain fault assumptions that restrict the occurrence of faults. For example, we would like to express that two components of a system can fail, but never both of them at the same time, or we want to express probabilities about the occurrence of faults, e.g. state that a transition can fail only once in n times, for some n.

To be able to formalize these fault assumptions, we suggest to introduce additional input channels used similar to *prophecies*. The enabledness of the fault transitions can be made dependent on the values received on these prophecy channels. We can then add an additional component that produces the prophecies that represent the fault assumption. During the verification, these virtual components and prophecy channels can be used as if they were normal components, even though they will never be implemented.

4.2   Detecting Errors

Error detection in our setting consists, in its simplest case, of finding an expression that is true iff the system is in an error state. The system itself must be able to evaluate this expression, so that this expression can be used as a precondition for error-correcting or -reporting transitions.

An easy way to detect errors is a modification of the fault transitions so that every fault transition assigns a certain value to an error-indicating variable. For example, a fault transition can set the variable *fault* to true, while normal transitions leave this variable unchanged, as suggested in [12]. But this approach assumes the fault transitions to be controllable, which is in general not the case: The faults are described according to experiences in the real world, e.g. messages are simply lost from a channel without any component reporting this event. We could change this lossy transition to one that reports its occurrence, but this new variable *fault* may only be used in proofs for investigating the correctness of the detection mechanism, but this is not a variable that is accessible by the system itself. We have to deal with given faults described by modifications that we must accept untouched, but nevertheless we want to detect them.

We suggest a way to handle errors that can be detected by finding inconsistencies in the state of the system. The consistency can be denoted as a formula Ψ that is an invariant of the unmodified system. It can be proved to be an invariant by the means of [3]. We can then remove all transitions with $\neg \Psi$ as precondition (via E) and add a new error reacting transition with an intended reaction (via F). Normally, a system occasionally contains transitions that are enabled if $\neg \Psi$, simply because a set of transitions can be indifferent to unspecified properties. Such a modification does not change the original system, but allows the specification of reactions, e.g. by sending an error message.

This approach is conceptually the easiest way, since error detection is immediate, but it is not always realistic. In [1] a more general approach is presented, that also allows delayed error detection. We have to integrate this idea also in our stream-based setting, being specially interested in a notion of a delayed detection that still occurs before an error becomes a failure.

4.3   Error Messages

Once we enabled a system to detect an error, we want it to react in an appropriate way. If errors cannot be corrected, they should at least be reported. Sending and receiving of error messages has to be integrated in the system without changing its fault-free behavior.

In Section 3.1 we already saw that by adding an additional output channel, with arbitrary messages sent, the behavior will only be refined. So, extending a system to send error reporting messages is easy: We can add a transition that sends an error message in the case an error is detected while it leaves all other variables in V unchanged, and we refine the other transitions to send no output on this channel.

We also want to react to error messages from other components. Therefore, we must be able to extend a component by a new input error message channel, and adapt the component to read error messages and react to them. A further transition in the system that reads from the new channel and reacts to it can easily be added while other transitions simply ignore the new channel.

4.4   Correcting Faults

We described ways how a system can be modified to contain anticipated faults already at the abstract level of specifications. The deviations of such a modified system can show different degrees of effect: The effects of the faults are harmless and preserve the properties of a specification, or the faults show effects that violate the specification, but they are correctable, or the faults lead to failures that are not correctable. The first case is of course the easiest since no countermeasures have to be taken for the system to fulfill its specification. In the last case, faults can only be detected and reported, as described in the previous sections.

For correctable faults the system usually must be extended by mechanisms that enable the system to tolerate the faults. Several mechanisms are known, implementing e.g. fail-stop behavior, restarts, forward or backward recovery, replication of components, voters and more. All of these are *correctors* in the sense of [1].

A methodology supporting the development of dependable systems should offer *patterns* that describe when and how these mechanisms can be integrated in a specified system, together with the impact on the black-box properties. For example, a fail-stop behavior can be modeled by introducing a new trap state that was not yet reachable before, and that does not consume or generate any messages, while safety properties are not compromised.

There is a special case of (local)correction of faults that can be done by new components in a system that catch the effect of faults of a component before they spread throughout the system. These new components, that we call *drivers*, are placed between the fault-affected component and the rest of the system. Depending on the characteristics and severity of the faults, the driver controls just the output of the component, or controls the output with the knowledge of the input, or even controls input and output, as showed in the following figure. The last variant is the most general one, and could tolerate arbitrary failures by totally ignoring the faulty component and simulating its correct functionality.

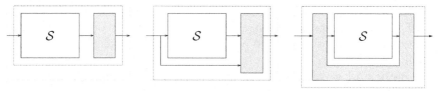

Since we already know how to specify components and how to compose components to systems, fault correction can be integrated as an ordinary development step, so that results concerning methodology [5], tool support [8] and proof support [3,4] can be used.

4.5   Fault-tolerance

Usually, fault-tolerance is interpreted as the property of a system to fulfill its purpose despite the presence of faults in the system, but also in their absence (as pointed out e.g. in [9]). In our formalism, this could be expressed by the following monotonicity property, stating that all partial modifications of a system should maintain a certain property.

$$\forall (E', F') \bullet E' \subseteq E \wedge F' \subseteq F \quad \Rightarrow \quad \mathcal{S} \triangle (E', F') \models \Phi$$

We think this condition is too strong, since too many partial modifications have to be considered. Assume a fault - being tolerable - that can be modeled by a change of a transition, expressed by removing the old and adding the new transition. If we just add the new one, but do not remove the old transition, we have a partial modification that could never happen in practice but results in a system with intolerable faults. Partial modifications are too fine-grained if they are based on single transitions.

We suggest that a statement about fault-tolerance must be made explicit by specifying the faults and combinations of faults for which the system should have certain properties. As opposed to other approaches [9,12], a modification (with a nonempty E) can change a system so that it cannot show any execution of the original system. So, if a property is valid for the modified system, it is possibly not valid for the unmodified system.

In our setting, explicit fault-tolerance can be expressed by generalizing our expressions to allow sets of modifications. The following expression is defined to be valid if $\forall i \bullet \mathcal{S} \triangle \mathcal{M}_i \models \Phi$.

$$\mathcal{S} \triangle \{\mathcal{M}_0, \mathcal{M}_1, \mathcal{M}_2, \ldots\} \models \Phi$$

For a statement about fault-tolerance, the empty modification $(\varnothing, \varnothing)$ has to be contained in the modification set, and the desired combinations of modifications must be explicitly included. The induced number of proof obligations needs further methodological support.

5   Proving Properties

The additional effort imposed by the use of formal methods for formalizing a system is rewarded by the possibility to *prove* that the systems have certain properties. While many formalisms offer this possibility theoretically, it is also important to offer methodology to find the proofs. In [3,4] we presented a way of proving properties for our system model, using proof rules, quite intuitive diagrams and tool support.

It is crucial for a successful methodology that proofs can be found with reasonable effort. For fault-tolerance, it is desirable that proof obligations can be shown in a modular way. Results for an unmodified system should be transferred to *modified results* for the *modified system*. If properties of the correct system are already shown, this result should not be invalidated totally by modifying the system so that the verification has to start again from scratch. The existing proof should only be adapted accordingly, reflecting the modifications, using already gained results.

So it seems to be an interesting research topic to find notions for modifying a proof. Since a proof can be represented by a proof diagram, it can be promising to investigate modifications of proof diagrams. If a transition is removed (by E), a safety diagram stays valid also without this transition. In a liveness diagram, new proof obligations emerge in this case, since the connectivity of the graph must be checked again. Adding a transition via F will - in most cases - destroy the validity of a safety diagram, and will even introduce new nodes. These new nodes have to be checked relative to all other transitions of the system, and they will also appear in the liveness diagram, leading to a bunch of additional proof obligations there. Nevertheless, parts of the diagram stay unchanged and valid, representing a reuse of the existing proof.

6 Conclusions

This paper discusses how faults can be modeled in the context of distributed systems, composed of components that interact by asynchronous message passing. We have shown how the behavior of such systems can be specified, using an abstract black-box view or an operational state-based view. Faults of a system are represented by the modifications that must be applied to the correct system to obtain the faulty system. Modifications can change both the interface and the behavior. For a modified system we can characterize its error states and failures. Once the faults resp. modifications of a system are identified, the ways how errors can be detected, reported, corrected and tolerated are also discussed, mostly informally, in this paper.

Future Work The topic of the formal development – including the specification, verification, and stepwise refinement – of fault tolerant systems is not yet explored to a satisfying degree with concrete help for developing systems with faults. It is a challenging task to combine various results found in literature with this paper's approach based on message streams and black-box views. An ideal formal framework combines the benefits of different approaches, and offers solutions to several aspects as formal foundation, methodology and verification support.

For a framework to be formal, precise definitions for all notions must be defined. We need a formal system model that is enriched by notions for faults and their effects, errors, failures, changes of interfaces and internals, fault assumptions, adaption of properties to modifications of the system, composition and refinement of faults. But a language to express statements about fault-affected or -tolerant systems is not enough, some methodological advice for its use is also needed, offering ideas how to use this language: When and why should faults be described, how can we refine a system to stay unchanged in the fault-free case, but improve its fault tolerance in the presence of faults? Formal methods allow for formal verification. This has to be supported by suitable proof rules, but even this is not enough: We also need description techniques for proofs and tool support for generating proof obligations and finding and checking proofs. Finally, only convincing case studies are able to show a recognizable benefit of the idea to formally develop fault-tolerant systems.

References

1. Anish Arora and Sandeep Kulkarni. Detectors and correctors: A theory of fault-tolerance components. *IEEE Transactions on Software Engineering*, 1999.
2. Max Breitling. Modellierung und Beschreibung von Soll-/Ist-Abweichungen. In Katharina Spies and Bernhard Schätz, editors, *Formale Beschreibungstechniken für verteilte Systeme. FBT'99*, pages 35–44. Herbert Utz Verlag, 1999.
3. Max Breitling and Jan Philipps. Step by step to histories. In T. Rus, editor, *AMAST2000 - Algebraic Methodology And Software Technology*, LNCS 1816, pages 11–25. Springer, 2000.
4. Max Breitling and Jan Philipps. Verification Diagrams for Dataflow Properties. Technical Report TUM-I0005, Technische Universität München, 2000.
5. Manfred Broy and Ketil Stølen. *Specification and Development of Interactive Systems - FOCUS on Streams, Interfaces and Refinement*. Springer, 2000. To appear.
6. Homepage of FOCUS. http://www4.in.tum.de/proj/focus/.
7. Felix C. Gärtner. A survey of transformational approaches to the specification and verification of fault-tolerant systems. Technical Report TUD-BS-1999-04, Darmstadt University of Technology, Darmstadt, Germany, April 1999.
8. Franz Huber, Bernhard Schätz, Alexander Schmidt, and Katharina Spies. Auto-Focus - A Tool for Distributed Systems Specification. In *FTRTFT'96*, LNCS 1135, pages 467–470. Springer, 1996.
9. Tomasz Janowski. On bisimulation, fault-monotonicity and provable fault-tolerance. In *6th International Conference on Algebraic Methodology and Software Technology*. LNCS, Springer, 1997.
10. J.C. Laprie. *Dependability: Basic Concepts and Terminology*, volume 5 of *Dependable Computing and Fault-Tolerant Systems*. Springer, 1992.
11. P.A. Lee and T. Anderson. *Fault Tolerance - Principles and Practice*. Springer, second, revised edition, 1990.
12. Zhiming Liu and Mathai Joseph. Specification and verification of recovery in asynchronous communicating systems. In Jan Vytopil, editor, *Formal Techniques in Real-Time and Fault-Tolerant Systems*, pages 137 – 166. Kluwer Academic Publishers, 1993.
13. Doron Peled and Mathai Joseph. A compositional framework for fault-tolerance by specification transformation. *Theoretical Computer Science*, 1994.

Acknowledgments I am grateful to Ingolf Krüger and Katharina Spies for inspiring discussions and their comments on this paper, and thank the anonymous referees for their very detailed and helpful remarks.

Threshold and Bounded-Delay Voting in Critical Control Systems[*]

Paul Caspi and Rym Salem

Laboratoire Verimag (CNRS, UJF, INPG)
{Caspi, Salem}@imag.fr
http://www-verimag.imag.fr

Abstract. This paper investigates the possibility of implementing fault tolerance in control systems without using clock synchronization. We first show that threshold voting applies to stable continuous systems and that bounded delay voting applies to combinational systems. We also show that 2/2 bounded delay voting is insensitive to Byzantine faults and applies to stable sequential systems. It thus allows the implementation of hybrid fault tolerance strategies.

1 Introduction

It seems that, from the very early times of SIFT and FTMP [10,7], it was assumed that highly fault-tolerant control systems had to be based on exact voting and clock synchronization. This led to the discovery of consensus problems and Byzantine faults [9], and produced an important academic activity [6], culminating in the time-triggered approach to the development of these systems [8].

However, it also seems that, in practice, at least in the domain of critical control systems, the use of clock synchronization is not so frequent [4,3]. We believe there are historical reasons for this fact, which can be found in the evolution of these systems: control systems formerly used to be implemented with analog techniques, that is to say without any clock at all. Then, these implementations smoothly evolved toward discrete digital ones, and then toward computing ones. When a computer replaced an analog board, it was usually based on periodic sampling according to a real-time clock, and, for the sake of modularity, when several computers replaced analog boards, each one came with its own real-time clock. Yet this raises the question of the techniques used in these systems for implementing fault-tolerance without clock synchronization, and of the well-foundedness of these techniques which equip, up to now, some of the most safety critical control systems ever designed (civil aircrafts [4], nuclear plants [3], etc.)

This paper aims at providing some answers to this question. It will be organized as follows: first we shall look at the architectural evolution from analog boards to distributed control systems. Then, we shall consider continuous control. This will lead us to the concept of threshold voting, based on accuracy estimates: two signals are considered to disagree if they differ for more than

---

[*] This work has been partially supported by the CRISYS Esprit Project

M. Joseph (Ed.): FTRTFT 2000, LNCS 1926, pp. 70–81, 2000.
© Springer-Verlag Berlin Heidelberg 2000

the maximum normal error. Then we shall look at discontinuous functions and take boolean ones as an illustration. Here, combinational functions appear as the analog of continuous ones. Yet boolean calculations are perfectly accurate but the analogy is based on a space-time trade-off and yields bounded-delay voting: two signals are considered to disagree if they remain different for more than the maximum normal delay. Extending this scheme to apply to sequential functions by transforming them into combinational ones, that is to say by bounded-delay voting on the state, leads to problems of Byzantine faults. However, we show here that 2/2 voting schemes are not sensitive to Byzantine faults and behave properly. This provides us with self-checking schemes which can then be used to build fault tolerant strategies by means of selective redundancy.

2   The Architectural Evolution

Analog/digital communication: Aircraft control systems illustrate this evolution which can also be found in many other fields of industrial control: starting from networks of analog boards, progressively some boards were replaced by discrete digital boards, and then by computers. Communication between the digital parts and the parts which remained analog was mainly based on periodic sampling (analog to digital conversion) and holding (digital to analog conversion), sampling periods being adapted to the frequency properties of the signals that traveled through the network. This allowed several technologies to smoothly cooperate.

Serial links: this technique was suitable up to the time when two connected analog boards were replaced by digital ones. Then these two also had to communicate and serial port communication appeared as the simplest way of replacing analog to digital and digital to analog communication as both can be seen as latches or memories.

Field busses: then for the sake of optimization, these serial links are replaced by busses of several standards, (aircraft, industrial, automotive). Most of them, like Arinc429, just "pack" together several serial links, thus providing a kind of "shared memory" service, on top of which synchronization services can be implemented on need.

Provision against Byzantine problems: In these very critical systems, Byzantine faults cannot be neglected and this is why some architectural precautions have to be taken in order to alleviate their consequences. For instance, these busses provide some protection against Byzantine problems [9], in the sense that they are based on broadcast: communication with several partners only involve one emission. Thus a failed unit cannot diversely lie to its partners. Then messages are protected by either error correcting and/or detecting codes which can be assumed to be powerful enough so that their failing be negligible with respect to the probabilistic fault tolerance requirements of the system under consideration.

Communication abstraction: according to what precedes, we can quite precisely state an abstract property of this kind of communication medium, which is a bounded delay communication property:

Property 1 *First, we assume that every process P is periodic with a period varying between small margins: $T_{Pm} \leq T_P \leq T_{PM}$*

Property 2 *Let T_{sM} and T_{rM} be the respective maximal periods of the sender and of the receiver, and n the maximum number of consecutive failed receives whose probability is not negligible with respect to fault tolerant requirements (in the case of error correction, $n = 1$). Then the value $x_r(t)$ known at any time t by the receiver of some signal x_s communicated by the sender is some $x_s(t')$, where $|t - t'| \leq T_{rM} + nT_{sM}$*

Definition 1. *A signal x' is a τ **bounded delay image** of a signal x if there exists a monotonic (retiming) function $t' : R^+ \rightarrow R^+$ such that*

$$\forall t \in R^+, 0 \leq t - t'(t) \leq \tau \text{ and } x'(t) = x(t'(t))$$

3 Continuous Control

3.1 Continuous Signals and Functions

Most basic accuracy computations on continuous signals and functions over signals can be based on standard uniform continuity:

Definition 2. *A function $f \in R^n \rightarrow R^m$ is **uniformly continuous** if there exists an error function $\eta_f \in R^+ \rightarrow R^+$ such that, for all $x, x' \in R^n$ and $\epsilon \in R^+$: $||x' - x|| \leq \eta_f(\epsilon) \Rightarrow ||f(x') - f(x)|| \leq \epsilon$*

As function composition preserves uniform continuity, this easily allows the computation of bounds for systems made of uniformly continuous static functions fed by uniformly continuous signals through bounded delay networks. This, in turn, allows the computation of voting thresholds or more precisely the computation of periods such as to reach some accuracy or some voting threshold. For instance, $|t' - t| \leq T = \eta_x(\eta_f(\epsilon)) \Rightarrow ||f(x(t')) - f(x(t))|| \leq \epsilon$

3.2 Dynamical Systems

However, static functions are quite rare in control algorithms, and one would rather find dynamical functions. There can be at least three different cases:

The stable case consists of seeing dynamic systems as uniformly continuous functions over normed spaces of time signals. If we want to compute deterministic voting thresholds, an adequate norm is the $\mathcal{L}_\infty$ one:

$$||x' - x||_\infty = sup\{||x'(t) - x(t)|| \mid t \in R^+\}$$

If f is an uniformly continuous dynamical function for this norm, fed with uniformly continuous signals, we can easily reach the same bound as for static ones:

Theorem 1. *If x' is a τ bounded delay image of x, if x is uniformly continuous with error function η_x, and if f is uniformly continuous with error function η_f, then $\tau \leq \eta_x(\eta_f(\epsilon)) \Rightarrow ||f(x') - f(x)||_\infty \leq \epsilon$*

In some sense, this uniform continuity is closely linked to stability: this could be rephrased by saying that stable dynamical functions behave like static ones.

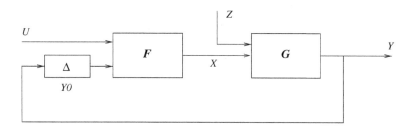

Fig. 1. A Control System

The stabilized case Unfortunately, controllers are often not stable: a typical situation is shown at figure 1. This closed-loop system computes the following functional equations: $X = F(U, \Delta_{Y0}^T Y)$ and $Y = G(X, Z)$, where F is the controller, G is the system under control, U is the vector of set values, X holds the control signals, Y contains the measurements from the process to be controlled that are fed back to the controller and Z contains the external perturbations that the system under control is subjected to. Δ is the unit delay for periodically sampled signals[1]:

$$\Delta_{x0}^T x(nT) = \texttt{if } n = 0$$
$$\texttt{then } x0$$
$$\texttt{else } x((n-1)T)$$

In order to yield an overall stable system, the system under control often requires a controller that, when viewed in isolation of the control system, is not stable. But the overall stable system still computes X as an uniformly continuous function of signals U and Z. This allows bounds and thresholds to be computed as before.

The unstable case However, even in the case of overall stable systems, it may be that some unstable variables are computed by the controller. Here, clock synchronization can be useful. But, in several cases, computing unstable values is a problem, regardless of fault tolerance, and some re-synchronization is algorithmically provided, so as to get stable computations, for instance thanks to Kalman filtering techniques. An example of such a situation can be found in [2].

---

[1] Indicating the sampling period allows mixing both time continuous and sampled systems within the same equational framework; this feature is currently provided in design tools such as Simulink and Matrix$_X$.

3.3   Threshold Voting

Knowing bounds on the normal deviation between values that should be equal, easily allows the design of threshold voters. For instance, a 2/3 voter for scalar values can be written:

$$voter2/3(x_1, x_2, x_3, \epsilon) = \textbf{if } (|x_2 - x_1| \leq \epsilon) or(|x_3 - x_2| \leq \epsilon) or(|x_1 - x_3| \leq \epsilon)$$
$$\textbf{then } median(x_1, x_2, x_3)$$
$$\textbf{else } alarm$$

where $median(x_1, x_2, x_3) = max(min(x_1, x_2), min(x_2, x_3), min(x_3, x_1))$

Notations: In the sequel, algorithms are expressed by abstracting over time indices, thus, $x_1 = x_2$ means $\forall n \in N : x_1(nT) = x_2(nT)$.

4   Combinational Boolean Functions

The case of combinational boolean functions closely looks like the static continuous ones, but for the fact that no error function is available. We thus need to elaborate some notions which will help in recovering it.

4.1   Uniform Bounded Variability

Periodically sampling boolean signals is only accurate if those signals do not vary too fast with respect to the sampling period. Bounded variability (closely linked to non Zenoness [1]) is intended to capture this fact. However, it is not strong enough a property in the same way as continuity is not strong enough for computing error bounds. What is needed in fact is the uniform version of it, a possible definition, which only presents a small deviation from the one in [5], being as follows:

Definition 3. *A signal $x \in R^+ \to B^n$ has* **uniform bounded variability** *if it is right-continuous and if there exists a discontinuity count function $c_x \in R^+ \to N$ such that any time interval of duration not larger than τ contains a number of discontinuities not larger than $c_x(\tau)$:*

$$\forall t_1, t_2 : t_2 - t_1 \leq \tau \Rightarrow |\{t \mid t \in [t_1, t_2] \wedge x(t^-) \neq x(t)\}| \leq c_x(\tau)$$

where $x(t^-)$ represents the left limit at time t. Thus, any time t such that $x(t^-) \neq x(t)$ is a discontinuity point.

This framework then allows us to define which boolean signals and tuples can be sampled without loosing too much information.

Definition 4. *A boolean signal x can be sampled with period T if $c_x(T) = 1$.*

This ensures that no value change will be lost by sampling. Another way, even more practical of defining the same thing is to define the minimum stable time interval:

Definition 5. *The* **minimum stable time interval** T_x *of a boolean signal* x *is the largest time interval such that* $c_x(T_x) = 1$: $T_x = sup\{T \,|c_x(T) \leq 1\}$

Thus the sampling period should be smaller than T_x. We can now relate bounded delays and minimum stable time interval:

Theorem 2 (Bounded delay and minimum stable time interval). *If* x' *is a* τ *bounded delay image of* x, *if* T_x *is the minimum stable time interval of* x *and if* $\tau < T_x$ *then the minimum stable time interval of* x' *is:* $T_{x'} = T_x - \tau$.

Remark: this result can be improved by considering both minimum τ_m and maximum τ_M delays: $T_{x'} = T_x - (\tau_M - \tau_m)$ Yet the extension to independent tuples is more difficult, since we cannot ensure that no value change will be lost. This is a general problem which arises in any periodically sampled system. In most cases, the best we can do is to choose the least period such that each component of the tuple is well sampled in the preceding sense. Nevertheless, we can relate the least minimum stable time interval T_x of each component of a n-tuple X to some time interval where the value of the tuple remains constant:

Theorem 3. *Let* X *be an* n-*tuple such that each component has a minimum stable interval larger that* T_x. *Then, in each time interval of duration larger than* T_x, *there exists a time interval of duration at least* $\frac{T_x}{n+1}$ *where the value of the tuple remains constant.*

4.2 Bounded Variability and Bounded Delays: Confirmation

However, delays do not combine nicely as errors do: the effect of errors on the arguments of a computation amounts to some error on the result. This is in general not true for delays: if the arguments of a computation come with distinct delays, the result may not always be a delayed image of the ideal (not delayed) result.

Fortunately, some filtering procedures make it possible to change incoherent delays into coherent ones: these are known as confirmation procedures. Assume a tuple $X' = \{x'_i, i = 1, n\}$ of boolean signals coming in one unit of period T from different units such that it is the image of an ideal tuple X through bounded delays: $\forall i = 1, n, \exists t'_i, \forall t, 0 \leq t - t'_i(t) \leq \tau_X : x'_i(t) = x_i(t'_i(t))$) where we assume that all delays have the same upper bound τ_X. We consider the following confirmation function:

Definition 6 (Confirmation function).

```
confirm(X', nmax) = X''
where X'', n       = if X' ≠ Δ^T_{X0} X'
                     then Δ^T_{X0} X'',  0
                     else if Δ^T_0 n < nmax − 1
                          then Δ^T_{X0} X'',  Δ^T_0 n + 1
                          else X',  Δ^T_0 n
```

- this confirm function stores a counter n with initial value 0, and its previous output, with some known initial value $X0$,
- whenever its input changes , it outputs its previous output and resets the counter,
- else, if the counter has not reached $nmax - 1$, it increments it and outputs the previous output,
- else it outputs the current input and leaves the counter unchanged.

We further assume that $nmax$ is the maximum number of samples that can occur within the maximum delay $nmax = E(\frac{\tau_X}{T_m}) + 1$, where E denotes the integer part function, and that the minimum stable interval of each component of the tuple T_x exceeds $(n.nmax + 1)T_M$. We then can prove:

Theorem 4. *The confirm function outputs a delayed image of the original tuple:*
$$\exists t', \forall t, 0 \leq t - t'(t) \leq (n.nmax + 1)T : confirm(X', nmax)(t) = X(t'(t))$$

This shows that incoherences due to variable delays can be changed into coherent delays. Once this coherent delay problem is solved, we can consider bounded delay voting. But we can note here an interesting by-product of this confirm function:

Corollary 1. *The output of a confirm function $confirm(X, nmax)$ remains constant for time intervals of duration at least $nmaxT_m$.*

4.3   Bounded Delay Voting

Let us consider several copies of a boolean signal x, received by some unit of period T with a maximum normal delay τ_x such that $\tau_x + T_M < T_x$. Then,

- the maximum time interval where two correct copies may continuously disagree is obviously τ_x,
- the maximum number of samples where two correct copies continuously disagree is $nmax = E(\frac{\tau_x}{T_m}) + 1$

This allows us to design **bounded-delay voters** for bounded-delay booleans signals. For instance, a 2/2 voter could be:

Definition 7 (2/2 bounded-delay voter).

$$voter2/2(x_1, x_2, nmax) = x$$
$$\texttt{where } x, \ n \qquad\qquad = \texttt{if } x_2 = x_1$$
$$\texttt{then } x_1, \ \ 0$$
$$\texttt{else if } \Delta_0^T n < nmax - 1$$
$$\texttt{then } \Delta_{x0}^T x, \ \ \Delta_0^T n + 1$$
$$\texttt{else } alarm$$

- this voter maintains a counter n with initial value 0, and its previous output, with some known initial value $x0$,

- whenever the two inputs agree , it outputs one input and resets the counter,
- else, if the counter has not reached $nmax - 1$, it increments it and outputs the previous output,
- else it raises an alarm.

Theorem 5. *voter2/2 raises an alarm if inputs disagree for more than $nmaxT_M$ otherwise it delivers the correct value with maximum delay $(nmax + 1)T_M$.*

4.4 Bounded Delay Voting on Tuples

Combining bounded delay voting on booleans and confirmation functions allows for the definition of voters for tuples and combinational functions:

Definition 8 (2/2 bounded-delay voter for tuples).

$$Voter2/2(X_1, X_2, nmax) = confirm(X'', nmax)$$
$$\texttt{where } \forall i \in \{1, n\} : x_i'' \quad = voter2/2(x_{1,i}, x_{2,i}, nmax)$$

Then the following theorem yields assuming:

- $X_i, i = 1, 2$ are τ_x bounded delay images of the same X,
- each component of X has minimum stable time interval T_x
- $nmax = E(\frac{\tau_x}{T_m}) + 1$
- $T_x > (n.nmax + 1)T_M$

Theorem 6. *Voter2/2 raises an alarm if any corresponding components of the two inputs disagree for more than $nmaxT_M$ and otherwise delivers the correct value with maximum delay $(n.nmax + 1)T_M$.*

This is the combination of theorems 4 and 5, but for the fact that we do not need to propagate the +1 additional delay from the voter to the confirmation function, because both occur in the same computing unit.

5 Sequential Functions

For the sake of simplicity, we do not distinguish here between states and outputs. Hence, a sequential function $\mathcal{F}$ will be defined by its transition function F: $\mathcal{F}(U) = X$, where $X = F(\Delta_{X0}^T X, U)$

Definition 9. *A 1_stable sequential function is a sequential function whose state only changes when its input changes. For all state X and input U:* $F(F(X, U), U) = F(X, U)$

5.1   Bounded-Delay Voting for Sequential Functions

An idea for applying bounded-delay voting to sequential functions would be to transform sequential functions into combinational ones by setting apart state memorization and voting on states as well as on inputs, *i.e.* instead of computing $x_i = F(\Delta_{x0}^T x_i, vote(U))$ compute $x_i = F(vote(\Delta_{X0}^T X), vote(U))$.

This does not work in general, for Byzantine-like reasons: our bounded-delay voters are sequential systems in the sense that they store as state variable the last value on which units agreed; then a malignant unit may successively agree with states of correct units, while these units disagree for delay reasons, leading the state voters of these correct units to store incoherent values.

5.2   2/2 Vote for Sequential Functions

Quite surprisingly, this phenomenon does not seem to appear for 2/2 bounded delay vote. 2/2 voting is in general not sensitive to Byzantine behaviors because a malignant unit only communicates with a correct one: either it agrees with it and behaves like the correct one or it disagrees and the fault is detected. This property of avoiding Byzantine problems may explain why this fault-detection strategy is very popular. Let us consider the **voting scheme**:

$$X_1 = F(\, vote2/2(\Delta_{X0}^T X_1, X_2', n(nmax_u + nmax_X)),$$
$$confirm(\, \{vote2/2(u_{1,i}', u_{2,i}', nmax_u), i = 1, n\},$$
$$nmax_u + nmax_X))$$

$$X_2 = F(\, vote2/2(\Delta_{X0}^T X_2, X_1', n(nmax_u + nmax_X)),$$
$$confirm(\, \{vote2/2(u_{1,i}'', u_{2,i}'', nmax_u), i = 1, n\},$$
$$nmax_u + nmax_X))$$

where

- F is a 1-stable transition function.
- U_i' and U_i'' are n-tuples linked to some U by bounded delays less than τ_u and $nmax_u = E(\frac{\tau_u}{T_m}) + 1$.
- X_i' are linked to X_i by bounded delays less than τ_X and $nmax_X = E(\frac{\tau_X}{T_m})+1$.
- we assume $\tau_X \leq \tau_u$
- the minimum stable interval of each component of U, T_u is larger than $(n.(nmax_u + nmax_X) + 1)T_M$.

Remark: we use here our simple boolean votes extended to tuples and not our tuple voters. The reasons are that, for states, we do not need confirmation, because one tuple comes from the very unit which computes the vote and the other one comes in one shot from the other unit, and for inputs, we set apart the confirmation because we need a longer stable delay.

Theorem 7. *In the absence of faults, any state voter delivers a correct state with maximum delay $(n.(nmax_u + nmax_X) + 1)T_M$ and delivers an alarm if some input components disagree for more than $nmax_u T_M$ or one of the two units does not compute as specified for more than $n.(nmax_u + nmax_X)T_M$.*

Proof: The proof is by induction on an execution path: Initially, inputs and states agree. Assume a time instant where inputs and states agree. From the stability assumption, nothing will change unless inputs change. Assume some input changes. It takes at most $(nmax_u+1)T$ for both units to agree on this input change and at most $(nmax_x + 1)T$ to agree on the corresponding state change. If this is the case we are done. Now it may be the case that meanwhile another input component changes. It the agreement on states has not been reached, no harm is done because, in both units, state voters still maintain the old state. If the agreement on states is reached in one unit, it will be certainly reached in the other one, because the "confirm" function freezes inputs for a sufficient delay for reaching an agreement in both units (this part of the proof is illustrated at figure 2). By induction on the number of components, if a state agreement has not been reached before, it will be reached when every input component have changed once, because no component can change again from the minimum stable interval assumption. Finally the alarm part of the theorem is obvious from the voting algorithm.

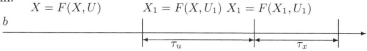

Fig. 2. Proof illustration: process a sees the input changing from U to U_1 first and computes X_1. Then process b sees the same change and also computes X_1. Having received X_1 from a, its state voter moves to X_1 but, for the sake of stability, it goes on computing X_1. Now this value will in turn reach a before the input changes again, thus allowing state voters to reach an agreement on X_1.

5.3   From Fault Detection to Fault Tolerance

2/2 voters account for fault detection and for the design of self-checking modules. Now these modules can be combined by means of selective redundancy so as to form fault-tolerant modules. In the Airbus architecture, this goal is achieved thanks to a global system approach: two self-checking computing systems are provided, each one being able to control the aircraft by itself.

Another possibility is to design hybrid redundancy voters: a primary self-checking system operates until it fails. Meanwhile a secondary system votes on the states of the primary one, so as to stay coherent with it. When the primary system fails, the control is moved to the secondary one which is hopefully still correct.

When designing it, one has to solve the following problem: we switch from the primary system to the secondary one when the watchdog counting the number of disagreements has expired. But then, it may be the case that, because of asynchrony, the secondary system is not yet coherent. We must not raise an alarm here, but, on the contrary leave this system the time to reach a coherent state. This is achieved by the following resetting 2/2 voter:

Definition 10 (2/2 Resetting Voter).

$$rvoter2/2(x_1, x_2, reset, nmax) = x$$

where x = if $x_2 = x_1$
then x_1
else if $\Delta_0^T n < nmax - 1$
then $\Delta_{x0}^T x$
else $alarm$

and n = if $x_2 = x_1 \vee reset$
then 0
else if $\Delta_0^T n < nmax - 1$
then $\Delta_0^T n + 1$
else $alarm$

We are now in a position to design the hybrid voter:

Definition 11 ($1/2 \times 2/2$Voter).

$$voter1/2 \times 2/2(X_1, X_2, X_3, X_4, nmax) = X$$

where X = $rvoter2/2(X_1', X_2', reset, nmax)$
and X_1', X_2' = if $primary$
then X_1, X_2
else X_3, X_4
and $primary$ = Δ_{true}^T if $X = alarm$
then $false$
else $primary$
and $reset$ = $(\neg primary) \wedge (\Delta_{true}^T primary)$

– $primary$ is initially true and the vote is performed on units 1 and 2.
– When one of these fails, primary becomes false for ever and the vote is performed on units 3 and 4.

6   Conclusion

Finally, it seems that we have been able to provide interesting fault tolerant schemes only based on the timing properties of periodic unsynchronized systems. This was quite easy to do for continuous and combinational systems. The problem was more involved for sequential stable systems, but, nevertheless we have found a fault detection scheme which applies to this case and is still only based on timing properties. This allows self-checking dual modules to be build that can serve as building blocks for more elaborated fault tolerant strategies.

One quite obvious possible use of this work is to help certification authorities in getting a better insight on these techniques which are still in use on many systems. Another possible one would be to help designers in choosing between clock synchronization techniques and the ones presented above: one outcome of this work is the computation of periods depending on some characteristics of the application, mainly the minimum stable time interval of the inputs, and the dimension of the involved tuples. This has clearly to be balanced with the cost of clock synchronization.

In this setting, a question left open in this work is the one of unstable sequential systems, for which our techniques clearly do not apply. But, this raises the question of when the implementation of critical control systems do require programming unstable systems. Our opinion is that, as for continuous control, this is seldom the case. More generally, the celebrated "Y2K" bug tells us that unstable systems should be avoided as most as possible.

Last but not least, we hope to attract the attention of computer scientist on this kind of techniques which seem to have been somewhat neglected in the past. It is our opinion that there is by now some revival of the asynchronous circuit culture to which this work may participate.

References

1. M. Abadi and L. Lamport. An old-fashioned recipe for real time. *ACM Transactions on Programming Languages and Systems*, 16(5):1543–1571, 1994.
2. S. Bensalem, P. Caspi, C. Dumas, and C. Parent-Vigouroux. A methodology for proving control programs with Lustre and PVS. In *Dependable Computing for Critical Applications, DCCA-7, San Jose*. IEEE Computer Society, January 1999.
3. J.-L. Bergerand and E. Pilaud. Saga : A software development environment for dependability in automatic control. In *IFAC-SAFECOMP'88*. Pergamon Press, 1988.
4. D. Brière, D. Ribot, D. Pilaud, and J.L. Camus. Methods and specification tools for Airbus on-board systems. In *Avionics Conference and Exhibition*, London, December 1994. ERA Technology.
5. P. Caspi and N. Halbwachs. A functional model for describing and reasoning about time behaviour of computing systems. *Acta Informatica*, 22:595–627, 1986.
6. M.J. Fisher, N.A. Lynch, and M.S. Patterson. Impossibility of distributed consensus with one faulty processor. *Journal of the ACM*, 32(2):374–382, 1985.
7. A.H. Hopkins, T. Basi Smith, and J.H. Lala. FTMP:a highly reliable fault-tolerant multiprocessor for aircraft. *Proceedings of the IEEE*, 66(10):1221–1239, 1978.
8. H. Kopetz, A. Damm, Ch. Koza, M. Mulazzani, W. Schwabl, Ch. Senft, and R. Zainlinger. Distributed fault-tolerant real-time systems: the MARS approach. *IEEE Micro*, 9(1):25–40, 1989.
9. M. Pease, R.E. Shostak, and L. Lamport. Reaching agreement in the presence of faults. *Journal of the ACM*, 27(2):228–237, 1980.
10. J.H. Wensley, L. Lamport, J. Goldberg, M.W. Green, K.N. Lewitt, P.M. Melliar-Smith, R.E Shostak, and Ch.B. Weinstock. SIFT: Design and analysis of a fault-tolerant computer for aircraft control. *Proceedings of the IEEE*, 66(10):1240–1255, 1978.

Automating the Addition of Fault-Tolerance

Sandeep S. Kulkarni
Department of Computer
Science and Engineering
Michigan State University
East Lansing MI 48824 USA

Anish Arora
Department of Computer
and Information Science
Ohio State University
Columbus Ohio 43210 USA

Abstract

In this paper, we focus on automating the transformation of a given fault-intolerant program into a fault-tolerant program. We show how such a transformation can be done for three levels of fault-tolerance properties, failsafe, nonmasking and masking. For the high atomicity model where the program can read all the variables and write all the variables in one atomic step, we show that all three transformations can be performed in polynomial time in the state space of the fault-intolerant program. For the low atomicity model where restrictions are imposed on the ability of programs to read and write variables, we show that all three transformations can be performed in exponential time in the state space of the fault-intolerant program. We also show that the the problem of adding masking fault-tolerance is NP-hard and, hence, exponential complexity is inevitable unless $P = NP$.

1 Introduction

In this paper, we focus on automating the transformation of a fault-intolerant program into a fault-tolerant program. The motivations behind this work are multi-fold. The first motivation comes from the fact that the designer of a fault-tolerant program is often aware of a corresponding fault-intolerant program that is known to be correct in the absence of faults. Or, the designer may be able to develop a fault-intolerant program and its manual proof in a simple way. In these cases, it is expected that the designer will benefit from reusing that fault-intolerant program rather than starting from scratch. Moreover, the reuse of the fault-intolerant program will be virtually mandatory if the designer has only an incomplete specification and the computations of the fault-intolerant program is the de-facto specification.

The second motivation is that the use of such automated transformation will obviate the need for manually constructing the proof of correctness of the synthesized fault-tolerant program as the synthesized program will be correct by construction. This advantage is especially useful when designing concurrent and fault-tolerant programs as it is well-understood that manually constructing proofs of correctness for such programs is especially hard.

---

[1] Email: sandeep@cse.msu.edu, anish@cis.ohio-state.edu. Web: http://www.cse.msu.edu/~sandeep, http://www.cis.ohio-state.edu/~anish. Tel: +1-517-355-2387. Arora is currently on sabbatical leave at Microsoft Research. This work was partially sponsored by NSA Grant MDA904-96-1-0111, NSF Grant NSF-CCR-9972368, an Ameritech Faculty Fellowship, a grant from Microsoft Research, and a grant from Michigan State University.

The third motivation stems from our previous work [1, 2] that shows that a fault-tolerant program can be expressed as a composition of a fault-intolerant program and a set of 'fault-tolerance components'. The fault-intolerant program is responsible for ensuring that the fault-tolerant program works correctly in the absence of faults; it plays no role in dealing with fault-tolerance. The fault-tolerance components are responsible for ensuring that the fault-tolerant program deals with the faults in accordance to the level of tolerance desired; they play no role in ensuring that the program works correctly in the absence of faults. We have also found that the fault-tolerance components help in manually designing fault-tolerant programs as well as in manually constructing their proofs [2]. Moreover, we have found that programs designed using fault-tolerance components are easier to understand and have a better structure [2] than programs designed from scratch.

The third motivation suggests that given a fault-intolerant program p, we should focus on transforming it to obtain a fault-tolerant program p' such that the transformation is done solely for the purpose of dealing with faults according to the level of fault-tolerance desired. More specifically, it suggests that p' should not introduce new ways to satisfy the specification in the absence of faults.

We study the problem of transforming a fault-intolerant program into a fault-tolerant program for three levels of fault-tolerance properties, namely, failsafe, nonmasking and masking. Intuitively, a failsafe fault-tolerant program only satisfies the safety of its specification, a nonmasking fault-tolerant program recovers to a state from where its subsequent computation is in the specification, and a masking fault-tolerant program satisfies the specification even in the presence of faults. (See Section 2 for precise definitions.)

For each of the three levels of fault-tolerance properties, we study the transformation problem in the context of two models; the high atomicity model and the low atomicity model. In the high atomicity model, the program can read and write all its variables in one atomic step. In the low atomicity model, the program consists of a set of processes, and the model specifies restrictions on the ability of processes to atomically read and write program variables. Thus, the transformation problem in the low atomicity model requires us to derive a fault-tolerant program that respects the restrictions imposed by the low atomicity model.

The main contributions are as follows: (1) For the high atomicity model, we present a sound and complete algorithm that solves the transformation problem. The complexity of our algorithm is polynomial in the state space of the fault-intolerant program (cf. Section 4). (2) For the low atomicity model, we present a sound and complete algorithm that solves the transformation problem. The complexity of our algorithm is exponential in the state space of the fault-intolerant program (cf. Section 5.1). (3) We also show that for the low atomicity model, the problem of transforming a fault-intolerant program into a masking fault-tolerant program is NP-hard. It follows that there is no sound and complete polynomial algorithm to solve the problem of adding masking fault-tolerance unless $P = NP$ (for reasons of space, we relegate the proof of NP-completeness to [3]).

Organization of the paper. This paper is organized as follows: We provide the definitions of programs, specifications, faults and fault-tolerance in Section 2. Using these definitions, we state the transformation problem in Section 3. In Section 4, we show how the transformation problem is solved in the high atomicity model. In Section 5, we show how to characterize the low atomicity model and sketch our algorithm for the low atomicity model. Finally, we discuss related work and concluding remarks in Section 6. (For reasons of space, we refer the reader to [3] for the proofs of correctness and the examples of programs constructed using our algorithms)

2   Programs, Specifications Faults, and Fault-Tolerance

In this section, we give formal definitions of programs, problem specifications, faults, and fault-tolerance. The programs are specified in terms of their state space and their transitions. The definition of specifications is adapted from Alpern and Schneider [4]. And, the definition of faults and fault-tolerances is adapted from our previous work.

2.1   Program

Definition. A program p is a tuple $\langle S_p, \delta_p \rangle$ where S_p is a finite set of states, and δ_p is a subset of $\{(s_0, s_1) : s_0, s_1 \in S_p\}$.   □

Definition (*State predicate*). A state predicate of $p(= \langle S_p, \delta_p \rangle)$ is any subset of S_p.   □

Notation.   A state predicate S is true in state s iff $s \in S$.

Definition (*Projection*).   Let $p(= \langle S_p, \delta_p \rangle)$ be a program, and let S be a state predicate of p. We define the projection of p on S, denoted as $p|S$, as the program $\langle S_p, \{(s_0, s_1) : (s_0, s_1) \in \delta_p \ \wedge \ s_0, s_1 \in S\} \rangle$.   □

Note that $p|S$ consists of transitions of p that start in S and end in S.

Definition (*Subset*).   Let $p(= \langle S_p, \delta_p \rangle)$ and $p'(= \langle S_p', \delta_p' \rangle)$ be programs. We say $p' \subseteq p$ iff $S_p' = S_p$ and $\delta_p' \subseteq \delta_p$.   □

Definition (*Closure*).   A state predicate S is closed in a set of transitions δ_p iff $(\forall(s_0, s_1) : (s_0, s_1) \in \delta_p : (s_0 \in S \Rightarrow s_1 \in S))$.   □

Definition. (*Computation*).   A sequence of states, $\langle s_0, s_1, ... \rangle$, is a computation of $p(= \langle S_p, \delta_p \rangle)$ iff the following two conditions are satisfied:

- $\forall j : j > 0 : (s_{j-1}, s_j) \in \delta_p$,
- if $\langle s_0, s_1, ... \rangle$ is finite and terminates in state s_l then there does not exist state s such that $(s_l, s) \in \delta_p$.   □

Notation. We call δ_p as the transitions of p. When it is clear from context, we use p and δ_p interchangeably, e.g., we say that a state predicate S is closed in $p(= \langle S_p, \delta_p \rangle)$ to mean that S is closed in δ_p.

2.2   Specification

Definition.   A specification is a set of infinite sequences of states that is suffix closed and fusion closed. Suffix closure of the set means that if a state sequence σ is in that set then so are all the suffixes of σ. Fusion closure of the set means that if state sequences α, x, γ and β, x, δ are in that set then so are the state sequences α, x, δ and β, x, γ, where α and β are finite prefixes of state sequences, γ and δ are suffixes of state sequences, x is a program state, and $\alpha x \gamma$ denotes a sequence obtained by concatenating α, x and γ.   □

Following Alpern and Schneider [4], it can be shown that any specification is the intersection of some "safety" specification that is suffix closed and fusion closed and some "liveness" specification. Intuitively, the safety specification identifies a set of bad prefixes. A sequence is in the safety specification iff none of its prefixes are identified as bad prefixes. Intuitively, a liveness specification requires that any finite sequence be extensible in order to satisfy that liveness specification. Formally,

Definition (*Safety*).   A safety specification is a set of state sequences that meets the following condition: for each state sequence σ not in that set, there exists a prefix α of σ, such that for all state sequences β, $\alpha\beta$ is not in that set   □

Definition (*Liveness*). A liveness specification is a set of state sequences that meets the following condition: for each finite state sequence α there exists a state sequence β such that $\alpha\beta$ is in that set. $\qquad\square$

Notation. Let *spec* be a specification. We use the term 'safety of *spec*' to mean the smallest safety specification that includes *spec*.

Note that the synthesis algorithm must be provided with a specification that is described in finite space. To simplify further presentation, however, we have defined specifications to contain infinite sequences of states. A concise representation of these infinite sequences is given in Section 2.6.

2.3   Program Correctness with respect to a Specification

Let *spec* be a specification.

Definition (*Refines*). p refines *spec* from S iff (1) S is closed in p, and (2) Every computation of p that starts in a state where S is true is in *spec*. $\qquad\square$

Definition (*Maintains*). Let α be a finite sequence of states. The prefix α maintains *spec* iff there exists a sequence of states β such that $\alpha\beta \in spec$. $\qquad\square$

Notation. We say that p maintains *spec* from S iff S is closed in p and every computation prefix of p that starts in a state in S maintains *spec*. We say that p violates *spec* from S iff it is not the case that p refines *spec* from S.

Definition (*Invariant*). S is an invariant of p for *spec* iff $S \neq \{\}$ and p refines *spec* from S. $\qquad\square$

Notation. Henceforth, whenever the specification is clear from the context, we will omit it; thus, "S is an invariant of p" abbreviates "S is an invariant of p for *spec*".

2.4   Faults

The faults that a program is subject to are systematically represented by transitions. We emphasize that such representation is possible notwithstanding the type of the faults (be they stuck-at, crash, fail-stop, omission, timing, performance, or Byzantine), the nature of the faults (be they permanent, transient, or intermittent), or the ability of the program to observe the effects of the faults (be they detectable or undetectable).

Definition (*Fault*). A fault for $p(=\langle S_p, \delta_p \rangle)$ is a subset of $\{(s_0, s_1) : s_0, s_1 \in S_p\}$. $\qquad\square$

For the rest of the section, let *spec* be a specification, T be a state predicate, S an invariant of p, and f a fault for p.

Definition (*Computation in the presence of faults*). A sequence of states, $\langle s_0, s_1, ... \rangle$, is a computation of $p(=\langle S_p, \delta_p \rangle)$ in the presence of f iff the following three conditions are satisfied:

- $\forall j : j > 0 : (s_{j-1}, s_j) \in (\delta_p \cup f)$,
- if $\langle s_0, s_1, ... \rangle$ is finite and terminates in state s_l then there does not exist state s such that $(s_l, s) \in \delta_p$, and
- $\exists n : n \geq 0 : (\forall j : j > n : (s_{j-1}, s_j) \in \delta_p)$. $\qquad\square$

Notation. For brevity, we use '$p[]f$' to mean 'p in the presence of f'. More specifically, a sequence is a computation of '$p[]f$' iff it is a computation of 'p in the presence of f'. And, the transitions of $p[]f$ are obtained by taking the union of the transitions of p and the transitions of f.

Definition (*Fault-span*). A predicate T is an f-span of p from S iff $S \Rightarrow T$ and T is closed in $p[]f$. $\qquad\square$

Thus, at each state where an invariant S of p is true, and an f-span T of p from S is also true. Also, T, like S, is also closed in p. Moreover, if any action in f is executed in a state where T is true, the resulting state is also one where T is true. It follows that for all computations of p that start at states where S is true, T is a boundary in the state space of p up to which (but not beyond which) the state of p may be perturbed by the occurrence of the actions in f.

Notation. Henceforth, whenever the program p is clear from the context, we will omit it; thus, "S is an invariant" abbreviates "S is an invariant of p" and "f is a fault" abbreviates "f is a fault for p".

2.5   Fault-Tolerance

In the absence of faults, a program should refine its specification. In the presence of faults, however, it may refine a weaker version of the specification as determined by the level of tolerance provided. With this notion, we define three levels of fault-tolerance below.

Definition (*failsafe f-tolerant for* spec *from* S). p is failsafe f-tolerant to *spec* from S iff (1) p refines *spec* from S, and (2) there exists T such that T is an f-span of p from S and $p[]f$ maintains *spec* from T.   □

Definition (*nonmasking f-tolerant for* spec *from* S). p is nonmasking f-tolerant to *spec* from S iff (1) p refines *spec* from S, and (2) there exists T such that T is an f-span of p from S and every computation of $p[]f$ that starts from a state in T has a state in S.   □

Definition (*masking f-tolerant for* spec *from* S). p is masking f-tolerant to *spec* from S iff (1) p refines *spec* from S, and (2) there exists T such that T is an f-span of p from S, $p[]f$ maintains *spec* from T, and every computation of $p[]f$ that starts from a state in T has a state in S.   □

Notation. In the sequel, whenever the specification *spec* and the invariant S are clear from the context, we omit them; thus, "masking f-tolerant" abbreviates "masking f-tolerant for *spec* from S", and so on.

2.6   Observations on Programs and Specifications

In this section, we summarize observations about our programs and specifications. Subsequently, we present the form in which specifications are given to the synthesis algorithm.

Note that a specification, say *spec*, is a set of infinite sequences of states. If p refines *spec* from S then all computations of p that start from a state in S are in *spec* and, hence, all computations of p that start from a state in S must be infinite. Using the same argument, we make the following two observations.

Observation 2.1 If p' is (failsafe, nonmasking or masking) f-tolerant for *spec* from S' then all computations of p' that start from a state in S' must be infinite.   □

Observation 2.2 If p' is (nonmasking or masking) f-tolerant for *spec* from S' then all computations of $p'[]f$ that start from a state in S' must be infinite.   □

Observe that we do not disallow fixed-point computations; we simply require that if s_0 is a fixed-point of p then the transition (s_0, s_0) should be included in the transitions of p.

Concise Representation for Specifications.   Recall that a safety specification identifies a set of bad prefixes that should not occur in program computations. For fusion closed and suffix closed specifications, we can focus on only prefixes of length 2. In other words, if we have a prefix $\langle \alpha, s_0 \rangle$ that maintains *spec* then we can determine whether an extended prefix $\langle \alpha, s_0, s_1 \rangle$ maintains *spec* by focusing on the transition (s_0, s_1), and ignoring α. Formally we state this in Lemma 2.3 as follows (cf. [2] for proof.):

Lemma 2.3. Let α be finite sequence of states, and let $spec$ be a specification.

If $\langle \alpha, s_0 \rangle$ maintains $spec$
Then $\langle \alpha, s_0, s_1 \rangle$ maintains $spec$ iff $\langle s_0, s_1 \rangle$ maintains $spec$.   □

From Lemma 2.3, it follows that the safety specification can be concisely represented by the set of 'bad transitions'. For simplicity, we assume that for a given $spec$ and a state space S_p, the set of bad transitions corresponding to the minimal safety specification that includes $spec$ are given. If this is not the case and $spec$ is given in terms of a temporal logic formula, the set of bad transitions can be computed in polynomial time by considering all transitions (s_0, s_1), where $s_0, s_1 \in S_p$.

Our proof that a fault-tolerant program refines the liveness specification solely depends on the fact that the fault-intolerant program refines the liveness specification. Therefore, our algorithm can transform a fault-intolerant program into a fault-tolerant program even if the liveness specification is unavailable.

3   Problem Statement

In this section, we formally specify the problem of deriving a fault-tolerant program from a fault-intolerant program. We first intuitively characterize what it means for a fault-tolerant program p' to be derived from a fault-intolerant program p. We use this characterization to precisely state the transformation problem. Finally, we also discuss the soundness and completeness issues in the context of the transformation problem.

Now, we consider what it means for a fault-tolerant program p' to be derived from p. As mentioned in the introduction, our derivation is based on the premise that p' is obtained by adding fault-tolerance alone to p, i.e., p' does not introduce new ways of refining $spec$ when no faults have occurred. We precisely state this concept based on the following two observations: (1) If S' contains states that are not in S then, in the absence of faults, p' will include computations that start outside S. Since p' refines $spec$ from S', it would imply that p' is using a new way to refine $spec$ in the absence of faults (since p refines $spec$ only from S). Therefore, we require that $S' \subseteq S$ (equivalently $S' \Rightarrow S$). (2) If $p'|S'$ contains a transition that is not in $p|S'$, p' can use this transition in order to refine $spec$ in the absence of faults. Since this was not permitted in p, we require that $p'|S' \subseteq p|S'$. Thus, we define the transformation problem as follows (This definition will be instantiated for failsafe, nonmasking and masking f-tolerance):

> **The Transformation Problem**
> Given p, S, $spec$ and f such that p refines $spec$ from S
> Identify p' and S' such that
> $S' \Rightarrow S$,
> $p'|S' \subseteq p|S'$, and
> p' is f-tolerant to $spec$ from S'.

We also define the corresponding decision problem as follows:(This definition will also be instantiated for failsafe f-tolerance, nonmasking f-tolerance and masking f-tolerance):

> **The Decision Problem**
> Given p, S, $spec$ and f such that p refines $spec$ from S
> Does there exist p' and S' such that
> $S' \Rightarrow S$,
> $p'|S' \subseteq p|S'$, and
> p' is f-tolerant to $spec$ from S'?

Notations.   Given a fault-intolerant program p, specification *spec*, invariant S and faults f, we say that program p' and predicate S' solve the transformation problem for a given input iff p' and S' satisfy the three conditions of the transformation problem. We say p' (respectively S') solves the transformation problem iff there exists S' (respectively p') such that p', S' solve the transformation problem.

Soundness and completeness.   An algorithm for the transformation problem is sound iff for any given input, its output, namely program p' and the state predicate S', solves the transformation problem. An algorithm for the transformation problem is complete iff for any given input if the answer to the decision problem is affirmative then the algorithm always finds program p' and state predicate S'.

4   Adding Fault-Tolerance in High Atomicity Model

In this section, we consider the transformation problem for programs in the high atomicity model, where a program transition can read any number of variables as well as update any number of variables in one atomic step. In other words, if the enumerated states of the program are $s_0, s_1, ... s_{max}$ then the program transitions can be any subset of $\{(s_j, s_k) : 0 \leq j \leq max\}$. We present our algorithm for adding failsafe, nonmasking and masking fault-tolerance in Sections 4.1, 4.2, and 4.3 respectively.

4.1   Problem of Designing Failsafe Tolerance

As shown in Section 2, the safety specification identifies a set of bad transitions that should not occur in program computations. Given a bad transition (s_0, s_1), we consider two cases: (1) (s_0, s_1) is not a transition of f, (2) (s_0, s_1) is a transition of f.

For case (1), we claim that (s_0, s_1) can be removed while obtaining p'. To see this consider two subcases: (a) state s_0 is ever reached in the computation of $p'[]f$, and (b) state s_0 is never reached in the computation of $p'[]f$. In the former subcase, the transition (s_0, s_1) must be removed as the safety of *spec* can be violated if $p'[]f$ ever reaches state s_0 and executes the transition (s_0, s_1). In the latter subcase, the transition (s_0, s_1) is irrelevant and, hence, can be removed.

For case (2), we cannot remove the transition (s_0, s_1) as it would mean removing a fault transition. Therefore, we must ensure that $p'[]f$ never reaches the state s_0. In other words, for all states s, the transition (s, s_0) must be removed in obtaining p'. Also, if any of these removed transitions, say (s'_0, s_0), is a fault transition then we must recursively remove all transitions of the form (s, s'_0) for each state s.

Using the above two cases, our algorithm to obtain the failsafe fault-tolerant program is as follows: it first identifies states, ms, from where execution of one or more fault transitions violates safety. Then, it removes transitions, mt, of p that reach these states as well as transitions of p that violate the safety of *spec*. (The latter part is included as transitions of p may violate the safety of *spec* in states outside S.) If there exist states in the invariant such that execution of one or more fault actions from those states violates the safety of *spec*, then we recalculate the invariant by removing those states. In this recalculation, we ensure that all computations of $p-mt$ within the new invariant, S', are infinite. In other words, the new invariant is the largest subset of $S-ms$ such that all computations of $p-mt$ when restricted to that subset are infinite. Thus, the detailed algorithm, *Add_failsafe*, is as shown in Figure 1. (As mentioned in Section 2, we use a program and its transitions interchangeably.):

4.2   Problem of Designing Nonmasking Tolerance

To design a nonmasking f-tolerant program p', we ensure that from any state p eventually recovers to a state in S. Thus, the detailed algorithm, *Add-nonmasking*, is as shown in Figure 1. (Note that the function RemoveCycles is defined in such a way that from each state outside S there is a path that reaches a state in S, and there are no cycles in states outside S.)

Add_failsafe(p, f : transitions, S : state predicate, $spec$: specification)
{

$\quad ms := \{s_0 : \exists s_1, s_2, \ldots s_n : (\forall j : 0 \leq j < n : (s_j, s_{(j+1)}) \in f) \ \wedge$
$\qquad\qquad (s_{(n-1)}, s_n) \text{ violates } spec \};$
$\quad mt := \{(s_0, s_1) : ((s_1 \in ms) \ \vee \ (s_0, s_1) \text{ violates } spec)\};$
$\quad S' := \mathsf{ConstructInvariant}(S - ms, p - mt);$
$\quad$ if $(S' = \{\})$ declare no failsafe f-tolerant program p' exists;
$\quad$ else $p' := \mathsf{ConstructTransitions}(p - mt, S')$

}

Add_nonmasking(p, f : transitions, S : state predicate, $spec$: specification)
{

$\quad \mathsf{RemoveCycles}(S, true, (p|S) \cup \{(s_0, s_1) : s_0 \notin S \wedge s_1 \notin S \}$

.}

Add_masking(p, f : transitions, S : state predicate, $spec$: specification)
{

$\quad$ Define ms and mt as in $Add\_failsafe$.
$\quad S_1, T_1 := \mathsf{ConstructInvariant}(S - ms, p - mt), true - ms;$
$\quad$ repeat
$\qquad T_2, S_2 := T_1, S_1;$
$\qquad p_1 := p|S_1 \ \cup \{(s_0, s_1) : s_0 \notin S_1 \ \wedge \ s_0 \in T_1 \ \wedge \ s_1 \in T_1\} - mt;$
$\qquad T_1 := \mathsf{ConstructFaultSpan}(T_1 - \{s : S_1 \text{ is not reachable from } s \text{ in } p_1 \}, f);$
$\qquad S_1 := \mathsf{ConstructInvariant}(S_1 \wedge T_1, p_1);$
$\qquad$ if $(S_1 = \{\} \ \vee \ T_1 = \{\})$ declare no masking f-tolerant program p' exists;
$\quad$ until $(T_1 = T_2 \ \wedge \ S_1 = S_2);$
$\quad p', S', T := \mathsf{RemoveCycles}(S_1, T_1, p_1), S_1, T_1$

}

$\mathsf{ConstructInvariant}(S$: state predicate, p : transitions)
// *Returns* the largest subset of S from where all computations of p are infinite
$\quad \{ \ \{ \text{ while } (\exists s_0 : s_0 \in S : (\forall s_1 : s_1 \in S : (s_0, s_1) \notin p)) \ S := S - \{s_0\} \}; \text{ return } S \quad \}$

$\mathsf{ConstructTransitions}(p$: transitions, S : set of states)
$\quad \{ \text{ return } p - \{(s_0, s_1) : s_0 \in S \ \wedge \ s_1 \notin S\} \}$

$\mathsf{ConstructFaultSpan}(T$: state predicate, f : transitions)
// *Returns* the largest subset of T that is closed in f.
$\quad \{ \ \{ \text{ while } (\exists s_0, s_1 : s_0 \in T \wedge s_1 \notin T \wedge (s_0, s_1) \in f) \qquad T := T - \{s_0\} \}; \text{ return } T \}$

$\mathsf{RemoveCycles}(S, T$: state predicates, p : program)
// *Requires* $(\forall s_0 : s_0 \in T : S$ is reachable from s_0 in $p)$
// *Returns* p_1 such that $p_1 \subseteq p$, $p_1|S = p|S$, $p_1|(T - S)$ is acyclic, and
// $(\forall s_0 : s_0 \in T : S$ is reachable from s_0 in $p_1)$.
$\quad$ (Since several implementations are possible and any one of them is acceptable, we let this procedure be non-deterministic in order to let the designer determinize it to obtain the best efficiency as well as to satisfy other constraints, e.g., further transformation to add tolerance to new faults.
$\quad$ One possible implementation in polynomial time is where each state is ranked based upon the shortest path from that state to a state in S, and transitions that increase the rank are removed.)

Fig. 1. Addition of Fault-Tolerance in High Atomicity

4.3   Problem of Designing Masking Tolerance

To design a masking f-tolerant program p', we proceed to identify the weakest invariant S' (which is stronger than S) and the weakest fault-span T'. To identify the first estimate for the invariant, S', we proceed as in the case of failsafe fault-tolerance. More specifically, we first compute states and transitions in S that need to be removed. Then, we recalculate the invariant to ensure that all computations within S' are infinite. We estimate T' to be T_1 where $T_1 = true - ms$, i.e., T_1 includes all states except those in ms.

We continue to strengthen our S_1 and T_1 while ensuring that if some S' solves the transformation problem then $S' \Rightarrow S_1$. We first identify and remove states in T_1 from where it is not possible to reach a state in S_1 without violating the safety of *spec*. We then find the largest subset of the remaining states that is closed in f. This represents the new estimate for fault-span. Since S_1 must be a subset of T_1, we recalculate S_1 to be the largest subset of $S_1 \wedge T_1$ such that all the computations from that subset are infinite. We continue this process until we reach a fixpoint. Now, p_1 is such that from every state in T_1 there is a path to a state in S_1. p_1 may, however, contain cycles that are entirely in $T_1 - S_1$. The function RemoveCycles removes the cycles while maintaining reachability. Thus, the detailed algorithm, *Add_masking*, is as shown in Figure 1.

While we leave the proof of soundness and completeness of algorithms *Add_failsafe*, *Add_nonmasking* and *Add_masking* to [3], we note that

Theorem 4.1 The algorithms *Add_nonmasking*, *Add_nonmasking* and *Add_masking* are sound, complete, and in P. □

5   Adding Fault-Tolerance in Low Atomicity Model

The synthesis algorithm in Section 4 assumes that the fault-tolerant program can contain a transition (s_0, s_1) for any two states s_0, s_1. If we think of the program state to consist of variables and their corresponding values, the synthesis algorithm assumes that the program can read the values of all variables and write the values of all variables in an atomic step. In this section, we first describe how a low atomicity model that imposes restrictions on how processes can read and write variables. Then, we will outline our algorithm in Section 5.1

We assume that the program consists of processes; each process can atomically read a subset of the program variables and write (a possibly different) set of variables. To systematically use these restrictions imposed by the model, we now define what it means for a process to read and write a variable. First, we define the following two notations.

Notation. Let x be a variable. $x(s_0)$ denotes the value of variable x in state s_0.

Notation. Let r_j denote the set of variables j is allowed to read and w_j denote the set of variables that j is allowed to write.

For simplicity, we assume that j can *atomically* read all variables in r_j and write all variables in w_j. If this is not the case, we split process j into multiple processes that satisfy this assumption. We leave it to the reader to verify that this can always be done.

Remark. Note that the above restrictions are for the program actions only. Faults are not restricted in any way, i.e., a fault transition could read and write all the variables in one atomic step.

Write-restrictions. If j can only write the subset of variables w_j and the value of a variable other than that in w_j is changed in the transition (s_0, s_1) then that transition cannot be used in synthesizing the transitions of j. In other words, being able to write the subset w_j is equivalent to providing a set of transitions $write(j, w_j)$ that j cannot use synthesis algorithm, where

$$write(j, w_j) = \{(s_0, s_1) : (\exists x : x \notin w_j : x(s_0) \neq x(s_1))\}$$

Read-restrictions.   Initially, we consider the case where $w_j \subseteq r_j$, i.e., j can write a variable only if it can read it. Let (s_0, s_1) be some transition of process j such that $s_0 \neq s_1$. Now, consider a state s_0' such that the values of all variables in r_j are identical to that in s_0. Since j can only read variables in r_j, j must have a transition of the form (s_0', s_1'). Moreover, the values of variables in r_j in s_1' must be the same as that in s_1. And, since $w_j \subseteq r_j$, the values of variables that are not in r_j must be the same as that in s_0'. Considering all states where the values of r_j are same, we get a group of transitions; if (s_0, s_1) is a transition of j then all transitions in that group must also be transitions of j. We define these transitions as $group(j, r_j)(s_0, s_1)$, for the case where $w_j \subseteq r_j$, where

$$group(j, r_j)(s_0, s_1) = \{(s_0', s_1') : (\forall x : x \in r_j : x(s_0) = x(s_0') \ \wedge x(s_1) = x(s_1')) \ \wedge \\ (\forall x : x \notin r_j : x(s_0') = x(s_1') \ \wedge \ x(s_0) = x(s_1)) \}$$

Now, we consider the case where $w_j \nsubseteq r_j$, i.e., j writes variables without reading them. To motivate such cases, consider the following scenario: Let $chan_j$ denote the sequence of messages on channel $chan$ which is an outgoing channel from process j. When j sends a message, it writes $chan_j$. However, j cannot read what messages are still pending on channel $chan$, i.e., j cannot read $chan_j$. When j updates $chan_j$, the new value of $chan_j$ depends upon the initial state of the program (including the initial value of $chan_j$). In other words, there exists a function f_{chan_j} such that when j executes in state s_0, j assigns the value $f_{chan_j}(s_0)$ to $chan_j$.

More generally, if j can write multiple variables, say $x_1, x_2, ...$, without being able to read any of them, the model provides a function f (or polynomial number of different functions) such that when j executes in state s_0, j assigns the value $x_i(f(s_0))$ to variable x_i. Using f (or for each possible function f), we now define a group of transitions, $group(j, f, r_j)(s_0, s_1)$, where

$$group(j, f, r_j)(s_0, s_1) = \{(s_0', s_1') : (\forall x : x \in r_j : x(s_0) = x(s_0') \ \wedge x(s_1) = x(s_1')) \ \wedge \\ (\forall x : x \notin r_j : x(s_1') = x(f(s_0')) \ \wedge \ x(s_1) = x(f(s_0))) \}$$

Remark.   The above grouping is done for the case where the transition is not a self-loop. Regarding the self-loop, there are no restrictions. We model this by introducing a group (s_0, s_0) for each state s_0. Note, however, given a program p with invariant S, the masking (respectively, nonmasking) fault-tolerant program p' can contain a self-loop only if it is in $p|S$.

Combining read-restrictions and write-restrictions.   The inability of a process to read is characterized in terms of grouping of transitions. Thus, if a transition in some group violates the restrictions imposed by the inability to write, then that entire group must be excluded in the design of fault-tolerant program. It follows that after combining the read restrictions and the write-restrictions, we get another grouping of transitions; we need to choose zero or more such groups to obtain the transitions of that process. Moreover, the time to compute these groups is polynomial in the size of the input. Thus, we have

Observation 5.1 The groups of transitions corresponding to the given fault-intolerant program and the low atomicity model describing the processes (with the restriction on their ability to read and write) can be computed in polynomial time.   □

5.1   Algorithm Sketch

Now, we sketch our algorithm for adding fault-tolerance in the low atomicity model. Our algorithm is in NP and, hence, the complexity of the corresponding (brute-force)

deterministic algorithm is at most exponential. Being in NP, we simply guess the solution, namely, the invariant S', the fault-span T', and the groups of transitions which would be included in the fault-tolerant program p'. Subsequently, we verify that the three conditions of the transformation problem are satisfied. In this verification, the first two conditions, closure of S' in p' and closure of T' in $p'[]f$ can be verified easily in polynomial time. The third condition about f-tolerance is verified by using T' as the fault-span. For failsafe and masking transformation, safety is verified by ensuring that $p'|T'$ does not contain transitions in mt (as defined in $Add\_failsafe$ in Figure 1). For nonmasking and masking transformation, convergence to S' is verified by checking (1) there is an outgoing edge from each state in T' and (2) $p'|(T'-S')$ is acyclic. (For reasons of space, we relegate the detailed algorithm to [3].)

5.2   NP-completeness of Adding Masking Fault-Tolerance

To show that the problem of adding masking fault-tolerance is NP-complete, we reduce the problem of 3-SAT to that of adding masking fault-tolerance. Given a 3-SAT problem consisting of literals $a_1, ... a_n$ (and respective complements $a'_1, ..., a'_n$), we construct a graph where there are three vertexes, a_i, b_i, s_i, for each a_i and one vertex for each clause c_i. (The vertices in this graph denote the program states and edges denote the program transitions.) We define faults in such a way that each of these vertices is reachable in the presence of faults. We then select processes and variables such that the edges (b_i, a_i), (a_i, b'_i) and (b'_i, s'_i) are grouped. Also, the graph contains edges from each clause c_i to each literal in that clause. The invariant of the fault-intolerant program consists of the s_i (and s'_i) states. From the possible permitted transitions, the program must first reach the vertex corresponding to some a_i (or a'_i), then reach b'_i and then s'_i. Due to grouping constraints, the edge (b_i, a_i) must also be included in the program. Observe that the truth value assigned to a_i determines whether the masking fault-tolerant program converges via a_i or a'_i. (Note that the program cannot converge via both a_i and a'_i as it would imply that there would be a cycle outside the invariant.) Thus, we construct an instance of the problem of adding masking fault-tolerance that has a solution iff the 3-SAT formula is satisfiable. For reasons of space, the detailed proof is in [3].

6   Conclusion and Future Work

In this paper, we focused on the problem of adding fault-tolerance to a fault-intolerant program for three levels of fault-tolerance, namely failsafe, nonmasking and masking. We showed that these transformations are feasible and their complexity depends upon underlying system model. More precisely, the complexity was polynomial in a model where a process could read and write all variables, and it was exponential for the case where restrictions were imposed on ability of processes to read and write. We also argued that there are system models for which complexiy of adding masking fault-tolerance will be exponential unless $P = NP$.

focused on transforming a fault-intolerant program into a fault-tolerant program. We considered three levels of fault-tolerance, namely failsafe, nonmasking and masking. We showed that in the high atomicity model, where the program can read and write all the variables in one atomic step, all these transformations can be performed in polynomial time in the size of the fault-intolerant program. We also showed that in the low atomicity model, where the program consists of processes each of which can only read and write a limited set of variables, all these transformations can be performed in exponential time in the size of the fault-intolerant program. For reasons of space, discussion about examples of programs that can be designed using these algorithms, namely, triple modular redundancy, byzantine agreemnt and token ring circulation, and the proof showing that the problem of adding masking fault-tolerance to a given fault-intolerant program is NP-hard is relegated to [3].

The main difference between our work and the previous work on program synthesis [5–10] is that we begin with a fault-intolerant program and transform it to obtain fault-tolerance. By way of contrast, algorithms in [5–10] deal with synthesizing a program from its specification (typically in a temporal logic). For this reason, we believe that our approach will be especially useful if a fault-intolerant program is already known or if other constraints (such as unavailability of a complete specification of the given fault-intolerant program) require that we reuse the fault-intolerant program. Also, due to the same reason, our algorithms only needed the safety specification that the program is supposed to satisfy in the presence of faults; the algorithms did not need the liveness specification.

Another difference between our work and previous work on synthesizing fault-tolerant programs [7–10] is the generality of our fault-model and that of the low atomicity model. Specifically, our low atomicity model is more general than the Read/Write model considered elsewhere [9, 11]. For example, our low atomicity model includes common shared memory models where process can atomicity read its neighbors' state and write its own state. This ability to design programs of atmocity higher than the Read/Write atomicity will be especially useful when adding fault-tolerance in Read/Write atomicity is impossible and adding it in higher atomicity is possible.

Our work on transformation raises the following open questions: Do there exist system models which are stronger than the high atomicity model but weaker than the (general) low atomicity model for which polynonmial transformations are possible? Do there exist specific fault-models for which polynomial transformation is possible? We will address these questions in the future work.

References

1. A. Arora and S. S. Kulkarni. Detectors and correctors: A theory of fault-tolerance components. *International Conference on Distributed Computing Systems*, pages 436–443, May 1998.
2. S. S. Kulkarni. *Component-based design of fault-tolerance.* PhD thesis, Ohio State University, 1999.
3. Sandeep S. Kulkarni and Anish Arora. Automating the addition of fault-tolerance. Technical Report MSU-CSE-00-13, Computer Science and Engineering, Michigan State University, East Lansing, Michigan, June 2000.
4. B. Alpern and F. B. Schneider. Defining liveness. *Information Processing Letters*, 21:181–185, 1985.
5. E. A. Emerson and E. M. Clarke. Using branching time temporal logic to synchronize synchronization skeletons. *Science of Computer Programming*, 2:241–266, 1982.
6. Z. Manna and P. Wolper. Synthesis of communicating processes from temporal logic specifications. *ACM Transactions on Programming Languages and Systems*, 6:68–93, 1984.
7. A. Pnueli and R. Rosner. On the synthesis of a reactive module. *ACM Symposium on Principles of Programming Languages*, pages 179–190, 1989.
8. A. Anuchitanukul and Z. Manna. Reliability and synthesis of reactive modules. *International Conference on Computer-Aided Verification*, pages 156–169, 1994.
9. A. Arora, P. C. Attie, and E. A. Emerson. Synthesis of fault-tolerant concurrent programs. *Proceedings of the 17th ACM Symposium on Principles of Distributed Computing (PODC)*, 1998.
10. O. Kupferman and M. Vardi. Synthesis with incomplete information. *ICTL*, 1997.
11. D. Dill and H. Wong-Toi. Synthesizing processes and schedulers from temporal specifications. *International Conference on Computer-Aided Verification*, 1990.

Reliability Modelling of Time-Critical Distributed Systems

Hans Hansson, Christer Norström, and Sasikumar Punnekkat

Mälardalen Real-Time Research Centre,
Department of Computer Engineering,
Mälardalen University, Västerås, SWEDEN,
han@idt.mdh.se, cen@mdh.se, spt@idt.mdh.se,
WWW home page: http://www.mrtc.mdh.se

Abstract. In cost conscious industries, such as automotive, it is imperative for designers to adhere to policies that reduce system resources to the extent feasible, even for safety-critical sub-systems. However, the overall reliability requirement, typically in the order of 10^{-9} faults/hour, must be both analysable and met. Faults can be hardware, software or timing faults. The latter being handled by hard-real time schedulability analysis, which is used to prove that no timing violations will occur. However, from a reliability and cost perspective there is a tradeoff between timing guarantees, the level of hardware and software faults, and the per-unit cost for meeting the overall reliability requirement.
This paper outlines a reliability analysis method that considers the effect of faults on schedulability analysis and its impact on the reliability estimation of the system. The ideas have general applicability, but the method has been developed with modeling of external interferences of automotive CAN buses in mind. We illustrate the method using the example of a distributed braking system.

1 Introduction

The parallel evolution of fault tolerance and real-time realms of research, though have been greatly successful independently, still fail to bring the necessary synergy between the two fields which both are of extreme importance in the design of safety-critical systems. Their mutual dependencies and interactions need to be analysed carefully for achieving predictable performance. The major stumbling block in having an intergrated approach is the orthogonal nature of two factors, viz., the stochastic nature of faults and the deterministic requirements on schedulability analysis. This calls for development of more realistic fault models which capture the nuances of the environment as well as methods for easy integration of such models into the timing analysis and finally, a unified and 'formal' approach in using them to obtain refined estimates for the system reliability.

During the last decade, schedulability analysis of real-time systems has developed into a mature discipline for determining whether a set of tasks executing on a single CPU or in a distributed system will meet their deadlines or not

M. Joseph (Ed.): FTRTFT 2000, LNCS 1926, pp. 94–105, 2000.

[2][1][6] [10]. The essence of the analysis is to investigate if the deadlines are met in a worst case scenario. Whether this worst case actually will occur during execution, or if it is likely to occur, is not normally considered (an exception being [3]). Reliability modeling, on the other hand involves study of fault models, characterization of distribution functions of faults and development of methods and tools for composing these distributions and models in estimating an overall reliability figure for the system.

We have recently [5] developed a model for calculating worst-case latencies of messages under error assumptions, for the Controller Area Network (CAN). This analysis might infer that a given message set is not feasible under worst case fault interferences. Such a result though correct, is only of limited help to system designers except to prompt them to overdesign the system and waste resources to tackle a situation, which might never happen during the life time of the system.

When performing schedulability analysis it is important to keep in mind that the analysis is only valid under some specific model assumptions. Behaviours outside these assumptions are typically catered for in the reliability analysis. This separation of deterministic (0/1) schedulability analysis and stochastic reliability analysis is a natural simplification of the the total analysis, which might be pessimistic. Consider, for instance, occasional external interference on a communication link. The effect will be increased message latencies which may lead to missed deadlines, especially if the interference coincides with the worst case message transmission scenario considered when performing schedulability analysis. In other scenarios, the interference might not increase the worst case message latency, as illustrated in Figure 1. The figure shows a system with 3 periodic messages M_1, M_2 and M_3 with descending priorities and with periods (equals to deadlines) of 5, 10 and 20 and worst-case transmission times of 2,1 and 1 respectively. Assuming an overhead, $O = 1$, for error signaling and recovery (but not including retransmission of the corrupted message), we have shown the effects of 3 different scenarios, corresponding to an external interference hitting the system at different points in time. In the first case, both M_2 and M_3 miss their deadlines. In the second case, though a re-transmission is necessitated, still the message set meets its deadlines, whereas in the third scenario, the error has no effect at all since it falls in a period of inactivity of the bus. Hence, schedulability analysis which only considers the worst-case phasing introduces pessimism by asuming that any interference will lead to a missed deadline.

The basic argument of our work, is that a system can only be guaranteed up to some level, after which we must resort to reliability analysis, and that the reliability analysis can be made more accurate if it considers schedulability. In this paper we present:

- An approach for integrating schedulability analysis and reliability models
- A systematic procedure for obtaining more accurate reliability estimates
- Modified response time modelling for CAN messages under our fault model
- An illustrative example presenting the usefulness of this method

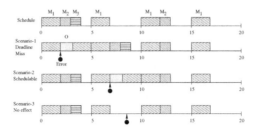

Fig. 1. Dependency of Effects of Faults on Phasings

The outline of the paper is as follows. Section 2 presents general reliability modelling for distributed real-time systems and introduces our approach. Section 3 specifically discusses the scheduling of message sets in Controller Area Networks under a general fault model and subsequently extends it to analyse arbitrary samples of phasings and interferences. Section 4 presents a case study of messages in a distributed computer network used in passenger cars. The concluding section 5, discusses some possible extensions.

2 Reliability Modelling

Reliability is defined as the probability that a system can perform its intended function, under given conditions, for a given time interval. In the context of an Antilock Braking System (ABS) for automobiles, this boils down to performing the tasks (mainly input_sensors, compute_control, and output_actuators etc.,) as per the specifications. Being part of a real-time system, the specifications for ABS, imply the necessity for the results to be both functionally correct and within timing specifications. A major issue here is how to compose hardware reliability, software reliability, environment model, and timing correctness to arrive at reasonable estimates of overall system reliability. Let us define

$$P_{HF}(t) = Probability(Hardware\ failure\ at\ t) \qquad (1)$$

$$P_{SF}(t) = Probability(Software\ failure\ at\ t) \qquad (2)$$

$$P_{CF}(t) = Probability(Communication\ failure\ at\ t) \qquad (3)$$

The reliability of the system, $R(t)$, is the probability that the system performs all its intended functions correctly for a period t. This is given by the product of cumulative probabilities that there are no failures in hardware, software and communication subsystem during the period $(0, t)$. That is,

$$R(t) = \left(1 - \int_0^t P_{HF}(t)\right) \left(1 - \int_0^t P_{SF}(t)\right) \left(1 - \int_0^t P_{CF}(t)\right) \qquad (4)$$

In this paper, we concentrate only on the final term in Equation 4, i.e, the probability that no errors occur in the communication subsystem. Please note that, when we talk about communication subsystem, we are not merely concentrating on the faults in the hardware or software of such a system. Instead we consider the probability of correct and timely delivery of message sets. Since the main cause for an incorrect (corrupted, missing or delayed) message delivery is environmental interferences, an appropriate modelling of such factors is essential.

The basis for our modelling and analysis will be an appropriate environment model and method to perform response time analysis of CAN messages under normal and error conditions[5], together with subsystem reliability requirements and timing specifications for the set of tasks and messages implementing the subsystem. These subsystem specifications and requirements are derived from overall system reliabilty and timing requirements.

The problem analysed is, given the above information, how to find a suitable way of predicting the reliability of the communication subsystem. The simple approach will be to give a 0/1 weight to the schedulability aspect in evaluating the system 'correctness' and calculate the reliability. However, the environment model provides worst case scenarios, which may not occur in practice and its impact may depend on the actual phasing of messages and the way in which they interact with the environment/fault model. So, we are faced with additional questions, such as:

- Can we partition the schedulability analysis under faults by considering a set of scenarios corresponding to message and fault model phasings and isolate the worst case as only one of several scenarios?
- Is it possible to get a more accurate reliability estimate by such an analysis?

2.1 Reliability Estimation

By definition, reliability is specified for a mission time. Normally we can assume a repetitive pattern of messages (over the least common multiple (LCM) of the message periods). Since such an LCM is typically a very small fraction of the mission time, it is sufficient to find the impact of environmental interferences over some constant k cycles of LCM, where $1 \leq k \leq \lceil \frac{Mission\ Time}{LCM} \rceil$. We can then extrapolate that data to get the projection over the entire mission time. The suitable value for k is one for which, $k \times LCM$ is large enough to contain any of the interference patterns, so that they do not spill over LCM boundaries.

Here we concentrate on $P_{CF}(t)$ and outline a methodology for estimating it. Let t represents an arbitrary time point in $(0, k \times LCM)$ that marks the time instance when the external interference hits the bus and causes an error. If we can assume zero error latency and instantaneous error detection then t becomes the time point of detection of an error in the bus. We define,

$$P_I(t) = Probability(Interference\ at\ t) \tag{5}$$
$$P_{TE}(t) = Probability(Deadline\ miss \mid Interference\ at\ t\ ) \tag{6}$$

By relying on the extensive error detection and handling features available in CAN, we can safely assume that an error in message corruption is either detected and corrected by re-transmission or will ultimately result in a timing error. So, the probability of communication failure due to interference starting at t is:

$$P_{CF}(t) = P_{TE}(t) \times P_I(t) \tag{7}$$

In our environment model [5], we have assumed the possibility of an interference I_1 from source 1, having a certain pattern hitting the message transmission. Let $P_I^1(t)$ be the probability of such an event occurring at time t. We also assume that another interference I_2 from source 2, having a different pattern, can hit the system at time t with a probability, say, $P_I^2(t)$. In [5], we assumed both these interferences hitting the message transmission resulting in the worst case impact on schedulability. In this paper, we will increase the realism in this modeling by relaxing the requirement on the phasing between schedule and interference. Note that, there is an implicit assumption that these interferences are independent.

2.2   Approach to Analysis

To calculate the subsystem reliability, first we need to calculate the failure probability, i.e. the probability of at least one failure (defined as a missed deadline) during the mission time, we use the following method:

1. We assume that the interference free system is schedulable, i.e. it meets all deadlines with probability 1.
2. For each interference source, we calculate the probability of interference in an arbitrary LCM. This could be given by:

$$\frac{\text{sum of interference periods during mission time}}{\text{mission time}}$$

   Here we will assume that the each interference source can be characterized by periods of relative frequent interferences (assumed to occur at least once every LCM) and interference free periods. The above "sum" denotes the total length of the former periods.

   Alternatively, the above probability for interference may, based on some other calculations or estimations, be provided by the designer.
3. Calculate probabilities for all combinations of interference sources. This is the product of individual probabilities, since we assume independent sources.
4. For each combination of interference sources, calculate the probability of an error in an LCM caused by the considered combination of interference. This is performed by the following procedure
   a) Do until required confidence level is reached[1]:
      i. Make a random selection of phasings by for each considered source making a random selection from the set of discrete time points (up to the granularity of the schedule) $(0, t_f]$, where t_f is the periodicity

---

[1] Since we are using random sampling, rather than complete analysis, keeping track of the confidence level of the analysis results is essential. However, to simplify this first presentation of our approach we will not here consider this further.

of the interference (as defined in Section 3.2). Each picked sample indicates the position in t_f of the corresponding source at time 0 in the LCM.

ii. Perform schedulability analysis (as detailed in subsequent sections)

iii. If not schedulable then increase *deadline_miss_count*.

iv. Failure probability is $\dfrac{deadline\_miss\_count}{number\ of\ samples}$

5. Total subsystem reliability with required confidence is 1 minus the weighted mean of calculated failure probabilities. This weighted mean is the sum of the probabilities for interference sources (as calculated in 3 above) multiplied with the corresponding failure probability (as defined in 4(a)iv above).

3   Schedulability Analysis of CAN Messages

The Controller Area Network (CAN) is a broadcast bus designed to operate at speeds of up to 1 Mbps. Each CAN message can contain 0 - 8 bytes of data. A unique 11 bit identifier is associated with each message, which assigns a priority to the message. CAN uses deterministic collision resolution to control access to the bus. During arbitration, competing stations are simultaneously putting their identifiers on the bus. The station with highest priority identifier will win the arbitration, and start transmitting the body of the message.

The CAN message format contains 47 bits of protocol control information. The data transmission protocol inserts a stuff bit after five consecutive bits of the same value. The frame format is specified such that only 34 of the 47 control bits are subject to bit stuffing. Hence, the maximum number of stuff bits in a message m_i with n bytes of data is $\lfloor \frac{(n*8+34-1)}{4} \rfloor$ (since the worst case bit pattern is '1111100001111...'). This means that a message is transmitted with between 0 and 24 stuff bits. Hence, the size of a transmitted CAN message is in the range 47..135 bits. The worst case transmission time, denoted C_i, of message m_i is given by the number of bits to be transmitted for the message multiplied by the time required to transmit one bit, denoted τ_{bit}. Hence, for a message with n bytes of data $C_i = (n*8 + 47 + \lfloor \frac{(n*8+34-1)}{4} \rfloor) * \tau_{bit}$.

3.1   Classical CAN Bus Analysis

Tindell et al. [7] [8] [9] present analysis to calculate the worst-case latencies of CAN messages. This analysis is based on the standard fixed priority response time analysis for CPU scheduling [1].

Calculating the response times requires a bounded worst case queuing pattern of messages. The standard way of expressing this is to assume a set of traffic streams, each generating messages with a fixed priority. The worst case behaviour of each stream is to periodically queue messages. In analogue with CPU scheduling, we obtain a model with a set $\mathcal{S}$ of streams. Each $S_i \in \mathcal{S}$ is a triple $< P_i, T_i, C_i >$, where P_i is the priority (defined by the message dentifier), T_i is the period and C_i the worst case transmission time of messages sent on stream S_i. The worst-case latency R_i of a CAN message stream S_i is defined by:

$$R_i = J_i + q_i + C_i \tag{8}$$

where J_i is the queuing jitter of the message, i.e., the maximum variation in queuing time relative T_i, inherited from the sender task which queues the message, and q_i represents the effective queuing time, given by:

$$q_i = B_i + \sum_{j \in hp(i)} \left\lceil \frac{q_i + J_j + \tau_{bit}}{T_j} \right\rceil C_j + E(q_i + C_i) \tag{9}$$

where the term B_i is the worst-case blocking time of messages sent on S_i, $hp(i)$ is the set of streams with priority higher than S_i, τ_{bit} (the bit-time) caters for the difference in arbitration start times at the different nodes due to propagation delays and protocol tolerances, and $E(q_i + C_i)$ is an error term denoting the time required for error signalling and recovery. The reason for the blocking factor is that transmissions are non-preemptive, i.e., after a bus arbitration has started the message with highest priority among competing messages will be transmitted, even if a higher priority message is queued before its completion.

3.2 Our Previous Generalization

In [5] we present a generalization of the relatively simplistic error model by Tindell and Burns [7], specifically addressing multiple sources of errors and considering the signalling pattern of individual sources. Each source can typically be characterized by a pattern of shorter or longer bursts, during which no signalling will be possible on the bus.

In this paper we will use a slightly simplified version of the error model introduced in [5]. Our definition of the error term $E_i(t)$ is based on the following:

- There are k sources of interference, with each source l contributing an error term $E_i^l(t)$. Their combined effect is $E_i(t) = E_i^1(t) \,|\, E_i^2(t) \,|\, \ldots \,|\, E_i^k(t)$, where $|$ denotes composition of error terms.
- Each source l interferes by inducing an undefined bus value during a characteristic time period I^l. Each such interference will (if it coincides with a transmission) lead to a transmission error. If I^l is larger than τ_{bit}, then the error recovery will be delayed accordingly.
- Patterns of interferences for each source l can independently be specified as a sequence of bursts with period T_f^l, where each group consists of n^l interferences of length I^l and with period t_f^l.

We can now define $E_i(t)$ for the case of k sources of interference:

$$E_i(t) = E_i^1(t)|E_i^2(t)|\ldots|E_i^k(t) \tag{10}$$

where

$$E_i^l(t) = Bu^l(t) * (O_i^b + max(0, I^l - \tau_{bit})) \tag{11}$$

where

$$Bu^l(t) = \left\lfloor \frac{t}{T_f^l} \right\rfloor * n^l + min \left(n^l, \left\lceil \frac{t \bmod T_f^l}{t_f^l} \right\rceil \right)$$ (12)

Some explanations:

1. $max(0, I^l - \tau_{bit})$ defines the length of I^l exceeding τ_{bit}.

2. $\left\lfloor \frac{t}{T_f^l} \right\rfloor$ is the number of full bursts until t.

3. $\left\lceil \frac{t \bmod T_f^l}{t_f^l} \right\rceil$ is the number of t_f^l periods that fit in the last (not completed) burst period in t.

We assume that the overheads O_i are given by:

$$O_i = 31 * \tau_{bit} + \max_{k \in hp(i) \cup \{i\}} (C_k)$$ (13)

where $31 * \tau_{bit}$ is the time required for error signalling in CAN and the max-term denotes the worst-case retransmission time.

3.3   Analysis with Random Phasings of Interferences

The analysis above assumes that interference hits the system in a worst case scenario. This assumption will now be relaxed. Our relaxed model will be based on

1. Worst-case phasings of queuings at time 0 in the LCM (actually this could be at any time, so why not choose 0). This introduces some pessimism, since the worst case may not occur in every LCM, but is consistent with the assumed traffic in the interference free model.
2. Random phasings of interferences. This can be expressed as an offset from the beginning of the LCM to when the first interference hits. For each source that hits the LCM, such an offset (offset$_l$) should be "sampled" (as outlined in Section 2.2).

Intuitively, extending the schedulability analysis equations to also cover random phasings of interferences seems the right approach to solve our problem. One candidate solution is the following minor modification of the schedulability formulas, by replacing, $E_i^l(t)$ with

$$E_i^l(t) = Bu^l(\max(0, t - \text{offset}_l) * (O_i^b + max(0, I^l - \tau_{bit}))$$ (14)

Unfortunately, there is a risk that the resulting analysis underestimates the probability of deadline misses, since it only considers the first invocation of each message in the LCM, and since the interference now may start later, a subsequent invocation may experience larger latency than the first one. To avoid optimism in the analysis we advocate other methods below, even though we think the schedulability analysis approach deserves further investigation and evaluation before being dismissed.

The following three approaches provide successively refined estimates of the probability of a deadline miss:

1. Use 1 if any message miss deadline under critical instant assumptions otherwise 0. This corresponds to the original analysis. But keep in mind that the result of a deadline miss here will not be 0, since we will only conclude a deadline violation in LCMs subjected to interference.
2. Add up all the idle time slots during LCM giving say I. If number of idle slots is n_I and error interference duration is E, calculate $I - n_I \times E$ (this is to remove the possibility of an error burst spilling to a busy period). Now $\frac{(I-n_I \times E)}{LCM}$ gives a crude, but better approximation.
3. Our final, and most accurate method, is based on a simulation of the message transfer and interference in the LCM. The basis is that for each combination of samples we will get a static scenario with fixed release times and parameters. The most efficient analysis is then probably a straight-forward simulation. Simulation possibly will provide best estimates for the probability of deadline miss, since it corresponds to actually running the system during an LCM. This allows more restricted traffic patterns to be handled (possibly better corresponding to reality).

3.4   Effects of Bit Stuffing

Another important factor which contributes pessimism is bit-stuffing overheads assumed for analysis. As mentioned in section 3, the worst case number of stuff bits is assumed to be $\lfloor \frac{(n*8+34-1)}{4} \rfloor$ and is accounted in the worst case transmission time, C_i. In applications where all the probable message bit patterns are known a priori, we can use that information to derive a new worst case transmission time. For systems where there is considerable amount of uncertainty in message patterns, we still can improve our results by using simple probabilistic estimates of the worst case transmission times. Since any bit can be '1' or '0', we can by assuming the probability for each to be $\frac{1}{2}$ estimate the probability for adding a certain number of stuff bits, e.g., the probability of adding one stuff bit after the 5 first bits subjected to bit-stuffing is $(\frac{1}{2})^5$. By providing probabilities for different message lengths (and in turn for the worst case transmission times), the simulation results can give closer match to the real scenario. Details of these calculations are provided in [4].

4   Example : A Distributed Braking System

We now present a case study of a simplified Antilock Braking System (ABS), where each separate brake is controlled by a computer. Furthermore, there is one computer that controls the brake pedal. All nodes are connected by a CAN-bus (see Figure 2). The application is a distributed control algorithm, which calculates the brake force for each wheel depending on the brake pressure achieved from the driver. Therefore, each wheel-computer has to receive information about the state of the other wheels, to be able to make correct calculation and actuation. Thus each wheel is equipped with a sensor that monitors the rotation of the wheel. Each node sends the monitored values periodically.

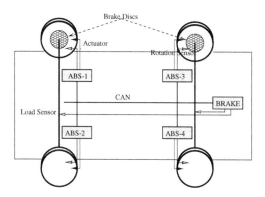

Fig. 2. Typical Computer Network in a Car with ABS

Since ABS is a subsystem of the entire vehicle system, we assume an appropriate reliability figure (say 10^{-9}) to be attained by the ABS. This figure is in fact mandated from an overall system reliability requirement of 10^{-7}.

Table 1 (left half) specifies a typical subset of messages sent through CAN in this simplified ABS and their timing details (in ms). The timing parameters are typically requirements derived from the vehicle dynamics by a control engineer. Priority 1 is assumed to be the highest and 6 is the lowest. We also assume that the CAN bus operates at 250 Kbps.

4.1   Interference Characteristics

In our example of the communication subsystem of a vehicle, two typical sources of interference could be from a mobile phone lying inside the vehicle or Radar transmissions from ships while the vehicle crosses bridges. Mobile phones (such as GSM-phones) typically operate at 900MHz - 1800 MHz frequencies. The carrier when transmission occurs is for a period of 500 μs duration out of a 4ms cycle. Also each half-an-hour or so, the mobile phone will send signals to the base station. In addition, on a moving vehicle extra signals are sent when the phone switches between base-stations. We assume 4 interferences in a burst and typical interval between bursts to be 30 secs. For the interference from radar, we assume the duration to be 1 ms with 1 interferences per burst and interval between bursts to be 1000 secs.

4.2 Reliability Analysis Results

A typical mission time for an ABS could be say less than 10 hours and our analysis is based on worst case scenarios in an LCM (which typically is in the order of a second). Table 1 shows the results of response time analysis. The column headed by '0' shows the message latencies under no errors, where as columns headed by '1', '2', and '3' show message latencies under interferences from source-1 (mobile phone), source - 2 (radar), and both sources respectively. A '*' indicates a deadline miss situation.

A typical Message Set									
Msg ID	Priority	T_i	D_i	size	C_i	Response Time			
						(0)	(1)	(2)	(3)
OPERATOR-1	1	8	8	8	0.54	1.08	2.24	2.74	3.908
ABS-1	2	4	4	8	0.54	1.64	2.78	3.28	* 4.448
ABS-2	3	4	4	8	0.54	2.16	3.32	3.82	* 6.692
ABS-3	4	4	4	8	0.54	2.70	3.86	* 4.36	* 7.772
ABS-4	5	4	4	8	0.54	3.24	* 4.40	* 6.52	* 12.176
OPERATOR-2	6	15	15	8	0.54	3.78	7.10	7.60	* 16.030

Table 1. Response Time Analysis- Normal and under Faults

Note that, 5 out of 6 messages miss their deadlines under the worst case phasing of combined interferences from both sources. We conducted simulation runs with and without random bit-stuffing and the results are shown in Table 2. Combining the obtained failure probabilities with resonable assumptions on

Interference Sources	Total Messages	Missed (worst-case)	Failure Probability	Missed (random)	Failure Probability
Source-I1	15064	5	0.00033	3	0.000199
Source-I2	15064	41	0.00272	14	0.000929
I1 and I2	15064	44	0.00292	16	0.001062

Table 2. Simulation results for worst-case and random bit-stuffing

occurence of interferences, we get the overall failure probability to be of the order 5×10^{-11}, which is quite negligible in relation to the admissible failure probability of 10^{-7}. Details on these calculations and the assumptions are provided in [4].

5   Conclusions

We have presented results from ongoing work to develop a framework that allows controlled relaxation of the timing requirements of safety-critical hard real-time systems. By integrating hard real-time schedulability with the reliability analysis normally used to estimate the imperfection of reality, we obtain a more accurate reliability analysis framework, which can provide reasonable arguments for making design trade-offs, e.g., choosing a slower (and less expensive) bus or CPU, even though the timing requirements are violated in some rare worst-case scenario.

Using traditional schedulability analysis techniques, the designer will have no other choice than to redesign the system (in hardware, software or both), if the emphasis is only on worst case interference hits. However, by resorting to our new analysis, if the probability of such an extreme situation arising is very low (in relation to the reliability requirements), then the designer may very well avoid such a costly step.

Further research planned on our approach include,

- Extensions by stochastic modeling of external interferences, and distributions of execution times of tasks, jitter, periods for sporadic tasks, etc. Some of these extensions require dependency issues to be carefully considered.
- A comparison of the schedulability and simulation based approaches.

References

1. N. C. Audsley, A. Burns, M.F. Richardson, K. Tindell, and A.J. Wellings. Applying New Scheduling Theory to Static Priority Pre-emptive Scheduling. *Software Engineering Journal*, 8(5):284–292, September 1993.
2. A. Burns. Preemptive Priority Based Scheduling: An Appropriate Engineering Approach. Technical Report YCS 214, University of York, 1993.
3. A. Burns, S. Punnekkat, L. Strigini, and D.R. Wright. Probabilistic scheduling guarantees for fault-tolerant real-time systems. *Proceedings of DCCS-7,IFIP International Working Conference on Dependable Computing for Critical Applications, California*, January 1999.
4. H. Hansson, C. Norström, and S. Punnekkat. Reliability Modelling of Time-Critical Distributed Systems. Technical report, MRTC, Mälardalen University, July 2000.
5. S. Punnekkat, H. Hansson, and C. Norström. Response Time Analysis under Errors for CAN. *Proceedings of IEEE Real-Time Technology and Applications Symposium(RTAS)*, page To appear, June 2000.
6. L. Sha, R. Rajkumar, and J.P. Lehoczky. Priority Inheritance Protocols: An Approach to Real-Time Synchronization. *IEEE Transactions on Computers*, 39(9):1175–1185, September 1990.
7. K. W. Tindell and A. Burns. Guaranteed message latencies for distributed safety-critical hard real-time control networks. Technical Report YCS229, Dept. of Computer Science, University of York, June 1994.
8. K. W. Tindell, A. Burns, and A. J. Wellings. Calculating Controller Area Network (CAN) Message Response Times. *Control Engineering Practice*, 3(8):1163–1169, 1995.
9. K. W. Tindell, H. Hansson, and A. J. Wellings. Analysing Real-Time Communications: Controller Area Network (CAN). *Proceedings 15th IEEE Real-Time Systems Symposium*, pages 259–265, December 1994.
10. J. Xu and D. L. Parnas. Priority scheduling versus pre-run-time scheduling. *Real-Time Systems Journal*, 18(1), January 2000.

A Methodology for the Construction of Scheduled Systems

K. Altisen, G. Gößler, and J. Sifakis

VERIMAG, 2 av. Vignates, 38610 Gières, France
{altisen, goessler, sifakis}@imag.fr

Abstract. We study a methodology for constructing scheduled systems by restricting successively the behavior of the processes to be scheduled. Restriction is used to guarantee the satisfaction of two types of constraints: schedulability constraints characterizing timing properties of the processes, and constraints characterizing particular scheduling algorithms including process priorities, non-idling, and preemption.
The methodology is based on a controller synthesis paradigm. The main results deal with the characterization of scheduling policies as safety constraints and the simplification of the synthesis process by applying a composability principle.

1 Introduction

Scheduling coordinates the execution of application and system activities, so as requirements about their temporal behavior are met. Guaranteeing correctness of schedulers is essential for the development of dependable real-time systems. In many application areas, well established theory and scheduling algorithms have been successfully applied to real-time systems development.

Existing scheduling theory is limited because it requires the system to fit into the mathematical framework of the schedulability criterion (e.g. all tasks are supposed periodic, worst case execution times are known). Studies to relax such hypotheses have been carried out but they generalize one hypothesis at a time, and no unified approach has been proposed.

To overcome limitations of scheduling theory, it is important to study its connections to specification theory and take advantage of their complementarity [8, 13, 4]. The specification based approach consists in building a timed model of the scheduled system or of an abstraction of it. Then, timed analysis tools are used either to check that the exact model meets scheduling requirements or to extract from the abstraction a scheduler [6, 10].

A major difficulty in applying this approach is the generation of the timed model from some description of the scheduling method. In fact, scheduling deals with the very dynamic nature of real-time systems, and behavior modeling requires a deep understanding of mechanisms such as priorities and preemption, as well of concepts such as urgency, idling, timeliness.

In this paper we propose a methodology for modeling scheduling algorithms that constructs compositionally the scheduled system from a global timed model based on

M. Joseph (Ed.): FTRTFT 2000, LNCS 1926, pp. 106–120, 2000.

1. A functional description of the processes to be scheduled, their resources, and the associated synchronization and management constraints;
2. Timing requirements added to the functional description and relating in particular execution speed with the dynamics of the external environment;
3. A description of a scheduling algorithm consisting of three types of requirements about
   (a) Fixed or dynamic priorities, for choosing between pending requests of the processes,
   (b) Possibility of idling, meaning that the scheduler may not satisfy a pending request anticipating the satisfaction of a forthcoming higher priority request,
   (c) Preemption, that is, for a given preemption order between processes, a process of lower priority is preempted when a process of higher priority raises a request.

In previous papers [3, 2] we have shown how a functional description can be extended into a timed one by preserving progress properties. In this paper we study a methodology for constructing a scheduled system from scheduling requirements and a timed specification of the processes to be scheduled. The methodology is based on the controller synthesis paradigm [11, 9, 1]. A scheduler is considered as a controller of the processes to be scheduled which restricts their behavior by triggering their controllable actions. The restricted behavior must respect the timing constraints of the processes as well as constraints characterizing the scheduling requirements.

We have shown in [1] how schedulers can be computed by applying a synthesis algorithm to timed automata. The synthesis algorithm computes iteratively from a constraint K characterizing scheduling requirements, the maximal *control invariant* K', K' $\Rightarrow$ K. The latter denotes the set of states from which K is guaranteed. The behavior of the scheduled system is obtained by restricting the controllable actions of the processes so as to respect the control invariant K'.

The application of synthesis techniques is limited for two reasons. First, the practical complexity of the synthesis algorithm is high even in the case of timed automata without scheduling policy constraints. Second, scheduling with preemption requires the use of automata with integrators [5] which implies that iterative computation of control invariants may not terminate.

The proposed methodology allows to decompose the global controller synthesis procedure into the application of simpler steps. At each step a control invariant corresponding to a particular class of constraints is applied to further restrict the behavior of the system of processes to be scheduled. The presented results can be summarized as follows:

1. Global scheduling requirements can be characterized by a constraint K of the form K = $K_{algo} \wedge K_{sched}$ where K_{algo} specifies a particular scheduling algorithm, and K_{sched} characterizes schedulability requirements of the processes. Furthermore, K_{algo} is a conjunction of constraints about the scheduling policy, the possibility of non-idling, and preemption;

2. A step of the method corresponds to the computation of a controller for some constraint. The control invariant corresponding to a constraint can be computed in a straightforward manner (without iterative fixpoint computation);
3. The scheduled system can be obtained by successive applications of steps restricting the process behavior by control invariants implying all the scheduling constraints, provided that some composability conditions are satisfied. In fact, the restriction by a control invariant does not necessarily preserve previously imposed control invariants.

The methodology allows an incremental construction of a scheduled system, or of an abstraction of it, if some steps fail.

The paper is composed of two sections. The first section presents basic results about control invariants and their composability. The second section shows how scheduling requirements can be expressed as constraints which are control invariants in some cases. The application of the methodology is illustrated by examples.

2   Control Invariants and Composability

2.1   Timed System

To model scheduling algorithms, we use reactive timed systems with two kinds of actions as in [1]: controllable actions that can be triggered by the scheduler, and uncontrollable actions that can be considered as internal actions of the processes to be scheduled. Controllable actions are typically resource allocations and process preemption, while uncontrollable actions are process arrival and termination.

Both controllable and uncontrollable actions are submitted to timing constraints expressed in terms of real-valued variables called *timers*. The derivatives of timers may take the values 0 or 1, as specified by a boolean vector.

Definition 2.1. *(X-constraint).* Let X be a finite set of timers, $\{x_1, \ldots, x_m\}$, real-valued variables defined on the set of non-negative reals $\mathbb{R}_+$. A predicate C generated by the grammar $C ::= x \# d \mid x - y \# d \mid C \wedge C \mid \neg C$, where $x, y \in X$, d is an integer, and $\# \in \{\leq, <\}$, is called a *X-constraint*.

Definition 2.2. *(Falling Edge).* Let C be a X-constraint, and b be a boolean derivative vector of $\{0,1\}^m$. The *closed* (resp. *open*) *falling edge* of C w.r.t. b, written $\updownarrow_b C$ (resp. $\updownarrow_b C$) is defined as $\forall x \in \mathbb{R}_+^m$,

$$\updownarrow_b C(x) \quad C(x) \wedge \exists t > 0 \ . \ \forall t' \in (0, t] \ . \ \neg C(x + t'b)$$
$$\updownarrow_b C(x) \quad \neg C(x) \wedge \exists t > 0 \ . \ \forall t' \in (0, t] \ . \ C(x - t'b) \ .$$

Example 2.1. Let $X = \{x_1, x_2\}$ be the set of real valued variables. $C = x_1 \leq 3$ and $C' = 2 \leq x_1 < 6 \wedge x_1 - x_2 \leq 4$ are X-constraints. For $b = (1, 1)$ and $b' = (1, 0)$, we have:

$$\updownarrow_b C = (x_1 = 3) \quad \updownarrow_b C = false \quad \Big| \quad \updownarrow_b C' = false \quad \quad \updownarrow_b C' = (x_1 = 6) \wedge (x_2 \geq 2)$$
$$\updownarrow_{b'} C = (x_1 = 3) \quad \updownarrow_{b'} C = false \quad \Big| \quad \updownarrow_{b'} C' = (x_1 - x_2 = 4) \updownarrow_{b'} C' = (x_1 = 6) \wedge (x_2 \geq 2)$$
$$\wedge \ (x_2 < 2)$$

Definition 2.3. *(Timed System)*. A *timed system* is

1. An untimed labeled transition system (S, A, T) where S is a finite set of control states; A is a finite vocabulary of actions partitioned into two sets of controllable and uncontrollable actions noted A^c and A^u; $T \subseteq S \times A \times S$ is an untimed transition relation;
2. A finite set of timers $X = \{x_1, \ldots, x_m\}$, as in definition 2.1;
3. A function b mapping S into $\{0, 1\}^m$. The image of $s \in S$ by b denoted b_s is a boolean derivative vector;
4. A labeling function h mapping untimed transitions of T into timed transitions: $h(s, a, s') = (s, a, g, \tau, r, s')$, where the guard g is a X-constraint; the reset $r \subseteq X$ is a set of timers to be reset; $\tau \in \{\lambda, \delta, \epsilon\}$ is an urgency type, respectively lazy, delayable, eager.

Semantics. A timed system defines a *transition graph* $(\mathcal{V}, \mathcal{E})$ constructed as follows. $\mathcal{V} = S \times \mathbb{R}_+^m$, that is, vertices (s, x) are states of the timed system.

The set $\mathcal{E} \subseteq \mathcal{V} \times (A \cup \mathbb{R}_+^*) \times \mathcal{V}$ of the edges of the graph is partitioned into three classes of edges: $\mathcal{E}^c$ controllable, $\mathcal{E}^u$ uncontrollable, and $\mathcal{E}^t$ timed, corresponding respectively to the case where the label is a controllable action, an uncontrollable action, and a (strictly) positive real.

Given $s \in S$, let J be the set of indices such that $\{(s, a_j, s_j)\}_{j \in J}$ is the set of all the untimed transitions departing from s. Also let $h(s, a_j, s_j) = (s, a_j, g_j, \tau_j, r_j, s_j)$. For all $j \in J$, $((s, x), a_j, (s_j, x[r_j])) \in \mathcal{E}^c \cup \mathcal{E}^u$ iff $g_j(x)$ and $x[r_j]$ is the timer valuation obtained from x when all the timers in r_j are set to zero and the others are left unchanged.

To define $\mathcal{E}^t$, we use the predicate φ, called *time progress function*. The notation $\varphi((s, x), t)$ means that time can progress from state (s, x) by t.

$$\varphi((s, x), t) - \bigwedge_{j \in J} \begin{cases} \tau_j = \delta \Rightarrow \begin{array}{l} \forall t' \in [0, t) \ . \ \neg\!\!\downarrow_{b_s} g_j(x + t'b_s) \wedge \\ \forall t' \in (0, t] \ . \ \neg\!\!\downarrow_{b_s} g_j(x + t'b_s) \end{array} \\ \tau_j = \epsilon \Rightarrow \forall t' \in [0, t) \ . \ \neg g_j(x + t'b_s) \end{cases}$$

If $\varphi((s, x), t)$, then $((s, x), t, (s, x + tb_s)) \in \mathcal{E}^t$ where $x + tb_s$ is the valuation obtained from x by increasing by t the timer values for which b_s elements are equal to one.

The above definition means that at control state s, time cannot progress whenever an eager transition is enabled, or beyond the falling edge of a delayable guard.

We will usually denote by TS a timed system. TS^c (resp. TS^u) represents the timed system composed of the controllable (resp. uncontrollable) transitions of TS only.

Proposition 2.1. If φ, φ^c, and φ^u are respectively the time progress functions of TS, TS^c, and TS^u then $\varphi = \varphi^c \wedge \varphi^u$.

Example 2.2. *(A Periodic Process)*. Let us model a periodic non-preemptible process P as a timed system. P is of period $T > 0$ and uses the CPU for an execution time E. It also has a relative deadline of D ($D \leq T$).

As shown in Fig. 2, the timed system
has three control states, s, w, and e where
P is respectively sleeping, waiting for the
CPU, and executing on the CPU. The actions a, b, and f stand for arrive, begin,
and finish. The timer x is used to measure
execution time while the timer t measures
the time elapsed since the process has arrived. In all states, both timers progress.
The only controllable action is b.

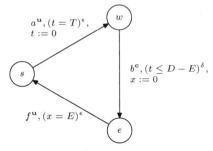

Fig. 2: A periodic process.

By convention, transition labels are of
the form $a^{\mathbf{x}}, g^{\tau}, r$, where $\mathbf{x}$ can be $\mathbf{u}$ (uncontrollable) or $\mathbf{c}$ (controllable), and τ
is an urgency type. The set r is omitted if it is empty.

Notice that since the transition b is delayable, the process might wait for a non-
zero time although the CPU is free: idling is permitted. A non-idling process is
modeled by changing the urgency type of the transition b to eager (see example 2.5
for further details). A preemptive periodic process is modeled in section 3.3.

2.2   Restriction and Control Invariants

Definition 2.4. *(Constraint).* Given a timed system with a set of timers X and
a set of control states $\{s_1, \ldots, s_n\}$, a *constraint* is a state predicate represented
as an expression of the form $\bigvee_{i=1}^{n} s_i \wedge C_i$ where C_i is a X-constraint and s_i is
(also) the boolean denoting presence at state s_i.

Definition 2.5. *(Restriction).* Let TS be a timed system and K be a constraint.
The *restriction* of TS by K denoted TS/K, is the timed system TS where each
guard g of a controllable transition (s, a, g, τ, r, s'), is replaced by

$$g'(x) = g(x) \wedge K(s', x[r]) \ .$$

Notice that in the restriction TS/K, the states reached right after execution
of a controllable transition satisfy K. Moreover, it follows from the definition that
$(\mathrm{TS}/\mathrm{K}_1)/\mathrm{K}_2 = \mathrm{TS}/(\mathrm{K}_1 \wedge \mathrm{K}_2)$.

Definition 2.6. *(Proper Invariant).* Let TS be a timed system and K be a constraint. We say that K is a *proper invariant* of TS, denoted by TS $\vDash$ inv(K), if
K is preserved by the edges of $\mathcal{E}$, i.e., $\forall (s, x) \ . \ \mathrm{K}(s, x) \Rightarrow \forall ((s, x), \gamma, (s', x')) \in$
$\mathcal{E} \ . \ \mathrm{K}(s', x')$.

Proper invariants, called simply invariants for closed systems, are constraints
preserved by all the transitions of the system. We use the term "proper" to
distinguish them from control invariants introduced in the following definition.
Control invariants are constraints that are satisfied by the restricted system.

Definition 2.7. *(Control Invariant).* Let TS be a timed system and K be a
constraint. K is a *control invariant* of TS if TS/K $\vDash$ inv(K).

Proposition 2.2. If K is a proper invariant of a timed system TS, then K is a control invariant of TS.

This property follows from the trivial observation that if TS and TS/K are initialized in K, then they have the same behavior. However, notice that control invariants are not proper invariants, in general.

Proposition 2.3. For any timed system TS and constraint K such that $\text{TS}^u \models \text{inv}(K)$, K is a control invariant of TS (i.e. $\text{TS}/K \models \text{inv}(K)$).

Proof (sketch). Assume $K(s,x)$ for some state (s,x). To prove $\text{TS}/K \models \text{inv}(K)$ it must be shown that K is preserved in TS/K by (1) controllable, (2) uncontrollable, and (3) timed edges of TS/K. By construction of TS/K, (1) is true. From $\text{TS}^u \models \text{inv}(K)$, (2) and (3) follow.

Definition 2.8. *(Timed System of Processes).* A timed system of processes is a timed system $\text{TS} = (S, A, T, X, b, h)$ obtained by composition of processes where a process P_i is a timed system $(S_i, A_i, T_i, X_i, b_i, h_i)$. TS is the timed system of n processes $\{P_1, \ldots, P_n\}$ if

$$S = S_1 \times \ldots \times S_n \; ; \; A = A_1 \cup \ldots \cup A_n \; ; \; X = X_1 \cup \ldots \cup X_n \; ;$$
$$\text{For } s = (s_1 \ldots s_n) \in S \text{ and } x \in X_i, b_s[x] = b_{i,s_i}[x];$$
$$\text{For } s = (s_1 \ldots s_i \ldots s_n), \text{ and } s' = (s_1 \ldots s_i' \ldots s_n) \in S,$$
$$\left| \begin{array}{ll} t = (s, a_i, s') \in T & - \; t_i = (s_i, a_i, s_i') \in T_i \\ h(t) = (s, a_i, g_i, \tau_i, r_i, s') & - \; h_i(t_i) = (s_i, a_i, g_i, \tau_i, r_i, s_i') \end{array} \right. .$$

We assume that processes have disjoint sets of control states, and timers. Moreover, we accept that guards are general constraints on timers and control states as in the definition 2.4.

Example 2.3. *(Mutual Exclusion).* Consider a timed system of n periodic non-preemptible processes $\{P_1, \ldots, P_n\}$, instances of the generic process of Fig. 2, and the constraint

$$\text{K}_{\text{mutex}} = \bigwedge_{i \neq j} \neg e_i \vee \neg e_j$$

expressing mutual exclusion. It is trivial to check that K_{mutex} is a control invariant, as $\text{TS}^u \models \text{inv}(\text{K}_{\text{mutex}})$. In fact, K_{mutex} is time invariant and is preserved by uncontrollable transitions.

If TS is the timed system of two processes — as in Fig. 2 for which the parameters (E, T, D) are equal to $(5, 15, 15)$ and $(2, 5, 5)$, resp. — and if $\text{K}_{\text{mutex}} = \neg e_1 \vee \neg e_2$, then $\text{TS}_1 = \text{TS}/\text{K}_{\text{mutex}}$ is obtained by restricting the controllable guards g_{b_1} and g_{b_2} to

$$g_{b_1}' = (t_1 \leq D_1 - E_1) \wedge \neg e_2 = (t_1 \leq 10) \wedge \neg e_2$$
$$g_{b_2}' = (t_2 \leq D_2 - E_2) \wedge \neg e_1 = (t_2 \leq 3) \wedge \neg e_1 .$$

2.3   Control Invariants and Synthesis

Following ideas in [11], synthesis is used to partially restrict the non-determinism of a system so as it satisfies a given invariant.

Problem 2.1. (SYNTH). Solving the *synthesis problem* for a timed system TS and a constraint K amounts to giving a non-empty control invariant K′ of TS which implies K, i.e. $K' \Rightarrow K$, $TS/K' \vDash inv(K')$.

We assume that the processes to be scheduled and their timing constraints are represented by a timed system of processes TS. Furthermore, we consider that scheduling requirements can be expressed as a constraint (safety property) K. A scheduled system can be obtained by solving the synthesis problem for TS and K, as explained in [1]. If K′ is a control invariant implying K, then TS/K′ describes a scheduled system.

We assume that the constraint K is in general the conjunction of two constraints $K = K_{algo} \wedge K_{sched}$. K_{algo} is an optional constraint characterizing a particular scheduling algorithm. We provide in section 3, a general framework for the decomposition of K_{algo} and the modeling of different scheduling policies.

K_{sched} expresses the fact that the timing requirements of the processes are satisfied. We consider that the processes to be scheduled are structurally time-lock-free [2]. This property means that time always eventually progresses. It is implied by the fact that at any control state, if no action is enabled then time can progress, and the requirement that in any circuit of the control graph a timer is reset and tested against some positive lower bound. For example, the periodic process of example 2.2 is structurally timelock-free.

Notice that structural timelock-freedom is preserved by restriction. For time-lock-free timed systems, K_{sched} can be formulated as a constraint expressing the property that each process always eventually executes some action. This property implies fairness of the scheduling algorithm.

Definition 2.9. *(◇)*. Let C be a X-constraint, $s \in S$ a control state, and $k \in \mathbb{N} \cup \{\infty\}$. We will use the notation

$$(\Diamond_k^s C)(x) = \exists t \in [0, k] \ . \ C(x + tb_s)$$

to express the property "eventually C within k in s". If the state s is clear from the context, we write $\Diamond_k$ instead of $\Diamond_k^s$. We use $(\Diamond C)(x)$ for $\exists t \geq 0 \ . \ C(x + t)$.

For a timed system of processes as in definition 2.8,

$$K_{sched} = \bigwedge_{P_i} K_{sched_i} \quad \text{where} \quad K_{sched_i} = \bigvee_{s \in S_i} s \wedge \left(\bigvee_{(s,a,s') \in T_i} \Diamond g_a \right) .$$

It can be shown that in general, K_{sched} is not a control invariant. We have shown in [1] how maximal schedulers for timed automata and their schedulability constraints can be computed. The synthesis algorithm has been implemented in the KRONOS tool.

Example 2.4. *(Schedulability).* The schedulability constraint for the timed system of n periodic processes TS as in example 2.3 is

$$K_{sched} = \bigwedge_{P_i} (s_i \wedge \Diamond g_{a_i} \vee e_i \wedge \Diamond g_{f_i} \vee w_i \wedge \Diamond g_{b_i}) \ .$$

We consider the timed system of two processes described in example 2.3 where the mutual exclusion constraint has been applied. We have

$$K_{sched} = \begin{bmatrix} s_1 \wedge t_1 \leq 15 \\ \vee \ e_1 \wedge x_1 \leq 5 \\ \vee \ w_1 \wedge t_1 \leq 10 \end{bmatrix} \wedge \begin{bmatrix} s_2 \wedge t_2 \leq 5 \\ \vee \ e_2 \wedge x_2 \leq 2 \\ \vee \ w_2 \wedge t_2 \leq 3 \end{bmatrix} \ .$$

The maximal control invariant implying K_{sched} computed by KRONOS is

$$K'_{sched} = \begin{bmatrix} (s_1 \wedge s_2 \ \wedge \ t_1 <= 15 \wedge t_2 <= 5) \\ \vee \ (w_1 \wedge s_2 \ \wedge \ (t_2 <= 3 \wedge t_1 \leq 10 \ \vee \ t_2 <= 5 \wedge t_1 <= t_2 + 3)) \\ \vee \ (s_1 \wedge w_2 \ \wedge \ t_1 <= 15 \wedge t_2 <= 3) \\ \vee \ (e_1 \wedge s_2 \ \wedge \ t_2 <= 5 \wedge x_1 <= 5 \wedge t_1 <= x_1 + 10 \wedge t_2 <= x_1 + 3) \\ \vee \ (w_1 \wedge w_2 \ \wedge \ (t_1 <= 8 \wedge t_2 <= 1 \ \vee \ t_2 <= 3 \wedge t_1 <= t_2 + 3)) \\ \vee \ (s_1 \wedge e_2 \ \wedge \ t_1 <= 15 \wedge x_2 <= 2 \wedge t_2 <= x_2 + 3) \\ \vee \ (e_1 \wedge w_2 \ \wedge \ x_1 <= 5 \wedge t_1 <= x_1 + 10 \wedge t_2 + 2 <= x_1) \\ \vee \ (w_1 \wedge e_2 \ \wedge \ (x_2 <= 2 \wedge t_1 <= x_2 + 8 \wedge t_2 <= x_2 + 1 \ \vee \\ \qquad x_2 <= 2 \wedge t_1 <= t_2 + 3 \wedge t_2 <= x_2 + 3)) \ . \end{bmatrix}$$

In the rest of the paper, we show how to construct control invariants for some frequently used scheduling algorithms *without* fixpoint computation.

2.4   Control Invariant Composability

Contrary to proper invariants, control invariants are not composable by conjunction. In general, it can not be inferred from $TS/K_i \vDash inv(K_i), i = 1, 2$ that $TS/(K_1 \wedge K_2) \vDash inv(K_1 \wedge K_2)$. We study a notion of control invariant composability.

Definition 2.10. *(Composable Invariant).* Let TS be a timed system and K_1 be a constraint. K_1 is a *composable invariant* of TS if for all constraints K_2, K_1 is a control invariant of TS/K_2 (i.e. if $TS/(K_1 \wedge K_2) \vDash inv(K_1)$).

Proposition 2.4. Let TS be a timed system and K_1 be a constraint on TS. K_1 is a composable invariant of TS iff $TS^u \vDash inv(K_1)$.

Proof. Let K_1 be a composable invariant of TS. By applying definition 2.10 with $K_2 = false$, we obtain: $TS/false = TS^u \vDash inv(K_1)$.

Conversely, assume that $TS^u \vDash inv(K_1)$ and let K_2 be some constraint. We show that $TS/(K_1 \wedge K_2) \vDash inv(K_1)$. Let (s, x) be a state of TS such that $K_1(s, x)$. (1) If there exists a controllable edge $((s, x), a_c, (s', x'))$ in the transition graph of $TS/(K_1 \wedge K_2)$, then by definition 2.5 of restriction, $(K_1 \wedge K_2)(s', x')$, thus $K_1(s', x')$. (2) An uncontrollable edge $((s, x), a_u, (s', x'))$ of $TS/(K_1 \wedge K_2)$ is also an uncontrollable edge of TS^u, thus $K_1(s', x')$. (3) Let $\varphi_{(K_1 \wedge K_2)}$ be the time progress function of $TS/(K_1 \wedge K_2)$. According to the property 2.1, we have

$$\varphi_{(K_1 \wedge K_2)} = \varphi^c_{(K_1 \wedge K_2)} \wedge \varphi^u_{(K_1 \wedge K_2)} = \varphi^c_{(K_1 \wedge K_2)} \wedge \varphi^u .$$

If $((s, x), t, (s, x + tb_s))$ is a timed edge of $TS/(K_1 \wedge K_2)$, then it is also a timed edge of TS^u because $\varphi_{(K_1 \wedge K_2)} = \varphi^c_{(K_1 \wedge K_2)} \wedge \varphi^u$. Thus, $K_1(s, x + tb_s)$ from $TS^u \vDash$ inv(K_1).

Corollary 2.1. For a timed system TS and constraints K_1 and K_2, $TS^u \vDash$ inv(K_1) and $(TS/K_1)/K_2 \vDash$ inv(K_2) implies that $TS/(K_1 \wedge K_2) \vDash$ inv$(K_1 \wedge K_2)$.

That is, if K_1 is composable and if K_2 is a control invariant of TS/K_1 then $(K_1 \wedge K_2)$ is control invariant of TS.

This corollary justifies the incremental methodology for restricting a timed system. To impose a control invariant $K_1 \wedge K_2$ on TS, if K_1 is a composable invariant of TS, the restriction by a control invariant K_2 does not destroy the invariance of K_1.

Example 2.5. *(Non-idling Constraint).* A scheduling algorithm is said to be non-idle if the CPU cannot remain free when there is a pending request. Let us consider the timed system of n processes as in example 2.3. As $TS^u \vDash$ inv(K_{mutex}), K_{mutex} is composable which means that K_{mutex} is a proper invariant of any system obtained by restriction of $TS_1 = TS/K_{\mathsf{mutex}}$.

In order to model non-idling, as remarked in example 2.2, all transitions b_i must have the urgency type *eager*. The non-idling constraint $K_{\mathsf{non\text{-}idle}}$ specifies that an enabled b_i action is fired as soon as the CPU is free.

$$K_{\mathsf{non\text{-}idle}} = \bigvee_{P_i} (e_i \vee x_i = E_i) \vee \bigwedge_{P_j} (s_j \vee w_j \wedge t_j = 0)$$

means that in a non-idling system, if no process P_i is executing or has just finished its execution, then any process P_j is either sleeping or waiting for zero time.

It can be shown that $K_{\mathsf{non\text{-}idle}}$ is a proper invariant of TS_1. However, it fails to be composable, in general. For the timed system of two processes described in example 2.3, the constraint $K_{\mathsf{non\text{-}idle}}$ becomes

$$K_{\mathsf{non\text{-}idle}} = \begin{bmatrix} (e_1 \vee e_2) \vee (x_1 = 5 \vee x_2 = 2) \\ \vee (s_1 \vee w_1 \wedge t_1 = 0) \wedge (s_2 \vee w_2 \wedge t_2 = 0) \end{bmatrix} .$$

Notice that $TS_1/K_{\mathsf{non\text{-}idle}} = TS_1$, that is, restricting by $K_{\mathsf{non\text{-}idle}}$ does not change controllable transitions of TS_1. It is easy to check that $TS_1/(K_{\mathsf{non\text{-}idle}} \wedge K_{\mathsf{sched}}) \nvDash$ inv$(K_{\mathsf{non\text{-}idle}})$: consider for instance the eager transition b_1 from the control state $(w_1 s_2)$ to $(e_1 s_2)$ with guard $g'_{b_1} = \underbrace{t_1 \leq 10}_{g_{b_1}} \wedge \underbrace{t_2 \leq 3}_{K'_{\mathsf{sched}}}$. When the system reaches the state $(w_1 s_2)$ with timer values $(t_1 = 0, t_2 = 4)$, the action b_1 is not enabled although the CPU is free due to the restriction $t_2 \leq 3$ imposed by K_{sched}. Thus, $K_{\mathsf{non\text{-}idle}}$ is violated.

Imposing K_{sched} has destroyed the property of the system to be non-idle. Thus the non-idling constraint is not composable. This is a consequence of the observation that a given scheduling problem with an idling solution may have no non-idling schedule.

The notion of composability described in this section allows to apply restrictions sequentially to build a system more and more close to the correct scheduler at each step.

3   Modeling Scheduling Algorithms

Timed systems with priorities are timed systems of processes with an associated set of priority orders on actions. They have been defined and studied in [3, 2]. We show how to model scheduling algorithms by specifying a timed system with priorities and that applying priorities is equivalent to restricting by a composable invariant.

3.1   Timed Systems with Priorities

Definition 3.1. *(Priority Order).* Let $\prec \subseteq A \times (\mathbb{N} \cup \{\infty\}) \times A$ be a relation. $a_1 \prec_k a_2$ is written for $(a_1, k, a_2) \in \prec$. The relation $\prec$ is a *priority order* if $\forall k \in \mathbb{R}_+ \cup \{\infty\}$,

1. $\prec_k$ is a partial order;
2. $a_1 \prec_k a_2 \Rightarrow \forall k' < k . a_1 \prec_{k'} a_2$;
3. $a_1 \prec_k a_2 \wedge a_2 \prec_l a_3 \Rightarrow a_1 \prec_{k+l} a_3$.

Definition 3.2. *(Timed System with Priorities).* A timed system with priorities (TS, pr) is the timed system of processes TS equipped with a *priority rule*, i.e., a finite set of pairs $pr = \{(C^i, \prec^i)\}_i$, where $\prec^i$ is a priority order, and C^i is a X-constraint that specifies when the priority order applies, such that

1. $C^i \wedge C^j \neq false \Rightarrow \prec^i \cup \prec^j$ is a priority order;
2. No uncontrollable action is dominated in $\prec^i$;
3. $(C^i, \prec^i) \in pr$ and $(a, k, b) \in \prec^i$ imply that transitions labeled by a do not reset any timer occurring in C^i.

For each state $s \in S$, let $\{(s, a_i, s_i)\}_{i \in I}$ be the set of the transitions departing from s, and $h(s, a_i, s_i) = (s, a_i, g_i, \tau_i, r_i, s_i)$. The timed system with priorities (TS, pr) represents a timed system TS' obtained from TS by replacing the guards g_j of TS by g'_j defined as follows:

$$g'_j = g_j \wedge \bigwedge_{(C, \prec) \in pr} \left(\neg C \vee \bigwedge_{\substack{\exists i \in I. \\ a_j \prec_k a_i}} \neg \Diamond^s_k g_i \right) .$$

This formula says that an action a_j is allowed if there is no transition a_i leaving s that has priority over a_j, and that will become enabled within a delay of k.

Example 3.1. *(The* edf *Policy).* Consider the timed system TS_1 of n non-preemptible periodic processes, on which K_{mutex} has already been applied, as in example 2.3.

We show how the basic earliest deadline first (edf, [7]) mechanism can be specified by using a priority rule. A scheduler follows an edf policy if the CPU is granted to the waiting process that is closest to its relative deadline.

The edf policy is partially specified by

$$pr^1_{\mathsf{edf}} = \{(D_i - t_i < D_j - t_j, \{b_j \prec_0 b_i\})\}_{i \neq j} ,$$

i.e., whenever there are two processes P_i and P_j waiting for the CPU, the action b_i has immediate priority over the action b_j if P_i is closer to its relative deadline than P_j (namely, $D_i - t_i < D_j - t_j$).

It is easy to check that pr satisfies the requirements of definition 3.2. In particular, note that the constraints $D_i - t_i < D_j - t_j$ define a partial order on the set of b_i actions. The complete specification of the edf policy is given in example 3.3.

3.2 Priorities as Restriction

We show that applying a priority rule amounts to restricting by a particular constraint. To obtain this result, we construct from (TS, pr) a timed system TS' that is *strongly equivalent* to TS, and a constraint K_{pr} such that (TS, pr) is strongly equivalent to TS'/K_{pr}. Strong equivalence means that for any state of TS there exists a state of TS' such that the transition graphs are strongly bisimilar from these states, and conversely. The construction has only a theoretical interest and is used to show that K_{pr} is a composable invariant.

Let (TS, pr) be a timed system with priorities. In order to interpret priorities on TS as a constraint, we have to identify the states reached right after firing a restricted transition.

For this we transform $TS = (S, A, T, X, b, h)$ into a strongly equivalent timed system $TS' = (S', A, T', X, b', h')$ with $S' \subseteq S \cup (S \times A)$, by iterative application of a state splitting procedure which creates for each transition a unique target control state.

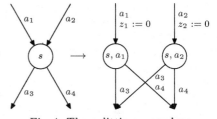

Fig. 4: The splitting procedure.

For each state $s \in S$ with an incident transition of the form $t = (ss, a_j, s)$ where $ss \in S'$ and $a_j \in A$, the splitting procedure removes t and creates a new transition $t' = (ss, a_j, (s, a_j))$. t' is labeled as t with in addition a reset of a new timer z_j. Notice that in TS' the set of states reached right after the execution of a_j is characterized by $((s, a_j) \wedge z_j = 0)$. For all states $s \in S'$, we take $b'_s[z_j] = 1$.

Proposition 3.1. Let (TS, pr) be a timed system with priorities, and TS' be the result of the splitting procedure on TS. The constraint

$$K_{pr} = \bigwedge_{s \in S'} \bigwedge_{(C, \prec) \in pr} \bigwedge_{\substack{i,j \in I \\ a_j \prec_k a_i}} \left(s_j \wedge z_j = 0 \Rightarrow (\neg \diamondsuit_k^s g_i \vee \neg C) \right) ,$$

is a composable invariant of TS', and $(TS', pr) = TS'/K_{pr}$, where for a given s, $\{(s, a_i, g_i, \tau_i, r_i, s_i)\}_{i \in I}$ is the set of transitions departing from s.

Proof. Notice that K_{pr} contains all the states but the ones that would be reached by firing a transition violating the priority rule.

$(TS', pr) = TS'/K_{pr}$ is obtained immediately by comparing syntactically the result of restriction by K_{pr} with the application of the priority rule pr.

To prove composability, we show that $TS'^u \models \mathsf{inv}(K_{pr})$. Let (s, x) be a state of TS'^u such that $K_{pr}(s, x)$. (2) If there exists an uncontrollable edge $((s, x), a_u, (s', x'))$ in TS'^u, then K_{pr} cannot contain a constraint of the form $s' \wedge z = 0 \Rightarrow \neg C \vee \neg \diamondsuit_k^{s''} g$, since a_u is the only transition leading to s' in TS'^u. Thus, $K_{pr}(s', x')$. (3) If time can progress by $t > 0$ from (s, x) in TS'^u, then $K_{pr}(s, x+tb_s)$ obviously holds.

Corollary 3.1. Let (TS, pr) be a timed system with priorities, K be a control invariant of (TS, pr), $((TS, pr)/K)'$ be the result of the splitting procedure on $(TS, pr)/K$, and K_{pr} the constraint associated to pr. Then $((TS, pr)/K)' \models \mathsf{inv}(K_{pr})$.

These results say that applying a priority rule can be seen as a restriction of a strongly equivalent timed system by a control invariant. Furthermore, whenever some other control invariant K is applied to (TS, pr), then $(TS, pr)/K$ still satisfies the priority rule pr. In some cases, the property 3.1 holds without applying the splitting procedure, as shown in the following examples.

3.3   Basic Scheduling Algorithms

Example 3.2. *(The* fifo *Policy).* A scheduler follows a first in first out policy (fifo) if the CPU is granted to the process that has been waiting for the longest time. For non-preemptible processes, fifo is specified by using priorities as follows

$$pr_{\mathsf{fifo}} = \{(t_j < t_i, \{b_j \prec_0 b_i\})\}_{i \neq j} .$$

This means that whenever two processes P_i and P_j are both waiting for the CPU, b_i has priority over b_j if process P_i has been waiting for longer time than process P_j, i.e. $t_j < t_i$.

Proposition 3.2. $(TS, pr_{\mathsf{fifo}}) = TS/K_{\mathsf{fifo}}$, where

$$K_{\mathsf{fifo}} = \bigwedge_{i \neq j} (w_i \wedge e_j \wedge x_j = 0 \Rightarrow t_i \leq t_j)$$

is the constraint associated with pr_{fifo}. Moreover, K_{fifo} is a composable control invariant for TS. (Proof omitted.)

Example 3.3. *(The* edf *Policy).* We showed in example 3.1 how to model partially the edf policy on TS as a priority rule, pr^1_{edf}. But this specification has to be completed since in case a process P_i arrives (transition a_i) exactly when the decision to allot the CPU to another process is made, this might be wrong depending on whether P_i was taken into account or not. This confusion situation can be prevented by a priority rule ensuring that the set of waiting processes is up to date before any decision is made. Therefore, processes arrival actions a_i are given priority over b_j actions:

$$pr_{\mathsf{edf}} = pr^1_{\mathsf{edf}} \cup \{(t_i = T_i, \{b_j \prec_0 a_i\})\}_{i \neq j} \ .$$

Let K_{edf} be the constraint associated with pr_{edf}. Thus,

$$K_{\mathsf{edf}} = \bigwedge_{i \neq j} w_i \wedge e_j \wedge x_j = 0 \ \Rightarrow \ D_j - t_j \leq D_i - t_i$$
$$\wedge \quad s_i \wedge e_j \wedge x_j = 0 \ \Rightarrow \ t_i \neq T_i \ .$$

Proposition 3.3. $(\mathrm{TS}, pr_{\mathsf{edf}}) = \mathrm{TS}/K_{\mathsf{edf}}$, and K_{edf} is a composable control invariant. (Proof omitted.)

Preemptive Fixed-priority Scheduling Preemptive fixed-priority scheduling assigns the CPU according to some fixed priority order between the processes to be scheduled. If the CPU is free, the highest priority process among the waiting processes is scheduled. An arriving process can preempt a running process of lower priority.

Fig. 6 shows the model of a preemptible process. It has an additional control state p (preempted), and two more transitions: pr (preempt) and rs (resume). The timer x is stopped in control state p, i.e. $b_p[x] = 0$. Everywhere else, timers progress. The timer x_{pr} measures the time elapsed since the process has been preempted.

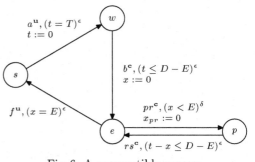

Fig. 6: A preemptible process.

Consider the timed system of n processes $P_1, \ldots, P_n$ as shown in fig. 6 with the given fixed priorities $\pi_1, \ldots, \pi_n$, where $\pi_i < \pi_j$ means that P_j has priority over P_i. As before, mutual exclusion is achieved by application of K_{mutex}. We construct the scheduled system of these processes according to the preemptive policy with the priorities $\pi_1, \ldots, \pi_n$ as follows.

Process Priorities. Priorities between the processes are specified by the priority rule pr_π on the CPU allocating actions b and rs:

$$pr_\pi = \{(true, \ \{b_i \prec_0 b_j, b_i \prec_0 rs_j, rs_i \prec_0 b_j, rs_i \prec_0 rs_j\}),$$
$$(t_j = T_j, \{b_i \prec_0 a_j, rs_i \prec a_j\})\}_{\pi_i < \pi_j} \ .$$

The first line says that the CPU is granted — by an action b_j or rs_j — to a process P_j that has highest priority among the waiting processes. Here, the constraint that specifies when the priority order applies is *true*, since the priorities are fixed and do not depend on timer valuations. The second line guarantees that the set of waiting processes is up to date before a new process is scheduled.

It is easy to show that pr_π satisfies the definition of a priority rule.

Proposition 3.4. Let K_{pr_π} be the constraint associated to pr_π. Then, (TS, pr_π) $= TS/K_{pr_\pi}$, and K_{pr_π} is a composable control invariant of TS. (Proof omitted.)

Preemption. pr_π only specifies the CPU allocation policy, but not the mechanism preempting a running process, which will be enforced by a further constraint

$$K_{\text{pmtn}} = \bigwedge_i \left(p_i \wedge x_{pr_i} = 0 \Rightarrow \exists j . \pi_j > \pi_i \wedge t_j = 0 \right) .$$

Notice that for given process priorities $\pi_1, \ldots, \pi_n$, the term $\exists j . \pi_j > \pi_i \wedge t_j = 0$ is a X-constraint. The constraint means that a process P_i must not take the pr_i action unless there is a higher priority process P_j that has just arrived. It implies that a running process is preempted as soon as a process of higher priority arrives. Immediately after that, since the a_i actions are eager, the CPU is assigned to a waiting process according to pr.

K_{pmtn} is a control invariant for TS, thus from corollary 2.1, $K_{\text{pmtn}} \wedge K_\pi$ is also a control invariant of TS. But K_{pmtn} is not composable, and neither is $K_{\text{pmtn}} \wedge K_\pi$.

Example 3.4. *(The* rms *Policy with Preemption).* The algorithm of preemptive rate-monotonic scheduling (rms, [7]) assigns to each process a fixed priority such that processes with shorter period have higher priority, i.e., $T_i > T_j \Rightarrow \pi_i < \pi_j$.

The invariant K_π can be obtained from pr_π as before. As remarked above, $K_{\text{pmtn}} \wedge K_\pi$ is not composable. However, the rms policy makes the scheduled system $(TS, pr_\pi)/K_{\text{pmtn}}$ nearly deterministic since π defines a total order. Therefore, there is no need to further restrict the system — it is either schedulable or not.

4   Conclusion

This work aims at bridging the gap between scheduling theory and timed systems specification and analysis. From the general idea that a scheduler is a controller of the scheduled processes, we elaborate a methodology for the construction of a scheduled system. The methodology is illustrated on periodic processes but it can be applied to arbitrary systems of structurally timelock-free processes.

A contribution of this work is the decomposition of scheduling requirements into classes of requirements that can be expressed as safety constraints. We believe that the decomposition allows better understanding of scheduling problems and clarification of the differences between the two approaches. Scheduling theory studies sufficient conditions guaranteeing K_{sched} for particular scheduling algorithms characterized by some K_{algo}. On the contrary, timed systems specification and analysis have focused so far on the extraction of behaviors satisfying K_{sched} from a global model.

This work relates controller synthesis by means of the notion of control invariant, to a methodology for constructing a scheduled system satisfying given requirements. The existence of composable control invariants allows the automatic application of the corresponding synthesis steps. Not surprisingly, finding control invariants for schedulability is the hard problem that deserves further investigation. Possible directions are the development of specific synthesis algorithms or the use of constructive correctness techniques as in [2].

This work is developed in the framework of a project on real-time systems modeling and validation. We have applied the methodology to the description of the ceiling protocol [12] and are currently developing tools supporting the methodology.

References

1. K. Altisen, G. Gößler, A. Pnueli, J. Sifakis, S. Tripakis, and S. Yovine. A framework for scheduler synthesis. In *IEEE RTSS 1999 proceedings*, 1999.
2. S. Bornot, G. Gößler, and J. Sifakis. On the construction of live timed systems. In *TACAS 2000*, volume 1785 of *LNCS*. Springer-Verlag, 2000.
3. S. Bornot and J. Sifakis. On the composition of hybrid systems. In *International NATO School on "Verification of Digital and Hybrid Systems"*, LNCS. Springer Verlag, 1997.
4. P.A. Hsiung, F. Wang, and Y.S. Kuo. Scheduling system verification. In *TACAS'99*, volume 1597 of *LNCS*. Springer-Verlag, 1999.
5. Y. Kesten, A. Pnueli, J. Sifakis, and S. Yovine. Integration graphs: A class of decidable hybrid systems. *Information and Computation*, 736, 1992.
6. H.-H. Kwak, I. Lee, A. Philippou, J.-Y. Choi, and O. Sokolsky. Symbolic schedulability analysis of real-time systems. In *IEEE RTSS 1998 proceedings*, 1998.
7. C.L. Liu and J.W. Layland. Scheduling algorithms for multiprogramming in a hard-real-time environment. *Journal of the ACM*, 20(1), 1973.
8. Z. Liu and M. Joseph. Specification and verification of fault-tolerance, timing, and scheduling. *ACM Transactions on Programming Languages and Systems*, 21(1):46–89, 1999.
9. O. Maler, A. Pnueli, and J. Sifakis. On the synthesis of discrete controllers for timed systems. In *STACS'95*, volume 900 of *LNCS*. Springer Verlag, 1995.
10. P. Niebert and S. Yovine. Computing optimal operation schemes for chemical plants in multi-batch mode. In *Hybrid Systems, Computation and Control*, volume 1790 of *LNCS*. Springer Verlag, 2000.
11. P.J. Ramadge and W.M. Wonham. Supervisory control of a class of discrete event systems. *Journal of Control and Optimization*, 25(1), 1987.
12. L. Sha, R. Rajkumar, and J. P. Lehoczky. Priority inheritance protocols: An approach to real-time synchronization. *IEEE Transactions on Computers*, 39(9), 1990.
13. S. Vestal. Modeling and verification of real-time software using extended linear hybrid automata. In *Fifth NASA Langley Formal Methods Workshop*, 2000.

A Dual Interpretation of "Standard Constraints" in Parametric Scheduling

K. Subramani[1] and Ashok Agrawala[2]

[1] Department of Computer Science and Electrical Engineering,
West Virginia University,
Morgantown, WV, USA
ksmani@csee.wvu.edu

[2] Department of Computer Science,
University of Maryland,
College Park, MD USA
agrawala@cs.umd.edu

Abstract. *Parametric scheduling* in real-time systems, in the presence of linear relative constraints between the start and execution times of tasks, is a well-studied problem. Prior research established the existence of polynomial time algorithms for the case when the constraints are restricted to be *standard* and the execution time vectors belong to an axis-parallel hyper-rectangle. In this paper we present a polynomial time algorithm for the case when the execution time vectors belong to arbitrary convex domains. Our insights into the problem occur primarily as a result of studying the dual polytope of the constraint system.

1 Introduction

The problem of *parametric scheduling* for hard real-time systems was introduced in [Sak94]. In particular, they considered the scheduling of processes subject to linear relative constraints between the start and execution times of tasks. In [GPS95], a polynomial time algorithm was presented for the case, where the constraints are "standard" (defined in Section §6). In this paper, we present a polynomial time algorithm for parametric scheduling when the execution time vectors belong to arbitrary convex domains. Our insights into the problem occur primarily as a result of studying the dual polytope of the constraint system.

The rest of this paper is organized as follows: In Section §2, we present the parametric scheduling model and pose the *parametric schedulability query.* In the succeeding section, viz. Section §3, we discuss the motivation behind the problem and related approaches in the literature. Section §4 commences our analysis by looking at the complement of the parametric scheduling problem. In Section §5, we study the dual of the complement problem and apply Farkas' lemma to derive the termination condition for our algorithm. Section §6 presents the "Standard Constraints Model". We also discuss the structure of the *standard constraint matrix* and interpret the complement of the parametric schedulability query in this model. We show that the infeasibility of the input constraint system coincides with the existence of a loop having infinite negative cost in a certain weighted graph. This implies that a *symbolic* version of the Bellman-Ford Algorithm for

M. Joseph (Ed.): FTRTFT 2000, LNCS 1926, pp. 121–133, 2000.

the Single-Source-Shortest-Paths problem (SSSP) in a network can be used to solve the parametric scheduling problem. Section §7 provides such an algorithm, while §7.1 discusses its correctness and complexity. We conclude in Section §8 by summarizing our results and posing problems for further research.

2   The Parametric Model

We are a given a set of ordered non-preemptive tasks $\mathcal{J} = \{J_1, J_2, \ldots J_n\}$, with linear constraints imposed on their respective start times $\{s_1, s_2, \ldots, s_n\}$ and execution times $\{e_1, e_2, \ldots, e_n\}$. The constraint system is expressed in matrix form as :

$$\mathbf{A}.[\vec{s}, \vec{e}] \leq \vec{b}, \tag{1}$$

where,

- $\vec{s} = [s_1, s_2, \ldots, s_n]$ is an $n-$vector of the start times of the tasks,
- $\vec{e} = [e_1, e_2, \ldots, e_n]$ is an $n-$vector of the execution time of the tasks,
- $\mathbf{A}$ is a $m \times 2.n$ matrix of rational numbers,
- $\vec{b} = [b_1, b_2, \ldots, b_m]$ is an $m-$vector of rational numbers.

System (1) is a convex polyhedron in the $2.n$ dimensional space, spanned by the start time axes $\{s_1, s_2, \ldots, s_n\}$ and the execution time axes $\{e_1, e_2, \ldots, e_n\}$. The execution time of the ith task e_i is *not constant*, but belongs to the set E_i where E_i is the projection of a convex set $\mathbf{E}$ on axis $\vec{e_i}$. The execution times are independent of the start times of the tasks; however they may have complex interdependencies among themselves. This interdependence is captured by the set $\mathbf{E}$. We regard the execution times as $n-$vectors belonging to the set $\mathbf{E}$.

The goal is to obtain a start time vector $\vec{s}$, that satisfes the constraint system (1), for all execution time vectors belonging to the set $\mathbf{E}$. One way of approaching this problem is through *Static Scheduling* techniques, as discussed in [SA00b]. However, Static Scheduling results in the phenomenon known as *loss of schedulability* discussed below.

Consider the two task system $J = \{J_1, J_2\}$ with start times $\{s_1, s_2\}$, execution times $\{e_1 \in [2, 4], e_2 \in [4, 5]\}$ and the following set of constraints:

- Task J_1 must finish before task J_2 commences; i.e. $s_1 + e_1 \leq s_2$;
- Task J_2 must commence within 1 unit of J_1 finishing; i.e. $s_2 \leq s_1 + e_1 + 1$;

A static approach forces the following two constraints:

- $s_1 + 4 \leq s_2$,
- $s_2 \leq s_1 + 2 + 1 \Rightarrow s_2 \leq s_1 + 3$

Clearly the resultant system is inconsistent and there is no static solution. Now consider the following start time vector assignment.

$$\vec{s} = \begin{bmatrix} s_1 \\ s_2 \end{bmatrix} = \begin{bmatrix} 0 \\ s_1 + e_1 \end{bmatrix} \tag{2}$$

This assignment clearly satisfies the input set of constraints and is hence a valid solution. The key feature of the solution provided by (2) is that the start time of task J_2 is no longer an absolute time, but a (parameterized) function of the start and execution times of task J_1. This phenomenon in which a static scheduler declares a system infeasible in the presence of a valid solution (albeit parameterized) is termed as *loss of schedulability*.

In the parametric scheduling model, we are interested in checking whether an input constraint system has a *parametric schedule*, i.e. a schedule in which the start time of a task can depend on the start and execution times of tasks that are sequenced before it.

Definition 1. *A parametric solution of an ordered set of tasks, subject to a set of linear relative constraints (expressed by (1)) is a vector* $\vec{s} = [s_1, s_2, \ldots, s_n]$, *where* s_1 *is a rational number and each* s_i, $i \neq 1$ *is a function of the variables* $\{s_1, e_1, s_2, e_2, \ldots, s_{i-1}, e_{i-1}\}$. *Further, this vector should satisfy the constraint system (1) for all vectors* $\vec{e} \in \mathbf{E}$.

Based on the discussion above, we are in a position to state the parametric schedulability query:

$$\exists s_1 \forall e_1 \in E_1 \ \exists s_2 \forall e_2 \in E_2, \ldots \exists s_n \forall e_n \in E_n \quad \mathbf{A}.[\vec{s}, \vec{e}] \leq \vec{\mathbf{b}} \quad ? \tag{3}$$

The elimination strategies used in [GPS95] establish that a parametric schedule need only have linear functions.

3 Motivation and Related Work

Our investigations have been motivated by two orthogonal concerns viz. real-time operating systems and real-time applications.

In real-time operating systems such as Maruti [LTCA89,MAT90,MKAT92] and MARS [DRSK89], the interaction of processes is constrained through linear relationships between their start and execution times. Real-time specification languages such as the Maruti Programming Language (MPL) [SdSA94] permit programmer constructs such as:

- **within** 10 ms; **do**
  Perform Task 1 od
- **Perform Task 1**;
  Delay at most 17 ms;
  Perform Task 2

These constructs are easily transformed into linear constraints between the start and execution times of the tasks. For instance, the first construct can be expressed as: $s_1 \geq 10$, while the second construct is captured through: $s_2 \geq f_1 + 17$. Note that f_1 is the finish time of task 1 and since we are dealing with non-preemptive tasks, we can write $f_i = s_i + e_i, \forall i$, where f_i denotes the finish time of task i.

The automation of machining operations [Y.K80,Kor83,SE87,SK90] provides a rich source of problems in which execution time vectors belong to convex domains. Consider the contouring system described in [TSYT97], in which the task is to machine a workpiece through cutting axes. In general, there are multiple axes of motion that move with different velocities. In a two axis system, a typical requirement would be to constrain the sum of the velocities of the axes to exceed a certain quantity. This is captured through:$e_1 + e_2 \geq a$.

Real-time database applications involve the scheduling of transactions and the execution of these transactions is constrained through linear relationships [BFW97].

Deterministic sequencing and scheduling have been studied extensively in the literature [BS74,DL78,Cof76]. Our focus is on a particular scheduling model viz. the *parametric scheduling* model proposed in [Sak94]. In [GPS95] a polynomial time algorithm is presented for the *standard constraints* case, in which the execution time vectors belong to an axis-parallel hyper-rectangle. They use the Fourier-Motzkin (FM) elimination method [Sch87] to successively eliminate the variables in query (3). The FM algorithm takes exponential time in the worst case; in the case where the constraints are *standard* they show that they can prevent the exponential increase in the number of constraints. Hochbaum, et. al. [HN94] have shown that it is possible to implement FM elimination in strongly polynomial time for *network* constraints. In a previous paper [SA00a], we showed that a restricted version of the parametric scheduling problem is NP-complete, when the constraints are arbitrary. It was also established that it is sufficient to determine whether a system is *parametrically schedulable*; explicit construction of the parametric functions is not necessary.

In this paper, we extend the results in [GPS95] to provide polynomial time algorithms for standard constraints in arbitrary convex domains

4   Complement of Parametric Scheduling

We commence our analysis by looking at the complement of the parametric scheduling query (3). Observe that a query is true iff its complement is false.

The complement of query (3) is:

$$\neg(\ \exists s_1 \forall e_1 \in E_1 \exists s_2 \forall e_2 \in E_2, \dots \exists s_n \forall e_n \in E_n \quad A[\vec{s}, \vec{e}] \leq \vec{b} \quad ? \ ), \qquad (4)$$

which gives

$$\forall s_1 \exists e_1 \in E \forall s_2 \exists e_2 \in E, \dots \forall s_n \exists e_n \in E \quad A[\vec{s}, \vec{e}] \not\leq \vec{b} \quad ?$$

where $\mathbf{A}.\vec{x} \not\leq \vec{b}$ means that the polyhedral set $\{\vec{x} : \mathbf{A}.\vec{x} \leq \vec{b}\}$ is empty.

As observed in [SA00a], when we restrict ourselves to the case in which the execution times are independent of the start times of the tasks, we can restate the query above as:

$$\exists e_1 \in E_1 \exists e_2 \in E_2, \dots \exists e_n \in E_n \forall s_1 \forall s_2, \dots \forall s_n \quad A[\vec{s}, \vec{e}] \not\leq \vec{b} \quad ? \qquad (5)$$

which implies

$$\exists \vec{e} = [e_1, e_2, \dots, e_n] \forall s_1 \forall s_2, \dots \forall s_n \quad A[\vec{s}, \vec{e}] \not\leq \vec{b} \quad ? \qquad (6)$$

Query (6) basically asks whether there exists an execution time vector $\vec{e} = [e_1', e_2', \dots, e_n'] \in \mathbf{E}$ such that the linear system resulting from substituting these execution times in $\mathbf{A}.[\vec{s}, \vec{e}] \leq \vec{b}$ is infeasible, i.e. as shown in [SA00a], (6) asks whether the polyhedral set

$$\vec{s} : \mathbf{A}.[\vec{s}.\vec{e}] \leq \vec{b} | \vec{e} = [e'_1, e'_2, \ldots, e'_n] \tag{7}$$

is empty.

For the rest of the paper, we focus on finding such a *witness* execution time vector; if we succeed in finding such a vector, it means that the input system does not have a parametric schedule. On the other hand, if we can definitely say that no such execution vector exists within the convex domain $\mathbf{E}$, then query (3) can be answered in the affirmative and the input system does have a parametric schedule.

5   The Parametric Dual

We rewrite the constraint system (1) in the form:

$$\mathbf{G}.\vec{s} \leq \vec{b} - \mathbf{B}.\vec{e} \tag{8}$$

where,

$$\mathbf{A}.[\vec{s}, \vec{e}] = \mathbf{G}.\vec{s} + \mathbf{B}.\vec{e}$$

Accordingly, query (6) gives

$$\exists \vec{e} = [e_1, e_2, \ldots, e_n] \forall s_1 \forall s_2, \ldots \forall s_n \quad \mathbf{G}.\vec{s} \not\leq \vec{b} - \mathbf{B}.\vec{e} \quad ? \tag{9}$$

Note that ($\vec{b} - \mathbf{B}.\vec{e}$) is an $m-$vector, with each element being an affine function in the e_i variables. We set $\vec{g} = (\vec{b} - \mathbf{B}.\vec{e})$, so that we can rewrite query (9) as

$$\exists \vec{e} = [e_1, e_2, \ldots, e_n] \forall s_1 \forall s_2, \ldots \forall s_n \quad \mathbf{G}.\vec{s} \not\leq \vec{g}? \tag{10}$$

The matrix $\mathbf{G}$ will henceforth be referred to as the *constraint matrix*. Note that $\mathbf{G}$ is a $m \times n$ rational matrix.

In order to find an execution time vector, which serves as a witness to the infeasibility of the input constraint system, we study the dual of the complement problem. The following lemma called Farkas' lemma [NW88,Sch87] is crucial to understanding and analyzing the dual.

Lemma 1. *Either* $\{\vec{x} \in \Re^n_+ : \mathbf{A}.\vec{x} \leq \vec{b}\} \neq \phi$ *or (exclusively)* $\exists \vec{y} \in \Re^m_+$, *such that,* $\vec{y}^{\mathbf{T}} \mathbf{A} \geq \vec{0}^T$ *and* $\vec{y}^{\mathbf{T}}.\vec{b} = -\infty$.

Proof: *See [Sch87,PS82,NW88].* □

The lemma is interpreted as follows: Either the primal system viz. $\{\mathbf{A}.[\vec{x}] \leq \vec{b}, \vec{x} \geq \vec{0}\}$ is feasible, in which case the associated polyhedron is non-empty *or* (exclusively) the vector $\vec{b}$ lies in the polar cone of the dual space viz. $\{\vec{y}^{\mathbf{T}}.\mathbf{A} \geq \vec{0}, \vec{y} \geq \vec{0}\}$ (See Figure (1)).

In the latter case, the function $\vec{y}^{\mathbf{T}}.\vec{b}$ is unbounded below and its minimum is $-\infty$. For a geometric interpretation of the lemma, refer [PS82].

Query (10) requires the system $\mathbf{G}.\vec{s} \leq \vec{g}$ to be infeasible for a particular $\vec{e} \in \mathbf{E}$. Farkas' lemma assures us that this is possible only if $\exists \vec{y}' \in R^+_m$, such that

$$\vec{y'}^T.\mathbf{G} \geq \vec{0}, \quad \vec{y'}^T.(\vec{b} - \mathbf{B}.\vec{e}) = -\infty \tag{11}$$

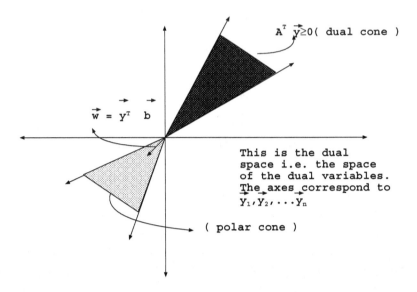

Fig. 1. Farkas' Lemma

which implies that

$$\mathbf{G^T}.\vec{y'} \geq \vec{0}, \quad \vec{y'}^{\mathbf{T}}.(\vec{b} - \mathbf{B}.\vec{e}) = -\infty. \tag{12}$$

Equation (12) is interpreted algorithmically in the following way:

> Let z be the minimum of the bilinear form $\vec{y'}^{\mathbf{T}}.(\vec{b} - \mathbf{B}.\vec{e})$ over the two convex bodies $\{\vec{y} : \vec{y} \geq \vec{0}, \mathbf{G^T}.\vec{y} \geq \vec{0}\}$ and E. If $z = -\infty$, the input system of constraints does not have a parametric schedule.

6 "Standard Constraints" Model

As discussed in [GPS95,Sch87] the Fourier-Motzkin elimination method suffers from the *curse of dimensionality* i.e. it is an exponential time method in the worst-case. [Sak94] shows that for an important subset of constraints, viz. *Standard Constraints*, the elimination method runs in polynomial time. As described in [Sak94],

Definition 2. *A standard constraint involves the start times of at most two tasks J_i and J_k, such that exactly one of s_i or s_j appears on one side of the $\leq$ relation. Further the coefficients of all start and execution variables are unity.*

For example, the following set of constraints are standard:

1. $s_i \leq s_j + 2$,
2. $s_i + e_i \leq s_j$,

3. $s_i + e_i \leq s_j + e_j + 2$

The constraint $s_i + s_j \leq 2$ is not standard, because both s_i and s_j appear on the same side of the relational operator $\leq$. *Absolute* constraints i.e. constraints in which the start time of a task is constrained by an absolute value (e.g. $s_1 \geq 5$) are also permitted and considered standard. In order to make the treatment of constraints (absolute and relative) uniform, we introduce an additional task J_0 with start time s_0 and execution time $e_0 = 0$. Further we impose the constraint $s_0 + e_0 \leq s_1$. Absolute constraints are modified as follows:

- Constraints of the form $s_i \leq a$ are replaced by $s_i - s_0 \leq a$;
- Constraints of the form $s_i \geq a$ are replaced by $s_0 - s_i \leq -a$

For the rest of the discussion, we assume that the matrix $\mathbf{G}$ in (12) has been altered to reflect the above changes. Accordingly, $\mathbf{G}^T$ has $n + 1$ rows 0 through n and $m + 1$ columns (m of the initial constraints and the additional constraint between s_0 and s_1.)

6.1   Structure of the Transpose of the Standard Constraint Matrix

When the constraints are standard, the transpose of the constraint matrix (i.e. $\mathbf{G}^T$ in (12)) has the following structure:

1. All entries belong to the set $\{0, 1, -1\}$.
2. There are *exactly* 2 non-zero entries in any column; one of the entries is 1 and the other entry is -1.

In this case, we can show that the problem: Is $z = \vec{\mathbf{y}}^T . \vec{\mathbf{b}} = -\infty$?, subject to :

$$\mathbf{G}^T . \vec{\mathbf{y}} = \vec{\mathbf{g}}, \quad \vec{\mathbf{y}} \geq \vec{\mathbf{0}} \tag{13}$$

where

- $\mathbf{G}^T$ is a $(n + 1) \times (m + 1)$ rational matrix, with the structure discussed above,
- $\vec{\mathbf{y}}$ is a $m + 1-$vector,
- $\vec{\mathbf{b}}$ is a rational $m + 1-$vector; $b_0 = 0$.
- $\vec{\mathbf{g}}$ is a rational $n + 1-$vector.

has a *min-cost flow* interpretation in a constraint network.[1] The network $G' = < V', E' >$ corresponding to the constraint system $\mathbf{G}^T . \vec{\mathbf{y}} = \vec{\mathbf{g}}$ is constructed as follows:

1. A vertex for v_j for the each row $j, j = 0, \ldots n$ of $\mathbf{G}^T$, giving a total of $n+1$ vertices. Note that v_i corresponds to row G_i i.e. task J_i.
2. Associated with each vertex v_j is a *supply* equal to g_j; Set $g_0 = 0$.
3. An edge r_i for each column of $i, i = 0, \ldots m$ of $\mathbf{G}^T$ giving a total of $m + 1$ edges. Let v_a denote the vertex corresponding to the $+1$ entry and v_b denote vertex corresponding to the -1 entry. Direct the edge from the vertex v_a to v_b.
4. Associated with edge r_i is *cost* b_i, where b_i is the coefficient of y_i;

---

[1] These constraints are a subset of *monotone constraints*, in which only relations of the form: $a.x_1 - b.x_2 \leq c, a, b > 0$ are allowed.

5. $y_i (\geq 0), \forall i = 0, \ldots, m$ represents the flow on edge r_i. The flow on the edge $v_0 - v_1$ i.e. y_0 does not contribute to the total cost as the cost on this edge is 0.

The vertex v_0 is the source of this network. Each constraint is now a *mass balance* condition i.e. it states that the net flow into node v_i which is the difference between the total flow into v_i and the total flow out of v_i must equal the supply at v_i. $z = \vec{y}^T.\vec{b}$ represents the cost of the flow.

Let us analyze the case where all vertices two special cases, which directly bear upon our scheduling problem:

1. $\vec{g} = \vec{0}$ i.e. the supply at all vertices is zero.

   Lemma 2. *In this case the condition $z = -\infty$ is possible only iff there is a negative cost loop in the network.*

   Proof: *Clearly, if there is a negative cost loop, we can pump flow in that loop decreasing the cost arbitrarily, while meeting the mass balance constraints.*
   Now assume that $z = -\infty$. This is possible only if the flow vector $\vec{y}$ is unbounded in some of its elements. Let us pick some element y_k that is unbounded i.e. $y_k = +\infty$. Thus there is an infinite flow on edge e_k. In order to satisfy the zero supply requirement at the vertices corresponding to its end-points, e_k must belong to a closed loop and all the edges in that loop have the same flow equal to $+\infty$. Since $z = -\infty$, it follows that the cost around that loop is negative. □

2. $g_1 = \alpha (\alpha \geq 0); g_i = 0, i = 2, \ldots n$. In this case the first node has a supply that could be non-zero. This is now a Single-Source Shortest Path Problem with vertex v_1 being the source. Using arguments identical to the case above, it is clear that that $z = -\infty$ coincides with the existence of a negative cost cycle i.e. the shortest path from the source v_0 to any vertex on this cycle is of length $-\infty$.

Our dual system (12) though is in the form $\mathbf{G}^T.\vec{y} \geq \vec{0}, \vec{y} \geq \vec{0}$. Before we apply the flow-related concepts and results derived above, the system needs to be converted into equality form. We use the *Complementary Slackness* property [Sch87,PS82] to aid us in this conversion. Observe that in the primal system, the start time variables are strictly ordered i.e. we have $s_i \leq s_{i+1}, i = 0, \ldots n - 1$. We impose $s_1 \geq \epsilon$ to simplify the analysis. Thus in any solution (including the optimal), we must have $s_i > 0, \forall i = 1, \ldots n$. According to the Complementary Slackness property, *if the primal variable is non-zero at optimality, then the corresponding constraint in the dual must be met with equality.* Thus, all the constraints in the system $G^T.\vec{y} \geq \vec{0}$, except the first one, are met with equality, which is exactly what we need. Hence, we can rewrite condition (12) for infeasibility in the primal as:

$$\exists \vec{y} \in \Re_+^{m+1} \quad \mathbf{G}^T.\vec{y'} = [\alpha, 0, \ldots, 0]^T \quad \vec{y'}^{\mathbf{T}}.(\vec{b} - \mathbf{B}.\vec{e}) = -\infty. \qquad (14)$$

Thus our problem is equivalent to the *SSSP* problem as discussed in case (2) of the above analysis. There is one major difference, viz. in our case the edge costs are *symbolic* (e.g. $e_1, e_1 - e_2$, etc.) and not rational numbers. However, if we can find values $e'_i \in \mathbf{E}$ for the e_i variables, then our techniques and results still hold. We now require an algorithm that detects *symbolic* negative cost cycles in the constraint graph corresponding to the given constraint system. We provide such an algorithm in the following section.

7   The Symbolic Bellman-Ford Algorithm

Algorithm (7.1) together with procedures (7.2) and (7.3) represents the Symbolic Bell-man-Ford Algorithm. The key modification to the algorithm in [CLR92] is the addition of procedure 7.3. In the case, where the edge weights are rational numbers, it is trivial to check whether $d[v]$ exceeds $d[u] + w(u, v)$.

The input to the algorithm is a graph $G' =< V', E' >$, with V' denoting the vertex set and E' denoting the edge set. The weights on the edges are parameterized linear functions in the execution times e_i as discussed above. The function INITIALIZE-SINGLE-SOURCE sets the source s to be at a distance of 0 from itself and all other vertices at a distance of ∞ from the source. A detailed exposition of the Bellman-Ford Algorithm is presented in [CLR92]. Let $\delta[v_0, v_i]$, $d[v_i]$ denote the length of the shortest path from v_0 to vertex v and the current estimate of the shortest path respectively.

Function SYMBOLIC-BELLMAN-FORD(G', w, s)

 1: INITIALIZE-SINGLE-SOURCE
 2: **for** ($i \leftarrow 1$ **to** $|V'(G)| - 1$) **do**
 3:    **for** (each edge $(u, v) \in E'[G]$) **do**
 4:       SYMBOLIC-RELAX(u, v, w)
 5:    **end for**
 6: **end for**
 7:
 8: **for** (each edge $(u, v) \in E[G]$) **do**
 9:    **if** ($d[v] >_{sym} d[u] + w(u, v)$) **then**
10:       **return(false)**
11:    **end if**
12: **end for**
13:
14: **return(true)**

Algorithm 7.1: Symbolic Bellman Ford

Procedure SYMBOLIC-RELAX(u, v, w)
  if ($d[v] >_{sym} d[u] + w(u, v)$) **then**
    $d[v] = d[u] + w(u, v)$
  end if

Algorithm 7.2: Symbolic-Relax

Assuming that all vertices are reachable from the source (a valid assumption in our case), a return value of **true** means that there is a finite shortest path from the source to every other vertex. Likewise, the detection of a negative cost cycle (indicating that certain vertices are at a distance of $-\infty$ from the source), causes the value **false** to be

---

Function SYMBOLIC $>(u, v, w)$
   if ($\min_{E'} .(d[v] - d[u] - w(u,v)) < 0$) **then**
      return(**true**)
   else
      return(**false**)
   end if

Algorithm 7.3: Implementation of $>_{sym}$

returned. When dealing with rational numbers, all the above operations are relatively straightforward. In our case, the weights on the edges are no longer rational numbers, but parameterized linear forms in the e_i variables, as indicated above. The algorithm implementing SYMBOLIC $>$ is a *convex minimization* algorithm [PS82,HuL93].

7.1 Analysis - Correctness and Complexity

The correctness of the algorithm follows from the correctness of the Bellman-Ford algorithm [CLR92]. The following two cases arise:

1. There is no point $\vec{e'} \in \mathbf{E}$ such that substituting $\vec{e'}$ on the edge costs results in a negative cost cycle.

    Claim: 71 *Algorithm (7.1) returns* true.

    <u>Proof</u>: *Observe that in the absence of a witness vector $\vec{e'} \in \mathbf{E}$, the shortest path from v_0 to every vertex is finite. Using the inductive technique from [CLR92], it is clear that after $|V'(G)| - 1$ iterations of the **for** loop in Step 2 of Algorithm (7.1) the distance of each vertex has converged to its true shortest path from the source. Consequently the test in the succeeding **for** loop fails and the value* true *is returned.*
    □

2. There exists a point $\vec{e'} = [e'_1, e'_2, \ldots, e'_n] \in \mathbf{E}$ such that substituting $\vec{e'}$ on the edge costs results in a negative cost cycle.

    Claim: 72 *Algorithm (7.1) returns* false.

    <u>Proof</u>: *Once again, we use the same technique as in [CLR92].* □

The time taken by the algorithm is dominated by the $O(n^3)$ loop represented by Steps $2 - 6$ of Algorithm 7.1. Each call to SYMBOLIC-RELAX takes time $O(\mathcal{C})$ where $\mathcal{C}$ is the time taken by the fastest convex programming algorithm [HuL93]. Accordingly, the total time taken by SYMBOLIC-BELLMAN-FORD is $O(n^3.\mathcal{C})$.

7.2 Example

Let us apply our techniques to the following problem.

We have four tasks $\{J_1, J_2, J_3, J_4\}$ with execution times $\{e_1 \in [4,8], e_2 \in [0,11], e_3 \in [10.13], e_4 \in [3,9]\}$ and start times $\{s_1, s_2, s_3, s_4\}$ constrained through:

(a) Task J_4 finishes before time 56; $s_4 + e_4 \leq 56$
(b) Task J_4 finishes within 12 units of J_3; $s_4 + e_4 \leq s_3 + e_3 + 12$
(c) Task J_4 starts no earlier than 18 units of T_2 completing: $s_2 + e_2 + 18 \leq s_4$
(d) Task J_3 finishes within 31 units of J_1 completing: $s_3 + e_3 \leq s_1 + e_1 + 31$
(e) Implicit are the ordering constraints:

$$0 \leq s_1, \ s_1 + e_1 \leq s_2, \ s_2 + e_2 \leq s_3, \ s_3 + e_3 \leq s_4$$

From (3), the parametric schedulability query is:

$$\exists s_1 \forall e_1 \in [4,8] \exists s_2 \forall e_2 \in [6,11] \exists s_3 \forall e_3 \in [10,13] \exists s_4 \forall e_4 \in [3,9] \{(a),(b),(c),(d),(e)\}$$
$$(15)$$

We construct the graph in Figure (2) as per the discussion in Section §6.1.

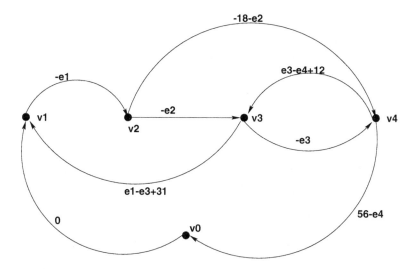

Fig. 2. Constraint Graph Corresponding to Example

In this case, the convex domain is the axis-parallel hyper-rectangle $\mathbf{E} = [4,8] \times [6,11] \times p10,13] \times [3,9]$. We provide the graph $M =< V', E' >$ and $\mathbf{E}$ as the input to Algorithm (7.1). The tables below (1-2) detail the iterations of the algorithm.

At the end of the 2nd iteration, the shortest path values converge and after applying Steps (8-12) of Algorithm (7.1), we conclude that there is no negative cost loop in the graph.

8   Concluding Remarks

In this paper, we set out to address the following question: Are there polynomial time algorithms for execution times in domains other than axis-parallel hyper-rectangles ?

Edge	Effect
$v_0 - v_1$	$v_1 = 0$
$v_1 - v_2$	$v_2 = -e_1$
$v_2 - v_3$	$v_3 = -e_1 - e_2$
$v_2 - v_4$	$v_4 = -18 - e_2$
$v_3 - v_4$	$v_4 = -e1 - e_2 - e_3$
$v_3 - v_1$	$v_1 = 0$
$v_4 - v_3$	$v_3 = -e_1 - e_2$
$v_4 - v_2$	$v_2 = -18 - 2.e_2 - e_3$
$v_4 - v_0$	$v_0 = 0$

Table 1. Iteration 1

Edge	Effect
$v_0 - v_1$	$v_1 = 0$
$v_1 - v_2$	$v_2 = -18 - 2.e_2 - e_3$
$v_2 - v_3$	$v_3 = -e_1 - e_2$
$v_2 - v_4$	$v_4 = -e1 - e_2 - e_3$
$v_3 - v_4$	$v_4 = -e1 - e_2 - e_3$
$v_3 - v_1$	$v_1 = 0$
$v_4 - v_3$	$v_3 = -e_1 - e_2$
$v_4 - v_2$	$v_2 = -18 - 2.e_2 - e_3$
$v_4 - v_0$	$v_0 = 0$

Table 2. Iteration 2 (Final iteration)

We answered this question by providing a polynomial algorithm for the case when the execution times belong to arbitrary convex domains. Our algorithms are simple and easy-to-implement extensions of existing algorithms for network problems. Our work is currently being implemented in the Maruti Operating System [2] [STA00].

It would be interesting to see if the techniques presented in this paper can be extended to a wider class of constraints in real-time scheduling.

References

BFW97.   Azer Bestavros and Victor Fay-Wolfe, editors. *Real-Time Database and Information Systems, Research Advances*. Kluwer Academic Publishers, 1997.

BS74.   K. R. Baker and Z. Su. Sequencing with Due-Date and Early Start Times to Minimize Maximum Tardiness. *Naval Res. Log. Quart.*, 21:171–176, 1974.

CLR92.   T. H. Cormen, C. E. Leiserson, and R. L. Rivest. *Introduction to algorithms*. MIT Press and McGraw-Hill Book Company, 6th edition, 1992.

Cof76.   E. G. Coffman. *Computer and Job-Shop Scheduling Theory, Ed.* Wiley, New York, 1976.

DL78.   S. K. Dhall and C. L. Liu. On a real-time scheduling problem. *Operations Research*, 26(1):127–140, Jan. 1978.

DRSK89. A. Damm, J. Reisinger, W. Schwabl, and H. Kopetz. The Real-Time Operating System of MARS. *ACM Special Interest Group on Operating Systems*, 23(3):141–157, July 1989.

GPS95.   R. Gerber, W. Pugh, and M. Saksena. Parametric Dispatching of Hard Real-Time Tasks. *IEEE Transactions on Computers*, 1995.

HN94.   Dorit S. Hochbaum and Joseph (Seffi) Naor. Simple and fast algorithms for linear and integer programs with two variables per inequality. *SIAM Journal on Computing*, 23(6):1179–1192, December 1994.

HuL93.   J. B. Hiriart-urruty and C. Lemarechal. *Convex Analysis and Minimization Algorithms*. Springer-Verlag, 1993.

Kor83.   Y. Koren. *Computer Control of Manufacturing Systems*. McGraw-Hill, New York, 1983.

---

[2] Maruti is the registered trademark of the Maruti Real-Time Operating System, developed at the University of Maryland, College Park; http://www.cs.umd.edu/projects/maruti

LTCA89.   S. T. Levi, S. K. Tripathi, S. D. Carson, and A. K. Agrawala. The Maruti Hard Real-Time Operating System. *ACM Special Interest Group on Operating Systems*, 23(3):90–106, July 1989.

MAT90.   D. Mosse, Ashok K. Agrawala, and Satish K. Tripathi. Maruti a hard real-time operating system. In *Second IEEE Workshop on Experimental Distributed Systems*, pages 29–34. IEEE, 1990.

MKAT92.   D. Mosse, Keng-Tai Ko, Ashok K. Agrawala, and Satish K. Tripathi. Maruti: An Environment for Hard Real-Time Applications. In Ashok K. Agrawala, Karen D. Gordon, and Phillip Hwang, editors, *Maruti OS*, pages 75–85. IOS Press, 1992.

NW88.   G. L. Nemhauser and L. A. Wolsey. *Integer and Combinatorial Optimization*. John Wiley & Sons, New York, 1988.

PS82.   C. H. Papadimitriou and K. Steiglitz. *Combinatorial Optimization*. Prentice Hall, 1982.

SA00a.   K. Subramani and A. K. Agrawala. The parametric polytope and its applications to a scheduling problem. Technical Report CS-TR-4116, University of Maryland, College Park, Department of Computer Science, March 2000. Submitted to the 7th International Conference on High Performance Computing (HIPC) 2000.

SA00b.   K. Subramani and A. K. Agrawala. The static polytope and its applications to a scheduling problem. 3rd *IEEE Workshop on Factory Communications*, September 2000.

Sak94.   Manas Saksena. *Parametric Scheduling in Hard Real-Time Systems*. PhD thesis, University of Maryland, College Park, June 1994.

Sch87.   Alexander Schrijver. *Theory of Linear and Integer Programming*. John Wiley and Sons, New York, 1987.

SdSA94.   M. Saksena, J. da Silva, and A. Agrawala. Design and Implementation of Maruti-II. In Sang Son, editor, *Principles of Real-Time Systems*. Prentice Hall, 1994. Also available as CS-TR-2845, University of Maryland.

SE87.   K. Shin and M. Epstein. Intertask communication in an integrated multi-robot system. *IEEE Journal of Robotics and Automation*, 1987.

SK90.   K. Srinivasan and P.K. Kulkarni. Cross-coupled control of biaxial feed drive mechanisms. *ASME Journal of Dynamic Systems, Measurement and Control*, 112:225–232, 1990.

STA00.   K. Subramani, Bao Trinh, and A. K. Agrawala. Implementation of static and parametric schedulers in maruti. *Manuscript in Preparation*, March 2000.

TSYT97.   M. Tayara, Nandit Soparkar, John Yook, and Dawn Tilbury. Real-time data and co-ordination control for reconfigurable manufacturing systems. In Azer Bestavros and Victor Fay-Wolfe, editors, *Real-Time Database and Information Systems, Research Advances*, pages 23–48. Kluwer Academic Publishers, 1997.

Y.K80.   Y.Koren. Cross-coupled biaxial computer control for manufacturing systems. *ASME Journal of Dynamic Systems, Measurement and Control*, 102:265–272, 1980.

Co-Simulation of Hybrid Systems: Signal-Simulink

Stéphane Tudoret[1], Simin Nadjm-Tehrani[1*], Albert Benveniste[2], and Jan-Erik Strömberg[3]

[1] Dept. of Computer & Information Science, Linköping University, S-581 83 Linköping, Sweden, e-mail: `simin@ida.liu.se`
[2] IRISA-INRIA, Campus de Beaulieu, Rennes, France
[3] DST Control AB, Mjärdevi Science Park, Linköping, Sweden

Abstract. This article presents an approach to simulating hybrid systems. We show how a discrete controller that controls a continuous environment can be co-simulated with the environment (plant) using C-code generated automatically from mathematical models. This approach uses SIGNAL with SIMULINK to model complex hybrid systems. The choices are motivated by the fact that SIGNAL is a powerful tool for modelling complex discrete behaviours and SIMULINK is well-suited to deal with continuous dynamics. In particular, progress in formal analysis of SIGNAL programs and the common availability of the SIMULINK tool makes these an interesting choice for combination. We present various alternatives for implementing communication between the underlying sub-models. Finally, we present interesting scenarios in the co-simulation of a discrete controller with its environment: a non-linear siphon pump originally designed by the Swedish engineer Christofer Polhem in 1697.

1 Introduction

The use of software and embedded electronics in many control applications leads to higher demands on analysis of system properties due to added complexity. Simple controller blocks in MATLAB are increasingly replaced by large programs with discrete mode changes realising non-linear, hierarchical control and supervision. The analysis of these design structures benefits from modelling environments using languages with formal semantics – for example, finite state machines (e.g. STATECHARTS [11], ESTEREL [5]), or clocked data flows (e.g. LUSTRE [9], SIGNAL [8]).

These (discrete-time) languages and associated tools provide support in programming the controller in many ways. To begin with, they provide an architectural view of the program in terms of hierarchical state machines or block

---

* This work was supported by the Esprit LTR research project SYRF. The second author was also supported by the Swedish research council for engineering sciences (TFR).

M. Joseph (Ed.): FTRTFT 2000, LNCS 1926, pp. 134–151, 2000.

diagrams. In recent years, certain modelling environments for continuous systems have also been augmented with versions inspired by these languages, e.g. MATLAB STATEFLOW [20] and MATRIXX [12] discrete-time superblocks.

In addition, formal semantics for the underlying languages allows the controller design to be formally analysed. Constructive semantics in ESTEREL and clock calculi in LUSTRE and SIGNAL, enable formal analysis directly at compilation stage [4]. Properties otherwise checked by formal verification at later stages of development [6], e.g. causal consistency or determinism, are checked much earlier. Also, results of these analyses are used at later stages of development – in particular, for automatic code generation (code optimisation) and code distribution [2,3,7,13]. Note that these types of formal analysis of a discrete controller are so far not supported in the traditional modelling environments (e.g. MATLAB and MATRIXX).

However, properties at the system level still have to be addressed by the analysis of the closed loop system. Formal verification of hybrid models is generating new techniques for this purpose. Restrictions on the class of differential and algebraic equations (DAE) for the plant or approximations on the model to get decidability are active areas of research [10,26,14].

In this paper we explore another direction aimed at applications where the DAE plant model is directly used for controller testing within the engineering design process. That is, we study the question of co-simulation. Formal verification can be a complement to, or make use of the knowledge obtained by integrated simulation environments. In this set-up the plant is specified as a set of DAE and the controller specified in a high level design language. The controller is subjected to formal verification supported by the discrete modelling tools, and the closed loop system is analysed by co-simulation. To this end, we propose a framework in which SIGNAL programs and MATLAB-SIMULINK [22] models can be co-simulated using automatically generated C-code. We present the application of the framework to a non-trivial example suggested earlier [27, 28].

2   Introduction to SIGNAL

SIGNAL is a data-flow style synchronous language specially suited for signal processing and control applications [1,16,18]. A SIGNAL program manipulates signals, which are unbounded series of typed values (**logical**, **integer**...), with an associated clock denoting the set of instants when values are present. Signals of a special kind called **event** characterised only by their clock i.e., their presence (when they occur, they give the Boolean value **true**). Given a signal X, its clock is obtained by the language expression *event* X, resulting in the event that is present simultaneously with X. To constrain signals X and Y to be synchronous, the SIGNAL language provides the operation: *synchro* X, Y. The absence of a signal is noted $\perp$.

2.1   The Kernel of SIGNAL

SIGNAL is built around a small kernel comprising five basic operators (functions, delay, selection, deterministic merge, and parallel composition). These operators allow to specify in an equational style the relations between signals, i.e., between their values and between their clocks.

Functions (e.g., addition, multiplication, conjunction, ...) are defined on the type of the language. For example, the Boolean negation of a signal E is *not E*.

$$X := f(X1, X2, \cdots, Xn)$$

The signals $X, X1, X2, \cdots, Xn$ must all be present at the same time, so they are constrained to have the same clock.

Delay gives the previous value ZX of a signal X, with initial value $V0$:

$$ZX := X \ \$1 \ init \ V0$$

Selection of a signal Y is possible according to a Boolean condition C:

$$X := Y \ when \ C$$

The clock of signal X is the intersection of the clock of Y and the clock of occurrences of C at the value *true*. When X is present, its value is that of Y.

$$Y : \perp 1 \ 2 \ 3 \ 4 \perp 5$$
$$C : t \perp t \ f \perp t \ t$$
$$X := Y \ when \ C : \perp \perp 2 \perp \perp \perp 5$$

Deterministic merge defines the union of two signals of the same type, with a priority on the first one if both are present simultaneously:

$$X := Y \ default \ Z$$

The clock of signal X is the union of that of Y and of that Z. The value of X is the value of Y when Y is present, or else the value of Z if Z is present and Y is not.

$$Y : 1 \perp 2 \ 3 \perp 4 \ 5$$
$$Z : \perp 10 \ 20 \perp 30 \perp 50$$
$$X := Y \ default \ Z : 1 \ 10 \ 2 \ 3 \ 30 \ 4 \ 5$$

Parallel composition of processes is made by the associative and commutative operator "|", denoting the union of the equation systems. In SIGNAL, the parallel composition of $P1$ and $P2$ is written:

$$(| \ P1 \ | \ P2 \ |)$$

Each equation from SIGNAL is like an elementary process. Parallel composition of processes is made by the associative and commutative operator "|", denoting the union of the equation systems. In SIGNAL, the parallel composition of $P1$ and $P2$ is denoted: $(| \ P1 \ | \ P2 \ |)$.

2.2   Tools

All the different tools which make up the SIGNAL environment use only one tree-like representation of programs, thus we can go from one tool to another without using an intermediate data structure. The principal tools are the compiler which allows to translate SIGNAL programs into C, the graphical interface and, for the classic temporal logic specifications, the verification tool SIGALI.

The most interesting tool from a formal verification point of view is the SIGALI tool supporting the formal calculus. It contains a verification and controller synthesis tool-box [17,15], and facilitates proving correctness of the dynamical behaviour of a system with respect to a temporal logic specification.

The equational nature of the SIGNAL language leads to the use of polynomial dynamical equation systems (PDS) over $\mathbb{Z}/3\mathbb{Z}$ as a formal model of program behaviour. Polynomial functions over $\mathbb{Z}/3\mathbb{Z}$ provides us with efficient algorithms to represent these functions and polynomial equations. Hence, instead of enumerating the elements of sets and manipulating them explicitly, this approach manipulates the polynomial functions characterising their set. This way, various properties can be efficiently proved on polynomial dynamical systems. The same formalism can also be efficiently used for solving the supervisory control problem.

3   Introduction to SIMULINK

SIMULINK is the part of the MATLAB toolbox for modelling, simulating, and analysing dynamical systems. It provides several solvers for the simulation of numeric integration of sets of Ordinary Differential Equations (ODEs). As SIGNAL, SIMULINK allows stand-alone generation in four steps, i.e. specify a model, generate C code, generate makefile and generate stand-alone program. For code generation, however, currently it is not possible to use variable-step solvers to build the stand-alone program. Thus, we had to use the fixed step size solvers, and therefore, the step size needs to be set accurately.

SIMULINK Real-Time Workshop (RTW) [19] is the setting for automatic C code generation from SIMULINK block diagrams via a Target Language Compiler (TLC) [21]. By default[1], the RTW gives mainly four C files : <Model>.c, <Model>.h, <Model>.prm and <Model>.reg. The function of these files in stand-alone simulation is fully described in [29]. Figure 1 summarises the architecture of the stand-alone code generation with SIMULINK. The makefile is automatically made from a template makefile (for example grt_unix.tmf is the generic real-time template makefile for UNIX).

By default, the run of a stand-alone program provides a MATLAB data file (<Model>.mat). Before building of the stand-alone program, it is possible to select which data we want to include in the MATLAB file. Then, one can use MATLAB to plot the result.

---

[1] It is possible to customise the C code generated from any SIMULINK model with the TLC which is a tool that is included in RTW.

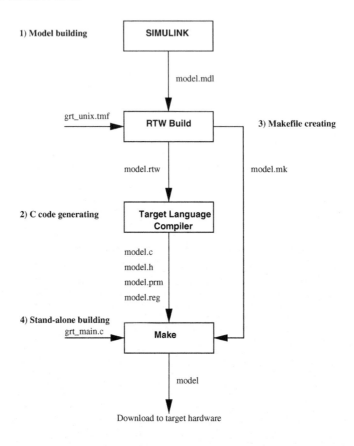

Fig. 1. Automatic code-generation within the Real-Time Workshop architecture

4   Modelling Multi-mode Hybrid Systems

SIGNAL and SIMULINK have both a data-flow oriented style. Here we present a mathematical framework in which both SIGNAL and SIMULINK sub-models can be plugged in to form a hybrid system.

Hybrid systems can be mathematically represented as follows:

$$\dot{x}_i = f_i(q, x_i, u_i, d_i) \, , \; x_i \in \mathbb{R}^{n_i} \, , \; q \in Q \tag{1}$$

$$y_i = h_i(q, x_i, u_i) \tag{2}$$

$$e_i = s_i(q, x_i, u_i, y_i) \tag{3}$$

$$\tau_i = e.\mathbf{1}_{\{e_i \neq e_{i_-}\}} \tag{4}$$

$$q' = T(q, \tau) \, , \; \tau = (\tau_i, i = 1, \dots, I) \tag{5}$$

Where:

(1): $i = 1, \ldots, I$ indexes a collection of continuous time subsystems (CTS),

$q \in Q$ is the discrete state, where Q is a finite alphabet,

$x_i \in \mathbb{R}^{n_i}$ is the vector continuous state of the ith CTS,

$u_i \in \mathbb{R}^{m_i}$ is the vector continuous control of the ith CTS,

$d_i \in \mathbb{R}^{o_i}$ is the vector continuous disturbance of the ith CTS.

(2): $y_i \in \mathbb{R}^{p_i}$ is the vector continuous output of the ith CTS,

(3): $e_i \in B^{r_i}$ where B is the Boolean domain. Thus at each instant an r-tuple of predicates depending on the current values of (q, x_i, u_i, y_i) is evaluated. Examples are $x_i^k > 0$ where superscript j refers to the kth component of x_i, if $x_i = (x^{1i}, \ldots, x^{n_i})$, or $g(q, x_i, u_i, y_i) > 0$ for $g(q, ., ., .) : \mathbb{R}^{n_i + m_i + p_i} \longmapsto \mathbb{R}$, and so on.

(4): $e_{i\_}(t)$ denotes the left limit of e_i at t, i.e., the limit of $e_i(s)$ for $s < t, s \nearrow t$. Assume that $e_{i\_}^k(t) \neq e_i^k(t)$ means that the kth predicate changes its status at instant t; this generates an event τ_i^k. The marked events τ_i^k together form a vector event τ_i (and the latter form the vector event τ). Thus trajectories e_i are piecewise constant.

(5): q, q' are the current and next discrete automaton state.

We use an architectural decomposition earlier used for several case studies [25]. Here we use it to discuss the way the communication between the two sub-models can be implemented for co-simulation.

In the generic architecture shown in Figure 2, the *Plant (P)* is the physical environment under control. The inputs u, the outputs y and the disturbances d all have continuous domains. The *Characterizer (C)* is the interface between the continuous plant and the discrete selector, including A/D converters. The *Selector (S)* is the purely discrete part of the controller – with discrete, input, state and output. The *Effector (E)* is the interface between the discrete selector commands and the continuous physical variables including actuators.

This architecture is a good starting point for hybrid system modelling. It remains to decide:

– How to map the mathematical representation above on the architecture?
– Which parts should be modelled in SIGNAL and which parts in SIMULINK?
– How the SIGNAL part should be activated? Which mechanism should be used including A/D convertors.

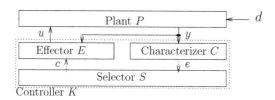

Fig. 2. General hybrid system architecture. Solid (dotted) arrows represent continuous (discrete) flows

From our introductory remarks it should be fairly obvious that selector modelling is best done in SIGNAL, and that SIMULINK is best for modelling the plant. Thus, it remains to determine how to implement the interface between the two, or rather, where and how to model the characterizer and the effector. Next, we need to determine how to generate runs of the hybrid system.

In this paper we adopt the scheme whereby the main module of the SIMULINK model is the master and the SIGNAL automaton is one of the many processes run in a pseudo-parallel fashion. This is realisable using the translation scheme in RTW. The SIMULINK model then contains input ports allowing SIMULINK subsystem blocks to be enabled and disabled, and output ports allowing subsystems to emit events to the controller. The connection can now be made by means of global variable passing.

5   Computational Model with Global Variable Passing

The mathematical model in section 4 is a natural way to conceptualise and model a multi-mode hybrid system. To implement such a system we have to transform these equations into a computational model. In this section we cast the generic mathematical model into the architectural framework presented earlier. In section 6 we provide three protocols for activation of the SIGNAL part of the model.

The plant is made of a collection of finite continuous time subsystems. As in the mathematical representation of section 4, let I be the cardinality of the collection and let i index over I. Each subsystem i contains a vector $x_i \in \mathbb{R}^{n_i}$ of n_i continuous state and also n_i differential equations. This set of equations can be rewritten as follows:

$$\begin{pmatrix} \dot{x}_i^1 \\ \vdots \\ \dot{x}_i^{n_i} \end{pmatrix} = \begin{pmatrix} f_i^1(q, x_i^1, u_i, d_i) \\ \vdots \\ f_i^{n_i}(q, x_i^{n_i}, u_i, d_i) \end{pmatrix} \tag{6}$$

Hence, the system contains $\sum_{k=1}^{I} n_k$ differential equations for each q. That is, $J = |Q| \sum_{k=1}^{I} n_k$ differential equations in the continuous system. However, the implementation needs to extract the discrete parameter $q \in Q$ of these differential equations.

At any time t, one or several equations among this collection forms the basis for computation. Consider the whole set of system equations as follows:

$$\begin{aligned} F_1(x_1^1, u_1, d_1) &= f_1^1(q_1, x_1^1, u_1, d_1) \\ F_2(x_1^1, u_1, d_1) &= f_1^1(q_2, x_1^1, u_1, d_1) \\ &\vdots \\ F_{|Q|}(x_1^1, u_1, d_1) &= f_1^1(q_{|Q|}, x_1^1, u_1, d_1) \\ F_{|Q|+1}(x_1^2, u_1, d_1) &= f_1^2(q_1, x_1^2, u_1, d_1) \\ &\vdots \end{aligned} \tag{7}$$

Let j be a new index for indexing the system equations. Then, we can define a new function F_j for the jth equation in the above list. Now we can rewrite each differential equation as follows:

$$\dot{x}_j = F_j(x_j, u_j, d_j) \tag{8}$$

which allows to calculate the vector continuous state x and the vector continuous output y thanks to equation $y = h(x, u)$. Then y feeds the characterizer, and the equation $e = s(y)$ defines the detection of event e.

Figure 3 shows one possible mapping of the mathematical representation into the architecture (later, we will see that this is not the only mapping). In comparison with Figure 2, a new component has been added in the controller, it is the *Edge detector* which corresponds to equation (4). The discrete state q is defined only in the selector which is the only purely discrete part. So, the selector contains the rewritten form of equation (5):

$$q' = T(q, \tau) \quad \tau = (\tau_j, j = 1, \ldots, J) \tag{9}$$

and the new equation below:

$$c = g(q') \tag{10}$$

where $c \in \mathbb{R}^J$ is the vector discrete control of the effector. The effector deduces from its input c two continuous vectors $u \in \mathbb{R}^J$ and $enabl \in B^J$ thanks to:

$$(u_j, enabl_j) = k(c_j) \tag{11}$$

$enabl_j$ is used by the plant to enable or disable the jth differential equation and u_j is the vector continuous control of the jth differential equation.

Since the discrete controller (the automaton) is in one state at any one computation point[2], it follows that the change in continuous state is well-defined, i.e. although several equations are enabled in parallel, only one equation at a time is chosen for *each* continuous state variable.

---

[2] This is a property of the data-flow program ensured by formal analysis built-in in the compilers for synchronous languages.

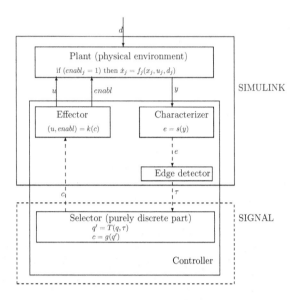

Fig. 3. Hybrid system representation

6   Selector Activations

The selector, i.e. the union of equations (9) and (10) is assumed to work in discrete time, meaning that continuous time t is sampled with period Δt. During each sampling period, the $(e_j(t), e_j(t+\Delta t))$ trajectory is recorded, and it is hoped that each component of e_j changes at most once during the sampling period. If e_j changes during the sampling period then the event τ_j is emitted. Then, there are several possibilities for checking the event τ_j by the selector. These possibilities depend on how the selector is activated. Here we discuss three activation methods – i.e., periodic, aperiodic and asynchronous selector activations.

6.1   Periodic Synchronous Selector Activations

Synchronous means here that the selector activation coincides with a tick of the clock of the sampled continuous system.

Protocol 1 *At each sampling period Δt, the selector senses the final value of vector τ_j, and applies its transition according to (9).*

This protocol is simple, but assumes that sampling period Δt is small enough to avoid missing events. This may typically lead to taking a Δt much smaller than really needed, i.e., to activate the automaton for nothing most of the time.

6.2   Aperiodic synchronous selector activations

Protocol 2 *Here the continuous time system (equations (8)) is the master, driven by continuous real time t. Each time some τ_j occurs a "wake_up" event is generated by the jth continuous time system in which τ_j was generated. Then selector (equation (9)) awaits for* wake_up, *so* wake_up *is the activation clock of the selector. When activated, the automaton checks which event τ_j is received, and moves accordingly, following equation (9).*

Within this protocol, the master is the continuous time system, and the selector reacts to the events output by the continuous time system. More precisely, the continuous time system outputs *wake_up* (in addition to τ_j), which in turn activates the selector.

6.3   Asynchronous Selector Activations

Here, continuous subsystems and the selector have independent SIMULINK threads, that means above all the selector has its own thread and its own activation clock.

Protocol 3 *At each round, the selector senses whether there is some event τ, if it is the case then the selector moves accordingly, following equation (9) and finally, it outputs the state changes to the effector following equation (10).*

It is important to note that with Protocol 3 the τ generation should be done in the SIGNAL part instead of the SIMULINK part (compare with Figure 3). Indeed, if the τ is provided by SIMULINK, there is a risk that the selector will miss some τ because no assumption can be made about when the selector will check its input channels. In the best case some τ are recognised with a delay of one tick in the selector.

7   Application: The Siphon Pump

The protocols for aperiodic and asynchronous selector activations have been implemented in our co-simulation environment [29]. In this section we give a brief exposition to application of the aperiodic protocol to a non-trivial example earlier introduced in [27,28]. This is a model of a siphon pump machine invented by the Swedish engineer Christofer Polhem in 1697. The purpose of the pump was to drain water from the Swedish copper mines with almost no movable parts. This works by having a system of interconnected open and closed tanks, and driving the water up to the ground level by adjusting the pressure in the closed tanks via shunt valves. The idea of the pump was so revolutionary in those times that the pump was never built. However, a model of the pump going back to the 17th century is the basis of the dimensions (and therefore the coefficients in the model) that we have used in our down-scaled model. Figure 4 shows a fragment of the pump consisting of the bottom three tanks.

The plant model has several interesting characteristics. First, even without the discrete controller, there are some discrete dynamic changes in the plant. These are brought about by the two check valves (hydro-mechanically) controlling the flow of water between each open and closed container. Secondly, the plant dynamics (and also the closed loop dynamics) is non-linear. When the check valve between container i and container $i + 1$ is cracked, the flow of water in that pipe, denoted by $q_{i(i+1)}$, is defined by $\dot{q}_{i(i+1)} = f(p_{i(i+1)}, q_{i(i+1)})$ where f is a non-linear function, and $p_{i(i+1)}$ is the pressure in the pipe between container i and container $i + 1$.

For closed-loop simulation we thus had to make an appropriate decomposition, placing the purely discrete parts (including switching in the plant) in the SIGNAL environment, and the purely continuous parts in the SIMULINK environment.

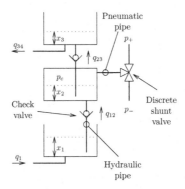

Fig. 4. A fraction of the siphon pump machine

7.1   Working Principles

The purpose of the pump is to lift the water which flows into the sump at the bottom of the mine to the drained ground level sump. This pump works in a two-phase (pull and push) manner as follows. The principle works for an arbitrary system of alternative closed and open tanks as follows.

The pull phase In the pull phase, the pressure vessels (the closed tanks) are de-pressurised by opening the p^- side of the shunt valve which drains the vessels (the p^- side is connected to a negative pressure source e.g. a vacuum tank). Now, the water will be lifted from all the open containers to the pressure vessels immediately above. Hence, as a result of this first phase, all the pressure vessels will be water-filled.

The push phase In the push phase, the pressure vessels are pressurised by opening the p^+ side of the shunt valve to fill the air-compressing vessel with air (the p^+ side represents a positive pressure source, e.g. created by an elevated lake above the mine). Now, all the pressure vessels will be emptied via the connections to the open containers immediately above. Hence, as a result of this second phase, all the open containers will again be filled with water. However, the water has now been shifted upwards half a section. By repeating these two phases the water is sequentially lifted to the ground level.

Figure 4 depicts a fraction of the siphon pump machine. The water entering the bottom container (flow q_1) is lifted to the top container by lowering and raising the pneumatic pressure P_c in the closed vessel. Due to the check valves (in between the open and closed valves), the water is forced to move upwards only. The reason why more than three containers and vessels are needed in practice, is that the vertical distance between any pair of vessel and container is strictly less than 10 meters since water can be lifted no higher than $\approx . 10$ meters by means of the atmospheric pressure (≈ 1 bar). In the sequel we assume that there are only three levels to the pump and the final flow variable $q_3 = q_{34}$.

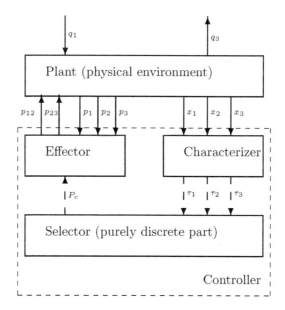

Fig. 5. General hybrid system architecture of the pump

7.2 Mathematical Models

From the high level description of the pump, it is possible to represent the simulated system by means of the architecture presented earlier. Thus, the system decomposition can be depicted as in Figure 5.

At the topmost block, the pump has the external flow $q_1 \, [m^3/s]$ entering container 1 as input and the external flow q_3 leaving the container 3 as output. The flow q_1 entering container 1 is determined by the environment (ground water entering the mine cannot be controlled but is defined by Mother Nature). Hence q_1 is a *disturbance* signal.

The closed loop system is modelled with the plant supplying control information to the effector, the characterizer and eventually to the selector. Obviously, the selector acts on the pneumatic pressure in container 2, i.e, increasing and decreasing P_c. Then the effector provides from P_c and from the gravity induced hydraulic pressure due to accumulated water in containers (p_1, p_2 and p_3) the net driving pressure of the vertical pipes (p_{12} and p_{23}). Hence, in addition to q_1, the plant uses p_{12} and p_{23} to calculate the output flow q_3. In order to stimulate the selector, the characterizer "watches" continuously the water levels of the containers (x_1, x_2 and x_3) and sends event τ to the selector when it is necessary.

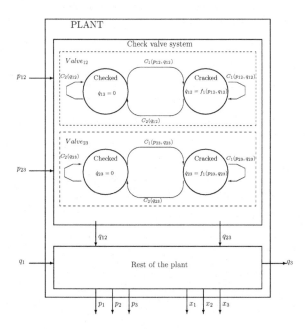

Fig. 6. The architecture of the plant

The refined model of the plant is depicted in Figure 6. It contains mainly two check valve systems. Each check valve system is a hybrid system. Indeed, the water flow through a check valve behaves differently according to the mode of the latter. In the checked mode the water flow is zero and in the cracked mode the water flow follows a non-linear differential equation (the interested reader is referred to the full report [29] for details of the plant model). Note that the check valve can be modelled using both SIMULINK and SIGNAL: The discrete mode changes are modelled in SIGNAL and the rest in SIMULINK.

7.3   The Control Strategy

Finding a safe and optimal controller is far from easy. One of the more important requirements is to maximise the output flow q_3 without risking that x_i will end up outside defined safe intervals. That is, to avoid overflow in the containers (and the mine), specially under all possible disturbances (q_1).

Another important requirement is related to energy consumption and maintainability. It is important to minimize the number of switches of the value of P_c. Changing P_c from $+50kPa$ to $-50kPa$ and vice versa results in a significant amount of energy loss. One solution is to maintain P_c constant over as long periods as possible.

A naive controller can be depicted by the automaton of Figure 7. This is not a robust controller and it was chosen to show the power of the co-simulation environment in illustrating its weaknesses.

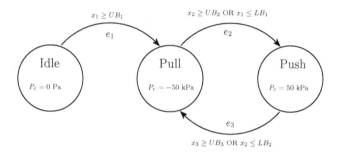

Fig. 7. Automaton implementing the control strategy in a selector, UB_i and LB_i are the level upper and lower limits in tank i respectively.

The behaviour of this controller can be informally described as follows.

1. The first discrete state, i.e., the **Idle** state, is the initialisation state. At the beginning, the three containers are empty. So it is necessary first to let the bottom containers fill. This is what is done in the **Idle** state.
2. When the first container is full enough, an event is broadcast by a level sensor (which is simulated by the characterizer) and the pump moves from the **Idle** state to the **Pull** state.
3. In the **Pull** state, container 2, i.e., the pressure vessel, is de-pressurised. Hence container 2 fills from container 1. Note that container 1 is continuously filled by the input flow q_1 which is uncontrollable. So the water level of container 1 moves according to the input flow q_1 and the flow q_{12} in the pipe between the two containers 1 and 2. When both are possible the level of container 1 either rises or falls.

4. If the water level of container 1 moves down until a given minimum threshold (detected by a sensor) or if the water level of container 2 is high enough then the pump moves from the **Pull** state to the **Push** state.
5. In the **Push** state, container 2 is pressurised. Hence container 2 stops filling from container 1 and fills container 3. So, container 1 continues to fill according to the flow q_1 and container 3 fills according to the flow q_{23} (in the pipe between the two containers 2 and 3) and the output flow q_3. Container 2 is of course emptied.
6. Finally, if the water level of container 2 reaches its minimum threshold or if the water level of container 3 is high enough then the pump comes back from the **Push** state to the **Pull** state. Thus, the loop is closed.

The above automaton shows which events lead to discrete state transitions of the selector and how these events are detected. Hence it is easy to model a characterizer which watches the different water levels and provides the suitable events.

8   Analysis Results and Future Works

In this section we present some co-simulation results. We study the behaviour of the closed loop system for given disturbance signals (incoming water into the bottom container) in presence of the naive controller. It is illustrated that while certain aspects of the behaviour are as expected, we also get unsatisfactory outputs.

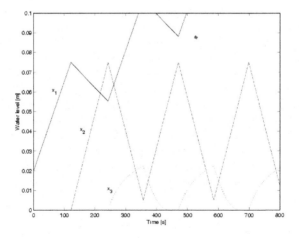

Fig. 8. Water levels of the system with $q_1 = 2.10^{-6}\, m^3/s$

First, observing the behaviour of the flow in the different pipes appears satisfactory. However, that in itself is not sufficient for correctness of the pump behaviour. Indeed, it is necessary to study the water levels in each container to check whether there is an overflow. Figure 8 shows such traces. The water level of the ith container is denoted by x_i and H denotes the height of the containers. At the beginning of the simulation, i.e., at time $t = 0$, the water level in container 1 is $0.02\,m$ and all the other containers are empty. What is important in these traces is that around $t = 350\,s$ container 1 overflows since x_1 reaches the value of H. Because water was not lifted fast enough against the input water flow q_1. The controller is not to blame, since overflow is due to q_1 which is uncontrollable.

The next plot shows that even if there is no overflow, the controller has a bad behaviour. That is, an infinitely fast switching behaviour in the shunt valve controller appears. This undesired behaviour of the system is a direct result of the naive control strategy adopted, not due to the chosen communication protocol. This lack of robustness in the controller is well-illustrated by the co-simulation, see Figure 9.

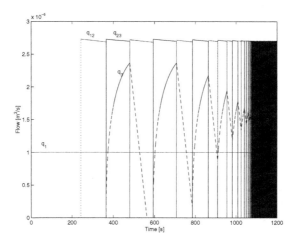

Fig. 9. The simulation result illustrating infinite switching.

Current work includes experiments using the asynchronous protocol. Another interesting problem is to study the range of values for q_1, for which the pump can work without problems; in particular, how simulation and formal verification can be combined to analyse such problems. Also, it is interesting to apply the combined environment to systems with more complex controller structure [24], where formal verification in SIGALI and co-simulation in the current environment are combined.

A survey of related works on simulation of hybrid systems can be found in [23]. A typical requirement in dealing with hybrid simulation is that systems with uneven dynamics be simulated with variable step solvers so that rapid simulation and accuracy can be combined. Our work points out a weakness in the code generation mechanism of MATLAB which restricts the ability to use variable solvers. On the other hand, this may not be a problem in some application areas. For example, it was not considered as a critical issue when this work was presented at a forum including our industrial partners from the aerospace sector.

References

1. T. Amagbegnon, P. Le Guernic, H. Marchand, and E. Rutten. Signal- the specification of a generic, verified production cell controller. In C. Lewerentz and T. Lindner, editors, *Formal Development of Reactive Systems - Case Study Production Cell*, number 891 in Lecture Notes in Computer Science, chapter 7, pages 115–129. Springer Verlag, January 1995.
2. A. Benveniste, B. Caillaud, and P. Le Guernic. Compositionality in Dataflow Synchronous Languages: Specification and Distributed Code Generation. *Information and Computation*. To appear.
3. A. Benveniste, B. Caillaud, and P. Le Guernic. From Synchrony to Asynchrony. In J.C.M. Baeten and S. Mauw, editors, *Proceedings of the 10th International Conference on Concurrency Theory, CONCUR'99, LNCS 1664*, pages 162–177. Springer Verlag, 1999.
4. G. Berry. The Constructive Semantics of Pure Esterel. Technical report, Centre de Mathematiques Appliquees, 1999. Draft book, available from `http://www-sop.inria.fr/meije/esterel/doc/main-papers.html`.
5. F. Boussinot and R. De Simone. The ESTEREL language. *Proceedings of the IEEE*, 79(9):1293–1304, September 1991.
6. W. Chan, R.J. Anderson, P. Beame, S. Burns, F. Modugno, D. Notkin, and J.D. Reese. Model Checking Large Software Specifications. *IEEE Transactions on Software Engineering*, 24:498–519, July 1998.
7. T. Gautier and P. Le Guernic. Code generation in the SACRES project. In F. Redmill and T. Andersson, editors, *Towards System Safety, Proceedings of the Safety-critical Systems Symposium, SSS'99*, pages 127–149, Huntingdon, UK, February 1999. Springer Verlag.
8. P. Le Guernic, T. Gautier, M. Le Borgne, and C. Le Maire. Programming real-time applications with SIGNAL. *Proceedings of the IEEE*, 79(9):1321–1336, September 1991.
9. N. Halbwachs, P. Caspi, P. Raymond, and D. Pilaud. The synchronous data flow programming language LUSTRE. *Proceedings of the IEEE*, 79(9):1305–1320, September 1991.
10. N. Halbwachs, P. Raymond, and Y.-E. Proy. Verification of Linear Hybrid Systems by means of Convex Approximations. In *In proceedings of the International Symposium on Static Analysis SAS'94, LNCS 864*. Springer Verlag, September 1993.
11. D. Harel. Statecharts: A visual formalism for complex systems. *Science of Computer Programming*, 8:231–274, 1987.
12. Integrated Systems Inc. *SystemBuild v 5.0 User's Guide*. Santa Clara, CA, USA, 1997.
13. A. Kountouris and C. Wolinski. Hierarchical conditional dependency graphs for mutual exclusiveness identification. In *12th International Conference on VLSI Design*, Goa, India, January 1999.

14. G. Lafferriere, G. J. Pappas, and S. Yovine. A New Class of Decidable Hybrid Systems. In *proceedings of Hybrid Systems: Computation and Control, LNCS 1569*, pages 137–151. Springer Verlag, March 1999.

15. M. Le Borgne, H. Marchand, E. Rutten, and M. Samaan. Formal verification of signal programs: Application to a power transformer station controller. In *Proceedings of AMAST'96, LNCS 1101*, pages 271–285, Munich, Germany, July 1996. Springer-Verlag.

16. E. Marchand, E. Rutten, and F. Chaumette. From data-flow task to multi-tasking: Applying the synchronous approach to active vision in robotics. *IEEE Trans. on Control Systems Technology*, 5(2):200–216, March 1997.

17. H. Marchand, P. Bournai, M. Le Borgne, and P. Le Guernic. A design environment for discrete-event controllers based on the signal language. In *1998 IEEE International Conf. On Systems, Man, And Cybernetics*, pages 770–775, San Diego, California, USA, October 1998.

18. H. Marchand and M. Samaan. On the incremental design of a power transformer station controller using controller synthesis methodology. In *World Congress on Formal Methods (FM'99)*, volume 1709 of *LNCS*, pages 1605–1624, Toulouse, France, September 1999. Springer Verlag.

19. The MathWorks, Inc. *Real-Time Workshop User's Guide*, May 1997.

20. The MathWorks, Inc. *Stateflow User's Guide*, May 1997.

21. The MathWorks, Inc. *Target Language Compiler Reference Guide*, May 1997.

22. The MathWorks, Inc. *Using Simulink*, January 1997.

23. P. Mosterman. An Overview of Hybrid Simulation Phenomena and Their Support by Simulation Packages. In *Hybrid Systems: Computation and Control, Proceedings of the second international workshop, March 1999, LNCS 1569*, pages 168–177. Springer Verlag, March 1999.

24. S. Nadjm-Tehrani and O. Åkerlund. Combining Theorem Proving and Continuous Models in Synchronous Design. In *Proceedings of the World Congress on Formal Methods, Volume II, LNCS 1709*, pages 1384–1399. Springer Verlag, September 1999.

25. S. Nadjm-Tehrani and J-E. Strömberg. Verification of Dynamic Properties in an Aerospace application. *Formal Methods in System Design*, 14(2):135–169, March 1999.

26. A. Puri and P. Varaiya. Verificaion of Hybrid Systems Using Abstractions. In *proceedings of Hybrid Systems II, LNCS 999*, pages 359–369. Springer Verlag, 1994.

27. J.-E. Strömberg. *A mode switching modelling philosophy*. PhD thesis, Linköping University, Linköping, 1994. Dissertation no. 353.

28. J.-E. Strömberg and S. Nadjm-Tehrani. On discrete and hybrid representation of hybrid systems. In *Proceedings of the SCS International Conference on Modeling and Simulation (ESM'94)*, pages 1085–1089, Barcelona, Spain, 1994.

29. S. Tudoret. Signal-simulink: Hybrid system co-simulation. Technical Report cis-1999-020, Dept. of Computer and Information Science, Linköpings University, December 1999. Currently available under Technical reports from http://www.ida.liu.se/~eslab/publications.shtml.

A System for Object Code Validation

A. K. Bhattacharjee[1], Gopa Sen[1], S. D. Dhodapkar[1]*, K. Karunakar[2],
Basant Rajan[3], and R. K. Shyamasundar[3]

[1] Reactor Control Division, Bhabha Atomic Research Centre, Mumbai 400 085, India
{anup,gopa,sdd}@magnum.barc.ernet.in
[2] Independent V&V Group, Aeronautical Development Agency, Bangalore, India
[3] STCS, Tata Institute of Fundamental Research, Mumbai 400 005, India
{basant,shyam}@tcs.tifr.res.in

Abstract. In several key safety-critical embedded applications, it has become mandatory to verify the process of translation by compilers since usually compilers are only certified rather than verified. In this paper, we shall describe a methodology and a system for the validation of translation of a safe-subset of Ada to assembly language programs. The work described here is an application of *Translation Validation* technique to safety-critical programs that are developed using standard software engineering practices using *safe* subsets of Ada such as SPARK Ada [3]. Our method consists of converting the high level language (HLL) program and its object code to a common semantic representation such as Fair Transition System (FTS) [6], and then establishing that the object code is a refinement of the HLL program. The proof of refinement is performed using STeP (Stanford Temporal Prover) theorem prover. The proposed approach also has the additional advantage that the embedded system remains unaffected by compiler revisions/updates. We conclude with a discussion of our practical experience, effectiveness and further possibilities.

1 Introduction

In the development of software for safety critical applications, very high levels of confidence in the correctness of code is essential. The two steps in the realization of object code (cf. Fig. 1) are:

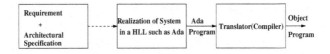

Fig. 1. Two Main Steps from Specification to Realization

---

* Corresponding Author

M. Joseph (Ed.): FTRTFT 2000, LNCS 1926, pp. 152–169, 2000.

1. Realizing a high level program from a given requirement specification and architectural specification.
2. Generating the object code using the translator (or compiler).

In Fig. 1, dotted lines are shown between the specification and the HLL realization to reflect several successive refinements whereas the solid arrow between the HLL and the translator shows the direct nature of the refinement (translation). To show that the object code indeed realizes the given specification, we need to establish that:

1. high level program is an implementation of the given specification,
2. object code derived is a correct translation of HLL program.

The first step depends upon the level of formalism at the specification level. In the current scenario, rigorous specification (e.g., B, Z, VDM *etc*) and development in high level languages (e.g., Ada, MISRA C[4] *etc*) is an industrial reality. The second step depends upon the correctness of the translator. In the context of compiler development, the step corresponds to the preservation of the meaning of program by the compiler. It may be noted that even certified compilers will have several known bugs many of which could affect executable code. Thus, one has to look for solutions such as:

1. Verification of Compiler
2. Formal verification of compiled code
3. Establishing the equivalence of the source and the object code.

Compiler verification is an extremely difficult task and almost impossible (undecidable in general) and formal verification of compiled code is again extremely difficult. *Translation Validation* is an approach proposed in [1] that intrinsically realizes (3) in a pragmatic manner. Translation validation is based on *Refinement Mappings* [7] and can be used to establish that the object code produced by the compiler on a given pass, is a correct implementation of the input program. *Refinement Mappings* have been used to prove that a lower-level specification correctly implements a higher-level specification. Pnueli et al. [1] proposed the technique of *Translation Validation* to show that a program in SIGNAL [8] – a synchronous language – is correctly translated into C – an asynchronous language.

In this paper, we shall propose a methodology supported with tools to establish *equivalence* of the given Ada source program with the corresponding object code. The rationale is based on the fact that usually in safety-critical embedded applications, it would suffice to establish correctness of compilation of a finite set of programs. In our approach, we basically find out whether the object code generated can be proved to be an implementation of the Ada source program restricted to a *safe* subset such as SPARK Ada [3]. For this, both the source and the object programs are brought under a common semantic framework of FTS and then it is shown that the transition system of the object program is a refinement of the transition system of the Ada source program. The contribution of the paper lies in the proposal of a methodology for Object Code Validation (OCV) with tool support for validating translations from a general purpose HLL to assembly language. Specifically, the contributions are:

1. A method for validating the translation of a safe-subset of Ada (SPARK subset) to i960 assembly programs.
2. A suite of tools for (a) Translation of the safe subset of Ada into FTS, (b) Translation of object program (i960 assembly) into FTS, that enable validation of the given Ada program through the STeP [5] theorem prover using *interface mapping* built using symbol tables generated by the compiler.

Rest of the paper is organized as follows: Section 2 gives an overview of translation validation and the related work. In section 3, an outline of the proposed OCV method is given. This is followed by a detailed treatment of refinements, proof obligations in STeP and a simple illustrative example of the method in section 4. In section 5, we give an example wherein the method detects translational errors. In section 6 implementation issues regarding support tools of OCV are discussed. The paper concludes with a summary of the experience, the status of the implementation and further possibilities.

2   Translation Validation: An Overview

For establishing the correctness of a compiler, one has to prove that the compiler always produces target code that correctly implements the source code. Owing to the intrinsic complexities of compiler verification, an alternative referred to as *Translation validation* has been explored in [1]. In this approach, each individual translation (i.e. a run of the compiler) is followed by a validation phase which verifies that the target code produced on this run correctly implements the source program. Such a possibility is particularly relevant for embedded systems where there is a need to execute a finite set of target programs. It must be pointed out that the validation task becomes increasingly difficult with the increase of sophistication and optimizations methods like scheduling of instructions as in RISC architectures or methods of code generation/optimization for super-scalar machines. In [1], the authors demonstrated the the practicability of translation validation for a translator/compiler that translates the synchronous language Signal to C without any optimizations[1]. The method exploits the special features of the SIGNAL compiler:

1. Each program consists of an initialization followed by an infinite loop consisting of phases like, calculating clock expressions,reading inputs, computing outputs, writing outputs and updating *previous* expressions.
2. The compiler translates a program structurally.

The question that arises is:

Is it possible to apply the above technique to a non-synchronous language that does not use such structural translation?

It is very clear that by the very facts of difficulties of compiler verification mentioned already, we cannot extend the method in an unconstrained manner. Our first attempt has been to consider general purpose programming languages instead of synchronous languages such as SPARK subset [3]. Here, we shall describe a method wherein the above approach can be used for a compiler that translates SPARK subset of Ada to i960 assembly. The basic characteristics of the underlying language and its translator that we have exploited are:

1. Source program satisfies *safeness* constraints as in SPARK Ada.
2. The programs also pass through some of the well-established metrics of software engineering required for certification.
3. The compiler is a certified industrial compiler that does not use complex optimizations; the assembler is a simple translator having almost a one-one correspondence between assembly and machine code.

The above characteristics are indeed the minimum requirements imposed on translators used in critical embedded applications.

2.1   Fair Transition System

The common semantic framework viz. FTS [6], is formally described as $\mathcal{F} = (V, \Theta, \Gamma, E)$ where,

---

[1] In [2], extension of the approach for TNI SIGNAL compiler is explored.

- $V = \{u_1, u_2 \cdots u_n\} \subseteq \nu$: A finite set of system variables consisting of *data variables*, and *control variables* and ν is the *vocabulary*.
- Θ: The initial condition characterizing the initial states.
- Γ: A finite set of transitions. $\tau \in \Gamma$ is a function $\tau : \Sigma \mapsto 2^\Sigma$ mapping each state $s \in \Sigma$ into a set of states $\tau(s) \subseteq \Sigma$.
- $E \subseteq V$: A set of externally observable variables.

A computation in FTS, $\mathcal{F}$, denotes an infinite sequence $\sigma = < s_0, s_1, s_2 \ldots >$, where $s_i \in \Sigma$ for each $i \in \mathcal{N}$ iff $s_0 \models \Theta$ and $(s_i, s_{i+1}) \models \Gamma$.

3   An Overview of the OCV Method

Our method for OCV consists of:

1. Translating the given Ada program into SPL(*Simple Programming Language* used in STeP) or FTS.
2. Translating the i960 program to SPL or FTS.
3. Deriving the *interface mapping* using the symbol table generated by the compiler.
4. Using STeP to show that the FTS for the object code is a refinement of the FTS for the source program.

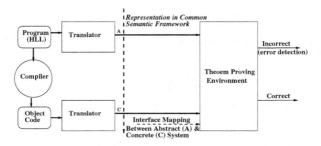

Fig. 2. Overall Object Code Validation Scheme

The overall OCV scheme is diagrammatically shown in Figure 2. The task of proving correctness of refinement in general is quite arduous and almost impossible. However, under some constraints , it is indeed possible is shown in the sequel. The feasibility of our approach relies on the following aspects:

1. Restricting the language subset to *safe subsets* enforces good structural relations on the FTS for the source and the object program since we also assume that there are no complex optimizing transformations.

2. The above structure also provides support for the *Interface Mapping* of variables. For instance, translations in an actual compiler like GNU gcc, that has options (eg, -gstabs, -gstabs+ *etc.*) for producing debugging information can be effectively used to derive correspondences between variables in the source and the object program.
3. Use of interactive theorem provers such a STeP to establish the equivalence.

4   Formal Description of the OCV Method

Firstly, the HLL program and it's object code are translated into FTS using the two translators shown in Figure 2. The two fair transition systems obtained become the input to the theorem proving tool STeP to carry out the proof of correctness of translation. The other input required is the *Interface Mapping* (cf. in Fig.2) that provides a mapping between the variables in the HLL program and the object code. Although FTS is the final representation used in the proof, it is also possible to first translate the HLL and it's object code into SPL, which is accepted by STeP as input. The translators shown in Figure 2 are designed to take one HLL program and it's object code as input and produce the corresponding SPL programs. The representations of the HLL and it's object code, in the form of FTS, could then be obtained using STeP. However, as explained later, we have found that in the case of object code it is easier to directly translate it to FTS. We illustrate the above concepts using a simple HLL program given below:

```
    int test(int a)
{ int i,j=1,k=2;
if(a) i=j*i +k;
else i=k*i +j;
}
```

The FTS of the above HLL program is shown in Fig.3 and is referred to as *Abstract System* denoted by A=$(V_A, \Theta_A, \Gamma_A, E_A)$, where $V_A = \{pi0, i, j, k, l, n, a\}$, $\Theta_A = \{pi0 = 0\}$, $\Gamma_A = \{T_1, T_2, T_3, T_4, T_5\}$ and $E_A = \{a, l, i, k, j\}$; pi0 denotes program location counter. The transition system shown in Fig.4 is obtained from the object code of the above HLL program. For lack of space, the object code is not shown here. In the sequel, the FTS corresponding to the object code is always referred to as *Concrete System* and is denoted by $C=(V_C, \Theta_C, \Gamma_C, E_C)$ where $V_C = \{$ pi0, ebp_4, ebp_8, ebp_12, ebp_16, ebp8, ecx, edx, eax, esp $\}, \Theta_C = \{pi0 = 0\}$,

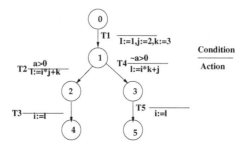

Fig. 3. Transition System for the Abstract System

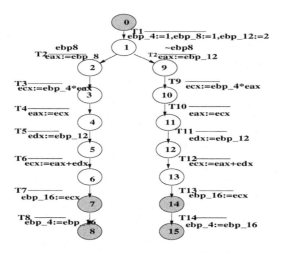

Fig. 4. Transition System for the Concrete System

$\Gamma_C = \{T_1, T_2, \ldots, T_{15}\}$ and $E_C = \{ebp\_4, ebp\_8, ebp\_12, ebp\_16, ebp8\}$. The *Concrete System* variables ebp_4, ebp_8, ebp_12, ebp_16 and $ebp8$ correspond to the variables in the *Abstract System*. The correspondence between variables of the A and C is $\{i \mapsto ebp\_4, j \mapsto ebp\_8, k \mapsto ebp\_12, l \mapsto ebp\_16, a \mapsto ebp8\}$. Thus, $V_A \subset V_C$. Even though in this example there is a direct one to one correspondence between the observables of the two systems, in general it need not be so. For example, HLL may support an abstract data type like a long integer (64 bit), which when mapped to a low level assembly program may be represented as two 32 bit integers (d1,d2) and the mapping will be an expression $(2^{32} * d2 + d1)$. It can be also observed that the number of states in the two transition systems are different ($\sharp \Sigma_C \geq \sharp \Sigma_A$). A state in the HLL program (or it's FTS) is said to correspond to a state in the object program (as represented by its FTS) when they agree on the values of the observable variables. Formally, if $s_A \in \Sigma_A$ and $s_C \in \Sigma_C$ are two states of HLL and object program then $s_A \mapsto s_C$ iff $\forall v_A \in E_A \bullet v_A(s_A) = v_C(s_C)$ where $v_C \in E_C \wedge v_A \mapsto v_C(s_C)$. Here $v(s)$ means the value of variable v interpreted in state s. Thus, in Figure 4 the shaded nodes $\{0,7,8,14,15\}$ are the states which correspond to states $\{0,2,4,3,5\}$ in abstract system in that order. The states of the *Concrete System* that do not have a correspondence with those of the *Abstract System* are unobservable and hence are local to it.

4.1 Correctness of Translation

Let us consider an *Abstract System A* representing a HLL program and *Concrete System C* representing the corresponding object code. The system A can be viewed as a specification for the implementation C. A refinement mapping [7] is defined as a function $(f : \Sigma_C \mapsto \Sigma_A)$ which maps concrete system states to abstract system states. If the translation is correct, C will preserve the essential features of A except for:

- The concrete system need not agree with the abstract system on the values of all variables. The refinement relation singles out the *observable variables* whose behavior should be preserved.
- In the course of computation, the concrete system may require data movement in temporary locations (registers). This leads to the possibility of loosing one to one correspondence between states in the two systems.
- The abstract system can operate in terms of high level abstract data types, while the concrete version is restricted to only those data types available in the particular architecture. Consequently, one should not always expect one to one correspondence between the concrete observable variables and the abstract ones.

From the theory of refinement mapping [1,7], we have:

- if $f : \Sigma_C \mapsto \Sigma_A$ is an inductive refinement mapping from C to A then C is said to be a refinement of A i.e $C \sqsubseteq A$
- A refinement mapping $f : \Sigma_C \mapsto \Sigma_A$ is called inductive iff **B-INV** rule given below is satisfied.:
  R1. *Initiation:* $s \models \Theta_C \rightarrow f(s) \models \Theta_A, \forall\ s \in \Sigma_C$ and
  R2. *Propagation:* $(s, s') \models \Gamma_C \rightarrow (f(s), f(s')) \models \Gamma_A$ for all $s, s' \in \Sigma_C$

Given two FTSs, A and C, we have to show that C is a correct implementation of A or in other words C refines A. We assume that $E_A = V_A - \{pi0\}$. Let $\alpha : V_A \rightarrow \varepsilon(V_C)$ be a substitution that replaces each abstract variable

$v \in V_A$ by an expression ε_v over the concrete variables. Such a substitution α induces a mapping $\tilde{\alpha}$ between states. To show that C refines A it is required to show that [7] R1: $\Theta_C \to \phi$, R2: $\forall \tau \in \Gamma_C \bullet \{\phi\}\tau\{\phi\}$, R3: $\Theta_C \to \Theta_A[\alpha]$ and R4: $\phi \to \phi[\alpha]$, where ϕ be an assertion on C and $\alpha : V_A \to \varepsilon(V_C)$ is a substitution. The rules R1-R2 express the requirement that ϕ is an invariant of system C and R3-R4 express the requirement that $\tilde{\alpha}$ is an inductive refinement mapping. We define ϕ to be an invariant defining the conditions under which observable variables are changed by the computation.

4.2   Proof of Validation Using STeP

Let u_A be an observable variable in A and u_C be the corresponding variable in C. Consider a state s_i in the abstract system where u_A is defined. Let $l_{u_A}(s_0 \hookrightarrow s_i)$ be the path condition (conjunction of all predicates on the path $(s_0 \hookrightarrow s_i)$) and $cond(u_A)$ be the disjunction of all such path conditions, because there can be more than one path from s_0 to s_i. Then an invariant can be defined by $\phi : at\_s_i \to cond(u_A) \wedge u_A = \ldots$. Thus taking the FTS in Fig. 3, we can have $\phi : pi0 = 2 \to a > 0 \wedge l = i * j + k$ and $\phi : pi0 = 3 \to \neg(a > 0) \wedge l = i * k + l$. Such invariants can also be defined for the concrete system. The fact that these invariants are indeed true in the respective systems can be verified by the B-INV rule. If for any transition $\tau \in \Gamma$, $\{\phi\}\tau\{\phi\}$ is not established, one can generate a weakest precondition (WPC)[9] which should hold good before the transition is taken so that ϕ remains true after the transition. The WPC itself can be checked by applying B-INV. These can be applied repeatedly till it is proved or disproved.

We define the substitution function $\alpha : V_A \to \varepsilon(V_C)$. This function defines the mapping between an abstract variable to its counterpart in the concrete system. In STeP this mapping is expressed by Simplify or Rewrite rules. These simplification rules are declared with the **SIMPLIFY, REWRITE** keywords. The **SIMPLIFY** rules are automatically and exhaustively applied when STeP simplifier is invoked. **REWRITE** rules are applied interactively. We also define a mapping of states in the two system where the values of the observables in the two systems are same. Now if $\phi(u_i^C)$ is an invariant in the concrete system for a concrete variable u_i^C and $\phi(u_i^A)$ is an invariant in the abstract system then if the translation is correct $\phi(u_i^C) \to \phi(\alpha(u_i^A))$ must be true by rule R4. This should be true for all observable variables. The technique by which this is carried out is the MON-I[6] rule (modus ponens) which says if p is true and $p \to q$ then q is true.

For the system shown in Fig. 3, we prove the following invariants (PROPERTY PA1-PA4) by using B-INV and WPC rules. For the systems shown in Fig. 3 and Fig 4 the script showing the proof requirement for correct implementation is given below:

```
(*These are the invariants of the Abstract System and
are shown in the syntax accepted by STeP.*)
PROPERTY PA1: [](pi0 = 2 --> a > 0 /\ 1 = i*j +k)
PROPERTY PA2: [](pi0 = 4 --> a > 0 /\ i = 1)
PROPERTY PA3: [](pi0 = 3 --> ~(a > 0) /\ 1 = i*k +j)
PROPERTY PA4: [](pi0 = 5 --> ~(a > 0) /\ i = 1)
( * Properties PC1-PC4 are invariants of the Concrete System *)
PROPERTY PC1:[](pi0=7 --> ebp8 >0 /\ (ebp_16=ebp_8*ebp_4 + ebp_12))
PROPERTY PC2:[](pi0=8 --> ebp8 >0 /\ ebp_4 = ebp_16)
PROPERTY PC3:[](pi0=14 --> ~(ebp8 > 0) /\ (ebp_16=ebp_12*ebp_4 +ebp_8))
PROPERTY PC4:[](pi0=15 --> ~(ebp8 > 0) /\ ebp_4=ebp_16)
(*Interface  mapping between abstract variables i,j,k,l,a and the
  concrete variables -4(ebp), -8(ebp), -12(ebp),-16(ebp) and 8(ebp).
  Here -1 means the variable is unobservable *)
value i:int*int --> int
value j:int*int --> int
value k:int*int --> int
value l:int*int --> int
value a:int*int --> int
SIMPLIFY S1: i(pi0, ebp_4) ---> if pi0 >= 0 then ebp_4 else -1
SIMPLIFY S2: j(pi0, ebp_8) ---> if pi0 >= 0 then ebp_8 else -1
SIMPLIFY S3: k(pi0, ebp_12) ---> if pi0 >= 0 then ebp_12 else -1
SIMPLIFY S4: l(pi0, ebp_16) ---> if (pi0=7 \/ pi0=8 \/ pi0=14
                                 \/ pi0=15) then ebp_16 else -1
SIMPLIFY S5: a(pi0, ebp8) ---> if pi0 >= 0 then ebp8 else -1
(* Axioms A1-A4 axiomatize the correspondence between observable states *)
control pca:[0..5] (* control variable *)
AXIOM A1: pi0=7 <==> pca=2
AXIOM A2: pi0=14 <==> pca=3
AXIOM A3: pi0=8 <==> pca=4
AXIOM A4: pi0=15 <==> pca=5
(* Properties P1-P4 are invariants of the Abstract System (written with
  mapping). Proof Obligation for correct refinement *)

PROPERTY P1:[](pca = 2 -->a(pi0,ebp8) > 0 /\ 1(pi0,ebp_16) =
                j(pi0,ebp_8)*i(pi0,ebp_4) + k(pi0,ebp_12))
PROPERTY P2:[](pca = 4 -->a(pi0,ebp8) > 0 /\ i(pi0,ebp_4) =
                l(pi0,ebp_16))
PROPERTY P3:[](pca = 3 --> ~(a(pi0,ebp8) > 0) /\ 1(pi0,ebp_16) =
                k(pi0,ebp_12)*i(pi0,ebp_4) + j(pi0,ebp_8))
PROPERTY P4:[](pca = 5 --> ~(a(pi0,ebp8) > 0) /\ i(pi0,ebp_4) =
                l(pi0,ebp_16))
```

Here properties PC1-PC4 are invariants of the concrete system. These are proved using B-INV and WPC as was done in proving properties PA1-PA4 for the abstract system. Properties P1-P4 are the properties of the abstract system (PA1-PA4) but written with substitution function. These properties are again proved using the properties PC1-PC4 and MON-I rule; note that premise R3 can be trivially proved.

5   Illustrative Example with Translation Error

The above technique was tested on experimental basis on a number of
test programs written in C language. The translations of C programs
were deliberately seeded with errors to test the efficacy of the method.
All seeded errors could be detected by carrying out the required proofs.
Later the method was tested on Ada examples, that had real translation
errors. One such example is given below in the form SPL representation
of Ada and its object code. It was found that the version of the Ada
compiler used, generated assembly code which executes a wrong path if
the value of the *case* predicate is more than the last allowed value. This
was detected during the proof.

SPL Representation of Ada Source Program (Abstract System)

```
macro LAST:int where LAST=1024
(*
macro C1: [0..999] where C1=10
macro C2: [0..999] where C2=15
macro C3: [0..999] where C3=20
macro const:int where const=1
*)
in param:int
local v1,pav1:[-LAST..LAST]
local v2,v3:[0..999]
local C1: [0..999] where C1=10
local C2: [0..999] where C2=15
local C3: [0..999] where C3=20
local const:int where const=1
case4:: [
v1:=param;
v2:=v2*8;
10: if v2 >= 1 /\ v2 <= 99 then
    [ v3:=C1;
11: skip ]
    else
    [ if v2>= 100 /\ v2 <= 199 \/ v2=201 then
        [ v3:=C2+C1;
12:      skip ]
      else
      [ if v2=0 then
        [ v3:= const;
13:      skip ]
        else
        [ if v2=200 then
          [ v3:=v2 div 4;
14:        skip]
          else
          [ if v2=202 then
            [ v1:=pav1;
15:          skip]
            else
            [ if v2>=203 /\ v2 <= 999 then
```

```
          [ v3:=v2+ const;
16:             skip]]]]]];
     pav1:=v1;
17: skip]
```

In the abstract system $A = \{V, \Theta, \Gamma, E\}$ where $V = \{pi0, param, v1, v2,$
$v3, C1, C2, C3, pav1\}$, $\Theta = pi0 = 0$, $\Gamma =$ the set of transitions and $E =$
$\{v1, v2, v3, C1, C2, C3\}$.
The following are the invariants of the abstract system as included in the
specification file (SPEC file) for the STeP.

```
PROPERTY P1: l1==>1<=v2 /\ v2 <= 99 /\ v3=C1
PROPERTY P2: l2==>((100<=v2 /\ v2<= 199) \/ v2=201) /\ v3=(C2+C1)
PROPERTY P3: l3==>v2=0 /\v3=const
PROPERTY P4: l4==>v2=200 /\ v3 = (v2 div 4)
PROPERTY P5: l5==>v2=202 /\ v1=pav1
PROPERTY P6: l6==>203<= v2 /\ v2 <= 999 /\ v3=(v2+const)
```

These invariants are proved using the rule `repeat(B-INV;Simplify;`
`Undo;WPC)`.

SPL Representation of i960 Object Program(Concrete System)

```
in g0:int
local r1,r2,r3,r4,r5,r6,r7,g1,g2,g3,g4,g5,g6,g7,v1,v2,v3,pav1:int
local temp:int
prog::
[ r5:=g0;temp:=r4 * 8;r4 := temp;r3:=r4;
l1:if r4>0 then
   [ g3:=99;
l2:   if r3 > 99 then
      [ g1 := 199;
l3:     if r3 > g1 then
        [ g6:=200;
          if r3 != g6 then
          [ g5 := 201;
l4:       skip;
l5:       if r3 = g5 then
          [ g6:=25;v3:=g6;
l6:         skip]
          else
          [ g3:=202;
l7:         if r3 != g3 then
            [ g6:= 203;
l8:           if g6 >= r3 then
              [g5:=v1;g4 := r4+g5;v3:=g4;
l9:             skip]
              else
              [ pav1:=r5;
l10:            skip]]
          else
          [ g1:= pav1;v1:=g1;
l11:        skip]]]
        else
        [ g6:=r4 div 4;v3:=g6;
```

```
112:          skip]]
          else
          [ g7:=100;
113:        if g7 <= r3 then
            [g6 := 25;v3 := g6;
114:          skip]]]
        else
        [ if 1 <= r3 then
          [ g7:=10;v3:=g7;
115:        skip]]]
        else
        [g4:=12;v3:=g4;
116: skip]]
```

In the above concrete system $C = \{V, \Theta, \Gamma, E\}$ where $V = \{pi0, r3, r4,$ $v1, C1, C2, C3, pav1\}$, $\Theta = \{pi0 = 0\}$, $\Gamma=$ the set of transitions, $E =$ $\{r3, v1, v2, v3, C1, C2, C3, pav1\}$. The following are the invariants of the system as included in the specification file (SPEC file) for the STeP. These are also proved using the same rules as in case of abstract system invariants.

```
macro C1: int where C1=10
macro C2: int where C2=15
macro C3: int where C3=20
macro const:int where const=12
control pca:[0..8]
AXIOM A1: []Forall i:int.(i=r4-->i=r3)
PROPERTY P1: 115==>1<=r3 /\ r3 <= 99 /\ v3=10
PROPERTY P2: 114==>(100<=r3 /\ r3<= 199)    /\ v3= 25
PROPERTY P3: 16==>r3=201 /\ v3=25
PROPERTY P4: 116==>r3<=0 /\ v3=12
PROPERTY P5: 112==>r3=200/\v3=(r4 div 4)
PROPERTY P6: 111==>r3=202 /\v1=pav1
PROPERTY P7: 19==>203<=r3 /\v3=(r4+v1)
```

The interface mapping between abstract system variables and the concrete system variables and the proof obligations are shown below.

```
local V1,V2,V3,PAV1:int
(* Interface Mapping between Abstract System variables
and Concrete System variables *)
value fv1:int*int*int-->int
value fv2:int*int*int-->int
value fV2:int*int*int-->int
value fv3:int*int*int-->int
value fpav1:int*int*int-->int
SIMPLIFY S1: fv1(pi0,V1,v1) ---> if pi0 >= 0 then v1 else -1
SIMPLIFY S2: fv2(pi0,V2,r3) ---> if pi0 >= 0 then r3 else -1
SIMPLIFY S3: fv3(pi0,V3,v3) ---> if pi0 >= 0 then v3 else -1
SIMPLIFY S4: fpav1(pi0,PAV1,pav1) ---> if pi0 > 0 then pav1 else -1
(* State Correspondence between Abstract States and Concrete States *)
AXIOM M1: [](pca=1<-->115)
AXIOM M2: [](pca=2<-->114)
AXIOM M3: [](pca=3<-->16)
```

```
AXIOM M4:[](pca=4<-->116)
AXIOM M5:[](pca=5<-->112)
AXIOM M6:[](pca=6<-->111)
AXIOM M7:[](pca=7<-->19)
(* Proof Obligation for correct translation *)
PROPERTY P1: pca=1==> 1 <= fv2(pi0,V2,r3)  /\ fv2(pi0,V2,r3)<= 99 /\
             fv3(pi0,V3,v3)=10
PROPERTY P2: pca=2==>(100<=fv2(pi0,V2,r3) /\ fv2(pi0,V2,r3)<= 199) /\
             fv3(pi0,V3,v3)=(C2+C1)
PROPERTY P7: pca=3==>fv2(pi0,V2,r3)=201 /\ fv3(pi0,V3,v3)= (C2+C1)
PROPERTY P3: pca=4==>fv2(pi0,V2,r3)=0 /\fv3(pi0,V3,v3)=const
PROPERTY P4: pca=12==>fv2(pi0,V2,r3)=200/\ fv3(pi0,V3,v3)=
             (fv2(pi0,V2,r3) div 4)
PROPERTY P5: pca=6==>fv2(pi0,V2,r3)=202 /\ fv1(pi0,V1,v1)=
             fpav1(pi0,PAV1,pav1)
PROPERTY P6: pca=7==>203<= fv2(pi0,V2,r3) /\ fv2(pi0,V2,r3) <= 999 /\
             fv3(pi0,V3,v3)=(fv2(pi0,V2,r3)+ fv1(pi0,V1,v1))
```

It is found that the property P3 and P6 could not be verified. The failure of P3 is because in the abstract system we have a state v3=const, with the path condition $l3 \longrightarrow v2 = 0 \wedge v3 = const$. Whereas in the concrete system, for the corresponding state where v3=const the path condition is $v2 \leq 0$. The failure of P6 is because the upper bound of v2 is 999 which is missing in the concrete system.

6   System for OCV: Implementation Features

The main tasks of the implementation lie in generating the FTS for the source and object code, extracting interface mapping, and the algorithm for proof. Extraction of interface mapping information is done closely to that discussed in Section 3 so as to achieve the mapping semi-automatically. The algorithm for proof of validity follows on the lines of STeP theorem prover [5]. The translators shown in Fig. 2 for the Ada subset and corresponding object code have been implemented. The translator for Ada produces SPL output while that for object code produces Fair Transition System (FTS) for reasons explained in section 6.2. The features of generating SPL/FTS and the underlying modeling are discussed in the following.

6.1   Generating SPL/FTS for the Ada Source

Some of the features of the translation scheme are discussed below:

- Each Ada function/procedure is translated into a SPL procedure.
- The Ada has support for many types of data structures like records, aggregates, enumerated types which do not have corresponding types

in SPL. Hence, the translators implemented for Ada handle only the basic data types which have corresponding types in SPL.

- The Ada has support for syntactic constructs like *case* ..., *do* ... *while* etc. which do not have corresponding statements in SPL. This requires that the translator use the concept of *abstract interpretation* to map a given construct into a set of equivalent statements. Thus, for example a *case* statement will be translated as a *if* ... *then* ... *else if* ... in SPL.
- The function invocations in Ada and object code are translated to corresponding function invocations in SPL or FTS. These functions are required not to have any side-effects (STeP assumption).
- Procedures are modeled as multiple functional assignments to **out** variables.

The **in** and **out** variables and their mutual dependencies are required to be explicitly annotated (as SPARK annotations) in the programs input to the translators, so that the functional assignment relationships between the **in** and **out** variables can be inferred. Some illustrative examples are shown in Table 1. Let us consider a procedure to multiply two matrices and the result returned in a third matrix. In SPL, the data type *Matrix* is to be specified as user defined type with corresponding axioms (not shown). The annotated Ada declaration and the corresponding SPL code is shown in Table 1.

Table 1. Ada-SPL mapping

Annotated Ada Declaration	SPL Translation
Multiply (X,Y: in Matrix,Z:out Matrix) -# derives Z from X,Y	in X,Y:Matrix out Z:Matrix Z:=Multiply_Z(X,Y)
Exchange(X,Y: in out float) -# derives X from Y & -# Y from X;	in X,Y:rat out_mX,_mY:rat _mX:=Exchange_X(Y) X:=_mX _mY:=Exchange_Y(X) Y:= _mY

Consider a procedure *Exchange* for exchanging two variables as shown in Table 1. which is called from a procedure being analyzed. The convention of naming the functions in SPL modeling the procedure is <procedure name_<Ada variable name which is exported > (list of variables modifying the exported variable). The assumptions made in translating functions and procedures can be easily ensured by using SPARK tools [3] for Ada.

Therefore, the analysis support provided by likes of SPARK environment is essential before the validation of object code is undertaken.

6.2   Generating FTS for the Object Code

The object code is translated directly into FTS for reasons explained below. The iterative type of statements from HLL program may be translated to object code by using conditional and unconditional branching statements because i960 processor has only binary branch statements and no *loop* statements. Since the predicates in the *loop* type of statement in the HLL (Ada) may be complex i.e. containing conjunction and disjunction of variables, it becomes very difficult to reconstruct a loop type construct in SPL from the form in which exists it in object code. This *reverse engineering* can only be done through extensive flow graph analysis. However, since the Fair Transition System syntax supports *goto*, it is straight forward to translate such constructs into Fair Transition Systems rather than into SPL. Hence the translator implemented for object code produces FTS directly instead of an SPL program.

In the implementation of the translator from i960 assembly instruction to FTS the main task lies in modelling the i960 assembly instructions and some illustrative instructions modelling are discussed in the following. Since many of the instructions in the instruction set have implicit operation, it is required to use SIMPLIFY/REWRITE rules to model the effect of the instruction. Some of the illustrative instructions are modelled as shown in Table.2. Let us take for example the `cmpi src1, src2` instruction which compares two integers and sets the condition flag `cc` to 4, 2 or 1 depending on the condition `src1 < src2, src1=src2` or `src1 > src2`. This is modelled as an assignment `cc:=cmp(src1,src2)` Let us

Table 2. i960 assembly-FTS mapping

Instruction	SPL/FTS Statement,	Declaration & Rule

cmpi src1,src2	cc:=cmp(src1,src2)	value $cmp : int * int \longrightarrow int$
		SIMPLIFY $cmp(src1, src2) \rightarrow$
		if($src1 < src2$) then 4 else
		if($src1 = src2$) then 2 else
		if ($src1 > src2$) then 1 else 0

shli len,src,dst
 	
shri len,src,dst
	dst:=src*power(2,len)
	
	dst:=src div power(2,len)
		value $power : int * int \longrightarrow$
		int
		REWRITE $\forall m, n : int\bullet$
		$power(m, n) \rightarrow$
		if($n = 0$) then 1 else
		if($n = 1$) then m else
		$m \star power(m, n - 1)$

consider the example of arithmetic shift **shli** and **shri** shown in Table 2. A multiplication or division by some power of two is usually implemented by an arithmetic shift left or right respectively when translated by the compiler.

The i960 processor supports movement of data between floating registers fp0-fp3 and other registers like r0-r15 and g0-g15. Since in our implementation the register sets r0-15 and g0-g15 are declared as integer types, operations involving this requires AXIOMs : $\forall m : rat \bullet (Real(Int(m)) = m)$ and $\forall m : int \bullet (Int(Real(m)) = m)$.

7   Conclusion and Future Work

OCV method was first tested successfully on test programs by carrying out manual translations to SPL or FTS. The implementation of translators from Ada subset to SPL and object code to FTS have been completed and trial proofs have been carried out. The translations are limited to data types supported in SPL. Using the system in the current form, we have been able to validate several Ada programs that are in actual use and had translation errors.

The object code validation is a task requiring special skills even in the presence of mechanized theorem provers. The implementation of the translators to SPL/FTS is a major step in reducing the total effort involved in object code validation. Human interaction is still required in constructing the interface mappings and in carrying out the proofs.

The technique generally works fine if there is a structural correspondence between the flow graph of the two programs. The common semantic representation should have capability to handle different type of data structures normally used in HLLs like Ada. Each verifiable unit, which is a function or procedure in our case, should be small enough, so that it is easily possible to establish state correspondence and construct interface mapping. This is not a problem if the software is nicely modularized following good software engineering practices where each module has a small cyclomatic number. This is generally a requirement for software to be used in safety-critical system.

The process of validation is quite arduous. However, even with our preliminary experience we find it to be very useful for the validator. On the fly validation[10] aids in generating correct code as large fraction of of target-dependent errors in compilers can be detected. Program annotation and assertions aid in the proof. If such assertions are carried into the object code, it will aid in handling optimizations, and also in certifying compilers that use the notions such as proof-carrying code.

References

1. Pneuli A., Siegel M., Singerman E.: *Translation validation* Proc. 4th TACAS, LNCS 1384, pp. 151-166. Springer-Verlag, 1998.
2. Pnueli A., Siegel M., and Shtrichman O.: *Translation Validation for Synchronous Languages*, Proc. 25th ICALP, LNCS, 1443, pp. 235-246, Springer-Verlag, 1998
3. Barnes John.:*High Integrity Ada: The SPARK Approach*, Addison-Wesley, 1997
4. Motor Industry Safety and Reliability Association(MISRA) of U.K., *Guidelines for the use of the C language in vehicle based software* MIRA, 1998
5. Manna Z. et. al.:*STeP : The Stanford Temporal Prover, version 1.2 Educational Release, Users Manual*, CS Dept., Standford Univ., 1996
6. Manna Z., Pneuli A. : *Temporal Verification of Reactive Systems* Springer Verlag, 1995
7. Abadi M., Lamport L. *The existance of refinement mappings*, Theoretical Computer Science, 82, pp. , Elsevier, 1991
8. Benvinste A., P. Le Guernic, Jacquemot C.: *Synchronous Programming with event and relations: the SIGNAL language and its semantics.* SCP, 16, pp. 1991.
9. Dijkstra E.W : *A Discipline of Programming*, Prentice Hall, 1967
10. G.C. Necula, *Compiling With Proofs*, Ph.D. Thesis, CMU, 1998

Real-Time Program Refinement
Using Auxiliary Variables

Ian Hayes

School of Computer Science and Electrical Engineering,
The University of Queensland, Brisbane, 4072, Australia.
ianh@csee.uq.edu.au

Abstract. Real-time program development can be split into a machine-independent phase, that derives a machine-independent real-time program from a specification, and a machine-dependent phase, that checks that the compiled program will meet its deadlines when executed on the target machine.

In this paper we extend a machine-independent real-time programming language with auxiliary variables. These are introduced to facilitate both reasoning about the correctness of real-time programs and the expression of timing deadlines, and hence the calculation of timing constraints on paths through a program. The auxiliary variable concept is extended to auxiliary parameters to procedures.

1 Introduction

Our overall goal is to provide a method for the formal development of real-time programs. One problem with real-time programming is that the timing characteristics of a program are not known until it is compiled for a particular machine, whereas we would prefer a *machine-independent* program development method. The approach we have taken is to partition program development into two phases: a *machine-independent phase*, in which a machine-independent program is derived from a specification; and a *machine-dependent phase*, in which the program is compiled and is checked to ensure that all deadlines within the program are met. The approach is facilitated by the use of a machine-independent real-time programming language, that extends a standard real-time programming language with constructs to allow the expression of deadlines. The crucial extension is a *deadline* command [6, 1], of the form '**deadline** D' that on execution takes no time and guarantees to complete by absolute time D. In isolation such a command cannot be implemented, but if it can be shown that all execution paths leading to the deadline reach it before time D, then it can be removed. This process can itself be split into two phases: *timing constraint analysis* which for each non-dead path [4] leading to a deadline determines the timing constraint that guarantees that the deadline will be met [2]; and *worst-case execution-time analysis*, which checks that the worst-case execution time of the code on each path meets its timing constraint [11].

M. Joseph (Ed.): FTRTFT 2000, LNCS 1926, pp. 170–184, 2000.

In addition to the deadline command, the machine-independent programming language may also contain logical constants and assumptions [12, 7]. These allow assumptions about the program state, including timing assumptions, to be expressed within the program and hence facilitate timing constraint analysis.

In this paper we add *auxiliary variables* to our machine-independent programming language. Auxiliary variables may only be used within specifications, assumptions, deadlines and assignments to auxiliary variables. Hence they do not have to be implemented in the compiled code. During the refinement process they can be introduced to simplify the development process and to allow the expression of timing deadlines. Auxiliary variables can be of any type, but of particular significance are auxiliary variables of type *Time*. These can be used to refer to the time of significant events in the environment of the program or to the time at which a point in the program is reached.

We also allow auxiliary parameters to procedures. These allow auxiliary information to be passed across a procedure's interface. The auxiliary parameters are used to facilitate the specification of timing deadlines in one component with respect to events in another. There is no need to actually pass auxiliary parameters in the compiled code.

Related work. Hooman and Van Roosmalen [10] have developed a platform-independent approach to real-time software development similar to ours. Their approach makes use of timing annotations that are associated with commands. The annotations allow the capture in auxiliary timing variables of the time of occurrence of significant events that occur with the associated command, and the expression of timing deadlines on the command relative to such timing variables. They give an example of a program that reads an input value x from d_1, calculates y as some function of x and outputs y to d_2.

$$in(d_1, x)[m?]; \; y := f(x); \; out(d_2, y)[< m + U]$$

The constructs in square brackets are timing annotations [10, Sect. 2]. On the input the annotation 'm?' indicates that the time at which the input occurs should be assigned to timing variable m, and on the output the annotation '$< m + U$' requires the output to take effect before $m + U$, i.e., within U time units of the input time. Hooman and Van Roosmalen keep timing annotations separate from the rest of the program. They recognise that this syntactic restriction is not necessary but advance the following arguments [10, Sect. 2].

1. By not introducing timing variables in the program domain it is possible to first construct a functionally correct program, and then consider timing requirements.
2. By forbidding the use of program variables in the time domain, it becomes syntactically impossible to introduce data dependencies in the timing requirements. Such data dependencies usually complicate correctness proofs considerably.

With regard to the first point, our experience indicates that the specification of a real-time program often combines both timing and functional requirements in an intertwined fashion. Part of the development process is separating out the timing requirements.

With regard to the second point, we agree that data dependencies can complicate correctness proofs, but for some applications they are unavoidable, and hence we would like our methods to allow them. For example, a real-time program handling a low-level communications protocol may read a value from an input channel that indicates the length of the rest of the message, and the time constraint on reading the rest of the message is dependent on its length.

Our work builds on all the above work to develop an approach that is more general. As in our earlier work timing deadlines are considered commands (rather than annotations) and given a semantics as for any other command. The generalisation introduced in this paper allows timing events, as well as other auxiliary information, to be captured and used in commands and as auxiliary parameters to procedures. The generalisations allow for a more flexible approach to specifying and reasoning about timing constraints.

Sect. 2 introduces the machine-independent, wide-spectrum language used for specification, and refinement to code. Sect. 3 presents an example refinement that makes use of auxiliary variables and auxiliary procedure parameters, and Sect. 4 discusses timing constraint analysis.

2   Language and semantics

We model time by nonnegative real numbers:

$$Time \mathrel{\widehat{=}} \{r : \textbf{real} \mid 0 \leq r < \infty\}.$$

The real-time refinement calculus makes use of a special real-valued variable, τ, for the current time. To allow for nonterminating programs, we allow τ to take on the value infinity (∞):

$$Time_\infty \mathrel{\widehat{=}} Time \cup \{\infty\}.$$

We refer to the set of variables in scope as the environment, and use the name ρ for the environment. In real-time programs we distinguish five kinds of variables: inputs, $\rho.in$, which are under external control; outputs, $\rho.out$, which are under the control of the program; local variables, $\rho.local$, which are under the control of the program, but unlike outputs are not externally visible; auxiliary variables, $\rho.aux$, which are similar to local variables, but are restricted to appear only in assumptions, specifications, deadline commands and assignments to auxiliary variables; and the current time variable, τ. Inputs and outputs are modelled as functions from $Time$ to the declared type of the variable, e.g., given the declaration, '**input** beam : boolean', beam is modelled as a function from $Time$ to boolean, with $beam(t)$ giving the value of beam at time t. Note that it is not meaningful to talk about the value of a variable at time infinity. Only the current time variable, τ, may take on the value infinity.

We use the term *state* to refer to the non-external variables, (i.e., the non-trace variables), $\rho.state = \rho.local \cup \rho.aux \cup \{\tau\}$. State variables are modelled by values of their declared type ($Time_\infty$ for τ).

In earlier work [13, 7] all variables (including locals) were modelled as functions of time (timed traces). For auxiliary variables this is not possible, because assignments to auxiliary variables take no time and a timed trace only allows a variable to have a single value at any one time. Hence within the semantics of a command, we represent an auxiliary variable, x, by its value before the execution of the command, x_0, and its value after the execution of the command, x. Having introduced this model for auxiliary variables, we decided to use the same model for local variables. Either model could be used for local variables, but choosing a similar model for auxiliary and local variables makes the semantics a little simpler.

In this paper we represent the semantics of a command by a predicate in a form similar to that of Hehner [8, 9]. The predicate relates the initial and final values of the state variables as well as constraining the traces of the outputs over time. All our commands insist that time does not go backwards: $\tau_0 \leq \tau$. The meaning function, $\mathcal{M}$, takes the variables in scope, ρ, and a command C and returns the corresponding predicate, $\mathcal{M}_\rho(C)$. As for Hehner, refinement of commands (in an environment, ρ) is defined as reverse entailment:

$$C \sqsubseteq_\rho D \,\widehat{=}\, \mathcal{M}_\rho(C) \Leftarrow \mathcal{M}_\rho(D)$$

where '$P \Leftarrow Q$' holds if for all possible values of the variables, whenever Q holds, P holds.

Real-time specification command. We define a possibly nonterminating real-time *specification command* similar to that of Morgan [12],

$$\infty x \colon [P, \ Q] \,,$$

where x is a vector of variables called the *frame*, the predicate P is the assumption made by the specification, and the predicate Q is its effect. The '∞' at the beginning is just part of the syntax; it reminds us that the command might not terminate. The assumption P is assumed to hold at the start time of the command. The frame, x, of a specification command lists those variables that may be modified by the command. The frame may not include inputs. The current time variable, τ, is implicitly in the frame. All outputs not in the frame, i.e., those in $\rho.out$ but not x, are defined to be stable for the duration of the command, provided the assumption holds initially. We define the predicate *stable* by

$$stable(v, S) \,\widehat{=}\, S \neq \{\} \Rightarrow (\exists x \bullet v(\!|S|\!) = \{x\})$$

where $v(\!|S|\!)$ is the image of the set S through the function v. We allow the first argument of stable to be a vector of variables, in which case all variables in the vector are stable. To specify the closed interval of times from s until t, we use the notation $\lceil s \ldots t \rceil$. The open interval is specified by $(\!\lceil s \ldots t \rceil\!)$. We also allow half-open, half-closed intervals. The operator '\' is set difference.

Definition 1 (real-time specification). *Given variables, ρ, a frame, x contained in $\rho.local \cup \rho.aux \cup \rho.out$, a predicate P involving the variables in ρ (including τ), and a predicate Q involving variables in ρ, and initial variables (zero-subscripted variables) corresponding to those in $\rho.state$, the meaning of a possibly nonterminating real-time specification command is defined by the following.*

$$\mathcal{M}_\rho\left(\infty x\colon [P, \ Q]\right) \ \widehat{=} \ \begin{array}{l} \tau_0 \leq \tau \ \wedge \\ ((\tau_0 < \infty \wedge P_0) \Rightarrow (Q \wedge stable(\rho.out \setminus x, \lfloor \tau_0 \ldots \tau \rfloor))) \end{array}$$

P_0 stands for the predicate P with all occurrences of τ, and local and auxiliary variables that are in the frame, replaced by their zero-subscripted forms.

Note that if P does not hold initially the command still guarantees that time does not go backwards. Because τ may take on the value infinity, the above specification command allows nontermination. As abbreviations, if P is omitted, then it is taken to be *true*, and if the frame is empty the ':' is omitted.

Primitive real-time commands can be defined in terms of equivalent specification commands. In Fig. 1 we define: a terminating specification command, $x\colon [P, \ Q]$; the null command, **skip**, that does nothing and takes no time; a command, **idle**, that does nothing but may take time; an absolute delay command; a multiple assignment; the deadline command; a command, **read**, to sample a value from an external input; a command, **write**, to output a value to an external output, o, (we allow references to o within the expression B – these refer to the initial value of o); a command, **gettime**, to obtain the current time; and an assumption. The expressions used in the commands are assumed to be idle-stable, that is, their value does not change over time provided all the variables under the control of the program are stable. In practice this means that the expressions cannot refer to τ or to the value of external inputs.

Definition 2 (idle-stable). *Given variables ρ, an expression E is idle-stable provided, $\tau_0 \leq \tau \wedge stable(\rho.out, \lfloor \tau_0 \ldots \tau \rfloor) \Rrightarrow E \left[\tau \backslash \tau_0 \right] = E.$*

The **deadline** command is unusual. It takes no time and guarantees to complete by the given deadline. It is not possible to implement a deadline command by generating code. Instead we need to check that the code generated for a program that contains a deadline command will always reach the deadline command by its deadline [2]. We discuss this further in Sect. 4.

Compound real-time commands. Because we allow nonterminating commands, we need to be careful with our definition of sequential composition. If the first command of the sequential composition does not terminate, then we want the effect of the sequential composition on the values of the outputs over time to be the same as the effect of the first command. This is achieved by ensuring that for any command in out language, if it is executed at $\tau = \infty$, it has no effect. (For the specification command this is achieved by the assumption $\tau_0 < \infty$ in its definition.) Here we provide a definition of sequential composition in terms of the effects of the two commands.

Definition 3 (primitive real-time commands). *Given a vector of variables, x, not including any inputs; a predicate, P, with no references to initial state variables; a predicate, Q, that may refer to initial state variables; an idle-stable, time-valued expression D; a vector of idle-stable expressions, E, of the same length as x and assignment compatible with x; a local variable, v; an input i that is assignment compatible with v; an output o; an idle-stable expression, B, that is assignment compatible with o; and a time-valued local variable, t; the real-time commands are defined as follows.*

$$x\colon \begin{bmatrix} P, & Q \end{bmatrix} \mathrel{\widehat{=}} \infty x\colon \begin{bmatrix} P, & Q \wedge \tau < \infty \end{bmatrix} \qquad \textbf{deadline } D \mathrel{\widehat{=}} \begin{bmatrix} \tau_0 = \tau \leq D \end{bmatrix}$$

$$\textbf{skip} \mathrel{\widehat{=}} \begin{bmatrix} \tau_0 = \tau \end{bmatrix} \qquad\qquad v : \textbf{read}(i) \mathrel{\widehat{=}} v\colon \begin{bmatrix} v \in i (\!(\tau_0 \dots \tau]\!) \end{bmatrix}$$

$$\textbf{idle} \mathrel{\widehat{=}} \begin{bmatrix} \tau_0 \leq \tau \end{bmatrix} \qquad\qquad o : \textbf{write}(B) \mathrel{\widehat{=}}$$

$$\textbf{delay until } D \mathrel{\widehat{=}} \begin{bmatrix} D \leq \tau \end{bmatrix} \qquad\qquad o\colon \begin{bmatrix} def(B_0), & o(\tau) = B_0 \end{bmatrix}$$

$$x := E \mathrel{\widehat{=}} x\colon \begin{bmatrix} def(E), & x = E\begin{bmatrix} \frac{x_0}{x} \end{bmatrix} \end{bmatrix}, \qquad t : \textbf{gettime} \mathrel{\widehat{=}} t\colon \begin{bmatrix} \tau_0 \leq t \leq \tau \end{bmatrix}$$

$$\text{where } x \text{ does not include outputs} \qquad \{P\} \mathrel{\widehat{=}} \begin{bmatrix} P, & \tau_0 = \tau \end{bmatrix}$$

Predicate $def(E)$ characterises those states in which the expressions E are well defined, i.e., there are no divisions by zero, etc. For the deadline command, D need not be idle-stable because a deadline takes no time. For the write command, B_0 stands for $B[o\backslash o(\tau_0)]$.

Fig. 1. Definition of primitive real-time commands

Definition 4 (sequential composition). *Given variables, ρ, and real-time commands, C and D, their sequential composition is defined by the following.*

$$\mathcal{M}_\rho (C; D) \mathrel{\widehat{=}} \exists \rho.state' \bullet \mathcal{M}_\rho (C) [\rho.state\backslash\rho.state'] \wedge$$
$$\mathcal{M}_\rho (D) [\rho.state_0\backslash\rho.state']$$

Recall that $\rho.state = \rho.local \cup \rho.aux \cup \{\tau\}$. Note that even if the precondition of the second command does not hold, the sequential composition still guarantees the effect of the first command and that the finish time is greater than or equal to the finish time of the first command.

A variable block introduces a new local or auxiliary variable. The allocation and deallocation of a local variable may take time. This is allowed for in the definition by the use of **idle** commands.

Definition 5 (block). *Given an environment, ρ, and a command, C,*

$$\mathcal{M}_\rho (\lbrack\!\lbrack \textbf{ var } v; \ C \ \rbrack\!\rbrack) \mathrel{\widehat{=}} (\exists v_0, v \bullet \mathcal{M}_{\rho'} (\textbf{idle}; C; \textbf{idle}))$$

where ρ' is ρ updated with the local variable v, and

$$\mathcal{M}_\rho (\lbrack\!\lbrack \textbf{ aux } x; \ C \ \rbrack\!\rbrack) \mathrel{\widehat{=}} (\exists x_0, x \bullet \mathcal{M}_{\rho''} (C))$$

where ρ'' is ρ updated with the auxiliary variable x.

We abbreviate multiple declarations with distinct names by merging them into a single block, e.g., $\lVert$ **var** v; **aux** x; $C \rVert = \lVert$ **var** v; $\lVert$ **aux** x; $C \rVert \rVert$.

Due to space limitations we do not attempt to give a complete definition of loops; more complete details can be found elsewhere [3]. Each iteration of a loop takes a minimum amount of time, d, which is strictly positive to avoid Zeno-like behaviour. A single branch loop, $DO \mathrel{\widehat{=}} \mathbf{do}\ B \to C\ \mathbf{od}$, can be characterised as follows: there exists a strictly positive time, d, such that

$$DO = \left(\lVert\ \mathbf{con}\ s;\ \{\tau = s\}\ ;\ [B]\ ;\ C;\ \mathbf{delay\ until}\ s + d\ \rVert;\ DO\right) \mathbin{\parallel} \left[\neg\ B\right]$$

There is a (deterministic) choice between two alternatives. The second alternative corresponds to the guard evaluating to false and termination of the loop. The first alternative corresponds to the guard evaluating to true. The logical constant s captures the start time of a single iteration. The guard evaluation (which typically takes time unless, for example, the guard is the constant $true$) is followed by the execution of the command, C. A delay is included at the end of an iteration to ensure the time is at least d time units later than the start time of the iteration, s. This ensures that even if the guard is the constant $true$ and the body is the null command **skip**, each iteration takes at least d time units and hence Zeno-like behaviour is avoided.

3   An example

Specification. To illustrate our approach we use the example of a conveyor belt that transports objects which are measured for their size and then sorted into a corresponding bin. A light beam is used to detect objects, and measure their size. The boolean input *beam* represents the detection of the light beam: its value is false (no light) at time t if and only if there is an object on the conveyor blocking the beam at time t. (We ignore failures of the light beam, etc.) The boolean output *lbin* selects between a bin for large objects (if it is true) and a bin for small objects (if it is false). The objects on the conveyor belt have a minimum length and separation. This translates to there being a minimum time, $MinW$, for which *beam* is false while an object passes the beam, and a minimum time, $MinS$, for which *beam* is true between objects.

To represent these properties we introduce two logical constants (specification variables) gs and ge, which represent the increasing sequences of times at which the beam goes true (no object) and false (object), respectively. The name gs (ge) abbreviates 'gap start' ('end'), where the gap in question is the gap between objects during which *beam* is true. We include the initial gap before the first object and after the last object (if there are a finite number of objects). Both gs and ge are completely derived from *beam*. They are used purely to simplify expression of the properties of *beam*. Logical constants can be used for specification purposes but cannot appear in the compiled code of a program. The sequences begin with index one, have the same domain, and may be infinite (indicating an infinite number of objects passing on the conveyor over all time). We assume that there is no object on the conveyor for an initial period of at least *MinS*, i.e., $gs(1)$ is zero and $ge(1)$ is greater than or equal to *MinS*. The value of $ge(1)$ represents the time at which the first object breaks the beam. If there are only a finite number of objects that pass on the conveyor then the value of the last element of *ge* will be infinity, e.g., if no objects at all pass the light beam, then $ge(1)$ would be infinity. The following gives a specification of these variables, and the assumptions we make about them. The notation seq$^\infty$ *Time* stands for the type of possibly infinite sequences of times, with indices starting at one. As well as giving the types of the variables and constants, we also give their units of measurement [5].

input *beam* : *boolean*; **output** *lbin* : *boolean*;
con *gs*, *ge* : seq$^\infty$ *Time*;
const $MinS = 40\,\mathrm{ms}$; $MinW = 20\,\mathrm{ms}$; $MaxW = 40\,\mathrm{ms}$;

$$\left\{ \begin{array}{l} \mathrm{dom}\ ge = \mathrm{dom}\ gs \wedge 1 \in \mathrm{dom}\ gs \wedge gs(1) = 0\ \wedge \\ (\forall\, i : \mathrm{dom}\ gs \bullet MinS \le ge(i) - gs(i)\ \wedge \\ \quad (i \ne 1 \Rightarrow MinW \le gs(i) - ge(i-1) \le MaxW))\ \wedge \\ (\forall\, t : Time \bullet beam(t) \quad (\exists\, i : \mathrm{dom}\ gs \bullet t \in \{gs(i) \dots ge(i)\})) \end{array} \right\}$$

The task of the program is to measure the size of the passing objects, and select the bin into which they are to be placed. We assume that the conveyor moves with velocity *vel* metres per second. The size of an object can only be measured approximately. Hence the specification allows a margin of error, *mrgn*, in determining whether an object is large or small. If an object is of size greater than or equal to $limit + mrgn$ then it must go in the large bin. If its size is less than or equal to $limit - mrgn$ it must go in the small bin. Objects with sizes between $limit - mrgn$ and $limit + mrgn$ can go in either bin. We assume that the value of *mrgn* has been adjusted (decreased) to take into account fluctuations in the velocity of the conveyor. The predicate *ObjSize* relates the jth object to the bins it is allowed to be placed in.

const $vel = 1\,\mathrm{m}\,/\,\mathrm{s}$; $limit = 30\,\mathrm{mm}$; $mrgn = 1\,\mathrm{mm}$; $bin\_limit = 10\,\mathrm{ms}$;
$ObjSize(j, b) \;\widehat{=}\; \textbf{let}\ sz = vel * (gs(j+1) - ge(j)) \bullet$
$\quad (sz > limit + mrgn \Rightarrow b) \wedge (sz < limit - mrgn \Rightarrow \neg\, b)$

The output *lbin* controls the bin selector. In order for the object to be placed in the correct bin, *lbin* should have the correct value from time bin_limit after the end of the jth object ($gs(j + 1)$) through until the next object is detected ($ge(j + 1)$). We introduce the predicate *ObjBin* to abbreviate this condition.

$ObjBin(j) \;\widehat{=}\; (\exists\, b : boolean \bullet ObjSize(j, b)\ \wedge$
$\qquad\qquad lbin(\{gs(j+1) + bin\_limit \dots ge(j+1)\}) = \{b\})$

The program is specified using a nonterminating specification command with a termination time, τ, of infinity.

$$\infty lbin : [\tau = \infty \wedge (\forall\, j : \mathbb{N} \bullet 1 \le j \wedge j + 1 \in \mathrm{dom}\ gs \Rightarrow ObjBin(j))] \qquad (1)$$

The main program code. Before going through the details of the refinement of the above specification, we give the final machine-independent program in Fig. 2. It makes use of a procedure *Await* (specified in Sect. 3.1) that waits for the beam to attain the value of its first parameter and returns an approximation to the time at which this occurs. The program makes use of the auxiliary variable *i* which counts the objects as they pass. The local variables *st* and *et* capture the start and finish times of the *i*th object (approximately), and the variable *size* is used to calculate the (approximate) size of the object from the time it took to pass and its velocity. If the calculated size is greater than or equal to *limit* then *lbin* is set to *true*, otherwise it is set to *false*. It is assumed that the program starts when the current time, τ, is at least *MinS* seconds before the first object passes through the beam.

$\|[$ **aux** $i : natural;$

$\quad A : \{\tau \leq ge(1) - MinS\}\ ;$

$\qquad i := 1;$

$\qquad$ **do** $true \rightarrow$

$\qquad\qquad$ **deadline** $ge(i);$

$\qquad\qquad \|[$ **var** $st, et : natural$ ms $;\ size : natural$ mm $;$

$\qquad\qquad\quad B : st \leftarrow Await(false,\ gs(i), ge(i)\ );$ -- start of object at $ge(i)$

$\qquad\qquad\quad C : et \leftarrow Await(true,\ ge(i), gs(i+1)\ );$ -- end of object at $gs(i+1)$

$\qquad\qquad\qquad size := (et - st) * vel;$

$\qquad\qquad\qquad lbin : \textbf{write}(limit \leq size);$

$\qquad\qquad\quad D : \boxed{\textbf{deadline}\ gs(i+1) + bin\_limit}\ ;$

$\qquad\qquad\qquad i := i + 1$

$\qquad\qquad]|$

$\qquad$ **od**

$]|$

Fig. 2. Main program

In addition to the expected standard code there are deadline commands and a number of uses of the auxiliary variable, *i*, and logical constants; these are highlighted within boxes. These are used to ensure that the operation of the program takes place in a timely fashion. No code needs to be generated for any of the highlighted constructs. Their purpose is to facilitate reasoning and to allow the specification of timing constraints via deadline commands.

3.1   Specification of procedure Await

The task of procedure *Await* is to wait until *beam* takes on the value of its first argument, *val*, and return in result *pt* (an approximation to) the time at which the value of *beam* changes to *val*. To allow simpler specification of the procedure, two auxiliary parameters are used: *prev* gives the (past) time at which *beam* previously changed, and *event* gives the (future) time of the awaited change. When *Await* is called, the time is after *prev*. The procedure may assume that *beam* is not equal to *val* from *prev* until *event*, and that once it changes to *val* it will remain equal to *val* for a time of at least *err*. If the value of *beam* never changes, then *Await* never returns. Otherwise it returns the result, *pt*, which is an approximation to *event*.

$$\textbf{const } err = 1\,\textsf{ms}\,;\ \big\{\, err \leq MinS \wedge err \leq MinW \wedge err * vel \leq mrgn \,\big\}\,;$$

$$\textbf{procedure } pt : time \leftarrow Await(val : \textbf{boolean};\ \textbf{aux } prev, event : Time) =$$

$$\infty pt: \begin{bmatrix} prev \leq \tau \wedge & event = \tau = \infty \vee \\ beam (\!(\vdash prev\,...\,event\,\dashv)\!) = \{\neg\,val\} \wedge & , \ (event < \infty \wedge \tau < \infty \wedge \\ beam (\!(\vdash event\,...\,event + err\,\dashv)\!) = \{val\} & event \leq pt \leq event + err) \end{bmatrix}$$

The implementation of *Await* in Fig. 3 loops while testing the value of *beam* until it changes to equal *val*. The time is initially (and hence always) after *prev*. Hence when a value equal to *val* is read from *beam*, the time must be after *event*. The read must be completed before *event + err* in order to ensure that the procedure is not detecting some later change of *beam* to *val*. Hence the deadline after the read. If the value read is equal to *val* the loop terminates and one can deduce that *event* is less than or equal to the current time, τ. The deadline after the **gettime** ensures that the value of *pt* is a close enough approximation to *event*. If the loop never terminates then for any time, t, there is a later time, t', at which both the condition for repeating ($p \neq val$) and the loop invariant (the assertion just before the **until**) hold, and hence, $t' \leq event + err$, holds for arbitrarily large values of t'. Therefore *event* must be infinity. Note that if the **repeat** loop never terminates then the deadline after the loop is never reached and does not have to be considered.

3.2   Refinement of the main program

To refine the specification of the main program we make use of a refinement rule for introducing a possibly non-terminating loop developed in earlier work [3]. The rule allows for the case in which the loop may terminate, although in our example the main program loop never terminates. Reasoning about a loop makes use of a loop invariant, but in the case of non-termination, the reasoning is quite different to what we are used to with a terminating loop. The loop invariant is required to be *idle-invariant*, that is, invariant over the passage of time if the program state and outputs are stable. This is so that if the invariant holds before evaluation of the guard, it holds after evaluation of the guard.

$\lVert$ **var** p : **boolean**;

   $\boxed{\textbf{aux } \textit{before} : \textit{Time};}$

  $\left\{ \textit{prev} \leq \tau \right\}$;

  repeat

     E : $\boxed{\textit{before} := \tau;}$

       p : **read**($\textit{beam}$);

    F : $\boxed{\textbf{deadline } \textit{event} + \textit{err};}$

       $\left\{ \begin{aligned} &(p = \textit{val} \Rightarrow \textit{event} \leq \tau) \wedge (p \neq \textit{val} \Rightarrow \textit{before} \leq \textit{event}) \wedge \\ &\tau \leq \textit{event} + \textit{err} \end{aligned} \right\}$

  until $p = \textit{val}$;

  $\left\{ \textit{event} \leq \tau \right\}$;

  pt : **gettime**;

  G : $\boxed{\textbf{deadline } \textit{event} + \textit{err}}$

$\rbrack\rbrack$

Fig. 3. Body of procedure Await

Definition 6 (idle-invariant). *A predicate* P *is* idle-invariant *provided,*

$$\tau_0 \leq \tau \wedge \textit{stable}(\rho.\textit{out}, [\tau_0 \ldots \tau]) \wedge P[\tau \backslash \tau_0] \Rrightarrow P.$$

Note that predicates of the form $\tau \leq D$ (where D is idle-stable) are not idle-invariant, but predicates of the form $D \leq \tau$ are.

If the loop body terminates, we require that it re-establishes the invariant, I, and hence if the loop terminates one can deduce $\tau < \infty \wedge \neg\, B \wedge I$. If the loop body does not terminate then it must establish some other condition, R. In this case the whole loop establishes $\tau = \infty \wedge R$. If the loop does not terminate but the loop body terminates on every iteration, then we can deduce the following predicate: $I_\infty \mathrel{\widehat{=}} (\forall\, t : \textit{Time} \bullet (\exists\, \rho.\textit{local}, \rho.\textit{aux}, \tau \bullet t \leq \tau \leq D \wedge B \wedge I))$. A deadline, D, is included at the start of the loop body. This allows the extra condition that the current time is before D to be included in I_∞, thus linking the invariant to the current time.

Law 7 (loop with nonterminating body). *Given an idle-stable, boolean-valued expression,* B; *an idle-invariant predicate,* I, *not involving* τ_0 *or initial (zero subscripted) variables; an time-valued expression,* D; *and a predicate* R *not involving* τ_0 *or any local or auxiliary variables (including initial variables); then*

$$\infty x\colon \left[I, \ (\tau < \infty \wedge \neg\, B \wedge I) \vee (\tau = \infty \wedge (I_\infty \vee R)) \right]$$

$\sqsubseteq$ **do** $B \to$ **deadline** D;

$$\infty x\colon \left[B \wedge I \wedge \tau \leq D, \ (\tau < \infty \wedge I) \vee (\tau = \infty \wedge R) \right]$$

  od

The predicate R may not depend on final state variables because the values of these are not defined at time infinity, and it may not refer to τ_0 or initial variables because R is used both in the specification, in which τ_0 is the start time of the whole loop, and in the body of the loop, in which τ_0 is the start time of an iteration. In order to refer to the start time of the whole loop within R it is necessary to introduce an explicit logical constant to stand for the start time.

To apply this law to our example we introduce an auxiliary variable, i, which contains the number of the next object to be recognised. The next object breaks the beam at time $ge(i)$. Hence this is a suitable deadline for the start of the loop body. The invariant states that all previous objects have been placed in the correct bin for their size. The most recent object, number $i - 1$, (if there was one) is special because the bin selector must be held at its current value until the start of the next object (within the next iteration).

$$I \,\widehat{=}\, 1 \leq i \wedge gs(i) \leq \tau \wedge i \in \mathrm{dom}\ gs \wedge (\forall j : \mathbb{N} \bullet 1 \leq j < i-1 \Rightarrow ObjBin(j))$$
$$\wedge\, (i \neq 1 \Rightarrow (\exists\, b : boolean \bullet ObjSize(i-1, b) \wedge$$
$$lbin(\!\lvert\!\leftarrow gs(i) + bin\_limit \dots \tau \dashv\!\rvert\!) = \{b\} \wedge lbin(\tau) = b)))$$

The final $lbin(\tau) = b$ allows for the case in which τ has not yet reached $gs(i) + bin\_limit$. The invariant is established by setting i to 1.

If there are no more objects on the conveyor (ever) then the body of the loop will not terminate. In this case the body of the loop must achieve the goal of the main program. The predicate R strengthens the goal with the condition that there are only a finite number of objects on the conveyor.

$$R \,\widehat{=}\, (\exists\, i : \mathrm{dom}\ gs \bullet i + 1 \notin \mathrm{dom}\ gs) \wedge$$
$$(\forall j : \mathbb{N} \bullet 1 \leq j \wedge j + 1 \in \mathrm{dom}\ gs \Rightarrow ObjBin(j))$$

For the loop in the example, the guard is the constant, $true$, and hence the postcondition in the specification in the law reduces to $\tau = \infty \wedge (I_\infty \vee R)$. This predicate must imply the goal of the main program specification (1). If R holds then this follows because R is a strengthening of the goal. If R does not hold, then it suffices to show

$$(\forall i : \mathrm{dom}\ gs \bullet i + 1 \in \mathrm{dom}\ gs) \wedge I_\infty$$
$$\Rightarrow (\forall j : \mathbb{N} \bullet 1 \leq j \wedge j + 1 \in \mathrm{dom}\ gs \Rightarrow ObjBin(j))$$

This condition expands and simplifies to

$$(\forall i : \mathrm{dom}\ gs \bullet i + 1 \in \mathrm{dom}\ gs) \wedge$$
$$(\forall t : Time \bullet$$
$$(\exists \tau : Time;\ i : \mathbb{N} \bullet t \leq \tau \leq ge(i) \wedge 1 \leq i \wedge gs(i) \leq \tau \wedge i \in \mathrm{dom}\ gs \wedge$$
$$(\forall j : \mathbb{N} \bullet 1 \leq j < i-1 \Rightarrow ObjBin(j)) \wedge (i \neq 1 \Rightarrow \dots)))$$
$$\Rightarrow (\forall j : \mathbb{N} \bullet 1 \leq j \Rightarrow ObjBin(j))$$

It suffices to show that for any positive j, that $ObjBin(j)$ holds. To do this we choose t such that $gs(j + 2) \leq t$. From the above condition there exist τ and i such that

$$gs(j + 2) \leq t \leq \tau \leq ge(i) \Rightarrow j + 2 \leq i \Rightarrow j < i - 1$$

and hence $ObjBin(j)$ follows from the remainder of the above condition.

After applying the law for introducing a nonterminating loop we are left with the following loop body.

deadline $ge(i)$;

$$\infty i, lbin: \left[I \wedge \tau \leq ge(i), \ (\tau < \infty \wedge I) \vee (\tau = \infty \wedge R) \right] \qquad (2)$$

We introduce three local variables, st, et and $size$ to store the start and finish times of the next object on the conveyor and the size of the object, respectively, and refine the body of the loop via the introduction of sequential compositions, procedure calls, assignments, a write and a deadline command. The details of these steps are similar to standard refinement steps and are omitted here.

4   Timing constraint analysis

Internal to the procedure. In order for compiled machine code to implement the machine-independent program it must guarantee to meet all the deadlines. The auxiliary variables and parameters introduced above aid this analysis. There are two deadlines within the procedure *Await* (Fig. 3). The deadline (F) within the **repeat** loop is reached initially from the entry to the procedure, and subsequently on each iteration. We defer analysis of the entry path to the analysis of the main program, because the context of the main program is necessary for the analysis. For an iteration we consider the path (shown in Fig. 4) that starts at the assignment to *before* (E), reads the value of *beam* into p, passes through the deadline (F), loops back to the start of the **repeat** because p is not equal to *val*, performs the assignment to *before* (E), reads the value of *beam*, and reaches the deadline (F). The guard evaluation is represented by $[p \neq val]$, which indicates that in order for the path to be followed, p must not be equal to *val* at that point in the path. (In refinement calculus terms $[p \neq val]$ is a coercion [12].) The initial

---

$E :$ *before* $:= \tau$;
  $p :$ **read**($beam$);
$F :$ **deadline** $event + err$;
  $\left\{ (p = val \Rightarrow event \leq \tau) \wedge (p \neq val \Rightarrow before \leq event) \wedge \tau \leq event + err \right\}$
  $[p \neq val]$;
$E :$ *before* $:= \tau$;
  $p :$ **read**($beam$);
$F :$ **deadline** $event + err$

Fig. 4. Repetition path in Await

---

time assigned to *before*, i.e., the time at which the path begins execution, must be before time *event* because the value of p was not equal to *val*, and the final deadline on the path is $event + err$. Hence, if the path is guaranteed to execute in less than time *err*, it will always meet its deadline. If this path is guaranteed to reach its deadline then any path with this as a suffix is also guaranteed to meet the final deadline.

A similar analysis can be performed for the path exiting the **repeat** loop to the final deadline in *Await*. The path is the same as that in Fig. 4 except that it is extended past the deadline within the loop (F), exits the loop because $p = val$, and reads the current time into pt, before reaching the final deadline (G). The constraint on this path is also *err*.

The main program. The analysis of the main program has to take into account deadlines within the procedure calls. There is a path that starts at (A) in Fig. 2. The path initialises i to 1, enters the loop, passes through the initial deadline, allocates the local variables *st*, *et* and *size*, makes the first call to *Await* (B), and within *Await* allocates and assigns the local and auxiliary variables corresponding to the formal value parameters, allocates the local variable p, extends the auxiliary variables with *before*, and follows the path into the **repeat** loop, ending at the first deadline (F) of $event + err$. The initial assertion guarantees the start time of the path is less than or equal to $ge(1) - MinS$. For this call to *Await*, *event* is $ge(1)$ and hence the final deadline is $ge(1) + err$. Therefore a suitable constraint on the path is $ge(1) + err - (ge(1) - MinS) = MinS + err = 41\text{ ms}$. If this path is guaranteed to execute in a time of less that 41 ms then the deadline is guaranteed to be reached. The remaining timing paths are analysed in a similar manner.

5   Conclusions

This paper has examined the addition of auxiliary variables to a machine-independent real-time programming language for use in specifying and reasoning about real-time programs, including timing constraint analysis. Auxiliary counter variables, such as i in the main program, can be used to relate the program state to the ith occurrence of an event. Auxiliary time variables can be used to keep track of times of relevant events. For example, auxiliary time parameters, *prev* and *event* in the procedure *Await* allowed the simplification of the specification of *Await* and allowed the expression of deadlines within the procedure relative to the time of occurrence of external events. In all cases the use of auxiliary variables/parameters does not generate any code in the final program. They are purely used to assist reasoning and timing constraint specification and analysis.

Acknowledgements. This research was funded by Australian Research Council (ARC) Large Grant A49937045, *Effective Real-Time Program Analysis.* I would like to thank Colin Fidge, Karl Lermer and Luke Wildman for feedback on earlier drafts of this paper, Brendan Mahony and Mark Utting for fruitful discussions on the topic of this paper, Andrew Lenart for his work on a summer project looking at auxiliary variables, and the members of IFIP Working Group 2.3 on Programming Methodology for feedback on this topic, especially Rick Hehner for his advice on how to simplify our approach.

References

[1] C. J. Fidge, I. J. Hayes, and G. Watson. The deadline command. *IEE Proceedings—Software*, 146(2):104–111, April 1999.

[2] S. Grundon, I. J. Hayes, and C. J. Fidge. Timing constraint analysis. In C. Mc-Donald, editor, *Computer Science '98: Proc. 21st Australasian Computer Science Conf. (ACSC'98)*, Perth, 4–6 Feb., pages 575–586. Springer-Verlag, 1998.

[3] I. J. Hayes. Reasoning about non-terminating loops using deadline commands. In Roland Backhouse and Jose Oliveira, editors, *Mathematics of Program Construction (MPC'2000)*, July 2000.

[4] I. J. Hayes, C. J. Fidge, and K. Lermer. Semantic identification of dead control-flow paths. Technical Report 99-32, Software Verification Research Centre, The University of Queensland, October 1999.

[5] I. J. Hayes and B. P. Mahony. Using units of measurement in formal specifications. *Formal Aspects of Computing*, 7(3):329–347, 1995.

[6] I. J. Hayes and M. Utting. Coercing real-time refinement: A transmitter. In D. J. Duke and A. S. Evans, editors, *BCS-FACS Northern Formal Methods Workshop (NFMW'96)*, Electronic Workshops in Computing. Springer Verlag, 1997.

[7] I. J. Hayes and M. Utting. A sequential real-time refinement calculus. Technical Report UQ-SVRC-97-33, Software Verification Research Centre, The University of Queensland, URL http://svrc.it.uq.edu.au, 1997.

[8] E. C. R. Hehner. Termination is timing. In J.L.A. van de Snepscheut, editor, *Mathematics of Program Construction*, volume 375 of *Lecture Notes in Computer Science*, pages 36–47. Springer-Verlag, June 1989.

[9] E. C. R. Hehner. *A Practical Theory of Programming*. Springer Verlag, 1993.

[10] J. Hooman and O. van Roosmalen. Formal design of real-time systems in a platform-independent way. *Parallel and Distributed Computing Practices*, 1(2):15–30, 1998.

[11] Sung-Soo Lim, Young Hyun Bae, Gyu Tae Jang, Byung-Do Rhee, Sang Lyul Min, Chang Yun Park, Heonshik Shin, Kunsoo Park, Soo-Mook Moon, and Chong Sang Kim. An accurate worst case timing analysis for RISC processors. *IEEE Trans. on Software Eng.*, 21(7):593–604, July 1995.

[12] C. C. Morgan. *Programming from Specifications*. Prentice Hall, second edition, 1994.

[13] M. Utting and C. J. Fidge. A real-time refinement calculus that changes only time. In He Jifeng, editor, *Proc. 7th BCS/FACS Refinement Workshop*, Electronic Workshops in Computing. Springer, July 1996. URL http://www.springer.co.uk/eWiC/Workshops/7RW.html.

On Refinement and Temporal Annotations [*]

Ron van der Meyden[1] and Yoram Moses[2]

[1] School of Computer Science and Engineering
The University of New South Wales, Sydney 2052, Australia
`meyden@cse.unsw.edu.au`
[2] Department of Electrical Engineering
Technion, Haifa, Israel
`moses@ee.technion.ac.il`

Abstract. This paper introduces the semantics of a wide spectrum language with a rich compositional structure that is able to represent both temporal specifications and sequential programs. A key feature of the language is the ability to represent partial correctness annotations expressed in temporal logic. A refinement relation is presented that enables refinement steps to make use of these partial correctness assertions. It is argued by means of an example that the approach presented allows for more flexible reasoning using temporal annotations than previous approaches, and that the added flexibility has significant value for program optimization.

Keywords: Refinement calculus, temporal logic, temporal refinement calculi

1   Introduction

Work on program refinement can be categorised into two classes. One of the most deeply explored approaches [Mor90,BvW98,Mor87] is *state-based*, premised on the use of predicate transformers and weakest preconditions as a semantic basis. This is natural for programs whose specifications are descriptions of input/output relations, of which predicate transformers are a generalization. One of the advantages of this approach is the ability to write specifications containing constructs modelling two distinct types of annotation. Annotations of one type, which we call *coercions*, are used to state properties that the program is *required* to satisfy. Annotations of the other type, which we call *assertions*, are more like conventional program annotations in that they are used to state properties that the program has been *proved* to satisfy.

Another class of refinement calculi, motivated directly by distributed programs, is *action-based* [GS86,Hol89,HL95,Win86,Lam94]. Work in this category typically begins with a process calculus. In a distributed setting, specifications and reasoning very frequently need to refer not just to the current state, but

[*] Work supported by an Australian Research Council Large Grant, and by the Technion fund for advancement of research. Thanks to Kai Engelhardt for helpful discussions on the topic of this paper.

M. Joseph (Ed.): FTRTFT 2000, LNCS 1926, pp. 185–202, 2000.

also to past and future events in the system. Thus, this approach enriches the process algebra with features of modal logic, typically Hennessy-Milner logic or the more expressive μ-calculus. On the other hand, these works do not contain the assertions available in the state-based approaches.

Our ultimate goal is to develop a framework for distributed programs that has both the rich compositional structure and temporal expressiveness of the process calculus based approaches and the ability to represent the two types of annotation available in the predicate transformer based approaches. Moreover, we aim for a high degree of flexibility in the use of assertions: given the temporal setting, we would like to be able to reason about, and refine, any program fragment based on properties established by any other program fragment, both past and future. Our contribution in this paper is to develop such a framework for sequential programs. There exist prior proposals [UF96] combining the expressive power of temporal formalisms and the annotational expressiveness of the predicate transformer based approaches to refinement, but we argue that our framework allows for some desirable modes of reasoning not available in these proposals. In particular, we show by means of an example (in Section 8) that it is possible in our framework to move annotations within the program in a manner that is not supported by other formalisms.

2   Syntax

The setting we are considering is one in which there is a single agent that performs actions, which in turn modify the state. We assume as given an *environment*, consisting of a tuple (S, A, R, π), where A is a set of basic *actions*, S is a set of *states*, $R \subseteq S \times A \times S$ is a transition relation describing the effect of actions on the state, and $\pi : Prop \to \mathcal{P}(S)$ is an *interpretation*, mapping each propositional constant in some set $Prop$ to a set of states. The environment will act as an implicit parameter in what follows.

Starting from a logical language $\mathcal{L}$ of formulas, which we shall define shortly, the set A of basic program actions, a set PV of *program variables* and a set CV of *constraint variables*, we define the class PT of *program templates* as follows.

$$P ::= \epsilon \mid a \mid Z \mid [\varphi, \psi]^X \mid [\varphi]^X \mid \{\varphi\}_J \mid P; P \mid P + P \mid P^\omega$$

where ϵ is a distinguished symbol representing the empty program, $a \in A$ is a basic action, $Z \in PV$ is a program variable, φ and ψ are formulae of $\mathcal{L}$, $X \in CV$ is a constraint variable, and $J \subseteq CV$ is a set of constraint variables. A program template containing no program variables will be called simply a *program*. The program $[\varphi]^X$ is called a *coercion*, while $[\varphi, \psi]^X$ is called a *specification*. We call these constructs *constraints*. A program of the form $\{\varphi\}_J$ is called an *assertion*. In contrast to coercions, an assertion does not constrain the execution. It is a statement, akin to a comment in the program text, whose truth depends on the rest of the program. The subscript J is called the *justification* of the assertion, and it keeps track of what constraints in the current program this assertion depends on. Intuitively, a program is called *valid* if the assertions in the program are all guaranteed to be satisfied. We will present a detailed motivation for the constraint variables and justifications in Section 5.

The operator ; represents sequential execution of programs. The operators +, representing nondeterministic choice, and $^\omega$, representing finite or infinite repetition, are nondeterministic. Together with coercions, they can be used to define the standard deterministic branching and looping operators **if- then - else** and **while**. We will use the following definitions of these constructs.

- **if**$^X\varphi$ **then** P **else** Q will stand for $([\varphi]^X; P) + ([\neg\varphi]^X; Q)$,   and
- **while**$^X\varphi$ **do** P will stand for $([\varphi]^X; P)^\omega; [\neg\varphi]^X$.

To define constraints and assertions, we use a modal logical language $\mathcal{L}$. For the sake of brevity, we use a simple version of propositional linear-time temporal logic. This language can be extended considerably without losing the properties we shall discuss. Given a set *Prop* of primitive propositions, the formulas of our language $\mathcal{L}$ are inductively defined as follows:

Every proposition in *Prop* is a formula, and if φ_1 and φ_2 are formulas then so are $\neg\varphi_1$, $\varphi_1 \wedge \varphi_2$, and $\Box\varphi_1$. We define **true** as $\neg(P \wedge \neg P)$, **false** as $\neg$**true**, $\varphi_1 \vee \varphi_2$ as $\neg(\neg\varphi_1 \wedge \neg\varphi_2)$, $\varphi_1 \rightarrow \varphi_2$ as $\neg\varphi_1 \vee \varphi_2$, and $\Diamond\varphi$ as $\neg\Box\neg\varphi$, as usual.

3   Semantics

3.1   Semantics of Formulas

Semantically, formulas of the modal language describe what is true at time points of the executions of programs in the environment (S, A, R, π). A *run* over (S, A, R, π) is defined by a pair $r = (h, \alpha)$ where $h : \mathbf{N} \rightarrow S$ and $\alpha : \mathbf{N} \rightarrow A$ such that $(h(n), \alpha(n), h(n+1)) \in R$ for all $n \in \mathbf{N}$. The h component is a *state history*, describing the sequence of states the system goes through. The component α is the *action history*, describing the sequence of actions taken. Intuitively, we think of $h(k)$ as the state at time k, and $\alpha(k)$ as the action performed at time k. A *point* is a pair (r, k) where r is a run and $k \in \mathbf{N}$ represents a time.

Formulas are said to be true or false at a point (r, k). The fact that φ is true at (r, k) is denoted by $r, k \models \varphi$, and is defined by induction on the structure of formulas as follows (here and elsewhere, we leave the environment implicit):

1. $r, k \models p$ for $p \in Prop$ if $h(k) \in \pi(p)$, where $r = (h, \alpha)$.
2. $r, k \models \neg\varphi$ if $r, k \not\models \varphi$.
3. $r, k \models \varphi_1 \wedge \varphi_2$ if both $r, k \models \varphi_1$ and $r, k \models \varphi_2$.
4. $r, k \models \Box\varphi$ if $r, k' \models \varphi$ holds for all $k' \geq k$.

3.2   Semantics of Programs

We will develop the complete meaning of the program constructs in a number of steps. We begin in this section by presenting a semantics of programs that ignores the role of assertions and constraint variables: we will introduce the semantic notions related to these once we have motivated them from some requirements on our approach to refinement.[1]

A *time interval* is a pair $[c, d]$ where c and d are elements of $\mathbf{N}^+ = \mathbf{N} \cup \{\infty\}$ with $c \leq d$. A *run interval* is a pair $r, [c, d]$ consisting of a run r and a time interval $[c, d]$. We will refer simply to "intervals" when the specific type of interval is clear from the context. We give semantics to programs in an operational style, by defining when an execution of a program P *occurs* over an interval $[c, d]$ in a run r, which we denote by $r, [c, d] \Vdash P$.

An *execution tree* for a program P is an ordered tree representing a possible execution of the program. Intuitively, such a tree describes one particular way in which the nondeterministic choices that may be made in running the program are resolved. The left to right ordering of nodes in a tree corresponds to precedence in time. Formally, an *execution tree* will be a finite or infinite tree T in which each node is adorned by a program template, subject to the following conditions on the nodes n of T:

1. If n is adorned by ϵ, by a program variable, a constraint, an assertion or a basic action, then n is a leaf.
2. If n is adorned by $P; Q$ then n has exactly two children, the leftmost adorned by P, the other adorned by Q.
3. If n is adorned by $P + Q$ then n has exactly one child, adorned by either P or Q.
4. If n is adorned by P^ω then n has exactly one child, adorned either by ϵ or by $P; (P^\omega)$.

An *execution tree for a program template* P is an execution tree whose root is adorned by P. We write $\mathcal{E}(P)$ for the set of execution trees of P.

Let T be an execution tree and $r = (h, \alpha)$ a run. We say that a mapping θ associating an interval with every node of T is an *embedding* of T in the interval $r, [c, d]$ if the following conditions are satisfied:

1. If n is the root of T then $\theta(n) = [c, d]$.
2. If n has a single child m then $\theta(n) = \theta(m)$.
3. If n has exactly two children m_1 and m_2 then there exists $e \leq f \leq g$ such that $\theta(m_1) = [e, f]$ and $\theta(m_2) = [f, g]$ and $\theta(n) = [e, g]$.
4. If n is adorned by the empty program ϵ and $\theta(n) = [e, f]$ then $e = f$.
5. If n is adorned by an assertion $\{\varphi\}_J$ and $\theta(n) = [e, f]$ then $e = f$.
6. If n is adorned by a basic action a and $\theta(n) = [e, f]$ then either $e = f = \infty$ or $e < \infty$, $f = e + 1$, and $\alpha(e) = a$.
7. If n is adorned by a coercion $[\varphi]^X$ and $\theta(n) = [e, f]$ then $e = f$ and if $e < \infty$ then $r, e \models \varphi$.
8. If n is adorned by a specification $[\varphi, \psi]^X$ and $\theta(n) = [e, f]$ then if $e < \infty$ and $r, e \models \varphi$ then $f < \infty$ and $r, f \models \psi$.

---

[1] Viewed in isolation, the definitions of this section could be given a simpler presentation: we go into the complexities of execution trees to prepare us for the later definition of validity.

9. If $\theta(n) = [e, f]$ then f is the least upper bound of the set of $g \in \mathbf{N}^+$ such that $\theta(m) = [g', g]$ for some *leaf* node m descended from n.

Notice that we made no special requirement about how θ should map a leaf adorned by a program variable $Z \in PV$. This is intentional, since in our view a program variable may be replaced by an arbitrary program, leading to an arbitrary mapping. In this sense, a program variable is treated just like a specification of the form $[\mathbf{false}, \mathbf{true}]$.

To understand the need for condition (9) of the definition of embedding, let P be the program $([\mathbf{true}]^X)^\omega$ and consider the infinite tree $T \in \mathcal{E}(P)$ depicted in Figure 1. (We omit the constraint variable X in this figure.) This tree depicts a computation in which a coercion is repeated infinitely often. Intuitively, as a coercion takes no time, this computation should take no time either. Suppose θ is an embedding of T into $r, [c, d]$. Thus, $\theta(\mathbf{root}(T)) = [c, d]$. It follows from conditions (2),(3) and (7) of the definition of embedding that $\theta(n) = [c, c]$ for all leaves n of T (each of which is adorned by $[\mathbf{true}]^X$). However, this still leaves open the possibility that $c < d$, which conflicts both with the intuition that the execution should take no time and with the intuition that the transition from time c to time d is effected by executing the sequence of statements represented at the leaves of the tree from left to right.

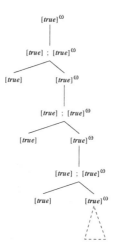

Fig. 1. A tree requiring a limit condition on embeddings

We write $r, [c, d] \Vdash_{T,\theta} P$ if $T \in \mathcal{E}(P)$ and θ is an embedding of T in the interval $r, [c, d]$. Intuitively, this means that T and θ describe an execution of P in this interval. We say that the program P *occurs* over $r, [c, d]$, denoted by $r, [c, d] \Vdash P$, if there exist T and θ such that $r, [c, d] \Vdash_{T,\theta} P$.

Define a program to be *concrete* if it does not contain assertions or specifications, it contains coercions only within **if** and **while** statements, and the formulas in these coercions contain no temporal operators. One can give a standard operational semantics to concrete programs, and establish its equivalence to the semantics presented above. We omit the details for reasons of space.

4   Refinement

In this section we consider some desiderata for the notion of program refinement for our framework. We propose some definitions in this section that are appropriate for programs not containing assertions. We will later need to adjust these definitions in order to accommodate assertions.

The notion of refinement we seek will be represented by means of a binary relation $\leq$ on programs, such that $P \leq Q$ when P is a refinement of Q. Intuitively, this means that the program P has less nondeterminism than Q, in the sense that every execution of P is an execution of Q. Recalling that our programs also function as specifications, an alternate way of phrasing this is that P carries more information, or is more constraining than Q. In order to support a reasonable calculus for refinement, we have the following desiderata for this refinement relation: it should be a reflexive, transitive relation satisfying

Monotonicity: If $P \leq Q$ and $C(Z)$ is a program template then $C(P) \leq C(Q)$.[2]
Reduction of Nondeterminism: $P \leq P + Q$ and $Q \leq P + Q$
Increase of Information: $[\varphi]^X \leq [\psi]^X$ if $\varphi \to \psi$ is valid.

We will say that a refinement relation is *adequate* if it satisfies the above conditions for programs not containing assertions.

Define a refinement relation $\sqsubseteq$ by having $P \sqsubseteq Q$ if for all intervals $r, [c, d]$, if $r, [c, d] \Vdash P$ then $r, [c, d] \Vdash Q$. We write $P \equiv Q$ when $P \sqsubseteq Q$ and $Q \sqsubseteq P$. It is not difficult to show that this definition satisfies all the properties above:

Theorem 1 *The binary relation $\sqsubseteq$ on program templates is adequate.*

Example 1. Consider a program that is to access a shared resource such as a printer, which is guarded by a locking mechanism. Only an application that has a lock on the resource can use it. Moreover, we wish to ensure that the program does not hold on to the lock indefinitely. We model this by a proposition have_lock which is defined to be true when the application has obtained a lock on the resource, and three (terminating) actions: get_lock, release_lock, and use_resource, corresponding to the action of fetching the lock, releasing the lock, and using the resource. Given an appropriate definition of the environment (omitted), the first two actions have the property that

$$\text{get\_lock} \ \sqsubseteq \ [\text{true}, \text{have\_lock}]^U \quad \text{and} \quad \text{release\_lock} \ \sqsubseteq \ [\text{true}, \neg\text{have\_lock}]^U$$

for any constraint variable U. Moreover,

$$\text{use\_resource} \ \sqsubseteq \ [\text{have\_lock}, \text{have\_lock}]^U$$

---

[2] We use the convention that if $C(Z)$ is a program template containing the program variable Z then $C(P)$ is the program template obtained by replacing every occurrence of Z in $C(Z)$ by P.

so that if started in a state where the application has the lock, the use of the resource will terminate in finite time, and does not relinquish the lock.

The restrictions on the use of the resource by the application can be guaranteed by requiring that the resource can only be used via a *legal access* procedure, defined by:

$$Access(X, Y) \quad = \quad [\mathbf{true}, \mathtt{have\_lock}]^X \; ; \; \mathtt{use\_resource} \; ; \; [\mathbf{true}, \Diamond \neg \mathtt{have\_lock}]^Y$$

Note that this allows that after using the resource the program need not release the lock immediately. However, it must ensure that the lock is eventually released. In a followup example in Section 8 we will demonstrate how this is possible. We now turn to implementing $Access(X, Y)$. From the fact that $\neg\mathtt{have\_lock} \rightarrow \Diamond\neg\mathtt{have\_lock}$ is a valid formula and the assumption that $\mathtt{release\_lock} \sqsubseteq [\mathbf{true}, \neg\mathtt{have\_lock}]^U$ we can show that $\mathtt{release\_lock} \sqsubseteq [\mathbf{true}, \Diamond\neg\mathtt{have\_lock}]^U$. Monotonicity of $\sqsubseteq$ now yields

$$(\mathtt{get\_lock} \; ; \; \mathtt{use\_resource} \; ; \; \mathtt{release\_lock}) \quad \sqsubseteq \quad Access(X, Y),$$

giving us one straightforward way of implementing $Access$.

The following example illustrates a sense in which our sequential framework is already able to capture some aspects of a distributed setting.

Example 2. The previous example treats the action of obtaining the lock as taking a single time step. This makes sense if time steps represent state transitions for the program we are developing, but if the program operates concurrently with other programs that may hold a lock on the resource, then we may wish to reason about the period during which the program waits for a lock held by another process to be released. This may be done by introducing another proposition $\mathtt{have\_lock}_e$ to represent that the environment of the program holds the lock, and an atomic action $\mathtt{lock}$ such that $\mathtt{lock} \sqsubseteq [\neg\mathtt{have\_lock}_e, \mathtt{have\_lock}]^X$, as well as an atomic action $\mathtt{skip}$ that does not change the value of $\mathtt{have\_lock}$ but may switch the value of $\mathtt{have\_lock}_e$. We may then implement the specification $[\mathbf{true}, \mathtt{have\_lock}]^U$ by the refinement

$$\Box(\mathtt{have\_lock}_e \rightarrow \Diamond\neg\mathtt{have\_lock}_e)]^X ; (\mathbf{while}^Y \, \mathtt{have\_lock}_e \, \mathbf{do} \, \mathtt{skip});$$
$$\mathtt{lock} \sqsubseteq [\mathbf{true}, \mathtt{have\_lock}]^U.$$

Note that the coercion in this program states that the environment of the program is required to eventually release any lock it may hold — this ensures eventual termination of the while loop and success of the $\mathtt{lock}$ action. (We could eliminate the need for such coercions by generalizing environments to include liveness conditions, but we will not pursue this here.)

5 Reasoning with Assertions

In deriving programs by refinement, it is frequently the case that one part of the program being developed ensures conditions that can be used to optimize other parts of the program. To take advantage of such opportunities for optimization, it is useful to have in a refinement calculus a facility for making assertions that are derivable from program fragments, and rules that allow such assertions to be exploited in refinement steps. The assertions $\{\phi\}_C$ in our framework are intended to play such a role. A further desideratum for our framework is that it should support reasoning about the temporal properties guaranteed by a program fragment based on the properties of program fragments that will run in the future. (We present an example of such reasoning later.) We now explain how this desideratum motivates our use of constraint variables and justifications. We suppose for the sake of the argument that constraints and assertions do not have these annotations.

Consider the program $[\mathbf{true}, \phi]$. When this program terminates (as it must) ϕ will be true. Thus, for a refinement relation $\leq$ that supports the introduction of assertions into the program text, we would like the rule $[\mathbf{true}, \phi]; \{\phi\} \leq [\mathbf{true}, \phi]$ to be sound. Intuitively, $\{\phi\}$ asserts that ϕ is guaranteed to hold at this location. Moreover, we would like to be able to exploit assertions to perform refinements. When $[\mathbf{true}, \phi]; \{\phi\}$ occurs within the context of a larger program, the reason for the assertion $\{\phi\}$ may be some following part of the program that guarantees that ϕ will hold at this location. (For example, ϕ might assert that a message will eventually be delivered, and the following code may send this message on a reliable channel.) In this situation, we would like to be able to use this fact to simplify the specification $[\mathbf{true}, \phi]$ to ϵ. Intuitively, this program fragment need do nothing, since its intended effect is taken care of by some other part of the program. This suggests that we want the rule $\epsilon \leq [\mathbf{true}, \phi]; \{\phi\}$ to be sound.

Of course, we cannot have both these rules, since we would obtain by transitivity that $\epsilon \leq [\mathbf{true}, \phi]$, which clearly cannot be sound. What has gone wrong is that we have attempted to refine a program fragment based on an assertion derived from that very program fragment. This is circular reasoning! To block such circularities, we keep track of the constraints that the truth of an assertion depends on, and allow refinement steps of this type only when they do not involve circular reasoning. We do this by labeling constraints by constraint variables, providing assertions with justifications, and carefully tracking the way that assertions depend on constraints by appropriately adjusting the justifications when refinement steps are performed. Intuitively, an assertion $\{\varphi\}_J$ in a program amounts to a claim that φ holds, with the proof depending on the fact that the requirements implied by the constraints associated with all $X \in J$ are satisfied. For example, if $Y \in J$ and $[\psi_1, \psi_2]^Y$ occurs in the program, then the proof of φ may depend on the segment of code that the designer ultimately substitutes for $[\psi_1, \psi_2]^Y$ having the property that if started in a state satisfying ψ_1, it will terminate in a state satisfying ψ_2.

Using this idea, the two refinements above become $[\mathbf{true}, \phi]^X; \{\phi\}_{\{X\}} \leq [\mathbf{true}, \phi]^X$, and $\epsilon \leq [\mathbf{true}, \phi]^X; \{\phi\}_J$ *provided* $X \notin J$. The latter still allows us to perform the optimization when the assertion is justified by some other part of the program, while blocking the undesirable refinement above.

The decision to track justifications of assertions and allow rules such as

$$\text{``} \epsilon \leq [\mathbf{true}, \phi]^X; \{\phi\}_J \quad \text{provided} \quad X \notin J \text{''}$$

leads to some further complexities. Note that this rule eliminates the constraint $[\mathbf{true}, \phi]^X$. The larger program within which this refinement occurs may contain assertions that depend on this constraint. These assertions are still valid, but the reason for the validity is now that ϵ runs in place of $[\mathbf{true}, \phi]^X$, and that this constitutes a correct implementation of $[\mathbf{true}, \phi]^X$ because of the condition ϕ guaranteed by the constraints in J. That is, J becomes part of the explanation for assertions that previously depended on X. This means that in applying this rule, we need to transform the justifications for assertions elsewhere in the program.

To formalize these transformations, define a *justification transformation* to be a mapping $\eta : \mathcal{P}(CV) \to \mathcal{P}(CV)$ that is *increasing*, i.e., satisfies $J \subseteq \eta(J)$ for all $J \subseteq CV$. The result of applying a justification transformation η to a program P (or, respectively, program template $C(Z)$), is the program $P\eta$ (respectively, the program template $C\eta(Z)$) obtained by replacing every assertion $\{\varphi\}_J$ in P (respectively, in C), by the corresponding assertion $\{\varphi\}_{\eta(J)}$ in which its justification set has been transformed by η. We write $C\eta(P)$ for the program obtained by substituting P for Z in $C\eta(Z)$.

The assumption that justification transformations are increasing arises from the fact that we allow more than one constraint to be associated with the same constraint variable. (Programs in which this is the case arise naturally from desirable program transformations, such as refining P^ω by $P; P^\omega$. This transformation would create copies of any constraints in P, resulting in multiple occurrences of constraint variables.) Consider a program such as

$$\{twice(\varphi)\}_{\{X\}} \; ; \; [\varphi]^Y \; ; \; \{\varphi\}_{\{Y\}} \; ; \; [\varphi]^X \; ; \; a \; ; \; [\varphi]^X$$

where a is any atomic action and $twice(\varphi)$ expresses that there are at least two distinct time points in the future at which φ holds. This program is valid. If we were to apply the coercion elimination rule discussed above, and apply a justification transformation η mapping $\{X\}$ to $\{Y\}$, we would obtain the program

$$P \; = \; \{twice(\varphi)\}_{\{Y\}} \; ; \; [\varphi]^Y \; ; \; \epsilon \; ; \; a \; ; \; [\varphi]^X$$

This program is not valid, because it states $\{Y\}$ as the justification set for the truth of the assertion $twice(\varphi)$. The program $P^{\{Y\}}$, which is obtained from P by replacing the coercion $[\varphi]^X$ by ϵ has executions in which φ holds only once and $twice(\varphi)$ is falsified. A sound refinement step would have stated that the assertion $twice(\varphi)$ depends on both X and Y. Hence, the appropriate justification transformation here is to map $\{X\}$ to $\{X, Y\}$; the elimination of a coercion $[\varphi]^X$ introduced a dependency on Y, but additional dependency on X still needs to be accounted for. More generally, when transforming justifications in refining a constraint with label X, we need to preserve instances of X, since occurrences of X in assertions may be due to X-constraints other than the one being refined.

It is convenient to introduce some notation for particular justification transformations that will occur frequently in what follows. The identity justification transformation, in which $\eta(J) = J$ for every $J \subseteq CV$, is denoted by ι. We will also represent justification transformations using expressions of the form $[X_1 \hookrightarrow S_1, \ldots, X_n \hookrightarrow S_n]$, where the $X_i \in CV$ are constraint variables and the $S_i \subseteq CV$ are sets of constraint variables. (In the simple case of $n = 1$, we write $X \hookrightarrow S$ instead of $[X \hookrightarrow S]$, and if S is a singleton $\{Y\}$ we write $X \hookrightarrow Y$.) Such an expression denotes the justification transformation η defined by $\eta(J) = J \cup \bigcup_{X_i \in J, i=1...n} S_i$ for all $J \subseteq CV$. It is also useful to talk about the *composition* of justification transformations. We define the composition $\eta \cdot \eta'$ by $\eta \cdot \eta'(J) = \eta(\eta'(J))$ for all $J \subseteq CV$.

6   Validity and Valid Refinement

We now provide a formal semantics for the ideas motivated in the previous section.

6.1   Validity

The semantics of assertions $\{\varphi\}_J$ can be made precise as follows. First, to help capture the dependency of the assertion on J, we define a program transformation that modifies a program to one in which the program structure is maintained, but only the constraints labelled by a variable in a given justification set are enforced. Let J be a justification set and P a program. We define the program P^J by a recursion on the structure of P. In the cases where P is the null program ϵ, an atomic action a, a program variable Z, or an assertion $\{\psi\}_{J'}$, we define $P^J = P$. The other base cases concern program constraints. In the case of coercions, we define $([\varphi]^X)^J$ to be $[\varphi]^X$ if $X \in J$ and ϵ otherwise. That is, if the constraint variable labeling a coercion is in the set J, then the coercion is preserved, otherwise it is eliminated. Note that ϵ and the coercion it replaces are programs requiring no time to execute, so the temporal behaviour of the program is not modified by this substitution. In the case of specifications, we define $([\varphi, \psi]^X)^J$ to be $[\varphi, \psi]^X$ if $X \in J$ and $[\mathbf{false}, \mathbf{true}]^X$ otherwise. Again, if the constraint variable X labeling the specification is in the set J, then the specification is preserved. If $X \notin J$, then the specification is replaced by $[\mathbf{false}, \mathbf{true}]^X$, which is the specification that does not impose any requirements. Intuitively, this specification may run for any finite or infinite amount of time, performing an arbitrary sequence of actions. More formally, it can be seen from the definition of occurrence that $r, [c, d] \Vdash [\mathbf{false}, \mathbf{true}]^X$ holds for *every* interval $r, [c, d]$.

The recursive cases of the definition of P^J are given by: (i) $(P; Q)^J = P^J; Q^J$, (ii) $(P+Q)^J = P^J + Q^J$ and (iii) $(P^\omega)^J = (P^J)^\omega$. Intuitively, these cases preserve the structure of the program and filter the transformation down to the base cases.

Notice that in moving from P to P^J we are *coarsening* the program:

Lemma 1. *For every program P and justification set J,* $P \sqsubseteq P^J$.

We define a program P to be *valid* if the following condition holds: for every assertion $\{\varphi\}_J$ appearing in P, for all $r, [c, d], T, \theta, n$ and e, if (i) $r, [c, d] \Vdash_{T,\theta} P^J$, (ii) n is a node of T adorned by $\{\varphi\}_J$ and (iii) $\theta(n) = [e, e]$ where $e < \infty$, then $r, e \models \varphi$.

Intuitively, this condition holds when the assertion φ holds at each point of an execution of the program P^J that corresponds to a location in the text of P^J at which the assertion $\{\varphi\}_J$ occurs. Note that we check assertions only at finite times, and do not require for validity that all assertions of the program be reached during the execution. In this respect, our notion of validity resembles *partial correctness* of program assertions [Hoa67].

Assuming the standard semantics for the assignment statement and the obvious interpretations of the propositions, the following is an example of a valid program:

$$P_1 \quad = \quad [x = 0]^X \; ; \; \{\Diamond(y > 1)\}_{\{X\}} \; ; \; y \leftarrow x + 1 \; ; \; y \leftarrow y + 1 \; ; \; \{y = 2\}_{\{X\}}$$

The justification of the assertions in this program is the singleton set $\{X\}$. The truth of the assertions in this program depends on more than just the coercion $[x = 0]^X$, but the other parts it depends on are concrete program segments, which cannot be modified at a later stage of a refinement process.

Program P_2 is another valid program, illustrating the sense in which validity represents a notion of partial correctness:

$$P_2 \quad = \quad [x = 0]^X \; ; \; (\textbf{while}^Y \; \textbf{true} \; \textbf{do} \; x \leftarrow x + 1) \; ; \{\textbf{false}\}_{\{Y\}}$$

To see that this program is valid, notice that $\{\textbf{false}\}_{\{Y\}}$ is the only assertion in P_2. In all execution trees of $P_2^{\{Y\}}$ that can be embedded in an interval r, $[c, d]$, the node adorned by this assertion is mapped to infinity, because it is preceded by infinitely many time steps in which x is incremented. The assertion is thus vacuously satisfied at all finite points that its nodes are mapped to, and it follows that P_2 is valid. Notice that this example also shows that the general problem of deciding whether a program is valid is at least as hard as proving nontermination of programs in our language.

The slight variant $\quad [x = 0]^X \; ; \; (\textbf{while}^Y \; \textbf{true} \; \textbf{do} \; x \leftarrow x + 1) \; ; \{\textbf{false}\}_{\{X\}}$ is not a valid program, however.

6.2   Valid Refinement

We are now ready to define a validity-preserving notion of refinement. As noted above, we need to apply a justification transformation η to the surrounding context in some cases. We will write $P \preceq_\eta Q$ to state that a program template P validly refines a program template Q, subject to a justification transformation η to be applied to the syntactic context in which the refinement is to be applied. We define $P \preceq_\eta Q$ to hold if for all program templates $C(Z)$, if $C(Q)$ is valid then (i) $C\eta(P) \sqsubseteq C(Q)$, and (ii) $C\eta(P)$ is valid. Notice that the transformation η affects only the form of assertions, which are effectively ignored by the refinement relation $\sqsubseteq$. As a result, $P \equiv P\eta$ and $C(P) \equiv C\eta(P)$ hold for every C, P, and η. Thus, condition (i) in the definition of valid refinement can equivalently be stated as (i') $C(P) \sqsubseteq C(Q)$. Moreover, since $\sqsubseteq$ is monotone, we can often obtain (i') from $P \sqsubseteq Q$. As we will see, however, there are important cases in which $P \preceq_\eta Q$ in cases where $P \not\sqsubseteq Q$.

Clearly, for every program template $C(Z)$, if $P \preceq_\eta Q$ and $C(Q)$ is valid then $C(P) \sqsubseteq C(Q)$. Thus, $P \preceq_\eta Q$ states in part that it is possible to obtain a refinement of any valid program by locally substituting P for Q. In addition to this, the definition requires that this substitution be validity preserving, provided we transform the justifications in the context by η. The following result shows that this relation has the transitivity and monotonicity properties, provided that we make appropriate allowance for the justification transformations.

Theorem 2 *The relations $\preceq_\eta$ satisfy the following:*

1. *If $P \preceq_\eta Q$ and $Q \preceq_{\eta'} R$ then $P \preceq_{\eta \cdot \eta'} R$.*
2. *If $P \preceq_\eta Q$ then $C\eta(P) \preceq_\eta C(Q)$ for all program templates $C(X)$.*

An easy corollary of Theorem 2 is that $\preceq_\iota$ is an adequate refinement relation. We write $P \preceq Q$ for $P \preceq_\iota Q$, and write $P \asymp Q$ when both $P \preceq_\iota Q$ and $Q \preceq_\iota P$.

The following example illustrates how assertions combine with the notion of valid refinement to enable refinement steps that exploit properties of the context in which the refinement takes place.

Example 3. In example 2, we refined a specification to a concrete program together with a coercion that states a property that the environment must have for this concrete program to implement the specification. We may restate this example using valid refinement as follows:

$$(\text{while}^Y \text{have\_lock}_e \text{ do skip}); \text{lock} \preceq \{\Box(\text{have\_lock}_e \rightarrow \Diamond \neg \text{have\_lock}_e)\}_J;$$
$$[\text{true}, \text{have\_lock}]^X$$

provided $X \notin J$. Intuitively, this states that the refinement is valid provided it is done in a context in which one can prove that the environment is guaranteed to eventually release the lock.

7   Rules for Valid Refinement

We now present a number of refinement rules sound with respect to the above semantics. (This is not a complete list of rules for our semantics.) First, we have a rule which enables one of the most basic steps used in top-down design of sequential programs (cf. [Mor90]):

Sequential composition: $[\varphi, \varphi_1]^X; \ [\varphi_1, \psi]^Y \ \preceq_{U \hookrightarrow \{X, Y\}} \ [\varphi, \psi]^U$

Many of the properties of $\sqsubseteq$ translate into valid refinements with the identity transformation:

Identity: $\epsilon; P \asymp P$ and $P; \epsilon \asymp P$

$^\omega$-rules: $P^\omega \asymp (\epsilon + P; P^\omega)$ and $P^\omega; P^\omega \asymp P^\omega$

Associativity: $(P; Q); R \asymp P; (Q; R)$ and $(P + Q) + R \asymp P + (Q + R)$

Commutativity and Idempotence of $+$: $P + Q \asymp Q + P$ and $P + P \asymp P$

Distribution: $P; (Q + R) \asymp (P; Q) + (P; R)$ and $(Q + R); P \asymp (Q; P) + (R; P)$

We say that a program is *vanishing* if it is the empty program ϵ, a coercion $[\varphi]^X$ or an assertion $\{\varphi\}_J$. These programs are called vanishing because they occur over point intervals and take no time to execute. The rules for vanishing programs do not hold in the formalism of Morgan [Mor90], for example.

<u>Commutativity and Idempotence of vanishing programs:</u>   for all vanishing P, Q, we have $P; Q \asymp Q; P$ and $P; P^{\omega} \asymp P$

The examples just given demonstrate standard refinements that still hold as valid refinements. Not every standard refinement translates into a valid refinement. For example, we clearly have $\{\mathbf{false}\} \sqsubseteq \epsilon$ but not $\{\mathbf{false}\} \preceq_{\iota} \epsilon$, since for the template $C(Z) = Z$ we have that $C(\epsilon)$ is a valid program, while $C(\{\mathbf{false}\})$ is not. But even for programs that do not contain assertions, one needs to be careful. For example, we have $[\varphi]^X \sqsubseteq [\varphi]^Y$. This does correspond to a valid refinement, but one in which anything that depends on Y should be made to depend on both X and Y. Thus, we have the valid refinement rule

<u>Renaming Constraint:</u> $[\varphi]^X \preceq_{Y \hookrightarrow X} [\varphi]^Y$ and $[\varphi, \psi]^X \preceq_{Y \hookrightarrow X} [\varphi, \psi]^Y$

A major reason for using valid refinement is for proving that $P \preceq_{\eta} Q$ in cases when $P \sqsubseteq Q$ *does not* hold. Intuitively, this will be the case for refinements that exploit properties of the context in which the refinement step is taking place. Examples of this are:

<u>Coercion Elimination:</u> $\epsilon \preceq_{X \hookrightarrow J} \{\varphi\}_J; [\varphi]^X$ provided $X \notin J$

<u>Specification Elimination:</u> $\epsilon \preceq_{X \hookrightarrow J} [\varphi, \psi]^X ; \{\varphi \rightarrow \psi\}_J$ and $\epsilon \preceq_{X \hookrightarrow J} \{\varphi \rightarrow \psi\}_J ; [\varphi, \psi]^X$, provided $X \notin J$

Of special interest are rules that allow us to move temporal assertions around the program text. One example is

<u>Advance Box:</u> $P; \{\Box\varphi\}_J \preceq \{\Box\varphi\}_J; P$

which moves a temporal assertion forward in time. It is also possible to move temporal assertions backwards.

<u>Regress Diamond:</u>   If $P \preceq_{X \hookrightarrow J_1} [\mathbf{true}, \mathbf{true}]^X$ then $\{\Diamond\varphi\}_{J_1 \cup J_2}; P \preceq P; \{\Diamond\varphi\}_{J_2}$

We remark that the statement $P \preceq_{X \hookrightarrow J_1} [\mathbf{true}, \mathbf{true}]^X$ ensures that P is a halting program, and so it provides one approach to expressing termination.

A few additional properties of $\preceq$ that we shall use in the following example are

<u>Strengthen Spec:</u>   If $\varphi_1 \rightarrow \varphi$ and $\psi \rightarrow \psi_1$ are valid formulae of the logic of $\mathcal{L}$ then $[\varphi, \psi]^X \preceq_{Y \hookrightarrow X} [\varphi_1, \psi_1]^Y$

<u>Specification Consequence:</u> $[\varphi, \psi]^X ; \{\psi\}_{J \cup \{X\}} \preceq \{\varphi\}_J ; [\varphi, \psi]^X$

<u>Valid Assertion:</u>   If φ is a valid formula of the logic of $\mathcal{L}$ then $\{\varphi\}_{\emptyset} \asymp \epsilon$.

As mentioned above, some of our rules are fairly standard, and appear in other refinement calculi. In the example presented in the next section we make effective use of two rules which do not hold in typical systems: The Regress Diamond and Specification Elimination rules.

8   Optimization Using Refinement

We now consider an example that illustrates some of the rules mentioned above and shows that our framework differs from others in useful ways. In the setting of Example 1 from Section 4, consider a case in which the resource needs to be used twice in a row. Thus, our goal is to implement the program *Access_twice* defined by

$$Access\_twice \quad = \quad Access(X1, Y1) \; ; \; Access(X2, Y2).$$

Recall from Example 1 that

$$Access(X2, Y2) \quad = \quad [\textbf{true}, \texttt{have\_lock}]^{X2} \; ; \; \texttt{use\_resource} \; ; \; [\textbf{true}, \Diamond \neg \texttt{have\_lock}]^{Y2}.$$

In Example 1 we argued that

$$(\texttt{get\_lock} \; ; \; \texttt{use\_resource} \; ; \; \texttt{release\_lock}) \quad \sqsubseteq \quad Access(X2, Y2),$$

A similar valid refinement can be established:

$$(\texttt{get\_lock} \; ; \; \texttt{use\_resource} \; ; \; \texttt{release\_lock}) \quad \preceq \quad Access(X2, Y2).$$

Indeed, one way to implement *Access_twice* would be to simply repeat this program twice in sequence. It is possible to do better, however. We now demonstrate how, with the aid of valid refinement, our framework can be used to obtain a more efficient implementation.

Let us first consider the final step of $Access(X2, Y2)$, i.e., the program $[\textbf{true}, \Diamond \neg \texttt{have\_lock}]^{Y2}$. Note that by using Identity and Valid Assertion (since **true** is a valid formula) we can obtain

$$\{\textbf{true}\}_\emptyset; [\textbf{true}, \Diamond \neg \texttt{have\_lock}]^{Y2} \preceq \epsilon; [\textbf{true}, \Diamond \neg \texttt{have\_lock}]^{Y2} \preceq [\textbf{true}, \Diamond \neg \texttt{have\_lock}]^{Y2},$$

and the Specification Consequence rule yields

$$[\textbf{true}, \Diamond \neg \texttt{have\_lock}]^{Y2}; \{\Diamond \neg \texttt{have\_lock}\}_{\{Y2\}} \quad \preceq \quad [\textbf{true}, \Diamond \neg \texttt{have\_lock}]^{Y2}.$$

By Monotonicity we thus have that

$$Access(X2, Y2); \{\Diamond \neg \texttt{have\_lock}\}_{\{Y2\}} \quad \preceq \quad Access(X2, Y2).$$

One of the strong points of our framework is that we can now use our rules to move the temporal assertion to the beginning of $Access(X2, Y2)$! The idea is to apply the Regress Diamond rule three times and thereby move the assertion back over each of the components of $Access(X2, Y2)$.

Notice that by Strengthen Spec we have[3]

$$[\textbf{true}, \Diamond \neg \texttt{have\_lock}]^{Y2} \quad \preceq \quad [\textbf{true}, \textbf{true}]^{Y2}.$$

---

[3] Strictly speaking, applying the rule we should write $\preceq_{Y2 \hookrightarrow Y2}$ in the valid refinement, but it is easy to check that the justification transformation $Y2 \hookrightarrow Y2$ is the identity transformation.

Hence, by Regress Diamond we have that

$$\{\Diamond\neg\textbf{have\_lock}\}_{\{Y2\}}; [\textbf{true}, \Diamond\neg\textbf{have\_lock}]^{Y2} \preceq [\textbf{true}, \Diamond\neg\textbf{have\_lock}]^{Y2};$$
$$\{\Diamond\neg\textbf{have\_lock}\}_{\{Y2\}},$$

so we can move the temporal assertion back over the last component of $Access(X2, Y2)$. Since use_resource is a basic (terminating) action, we have use_resource $\preceq [\textbf{true}, \textbf{true}]^{Y2}$. Thus, again by Regress Diamond we can derive

$$\{\Diamond\neg\textbf{have\_lock}\}_{\{Y2\}}; \text{use\_resource} \preceq \text{use\_resource}; \{\Diamond\neg\textbf{have\_lock}\}_{\{Y2\}},$$

Finally, we again apply Strengthen Spec to obtain that

$$[\textbf{true}, \textbf{have\_lock}]^{X2} \preceq [\textbf{true}, \textbf{true}]^{X2}$$

and hence

$$\{\Diamond\neg\textbf{have\_lock}\}_{\{X2,Y2\}}; [\textbf{true}, \textbf{have\_lock}]^{X2} \preceq [\textbf{true}, \textbf{have\_lock}]^{X2}; \{\Diamond\neg\textbf{have\_lock}\}\{Y2\}.$$

The end result of moving the temporal assertion back over these three clauses yields:

$$\{\Diamond\neg\textbf{have\_lock}\}_{\{X2,Y2\}}; Access(X2, Y2) \preceq Access(X2, Y2).$$

By monotonicity, it follows that

$$Access(X1, Y1); \{\Diamond\neg\textbf{have\_lock}\}_{\{X2,Y2\}}; Access(X2, Y2) \preceq Access\_twice.$$

Let us now focus on the interaction of the assertion in this program with the final statement in $Access(X1, Y1)$. Since $Y1 \notin \{X2, Y2\}$, we have by Specification Elimination that

$$\epsilon \preceq_{Y1\hookrightarrow\{X2,Y2\}} [\textbf{true}, \Diamond\neg\textbf{have\_lock}]^{Y1}; \{\Diamond\neg\textbf{have\_lock}\}_{\{X2,Y2\}}$$

so that we can eliminate the third clause in $Access(X1, Y1)$ and derive

$$[\textbf{true}, \textbf{have\_lock}]^{X1}; \text{use\_resource}; Access(X2, Y2) \preceq_{Y1\hookrightarrow\{X2,Y2\}} Access\_twice.$$

One further improvement is now possible. As we did for the final step of $Access(X2, Y2)$, we can apply the Identity, Valid Assertion and Specification Consequence rules to $[\textbf{true}, \textbf{have\_lock}]^{X1}$—the first step of $Access(X1, Y1)$, and obtain:

$$[\textbf{true}, \textbf{have\_lock}]^{X1}; \{\textbf{have\_lock}\}_{\{X1\}} \preceq [\textbf{true}, \textbf{have\_lock}]^{X1}.$$

With an additional application of Specification Consequence, using the property

$$\text{use\_resource} \preceq [\textbf{have\_lock}, \textbf{have\_lock}]^{X1}$$

which was one of the given assumptions, we can derive

$[\textbf{true}, \texttt{have\_lock}]^{X1}; \texttt{use\_resource}; \{\texttt{have\_lock}\}_{\{X1\}} \preceq [\textbf{true}, \texttt{have\_lock}]^{X1}; \texttt{use\_resource}.$

We can now apply the assertion $\{\texttt{have\_lock}\}_{\{X1\}}$ to the first statement in $Access(X2, Y2)$, using Specification Elimination to obtain

$$\epsilon \quad \preceq_{X2 \hookrightarrow X1} \quad \{\texttt{have\_lock}\}_{\{X1\}}; [\textbf{true}, \texttt{have\_lock}]^{X2},$$

and we can use this to derive that

$[\textbf{true}, \texttt{have\_lock}]^{X1}; \texttt{use\_resource}; \texttt{use\_resource} \ ; \ [\textbf{true}, \Diamond\neg\texttt{have\_lock}]^{Y2} \ \preceq_{\eta} \ Access\_twice$

where $\eta = [X2 \hookrightarrow X1] \cdot [Y1 \hookrightarrow \{X2, Y2\}] = [X2 \hookrightarrow X1, \ Y1 \hookrightarrow \{X1, X2, Y2\}]$. The first and last steps of this program may be refined to get_lock and release_lock, respectively, as before, yielding a concrete implementation of $Access\_twice$:

$$\texttt{get\_lock} \ ; \ \texttt{use\_resource} \ ; \ \texttt{use\_resource} \ ; \ \texttt{release\_lock} \quad \preceq_{\eta} \ Access\_twice.$$

Note that we have achieved an interesting optimization by means of this reasoning: instead of releasing the lock after the first use and then re-acquiring it immediately, we simply hold onto the lock and use the resource twice. This optimization made essential use of valid refinement. Moreover, moving *temporal* assertions (both forward and backward) in the program text played an important role.

9   Conclusion

As discussed in the introduction, there exist many approaches to program refinement. Perhaps the work most closely related to ours is the work on real-time refinement originated by Utting and Fidge [UF96,UF97,HU97,Hay98]. This work shares our objective of developing a Back/Morgan-style framework with temporal features. In particular, Utting and Fidge define a real time specification construct $\star[\varphi, \psi]$, similar to our $[\varphi, \psi]$ in that φ and ψ may be formulae expressing properties not just of the current state, but also of the run. They give semantics to this construct by translation to an instance of Morgan's refinement calculus in which states are taken to correspond to what we have called "points" in this paper, i.e. a run together with a "current time" variable. The construct $\star[\varphi, \psi]$ is represented by a predicate transformer over such states that "changes only the current time." The resulting calculus is like ours in many ways. A crucial difference, however, is that it does not support refinements like $\{\Diamond\varphi\}; \star[\textbf{true}, \varphi] \preceq \star[\textbf{true}, \varphi]$ which are essential to the example in Section 8. Their framework does not make use of explicit justifications, but, intuitively, it avoids circular temporal refinements like that discussed in Section 5 by allowing assertions to be "justified" only by constraints that have "executed" at an earlier time. Thus, in the refinement above, while φ can be asserted after the specification $\star[\textbf{true}, \varphi]$, we cannot assert $\Diamond\varphi$ before it.

We believe that examples similar to that of Section 8 will be quite significant in practice. For example, it is common to optimize protocols in distributed systems by noting that in certain circumstances, one can omit sending a message because its intended effect is already guaranteed to occur (perhaps because of actions and events due to occur in the future). This is particularly useful when developing protocols that optimize use of bandwidth by minimizing the number of messages sent. Of course, our framework needs generalization to be applied to such protocols — this is a topic of current work; we have discussed considerations applying to the generalization elsewhere [MM98]. The example in Section 8 already suggests that mechanical assistance for the bookkeeping involved in maintaining and updating justification sets and justification transformations. In addition, we believe that results derived using temporal logic theorem provers and related tools can be incorporated in derivations in our framework by providing input into rules such as Strengthen Spec and Valid Assertion. There is clearly a wide range of topics and issues to explore in developing this topic.

The definition of valid refinement we have introduced here demonstrates that it is possible to develop a refinement calculus involving temporal assertions that has an easily understood semantics and supports some quite intuitive reasoning. One point is worth making however: because it involves a quantification over the syntactic contexts $C(\cdot)$, our definition of valid refinement is likely to be sensitive to the syntax of programs. It is therefore worthwhile to consider more semantic notions of valid refinement. In a followup paper we will define a semantic counterpart of valid refinement, and prove the soundness of the rules used in this paper, as well as a host of other rules, with respect to this semantic notion.

We are also in the process of developing the framework to deal with several extensions of the language studied here. One extension introduces a way of placing labels within a program and enriches the assertion language to allow it to express properties of the program locations corresponding to these labels. This allows some interesting properties such as termination to be expressed directly in the programming language (rather than indirectly, through a statement about refinement, as we have done here in the Regress Diamond rule). Use of labels also provides a tighter coupling between program structure and temporal assertions that enables some quite useful refinement rules. Finally, we are also in the process of extending the framework developed here to include quantification over "local predicates" [EvdMM98,EvdMM00]: this provides a framework generalizing knowledge-based [FHMV95] and knowledge-oriented programs [MK93].

References

[BvW98]   R. J. Back and von Wright. *Refinement Calculus: A systematic approach.* Graduate Texts in Computer Science. Springer Verlag, 1998.

[EvdMM98]   K. Engelhardt, R. van der Meyden, and Y. Moses. Knowledge and the logic of local propositions. In I. Gilboa, editor, *Proc. Conf on Theoretical Aspects of Reasoning about Knowledge*, pages 29–41. Morgan Kauffman, July 1998.

[EvdMM00]   K. Engelhardt, R. van der Meyden, and Y. Moses. A refinement framework supporting reasoning about knowledge and time. In *Proc. of FOSSACS '2000.* Springer Verlag, March 2000.

[FHMV95]   R. Fagin, J. Y. Halpern, Y. Moses, and M. Y. Vardi. *Reasoning about Knowledge.* MIT Press, Cambridge, Mass., 1995.

[GS86]   S. Graf and J. Sifakis. A logic for the description of non-deterministic programs and their properties. *Information and Control*, 68(1–3):254–270, January/February/March 1986.

[Hay98]   I. Hayes. Separating timing and calculation in real-time refinement. In J. Grundy et al, editor, *International Refinement Workshop & Formal Methods Pacific, Proc. IRW/FMP'98*, Series in Discrete Mathematics and Theoretical Computer Science, 1998.

[HL95]   K. Havelund and K. Larsen. A refinement logic for the fork calculus. In S. T. Vuong and S. T. Chanson, editors, *Protocol Specification, Testing and Verification XIV*, pages 5–20. Chapman and Hall, 1995. IFIP WG 6.1 Symposium.

[Hoa67]   C.A.R. Hoare. An axiomatic basis for computer programming. *Comm. ACM*, 12:516–580, 1967.

[Hol89]   S. Holström. A refinement calculus for specifications in Henessy-Milner logic with recursion. *Formal Aspects of Computing*, 1:242–272, 1989.

[HU97]   I. Hayes and M. Utting. A sequential real-time refinement calculus. Technical Report UQ-SVRC-97-33, Software Verification Research Centre, University of Queensland, 1997. URL http://www.svrc.it.uq.edu.au/.

[Lam94]   Leslie Lamport. The temporal logic of actions. *ACM Transactions on Programming Languages and Systems*, 16(3):872–923, May 1994. Also appeared as DEC SRC Research Report 79.

[MK93]   Y. Moses and O. Kislev. Knowledge-oriented programming. In *Proc. 12th ACM Symp. on Principles of Distributed Computing*, pages 261–270, 1993.

[MM98]   R. van der Meyden and Y. Moses. Top-down considerations on distributed systems. In *Proc. 12th Int. Symp. on Distributed Computing, DISC'98*, pages 16–19, Andros, Greece, Sept 1998. Springer LNCS No. 1499.

[Mor87]   J. M. Morris. A theoretical basis for refinement and the programming calculus. *Science of Computer Programming*, 9(3):287–306, 1987.

[Mor90]   C. Morgan. *Programming from Specifications*. Prentice Hall, New York, 1990.

[UF96]   M. Utting and C. Fidge. A real-time refinement calculus that changes only time. In He Jifeng, editor, *Proc. 7th BCS/FACS Refinement Workshop*, Electronic Workshops in Computing. Springer, 1996.

[UF97]   M. Utting and C. Fidge. Refinement of infeasible real-time programs. In *Proc. Formal Methods Pacific '97*, Series in Discrete Mathematics and Theoretical Computer Science, pages 243–262, 1997.

[Win86]   G. Winskel. A complete proof system for SCSS with modal assertions. *Fundamenta Informaticae*, IX:401–419, 1986.

Generalizing Action Systems to Hybrid Systems

R.-J. Back, L. Petre and I. Porres

Turku Centre for Computer Science (TUCS)
Lemminkäisenkatu 14A, FIN-20520 Turku, Finland
{Ralph-Johan.Back,Luigia.Petre,Ivan.Porres}@abo.fi

Abstract. Action systems have been used successfully to describe discrete systems, i.e.,systems with discrete control acting upon a discrete state space. In this paper we extend the action system approach to hybrid systems by defining *continuous action systems*. These are systems with discrete control over a continuously evolving state, whose semantics is defined in terms of traditional action systems. We show that continuous action systems are very general and can be used to describe a diverse range of hybrid systems. Moreover, the properties of continuous action systems are proved using standard action systems proof techniques.

1 Introduction

A system using discrete control over continuously evolving processes is referred to as a *hybrid system*. The use of formal methods and models to describe hybrid systems has attracted quite a lot of attention in the last years, with a number of different models and formalisms being proposed in the literature (see e.g., [2, 13,9]). We continue this line of research, essentially proposing what we believe is a new and very general model for hybrid systems, based on the *action systems* paradigm.

Action systems [4] have been used successfully to model discrete systems, i.e., systems that use a discrete control upon a discrete state space. Their original purpose was to model concurrent and distributed systems. In this paper we show that the action system model can be adapted to model hybrid systems. An important advantage of this adaption is that standard modeling and proof techniques, developed for ordinary action systems, can be reused to model and reason about hybrid systems.

Our extension of action systems to hybrid systems is based on a new approach to describing the state of a system. Essentially, our state variables will range over functions over time, rather than just over values. This allows a variable to capture not only its present value, but also the whole history of values that the variable has had, as well as the default future values that the variable will receive. Updating a state variable is restricted so that only the future behavior of the variable can be changed, not its past behavior. We will refer to action systems with this model of state as *continuous action systems*. Continuous action systems are inspired by, but differ from, the extension of action systems to hybrid systems described in [14].

M. Joseph (Ed.): FTRTFT 2000, LNCS 1926, pp. 202–213, 2000.

Proofs about action system properties are based on the refinement calculus [7]. This extends the programming logic based on weakest precondition predicate transformers that was proposed in [10]. Action systems are intended to be stepwise developed, the correctness of these refinement steps being verified within the refinement calculus. Thereby, we get an implicit notion of refinement also for continuous action systems. Even though the refinement of hybrid systems is not the purpose of this paper, the approach we adopt for hybrid systems fits well into the refinement calculus and it can be used for systems where correct construction is a central concern.

The refinement calculus is based on higher-order logic, which in turn is an extension of simply typed lambda calculus. Functions are defined by λ-abstraction and can be used without explicit definition and naming. As an example, the function that calculates the successor of a natural number is defined as $(\lambda n \cdot n + 1)$. We denote by $f.x$ the application of the function f to the argument x so that, e.g., $(\lambda n \cdot n + 1).1 = 2$. A binary relation $R \subseteq A \times B$ is here considered as a function $R : A \to \mathcal{P}B$, i.e., mapping elements in A to sets of elements in B.

We proceed as follows. The action system model is briefly reviewed in Section 2. We define the continuous action systems in Section 3. Their semantics is specified by explaining how to translate them into ordinary action systems. Section 4 contains examples of hybrid systems, modeled using our framework. In Section 5 we show how to prove safety properties for continuous action systems. Conclusions and comparisons to related work are presented in Section 6.

2 Action Systems

We start by giving a brief overview of the action systems formalism. An action system is essentially a *discrete state space* updated by a *discrete control* mechanism. The state of the system is described using *attributes* or *program variables*. We define a finite set *Attr* of *attribute names* and assume that each attribute name in *Attr* is associated with a non-empty set of *values*. This set of values is the *type* of the attribute. If the attribute x takes values from *Val*, we say that x has the type *Val* and we write it as $x : Val$. We consider several predefined types, like Real for the set of real numbers, Real$_+$ for the set of non-negative real numbers, and Bool for the boolean values $\{F, T\}$.

An *action system* consists of a finite set of attributes, used to observe and manipulate the *state* of the system, and a finite set of *actions* that act upon the attributes. This set of actions models the *control mechanism* over the state of the system. An action system $\mathcal{A}$ has the following form:

$$\mathcal{A} \triangleq \|[\mathsf{var}\ x : Val \bullet S_0\ ;\ \mathsf{do}\ A_1 \square\ \ldots \square\ A_m\ \mathsf{od}\ ]\| : y$$

Here $x : Val = x_1 : Val_1, \ldots, x_n : Val_n$ are the *local attributes* of the system, S_0 is a statement that initializes the attributes, while '$A_i = g_i \to S_i$', $i = 1, \ldots, m$, are the *actions* of the system. The boolean expression g_i is the *guard* of the action A_i and S_i is the *body* of the action. The attributes $y = y_1, \ldots, y_k$ are defined in the environment of the action system and called *imported attributes*.

Attributes in x may be *exported*, in the sense that they can be read, or written, or both read and written by environment actions. In this case, we decorate these attributes with $-$, $+$ or $*$, respectively. An action A of the form '$g \to S$' is a guarded statement that can be executed only when g is enabled, i.e., when g evaluates to T. The body S of an action is defined by the following syntax:

$$S ::= \text{abort} \mid \text{skip} \mid x : = e \mid [x : = x'|R] \mid \text{if } g \text{ then } S_1 \text{ else } S_2 \text{ fi} \mid S_1 ; S_2$$

Here x is a list of attributes, e is a corresponding list of expressions, x' is a list of variables standing for unknown values, and R is a relation specified in terms of x and x'. Intuitively 'skip' is the stuttering action, '$x : = e$' is a multiple assignment, 'if g then S_1 else S_2 fi' is the conditional composition of two statements, and '$S_1;S_2$' is the sequential composition of two statements. The action 'abort' always fails and is used to model disallowed behaviors. Given a relation $R(x, x')$ and a list of attributes x, we denote by $[x : = x'|R]$ the *non-deterministic assignment* of some value $x' \in R.x$ to x (the effect is the same as abort, if $R.x = \emptyset$). The semantics of the actions language has been defined in terms of weakest preconditions in a standard way [10]. Thus, for any predicate q, we define

$$
\begin{aligned}
wp(\text{abort}, q) \quad &= \text{F} \\
wp(\text{skip}, q) \quad &= q \\
wp(x : = e, q) \quad &= q[x := e] \\
wp([x : = x'|R], q) &= (\forall x' \in R.x \cdot q[x := x']) \\
wp(S_1 ; S_2, q) \quad &= wp(S_1, wp(S_2, q)) \\
wp(\text{if } g \text{ then } S_1 \text{ else } S_2 \text{ fi}, q) &= \text{if } g \text{ then } wp(S_1, q) \text{ else } wp(S_2, q) \text{ fi}
\end{aligned}
$$

The term $q[x := e]$ stands for the result of substituting e for all free occurrences of variable x in predicate q.

The execution of an action system is as follows. The initialization S_0 will set the attributes x to some specific values, using a sequence of possibly non-deterministic assignments. Then, enabled actions are repeatedly chosen and executed. The chosen actions will change the values of the attributes in a way that is determined by the action body. Two or more actions can be enabled at the same time, in which case one of them is chosen for execution, in a demonically non-deterministic way. The computation terminates when no action is enabled. Actions systems model parallel execution by interleaving atomic actions in a demonically non-deterministic fashion.

In the following, we specify a notion of time and show how to model attributes that are functions of time. These extensions to the action systems formalism define a new model for hybrid systems.

3   Continuous Action Systems

A system using a discrete control mechanism over a continuously evolving state is referred to as a hybrid system. In this section we introduce *continuous action systems*, an extension of the action system formalism to model hybrid systems.

A continuous action system consists of a finite set of time-dependent attributes together with a finite set of actions that act upon them. The attributes

can range over discrete or continuous domains and form the state of the system.
A continuous action system is of the form:

$$\mathcal{C} \stackrel{\triangle}{=} |(\text{var } x : \text{Real}_+ \rightarrow Val \bullet S_0 \,; \text{do } g_1 \rightarrow S_1 \square \ldots \square \ g_m \rightarrow S_m \text{od })| : y \qquad (1)$$

Intuitively, executing a continuous action system proceeds as follows. There
is an implicit variable now, that shows the present time. Initially $now = 0$.
The initialization S_0 assigns initial time functions to the attributes $x_1, \ldots, x_n$.
These time functions describe the default future behavior of the attributes, whose
values may, thereby, change with the progress of time. The system will then start
evolving according to these functions, with time (as measured by now) moving
forward continuously. The guards of the actions may refer the value of now, as
may expressions in the action bodies and the initialization statements.

As soon as one of the conditions $g_1, \ldots, g_m$ becomes true, the system chooses one of the *enabled* actions, say $g_i \rightarrow S_i$, for execution. The choice is non-
deterministic if there is more than one such action. The body S_i of the action
is then executed. Execution is atomic and instantaneous. It will usually change
some attributes by changing their future behavior. We write $x :- e$ for an assignment rather than $x := e$, to emphasize that only the future behavior of the
attribute x is changed to the function e and the past behavior remains unchanged. Attributes that are not changed will behave as before. After the changes
stipulated by S_i have been done, the system will evolve to the next time instance
when one of the actions is enabled, and the process is repeated. The next time
instance when an action is enabled may well be the same as the previous, i.e.,
time does not need to progress between the execution of two enabled actions.
This is usually the case when the system is doing some (discrete, logical) computation to determine how to proceed next. Such computation does not take any
time. It is possible that after a certain time instance, none of the actions will
be enabled anymore. This just means that the system will continue to evolve
forever according to the functions last assigned to the attributes.

As an example of a continuous action system consider the system in Fig. 1.
The attributes x and *clock* are first initialized to the constant function $(\lambda t \cdot 0)$
and the switching function up is set to the constant function $(\lambda t \cdot \text{F})$. The guard
of the first action is immediately enabled at time 0, so the first action's body
is executed immediately. The future behaviors of *clock* and x are changed to
increase linearly from 0, and the future behavior of up is changed to the constant
function $(\lambda t \cdot \text{T})$, i.e., up is set to be T in all the future time instances. After
this, the system starts to evolve by advancing time continuously. In particular,
the value of x increases linearly, depending on time. When x gets value 1, the
second action is enabled. The clock is then first reset, the future behavior of
x is changed to decrease linearly with the clock value, and the future value of
up is set to the constant F. This continues until x reaches 0, when the first
action is again enabled, changing x to increase again, and so on. The effect of
these two actions is a sawtooth-like behavior, where the value of x alternatively
increases and decreases forever. The evolution of the system is also described in
Fig. 1, showing each attribute on the same time domain together with the points

$Saw \stackrel{\triangle}{=} |($ var $x, clock : \mathsf{Real}_+ \to \mathsf{Real}$; $up : \mathsf{Real}_+ \to \mathsf{Bool}$

$\bullet\ x :- (\lambda t \cdot 0)$; $clock :- (\lambda t \cdot 0)$; $up :- (\lambda t \cdot \mathsf{F})$;

do $x.now = 0 \wedge \neg up.now \to$

$\quad clock :- (\lambda t \cdot t - now)$;

$\quad x :- clock$; $up :- (\lambda t \cdot \mathsf{T})$

$\square\ \ x.now = 1 \wedge up.now \to$

$\quad clock :- (\lambda t \cdot t - now)$;

$\quad x :- (\lambda t \cdot 1 - clock.t)$;

$\quad up :- (\lambda t \cdot \mathsf{F})$

od

$)|$

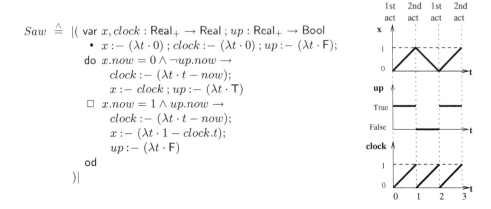

Fig. 1. Continuous action system *Saw* (left) and its behavior (right).

in time where a discrete action is performed. We see that a continuous action system is just a non-deterministic way of defining a collection of time dependent functions. One of the main advantages of this model for hybrid computation is that both discrete and continuous behavior can be described in the same way. In particular, if the attributes are assigned only constant functions, we obtain a discrete computation.

Semantics of continuous action systems. Let $\mathcal{C}$ be the continuous action system in (1). We explain the meaning of $\mathcal{C}$ by translating it into an ordinary action system. Its semantical interpretation is given by the following (discrete) action system $\bar{\mathcal{C}}$:

$$\bar{\mathcal{C}} \stackrel{\triangle}{=} |[\ \text{var}\ now : \mathsf{Real}_+, x : \mathsf{Real}_+ \to Val$$
$$\bullet\quad now := 0\ ; S_0\ ; N;$$
$$\text{do}\ \ g_1 \to S_1\ ; N\square\ \ ...\square\ g_m \to S_m\ ; N\ \text{od}$$
$$]|\ :\ y \tag{2}$$

Here the attribute *now* is declared, initialized, and updated explicitly. It models the time moments that are of interest for the system, i.e., the starting time and the succeeding moments when some action is enabled. The value of *now* is updated by the statement $N \stackrel{\triangle}{=}\ now := \mathsf{next}.gg.now$. Here $gg = g_1 \vee ... \vee g_m$ is the disjunction of all guards of the actions and next is defined by

$$\mathsf{next}.gg.t \stackrel{\triangle}{=} \begin{cases} min\{t' \ge t\ |\ gg.t'\}, & \text{if}\ \exists\ t' \ge t\ \text{such that}\ gg.t' \\ t, & \text{otherwise.} \end{cases} \tag{3}$$

The function next models the moments of time when at least one action is enabled. Only at these moments can the future behavior of attributes be modified. If no action will ever be enabled, then the second branch of the definition will be followed, and the attribute *now* will denote the moment of time when the last discrete action was executed. In this case the discrete control terminates and the attributes will evolve forever according to the functions last assigned. We assume in this paper that the minimum in the definition of next always exists when at least one guard is enabled in the present or future. Continuous action systems that do not satisfy this requirement are considered ill-defined.

The *future update* $x :- e$ is defined by $x :- e \stackrel{\wedge}{=} x := x/now/e$ where $x/t_0/e \stackrel{\wedge}{=} (\lambda t \cdot \text{if } t < t_0 \text{ then } x.t \text{ else } e.t \text{ fi})$. Thus, only the future behavior of x is changed by the future update. It is important to note that all the attributes of a continuous action system are functions of time, except for *now*. As an example, the statement $x :- (\lambda t \cdot t)$ updates the default future of x with an increasing function, while $x :- (\lambda t \cdot now)$ updates it with a constant function. We write $x :- c$ as a shorthand for $x :- (\lambda t \cdot c)$ when c is a constant function.

This explication of a continuous action system shows it essentially as a collection of time functions $x_0, \ldots, x_n$ over the non-negative reals, defined in a stepwise manner. The steps form a sequence of intervals $I_0, I_1, I_2, \ldots$, where each interval I_k is either a left closed interval of the form $[t_i \ldots t_{i+1})$ or a closed interval of the form $[t_i, t_i]$, i.e., a point. The action system determines a family of functions $x_0, \ldots, x_n$ which are stepwise defined over this sequence of intervals and points. The extremes of these intervals correspond to the control points of the system where a discrete action is performed. In the *Saw* example, the sequence of intervals is $[0], [0 \ldots 1), [1 \ldots 2), [2 \ldots 3), \ldots$ As such, the continuous action system can be best understood as the limit of a sequence of approximations of the time functions $x_0, \ldots, x_n$, defined over successively longer and longer intervals $[0 \ldots t_i)$, where $i = 0, 1, 2, \ldots$. Looking at the example in this way, its sequence of initial segments is $[0], [0 \ldots 1), [0 \ldots 2), [0 \ldots 3), \ldots$ and the defined approximations are successively:

$$x_0.t = 0, 0 \leq t; \quad x_1.t = t, 0 \leq t; \quad x_2.t = \begin{cases} t, & 0 \leq t < 1 \\ 1 - t, 1 \leq t \end{cases} ; \quad x_3.t = \begin{cases} t, & 0 \leq t < 1 \\ 1 - t, 1 \leq t < 2 \\ t - 2, 2 \leq t \end{cases}$$

For each attribute x_i there is a defined history of its past, i.e. the interval $[0, now)$, its present value in the point $[now]$, and a default future. The execution of an action can modify the present value of an attribute and its default future, but not its past. It is important to note that such a definition does not necessarily determine a single function for x_i. Because of the non-deterministic choices involved, there might be a collection of such function tuples that are allowed by the continuous action system, and we cannot know which one of these will actually be the one the system follows. Thus, the system behavior may only be determined up to a certain tolerance, and any system behavior that is within these limits is possible.

Another important observation regards the possibility of *Zeno behavior*. That is, our definition does not guarantee that the sequence of generated intervals will cover all the non-negative reals. They might only cover an initial segment of these. In this case, there is a limit point of time that the action system reaches when the number of iterations reaches infinity. These systems are well-defined but the simple explication of the behavior of the hybrid system is then not sufficient. For this, we further assume that the system is restarted at the limit point, and repeat the process again. This is meaningful if all the attribute values converge to a well-defined value in the limit. This restart can be carried out as many times as needed. Thus, a continuous action systems may have multiple limit points in its execution. However, the standard action system semantics does not allow multiple limit points, so this is a point where the semantics has to be extended. For simplicity, we assume in the sequel that there is no Zeno-behavior and a single limit point is sufficient. The absence of Zeno behavior means that the action system will define the values of the attributes for the whole domain of $Real_+$.

A simple way of reaching a limit point is when a control computation (where the time does not advance) does not terminate. This means that the continuous behavior of the system is stuck at the last time instance reached. Nontermination of the control computation is most certainly undesired and unintended. This means that is desirable to prove that control computations where time does not advance always terminate.

Composing continuous action systems In order to model complex hybrid systems, where several different subsystems or components evolve concurrently, we need to formally define the composition of continuous action systems. Two actions systems communicate by means of imported and exported variables. We can also model other means of communication using the action systems framework [6], but this is out of the scope of this paper. For parallel composition, we may also need to rename certain attributes of the system when describing more complex systems, but we ignore this aspect here for brevity.

We define the parallel composition of two continuous systems by using essentially the parallel composition operator for ordinary action systems [5]. Thus, if we have two continuous action systems $\mathcal{C}$ and $\mathcal{C}'$ as in (1), then their parallel composition is the continuous action system $\mathcal{C} \parallel \mathcal{C}'$ defined as follows:

$$\mathcal{C} \parallel \mathcal{C}' \stackrel{\triangle}{=} |(\text{var } x : \text{Real}_+ \to \mathit{Val}, x' : \text{Real}_+ \to \mathit{Val}';$$
$$\bullet \; S_0 \, ; S_0';$$
$$\text{do } g_1 \to S_1 \square \, \ldots \square \, g_m \to S_m \square \, g_1' \to S_1' \square \, \ldots \square \, g_n' \to S_n' \text{ od} \tag{4}$$
$$)| : (y \cup y') - (z \cup z')$$

where the unprimed entities originally belonged to $\mathcal{C}$ and the primed entities to $\mathcal{C}'$. We assume here that the variables x and x' are disjoint. We need to combine the continuous action systems before we translate them into discrete action systems, because the local variable *now* appears in both $\bar{\mathcal{C}}$ and $\bar{\mathcal{C}}'$. By combining the continuous action systems first, we ensure that $\mathcal{C} \parallel \mathcal{C}'$ uses a single *now* variable, which is checked by actions from both components.

Thus, parallel composition essentially combines the attributes of the two component systems and, therefore, their continuous evolution. Because the actions in the parallel composition are the combined actions of the two systems, discrete changes will usually occur more frequently. An action in one component system may depend on an attribute in the other component system, which may be again modified by actions of the former system. This means that the behavior of a system in a parallel composition is usually different from the behavior of the system when it is alone.

4   Modeling Systems

In this section we illustrate how a hybrid system can be described as a continuous action system. We show how to model real-time systems, systems using differential equations, and also a press that reacts to external signals from the environment.

We can use clock variables to measure the passage of time and to correlate the execution of an action with the time. A *clock variable* is an attribute that measures the time elapsed since it was set to zero. Assume that c is an attribute of type Real. We then use the following definition for resetting the clock c:

$$reset(c) \; \stackrel{\wedge}{=} \; c :- (\lambda t \cdot t - now)$$

This definition is just a convenience for correlating the behavior of a system with the passage of the time. Since a clock variable is a regular attribute, we can define as many clocks as needed and reset them independently. It is also possible to do arithmetic operations with clock variables, to use time constrains as guards, or to refer to past values of an attribute, e.g. $x.(now - 1)$. Hence, continuous action systems can be used to model real-time systems.

The behavior of a dynamic system is often described using a system of differential equations. We can allow this kind of definitions by introducing the shorthand

$$\dot{x} :- f \; \stackrel{\wedge}{=} \; [x :- y \mid y.now = x.now \wedge \dot{y} = f.y, y \geq now]$$

This will assign to x a time function that satisfies the given differential equation and which is such that the function x is continuous at now. As an example, if $f = (\lambda t \cdot c)$, where c is a constant value, then we have that $\dot{x} :- (\lambda t \cdot c) \equiv x :- (\lambda t \cdot x.now + c * (t - now))$. Thus, we can use continuous action systems to express hybrid systems using either explicit functional expressions or implicit differential equations.

An example of a press from a metal processing factory [12] is shown in Fig. 2. The press works as follows. First, its lower part is raised until the middle position. Then an upper conveyor belt feeds a metal blank into the press. When the press is loaded (signalled by $sensor_1$ being T), the lower part of the press is raised until the top position and the blank is forged. The press will then move down until the bottom position and the forged blank is placed into a lower conveyor belt. When the press is unloaded (signalled by $sensor_2$ being T), its lower part is raised to the middle position, ready for being loaded again.

The press works cyclically and keeps evolving from one phase to another. We model these phases with a *task* attribute in the continuous action system $\mathcal{P}ress$

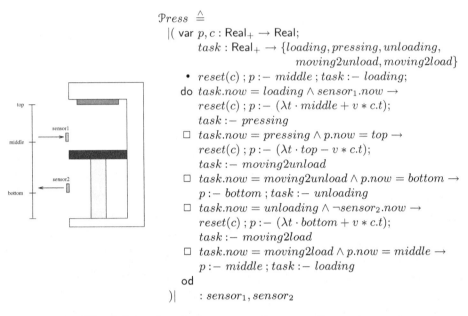

$$\mathcal{P}ress \overset{\triangle}{=}$$
$$|(\ \text{var}\ p, c : \mathsf{Real}_+ \rightarrow \mathsf{Real};$$
$$task : \mathsf{Real}_+ \rightarrow \{loading, pressing, unloading,$$
$$moving2unload, moving2load\}$$

- $reset(c)\ ;\ p :-\ middle\ ;\ task :-\ loading;$

do $task.now = loading \wedge sensor_1.now \rightarrow$
$reset(c)\ ;\ p :-\ (\lambda t \cdot middle + v * c.t);$
$task :-\ pressing$

□ $task.now = pressing \wedge p.now = top \rightarrow$
$reset(c)\ ;\ p :-\ (\lambda t \cdot top - v * c.t);$
$task :-\ moving2unload$

□ $task.now = moving2unload \wedge p.now = bottom \rightarrow$
$p :-\ bottom\ ;\ task :-\ unloading$

□ $task.now = unloading \wedge \neg sensor_2.now \rightarrow$
$reset(c)\ ;\ p :-\ (\lambda t \cdot bottom + v * c.t);$
$task :-\ moving2load$

□ $task.now = moving2load \wedge p.now = middle \rightarrow$
$p :-\ middle\ ;\ task :-\ loading$

od

$)|\qquad : sensor_1, sensor_2$

Fig. 2. Press functioning as a continuous action system.

shown in Fig. 2. This attribute can have the discrete values *loading, pressing, moving2unload, unloading, moving2load*. The continuous attribute p shows the position of the press plate and is, at different moments in time, a linearly increasing, a linearly decreasing or a constant function of time. The positions of reference for the press, i.e. *bottom, middle,* and *top*, are given as parameters.

The press example is a typical part of a control system. This kind of systems are essentially composed from several components that work together in order to meet the requirements of the overall system. Thus, an important feature of a component is its interaction with the environment. In the case of the press the interaction with the environment (two conveyor belts) is modeled with several sensors. The sensors are modeled as imported attributes that can be changed by the environment at any time. The press reads the values that $sensor_1$ and $sensor_2$ display, but these values are updated by the environment in a way we are not interested in here.

Other types of hybrid systems can be modelled as well using continuous action systems. Some more examples can be found in [8,14].

5   Safety Properties

Properties of continuous action systems can be established by proving that these properties hold for the corresponding discrete action systems. Hence, there is no special proof theory for continuous action systems, but the standard proof theory for action systems suffices (with the exception that we may need to consider multiple limit points, as was mentioned earlier). In this paper, we concentrate on safety properties, as in many cases they are the kind of properties that we want to initially establish for hybrid systems.

A common characterization for a safety property is that nothing 'bad' happens during the lifetime of the system. Put in another way, a safety property is a 'good' property G that always holds, i.e., $(\forall t \geq 0 \cdot G.t)$. We can establish this property for the action system $\mathcal{C}$ in (1) by proving that a property $I \stackrel{\wedge}{=} (\forall t \mid 0 \leq t < now \cdot G'.t)$ is an invariant of the corresponding discrete action system $\bar{\mathcal{C}}$, where $(\forall t \geq 0 \cdot G'.t \Rightarrow G.t)$. This implies the safety property, provided that the system does not have a Zeno behavior and does not terminate (i.e., now will go to infinity in the system). More precisely, the safety property G holds when the system is started in an initial state satisfying P, if and only if the following three conditions are satisfied for $\bar{\mathcal{C}}$:

$$\forall t \geq 0 \cdot G'.t \Rightarrow G.t$$
$$P \Rightarrow wp(now := 0 ; S_0 ; N, I)$$
$$I \wedge g_i \Rightarrow wp(S_i ; N, I), \quad i = 1, \dots, m$$

Consider the press example in Fig. 2. We consider two safety properties. First, we want to prove that the movable plate of the press does not pass the limits of the machine. Formally this is expressed by $(\forall t \geq 0 \cdot bottom \leq p.t \leq top)$, where p is the vertical position of the plate. Second, we want to prove that p is a continuous function on Real_+. We need to choose an invariant I that allows us to establish the safety property $(\forall t \geq 0 \cdot bottom \leq p.t \leq top) \wedge (p \ continuous \ on \ \mathsf{Real}_+)$ using the proof rule above.

For the first conjunct of the safety property, an invariant of the form $(\forall t \mid 0 \leq t \leq now \cdot bottom \leq p.t \leq top)$ would be sufficient. However, to prove the global continuity property, we need a stronger invariant, which also ensures that the press remains in the correct position during the loading and unloading operations. The following invariant I is sufficient for establishing the required safety property:

$$
\begin{aligned}
I \stackrel{\wedge}{=} \ & (p \ continuous \ on \ [0, now] \wedge (\forall t \mid 0 \leq t \leq now \cdot bottom \leq p.t \leq top) \wedge \\
& (\forall t \mid 0 \leq t \leq now \cdot task.t = loading \Rightarrow p.t = middle) \wedge \\
& (\forall t \mid 0 \leq t \leq now \cdot task.t = unloading \Rightarrow p.t = bottom))
\end{aligned}
$$

The proof must establish that the invariant is satisfied by the initialization from the moment 0 until the first moment an action is enabled and during the time elapsed between the execution of two actions. The discharging of the proof obligations can be found in [8].

6 Conclusions and Related Work

In this paper we have shown how to generalize the action systems framework for modeling hybrid systems, by introducing the notion of continuous action systems. We model attributes in continuous action systems as functions over time that are updated in a way that only changes their present and future behavior. Essentially, this amounts to extending the notion of state with both an history and a default future, thus generalizing the classical action systems approach that only handles the present state.

This extension allows us to model systems that combine discrete control with continuous behavior, the latter either defined by explicit functions of time or by differential equations. We have also shown that the continuous action systems model provides a simple way of defining the parallel composition of hybrid systems, using communication by means of imported and exported attributes. Finally, we explained how to prove safety properties of continuous action systems using the classical invariant method. We illustrated these concepts with a simple example, while a complete case study can be found in [3].

The idea of extending an existing formalism to model real-time systems by introducing a variable representing the time was presented by Abadi and Lamport in [1]. We follow the same approach here, extending an existing formalism to handle hybrid systems instead of creating a new formalism specific for such systems. This provides a clear advantage, as we can reuse all the previous results on action systems to study real-time and hybrid systems models.

Rönkkö and Ravn [14] have already proposed a model for combining action systems and continuous behavior, called *hybrid action systems*. In their model, the continuous evolution of a variable is modeled as a special kind of atomic action. An atomic action cannot be interrupted and its bounds are specified in advance. This affects the parallel composition of systems, since different simultaneous actions must be combined into a sequence of atomic actions. In the worst case, the parallel composition of two systems with n and m actions leads to a system with $n * m$ actions. Also, there is no implicit notion of time in their approach, which is not intended for modeling real-time systems. In our model, parallel composition of two such systems gives a continuous action system with $n + m$ actions. This is a major simplification for handling large systems.

These advantages still exist when comparing our formalism with the *hybrid automata* [2]. The number of states in the parallel composition of two hybrid automata is also the product of the number of states of the original automata. Note that in the hybrid automata formalism, transitions are fired synchronously, while in the action system formalism actions are selected and executed asynchronously. The continuous action system formalism is more expressive than hybrid automata, as it allows references to historical values of the attributes in guards and expressions. Compared to hybrid automata, our model also allows the attributes to be selectively updated: only those attributes that are changed need to be mentioned in an action.

Another interesting model for hybrid systems is provided by *phase transition systems* [11]. In this model, the continuous behavior of the system is modeled using a finite set of activities. However, only one activity can be enabled at a certain time. Thus, a single activity completely defines the continuous behavior of a system. Again, our model allows the attributes to be selectively updated.

The next step in the development of the continuous action systems formalism is to illustrate their stepwise refinement. This will provide for the derivation of executable control programs that are correct with respect to their specification, given as a continuous action system.

Acknowledgement We would like to thank Cristina Cerschi, Mauno Rönkkö and Hannu Toivonen for our inspiring discussions as well as to the anonymous referees for their useful comments on the topics covered in this paper.

References

1. M. Abadi and L. Lamport. An old-fashioned receipe for real time. *ACM Transactions on Programming Languages and Systems*, 16(5):1543–1571, 1994.
2. R. Alur, C. Courcoubetis, T.A. Henzinger, and P.H. Ho. Hybrid automata: an algorithmic approach to the specification and verification of hybrid systems. In R.L. Grossman, A. Nerode, A.P. Revn, and H. Rischel, editors, *Hybrid Systems I*, volume LNCS 736, pages 209–229. Springer-Verlag, 1993.
3. R. J. R. Back and C. Cerschi. Modeling and verifying a temperature control system using hybrid action systems. In *Proc. of the 5th Int. Workshop in Formal Methods for Industrial Critical Systems*, 2000, to appear.
4. R. J. R. Back and R. Kurki-Suonio. Decentralization of process nets with centralized control. In *2nd Symp. on Principles of Distributed Computing*, volume LNCS 873, pages 131–142. ACM SIGACT-SIGOPS, 1983.
5. R. J. R. Back and K. Sere. Stepwise refinement of parallel algorithms. In *Science of Computer Programming 13*, pages 133–180, 1991.
6. R. J. R. Back and K. Sere. From action systems to modular systems. In *Formal Methods Europe (FME '94)*, volume LNCS 873, pages 1–25. Springer-Verlag, 1994.
7. R. J. R. Back and J. von Wright. *Refinement Calculus - A Systematic Introduction*. Springer-Verlag, 1998.
8. R.J. Back, L. Petre, and I. Porres. Generalizing action systems to hybrid systems. Technical Report 307, TUCS Turku Centre for Computer Science, 1999.
9. M.S. Branicky. General hybrid dynamical systems: modeling, analysis and control. In R. Alur, T. A. Henzinger, and E. D. Sontag, editors, *Hybrid Systems III*, volume LNCS 1066, pages 186–200. Springer-Verlag, 1996.
10. E. W. Dijkstra. *A Discipline of Programming*. Prentice-Hall International, 1976.
11. Y. Kesten, Z. Manna, and A. Pnueli. Verification of clocked and hybrid systems. In *Lectures on Embedded Systems*, volume LNCS 1494, pages 4–73. Springer-Verlag, 1998.
12. C. Lewerentz and T. Lindner. *Formal Development of Reactive Systems: Case Study Production Cell.*, volume LNCS 891. Springer-Verlag, 1995.
13. A. Nerode and W. Kohn. Models for hybrid systems: automata, topologies, controllability, observability. In R.L. Grossman, A. Nerode, A.P. Revn, and H. Rischel, editors, *Hybrid Systems I*, volume LNCS 736, pages 317–356. Springer-Verlag, 1993.
14. M. Rönkkö and A.P. Ravn. Action systems with continuous behaviour. In P. J. Antsaklis, W. Kohn, M. Lemmon, A. Nerode, and S. Sastry, editors, *Hybrid Systems V*, volume LNCS 1567, pages 304–323. Springer-Verlag, 1999.

Compositional Verification of Synchronous Networks

Leszek Holenderski

Dept. of Computing Sci., Technical University of Eindhoven
PO Box 513, 5600 MB Eindhoven, The Netherlands
L.Holenderski@tue.nl

Abstract. We present a logical framework for the verification of synchronous networks in an assert-commit style. It is based on the known observation that the Hoare rule for sequential composition is sound and complete for parallel composition as well. The calculus we develop inside the framework is extremely simple, based on just one propositional tautology. Nevertheless, it is powerful enough to analyze the common proof strategies (monolithic, forward and backward) applied in automated verification of such networks. This analysis leads to an incremental verification method, based on successive construction of the weakest preconditions, in which the backward proof is driven by the property being verified. In the case of finite synchronous networks this construction can be carried out via simple manipulations on circuits, and circuit optimizers can be used incrementally to simplify the complexity of such backward proofs. The method should hopefully be applicable in verification of software synchronous systems, since the current compilers for synchronous languages generate quite redundant circuits.

1 Introduction

We present a simple logical framework in which we study the problem of formal verification of reactive networks (systems formed as a hierarchy of reactive processes run in parallel). We consider only *synchronous* networks, i.e., systems obtained by parallel synchronous composition $P||Q$, where P and Q are synchronous processes (or synchronous networks themselves). We are not concerned with the exact nature of the processes. For example, they can be specified in any of the common notations used for programming synchronous processes, like ARGOS [14,9], ESTEREL [7,9], LUSTRE [10,9] or SIGNAL [6,9].

Properties of reactive systems can conveniently be specified in assert-commit style, by Hoare triples $\alpha P \beta$, where α and β are formulae in some logic and P is a process (or a network). Assertion α specifies a property of the environment in which P is executed, and commitment β specifies a property guaranteed by P. More precisely, $\alpha P \beta$ is valid iff $E||P$ satisfies β, for any environment E which satisfies α.

Our approach is based on the old observation [20] that under the above interpretation of Hoare triples the following inference rule is both sound and

M. Joseph (Ed.): FTRTFT 2000, LNCS 1926, pp. 214–227, 2000.

(relatively) complete for a parallel composition of processes P and Q:

$$\frac{\alpha P\gamma, \quad \gamma Q\beta}{\alpha(P||Q)\beta}$$

Thus, in order to prove $\alpha(P||Q)\beta$, it suffices to find an intermediate formula γ such that $\alpha P\gamma$ and $\gamma Q\beta$.

The above rule is analogous to the well known rule for the sequential composition of iterative programs. We draw on this analogy, by considering the strongest post-condition of α w.r.t. P (denoted by $\alpha\vec{P}$) and the weakest precondition of β w.r.t. Q (denoted by $\overleftarrow{Q}\beta$) in order to automate the task of finding the intermediate formula γ.

When verifying complex systems, especially software safety-critical systems, one is usually interested in verifying many relatively simple commitments under the same assertion. By a relatively simple commitment we mean the property which only a small part of the system contributes to. In this typical scenario, synthesis of γ as $\overleftarrow{Q}\beta$ turns out to be particularly useful: by considering successive weakest pre-conditions $\overleftarrow{Q}\beta$ and $\overleftarrow{P}(\overleftarrow{Q}\beta)$, one in fact considers automatically how the component processes contribute to property β.

On the way, we develop a logical framework to study proof strategies for $\alpha(P||Q)\beta$. This framework leads to a simple calculus in which such strategies can be derived formally, just by manipulating propositional logic formulae. In fact, the whole calculus is based on just one propositional tautology: $(p \wedge q) \to r$ is equivalent to $p \to (q \to r)$. The reason for this simplicity is given in Section 3.2.

The logical framework is developed in two steps. First we consider the general case in which we are not concerned with any particular notation used to specify components of $\alpha(P||Q)\beta$. Next we instantiate the general framework in the context where processes P and Q are specified by synchronous sequential circuits, and formulae α and β are specified by synchronous observers [12]. Since synchronous observers can be translated to circuits, all the components of $\alpha(P||Q)\beta$ can be represented by circuits, and this allows to simplify the proof of $\alpha(P||Q)\beta$ via manipulations on circuits.

The paper is organized as follows. In Section 2 we recall some basic theory of synchronous networks. In Section 3, the logical framework is developed, and three common strategies to prove $\alpha(P||Q)\beta$ are derived. One of the strategies, which we call a backward proof with weakest observers, turns out to be more efficient than the other two, so we analyze it in more detail, in Section 5. We conclude with the proposal of a simple software tool to implement the strategy.

2   Preliminaries

We recall those parts of the theory of synchronous networks which establish the equivalence between the three views of synchronous processes: (1) as sets of traces, (2) as sequential circuits and (3) as temporal logic formulae. In summary, synchronous parallel composition $P||Q$ can be described as $[\![P]\!] \cap [\![Q]\!]$ (the intersection of sets of traces), $\mathbf{P} \cup \mathbf{Q}$ (the union of circuits understood as sets of boolean clauses), and $\mathcal{P} \wedge \mathcal{Q}$ (the conjunction of characteristic formulae).

2.1   Processes as Traces

We only consider *pure* reactive processes (i.e. those which manipulate boolean values or, more generally, values from finite domains). A process, say P, operates on a finite set of boolean variables (from some alphabet V) that represent the signals used by P to interact with its environment. We use the notation $P(I; O)$ to indicate that process P has inputs I and outputs O, for $I, O \subseteq V$ and $I \cap O = \emptyset$. (For now, in order to simplify presentation, we do not consider processes with local variables. We postpone them till Section 8.)

The semantics of synchronous processes we use in this paper is borrowed from [11]. In synchronous computations time is assumed to be *discrete*. In any instant of time, every signal is either true or false (present/absent, on/off, up/down, ...). A computation of $P(I; O)$ is represented by a *trace* which is an infinite sequence of reactions $\langle r_1, r_2, \ldots \rangle$, for $r_i \subseteq V$. Reaction r_i consists of all the signals present in the i'th instant of time; $r_i \cap I$ is the stimulus of P and $r_i \cap O$ is the response of P to the stimulus.

Let $\mathcal{T} := (2^V)^\omega$ denote the set of all traces (over alphabet V). Traces t and t' are called *compatible* on variables $X \subseteq V$, denoted by $t \sim_X t'$, iff they differ only on variables from $V \setminus X$. Formally, for $t = \langle r_1, r_2, \ldots \rangle$ and $t' = \langle r_1', r_2', \ldots \rangle$,

$$t \sim_X t' \quad \text{iff} \quad \forall i \geq 1 (r_i \cap X = r_i' \cap X)$$

Let $\llbracket P \rrbracket \subseteq \mathcal{T}$ denote the *behaviour* of $P(I; O)$ (the set of all its traces). We assume that the behaviour is always closed w.r.t. $\sim_{I \cup O}$ (if $t \in \llbracket P \rrbracket$ and $t \sim_{I \cup O} t'$ then $t' \in \llbracket P \rrbracket$).

Processes can be put in parallel to form networks, say $P \| Q$. A reaction of a network, in some instant of time, consists in simultaneous execution of reactions by all its processes. Communication is realized by sharing signals with the same name. The communication protocol is that of instantaneous broadcast: a signal emitted by one process is perceived as present, in the same instant it was emitted, by all the processes that share the signal.

In the sequel we assume that each signal can be emitted by at most one process. This data-flow model is directly applicable only to data-flow synchronous languages, like LUSTRE and SIGNAL. However, the imperative model employed in ARGOS and ESTEREL (where a signal can be emitted by several processes) can easily be reduced to the data-flow model. Replace $P_1(\ldots; o) \| P_2(\ldots; o)$ with $P_1(\ldots; o)[o_1/o] \| P_2(\ldots; o)[o_2/o] \| Q(o_1, o_2; o)$, where $[x/y]$ denotes the substitution of x for y, and Q is a process which emits o whenever o_1 or o_2 is present.

Under this assumption, together with the assumption about the behaviors being closed w.r.t. compatible traces, the behaviour of $P \| Q$ can simply be formalized as $\llbracket P \| Q \rrbracket := \llbracket P \rrbracket \cap \llbracket Q \rrbracket$.

2.2   Processes as Circuits

The behaviors of synchronous networks can be specified in many ways [9]. In this paper we prefer to use synchronous sequential circuits since it is a common formalism to which other (pure) synchronous formalisms can be translated, as in [8,15].

By a circuit we mean a set of boolean clauses that specify both the combinational and sequential part of the circuit. In order to avoid potential problems with causal correctness, we assume that all synchronous processes and networks we consider have no combinational cycles, when translated to circuits.

In the sequel we use bold letters $\mathbf{O}$, $\mathbf{P}$ and $\mathbf{Q}$ to denote circuits representing processes O, P and Q, respectively. Under the data-flow assumption, $P\|Q$ can simply be specified by $\mathbf{P} \cup \mathbf{Q}$. (Formally, one can give the trace semantics to circuits, such that $[\![\mathbf{P} \cup \mathbf{Q}]\!] = [\![\mathbf{P}]\!] \cap [\![\mathbf{Q}]\!]$.)

2.3 Processes as Formulae

The behaviors of synchronous networks can also be specified by formulae in some logic $\mathcal{L}$ of traces. Usually, $\mathcal{L}$ is some variant of linear temporal logic. The simple logical framework we develop in this paper does not rely on any particular logic of traces. Although we need some assumptions about $\mathcal{L}$, the assumptions are fairly standard and are satisfied by most temporal logics.

Let α, β, γ be formulae of $\mathcal{L}$. As usual, $t \models \alpha$ stands for "trace t satisfies α". Let $[\![\alpha]\!]$ denote the set of all traces which satisfy α. As usual, $\models \alpha$ stands for "α is valid", and denotes $[\![\alpha]\!] = \mathcal{T}$.

We assume that $\mathcal{L}$ contains at least the following connectives: $\wedge$, $\rightarrow$ and $\square$, and they are interpreted such that $[\![\alpha \wedge \beta]\!] = [\![\alpha]\!] \cap [\![\beta]\!]$, $\models \alpha \rightarrow \beta$ iff $[\![\alpha]\!] \subseteq [\![\beta]\!]$, $t \models \square\alpha$ iff α is satisfied by all suffixes of t. In addition, we require that

$$\models \alpha \wedge \beta \rightarrow \gamma \quad \text{iff} \quad \models \alpha \rightarrow (\beta \rightarrow \gamma) \tag{1}$$

We also assume that $\mathcal{L}$ is expressive enough to characterize synchronous processes, in the sense that for any process, say P, there exists a formula, say $\mathcal{P}$, such that $[\![P]\!] = [\![\mathcal{P}]\!]$. Such a formula is called a *characteristic formula* of a process. For example, the logic given in [11] is expressive in this sense.

In the sequel we use calligraphic letters $\mathcal{O}$, $\mathcal{P}$ and $\mathcal{Q}$ to denote characteristic formulae of processes O, P and Q, respectively. Obviously, $\mathcal{P} \wedge \mathcal{Q}$ is a characteristic formula of $P\|Q$.

3 Logical framework

3.1 Assert-commit Formulae

A property of a reactive process can be regarded as a set of traces that have the property. As usual, we say that process P has property X iff $[\![P]\!] \subseteq X$. We assume that properties are specified by formulae in the logic $\mathcal{L}$ described in the previous section. As usual, we say that process P satisfies formula α, denoted by $P \models \alpha$, iff $[\![P]\!] \subseteq [\![\alpha]\!]$.

In fact, we will specify behaviors of processes in the assert-commit style, by formulae of the form $\alpha P \beta$, where $\alpha, \beta \in \mathcal{L}$. Intuitive meaning of such Hoare triples is the following: $\alpha P \beta$ is valid iff P has property β whenever executed in an environment which has property α. Formally,

$$\models \alpha P \beta \quad \text{iff} \quad \forall E (\text{if } E \models \alpha \text{ then } E \| P \models \beta) \tag{2}$$

The meaning of triple $\alpha P \beta$ can also be formalized in logic $\mathcal{L}$, as

$$\models \alpha P \beta \quad \text{iff} \quad \models \alpha \wedge \mathcal{P} \to \beta \tag{3}$$

or equivalently, by (1), as

$$\models \alpha P \beta \quad \text{iff} \quad \models \mathcal{P} \to (\alpha \to \beta) \tag{4}$$

The semantical and logical characterization of validity of $\alpha P \beta$ are (almost) equivalent:

Lemma 1. $\models \alpha \wedge \mathcal{P} \to \beta$ *implies* $\forall E (\text{if } E \models \alpha \text{ then } E \| P \models \beta)$.

Proof. If $E \models \alpha$ then $E \| P \models \alpha \wedge \mathcal{P}$, hence $E \| P \models \beta$.   □

Lemma 2. *If logic $\mathcal{L}$ is realizable, in the sense that any formula $\alpha \in \mathcal{L}$ is a characteristic formula of some process, then $\forall E (\text{if } E \models \alpha \text{ then } E \| P \models \beta)$ implies* $\models \alpha \wedge \mathcal{P} \to \beta$.

Proof. Take as E the process characterized by α, then $E \| P \models \beta$ is equivalent to $[\![\alpha]\!] \cap [\![P]\!] \subseteq [\![\beta]\!]$ which is equivalent to $\models \alpha \wedge \mathcal{P} \to \beta$.   □

In order to resolve the "almost" issue, in the rest of the paper we assume that $\mathcal{L}$ is realizable, and thus the meaning of $\alpha P \beta$ is defined equivalently by (2), (3) or (4).

3.2   Strongest Post-Condition and weakest Pre-Condition

Intuitively, the strongest post-condition of α w.r.t. P, denoted by $\alpha \vec{P}$, is the strongest property guaranteed by P, when P is executed in the environment which has property α. Dually, the weakest pre-condition of β w.r.t. P, denoted by $\overleftarrow{P}\beta$, is the weakest property of the environment, in order for P to guarantee property β.

Formally, $\alpha \vec{P}$ and $\overleftarrow{P}\beta$ are formulae such that $\models \alpha \vec{P} \to \beta$ iff $\models \alpha P \beta$, and $\models \alpha \to \overleftarrow{P}\beta$ iff $\models \alpha P \beta$. From (3) and (4) it follows that

$$\alpha \vec{P} = \alpha \wedge \mathcal{P} \tag{5}$$

$$\overleftarrow{P}\beta = \mathcal{P} \to \beta \tag{6}$$

Notice that $\vec{P}$ and $\overleftarrow{P}$ form a well known Galois connection (by the equivalence $\models \alpha \vec{P} \to \beta$ iff $\models \alpha \to \overleftarrow{P}\beta$). Also $\wedge$ and $\to$ form a well known Galois connection (by the tautology (1)). In the presented framework, both Galois connections coincide, and the simplicity of our calculus follows from the fact that we can use them interchangeably.

3.3   The Inference Rule

The following rule is both sound and complete:

$$\frac{\alpha P \gamma, \quad \gamma Q \beta}{\alpha (P || Q) \beta}$$

The soundness of the rule follows directly from (3), by a simple propositional reasoning to justify that $\models \alpha \wedge \mathcal{P} \wedge \mathcal{Q} \rightarrow \beta$ follows from $\models \alpha \wedge \mathcal{P} \rightarrow \gamma$ and $\models \gamma \wedge \mathcal{Q} \rightarrow \beta$.

For completeness it suffices to assume $\models \alpha (P || Q) \beta$ and take as γ either $\alpha \vec{P}$ or $\overleftarrow{Q} \beta$. For example, let $\gamma := \alpha \vec{P} = \alpha \wedge \mathcal{P}$. Then, $\alpha P \gamma$ is valid (as equivalent to the validity of $\alpha \wedge \mathcal{P} \rightarrow \alpha \wedge \mathcal{P}$) and $\gamma Q \beta$ is valid (as equivalent to the validity of $\alpha \wedge \mathcal{P} \wedge \mathcal{Q} \rightarrow \beta$ which follows from the assumption $\models \alpha (P || Q) \beta$).

3.4   Proof Strategies

In this section, we analyze the well-known proof strategies for establishing validity of $\alpha (P || Q) \beta$. The analysis can be done in a very simple way, using the simple logical framework we have developed so far.

Directly from definition (3),

$$\models \alpha (P || Q) \beta \quad \text{iff} \quad \models \alpha \wedge \mathcal{P} \wedge \mathcal{Q} \rightarrow \beta$$

and formula $\alpha \wedge \mathcal{P} \wedge \mathcal{Q} \rightarrow \beta$ is equivalent, again by (1), to the following formulae:

$$\begin{array}{ll}
\text{(monolithic)} & \mathcal{P} \wedge \mathcal{Q} \rightarrow (\alpha \rightarrow \beta) \\
\text{(forward)} & ((\alpha \wedge \mathcal{P}) \wedge \mathcal{Q}) \rightarrow \beta \\
\text{(backward)} & \alpha \rightarrow (\mathcal{P} \rightarrow (\mathcal{Q} \rightarrow \beta))
\end{array}$$

The first formula represents a monolithic proof strategy since it can be rewritten as $P || Q \models \alpha \rightarrow \beta$, and this can be proved by using a model checker for the model $P || Q$ and property $\alpha \rightarrow \beta$.

The second formula represents a forward proof strategy since it can be rewritten as $((\alpha \vec{P}) \vec{Q}) \rightarrow \beta$, and this represents the method of pushing α forward, towards β, via the chain $P || Q$.

The third formula represents a backward proof strategy since it can be rewritten as $\alpha \rightarrow (\overleftarrow{P}(\overleftarrow{Q} \beta))$, and this represents the method of pulling β backward, towards α, via the chain $P || Q$.

The three strategies seem to be equally difficult since the formulae which characterize them have the same complexity, in terms of their size. However, the forward and backward strategies can easily be improved, and thus have an advantage over the monolithic strategy.

In case of the forward proof, instead of forming the whole implication $((\alpha \wedge \mathcal{P}) \wedge \mathcal{Q}) \rightarrow \beta$ in one step, one can first form $\alpha \wedge \mathcal{P}$ (thus, $\alpha \vec{P}$), simplify it to some γ, then form $\gamma \wedge \mathcal{Q}$ (thus, $\gamma \vec{Q}$), simplify it to some γ', and finally form the simpler implication $\gamma' \rightarrow \beta$.

Similarly, in case of the backward proof, instead of forming the whole impli-
cation $\alpha \rightarrow (\mathcal{P} \rightarrow (\mathcal{Q} \rightarrow \beta))$ in one step, one can first form $\mathcal{Q} \rightarrow \beta$ (thus, $\overleftarrow{\mathcal{Q}}\beta$),
simplify it to some γ, then form $\mathcal{P} \rightarrow \gamma$ (thus, $\overleftarrow{\mathcal{P}}\gamma$), simplify it to some γ', and
finally form the simpler implication $\alpha \rightarrow \gamma'$.

In Section 5 we show how to incrementally use circuit optimizers as the
simplifying devices. Such optimizers can be perceived as automated theorem
provers in propositional logic. They are usually incomplete, due to the use of
more efficient, non-exponential, algorithms.

The improved forward and backward strategies are very similar. However, the
backward proof turns out to have an advantage over the forward proof, under the
verification scenario presented in the Introduction. This is quite obvious since
the forward proof is usually too general (α is too strong), quite unnecessarily.

4   Synchronous Observers

In the rest of this paper we will analyze the backward proof strategy in the
context where both α and β, in $\alpha \mathcal{P} \beta$, are synchronous observers [12]. (Note that
our formalization of observers is much simpler than the one given in [12].)

An observer is a pair $(O\!:\!o)$ where O is a process with a distinguished output
o. Observers specify safety properties of processes. Intuitively, process P satisfies
property $(O\!:\!o)$ iff $P\|O$ always emits o. Formally,

$$
\begin{aligned}
P \models (O\!:\!o) \quad &\text{iff} \quad P\|O \models \Box o \\
&\text{iff} \quad \models \mathcal{P} \wedge \mathcal{O} \rightarrow \Box o \\
&\text{iff} \quad \models \mathcal{P} \rightarrow (\mathcal{O} \rightarrow \Box o) \\
&\text{iff} \quad P \models \mathcal{O} \rightarrow \Box o
\end{aligned}
$$

Thus, the property specified by the observer $(O\!:\!o)$ can be defined by formula
$\mathcal{O} \rightarrow \Box o$. We call this semantics a *weak* interpretation of observer $(O\!:\!o)$, and
denote the formula by $(O \triangleleft o)$. Another semantics of observer $(O\!:\!o)$ can be
given by formula $\mathcal{O} \wedge \Box o$, denoted by $(O \triangleright o)$. We call this semantics a *strong*
interpretation of observer $(O\!:\!o)$.

We use strong observers to specify assertions and weak observers are used to
specify commitments. In other words, we only consider triples $(A \triangleright a)P(B \triangleleft b)$,
for some observers $(A\!:\!a)$ and $(B\!:\!b)$. Such triples are characterized by formula

$$
\mathcal{A} \wedge \Box a \wedge \mathcal{P} \rightarrow (\mathcal{B} \rightarrow \Box b),
$$

or equivalently, by

$$
\mathcal{A} \wedge \mathcal{P} \wedge \mathcal{B} \rightarrow (\Box a \rightarrow \Box b).
$$

This particular choice is one of the main reasons for the simplicity of our
calculus, as manifested in the sequel.

4.1   The Strongest and Weakest Observers

It turns out that the construction of the strongest post-condition $\alpha\vec{P}$ and the weakest pre-condition $\overleftarrow{P}\beta$ is surprisingly easy when α and β are observers and P, α and β are specified by circuits. This is in contrast with the methods of synthesizing the weakest-precondition via manipulations on Mealy machines, as presented in [12,5].

Consider the following calculations:

$$(O \triangleright o)\vec{P} = (\mathcal{O} \wedge \Box o) \wedge \mathcal{P} = (\mathcal{O} \wedge \mathcal{P}) \wedge \Box o = (O||P \triangleright o)$$
$$\overleftarrow{P}(O \triangleleft o) = \mathcal{P} \rightarrow (\mathcal{O} \rightarrow \Box o) = (\mathcal{P} \wedge \mathcal{O}) \rightarrow \Box o = (P||O \triangleleft o)$$

The calculations show that the same construction, namely the observer $(O||P\!:\!o)$ obtained by putting process O in parallel with process P, leads to both the strongest post-condition and the weakest pre-condition (provided one applies $\vec{P}$ to a strong observer and $\overleftarrow{P}$ to a weak observer). Notice that since P and O are specified as circuits, we could equally well write $(\mathbf{O} \cup \mathbf{P}\!:\!o)$ instead of $(O||P\!:\!o)$, and thus the cost of this construction is linear in size of P and O.

5   Backward Proofs with the Weakest Observers

The proof of $\models (A \triangleright a)(P||Q)(B \triangleleft b)$ can proceed as follows:

- Form the weakest observer

$$\overleftarrow{Q}\beta := (Q||B \triangleleft b)$$

  and simplify $Q||B$ to $Q'||B'$, using some sequential circuit optimizer, such as [19]. In addition, one can use some special-purpose algorithms, for example [17,16], to further reduce the number of latches in $Q||B$.
- Form the weakest observer

$$\overleftarrow{P}(\overleftarrow{Q}\beta) := \overleftarrow{P}(Q'||B' \triangleleft b) = (P||Q'||B' \triangleleft b)$$

  and simplify $P||Q'||B'$ to $P'||Q''||B''$, as above.
- Prove $\models \alpha \rightarrow \overleftarrow{P}(\overleftarrow{Q}\beta)$ by using either a tautology checker on formula

$$\mathcal{A} \wedge \Box a \rightarrow (\mathcal{P}' \wedge \mathcal{Q}'' \wedge \mathcal{B}'' \rightarrow \Box b)$$

  or a model checker on

$$A||P'||Q''||B'' \models \Box a \rightarrow \Box b$$

In the above scenario, the assertion $(A \triangleright a)$ is only used at the end of a proof. If $\Box a$ was used during the optimization, as an additional "don't care" condition, the optimization of the weakest observers constructed in the backward proof could lead to more simplifications. Such an improvement can easily be derived in our calculus, as shown below.

Let $(D\!:\!d_1, d_2)$ denote a *double observer* which is a process D with two distinguished outputs d_1 and d_2. Its (weak) semantics is denoted by $(D \lhd d_1, d_2)$, and is defined by the formula $\mathcal{D} \to (\Box d_1 \to \Box d_2)$.

It is easy to check that the weakest double observer can be constructed in the same way as the weakest single observer: $\overleftarrow{P}(D \lhd d_1, d_2) = (P || D \lhd d_1, d_2)$, for any process P. It is also easy to check that $\models (A \rhd a)P(B \lhd b)$ is equivalent to $\models (true)P(A || B \lhd a, b)$. Thus, the proof of $\models (A \rhd a)(P || Q)(B \lhd b)$ can proceed as above, by pulling backward $(A || B \lhd a, b)$ through the chain $P || Q$, and optimize the intermediate circuits under the "don't care" condition $\Box a$.

6   The Software Tool

The software tool which might implement our incremental method is quite simple. It is fed with the formula $(A \rhd a)(P_1 || \cdots || P_n)(B \lhd b)$, given as $n + 2$ files which contain descriptions of respective circuits, and returns either a confirmation that the formula is valid, or a counter-example trace if the formula is not valid.

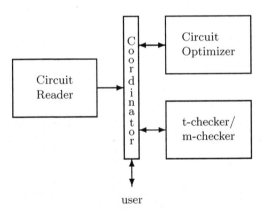

Fig. 1. The software tool

The tool consists of four main software components arranged in the structure depicted in Fig. 1. The input circuits are read in by `CircuitReader` and converted to the form suitable as input to `CircuitOptimizer`. `Coordinator` implements the loop in which the successive weakest observers are formed and fed to the optimizer. The loop is finished if either the optimizer returns the "empty" observer *true*, in which case the input formula is valid, or there are no more processes to be processed. In the later case, the coordinator invokes the tautology (or model) checker (component `t-checker/m-checker`) and reports the result.

Notice that this simple architecture allows to parameterize the tool, in a relatively easy way, with different combinations of `CircuitOptimizer` and `checker`.

The tool can be used to experiment with different heuristics (expressed as scripts for hardware optimizer) for improving efficiency of proving $\alpha(P\|Q)\beta$, compared to the usual monolithic strategy.

7 Possible Optimization Strategies

The incremental method of constructing the weakest observer of a network is sensitive to the order in which processes are applied and to the optimization strategy.

The order in which processes are applied to construct the intermediate weakest observers may influence their size, much the same as the order of variables may influence the size of BDDs. Usually, the process which influences the most variables appearing in the initial observer should be applied first since this will usually lead to maximal reductions during the optimization phase. The second process should influence the most variables appearing in the optimized observer obtained in the previous step, and so on.

The optimization strategy should try to minimize the number of latches, according to the common belief that the number of state bits in a model is the most important factor which contributes to the state explosion problem in model checkers. So far we have only considered two optimization algorithms: the Incompatible Sets algorithms for removal of redundant latches, as described in [17,16], and retiming.

The Incompatible Sets algorithms were designed for optimizing circuits obtained from imperative synchronous programs, written in ESTEREL and ARGOS, for example. Their efficiency in removing latches is due to the fact that current compilers for imperative synchronous languages employ quite simple state encoding techniques, usually the hot-state encoding, and thus introduce many redundant latches. Encouraging experimental results are well documented in [17,16], and we hope that applying the algorithms incrementally should in many cases produce even better results.

On the other hand, the Incompatible Sets algorithms do not seem to be much helpful in optimizing the number of latches in declarative (data flow) synchronous programs, where there are no explicit control states to encode, and instead, latches are introduced to implement the delay operators. In this case, retiming can be helpful in removing redundant latches, as explained below.

In what follows, we use **pre** to denote the delay operator. (This notation is borrowed from LUSTRE where **pre**(e) is an expression which gives the value of expression e in the previous instant.) Recall that **pre** distributes w.r.t. most operators, and this can be used to optimize the number of latches needed to compute complex expressions which involve **pre**. For example, **pre**$(a) \vee$ **pre**$(b) =$ **pre**$(a \vee b)$, and thus only 1 latch is needed for expression **pre**$(a) \vee$ **pre**(b).

Since the retiming algorithm can be perceived as exactly this kind of simplifier, it can often substantially reduce the number of latches in declarative programs with complex expressions involving **pre**. Although a programmer will seldom write such unoptimized expressions himself, nevertheless they may appear implicitly, as a result of compilation. This is illustrated by the following example.

7.1 An Example of Optimization by Retiming

We consider a simple example of a pipelined computing device (it comes from a very high level abstraction of a pipelined microprocessor).

Let *comp* (which stands for component) denote a process which gets a vector of bits (the input word) and produces a vector of bits (the output word). Both words have the same length w (which stands for width), and the bits are numbered from 0 to $w - 1$. If *in* is the input word and *out* is the output word then

$$out[i] = \mathbf{pre}(\neg in[i - 1]), \quad \text{for } 0 \leq i < w$$

where $\neg$ is negation and $in[-1] = in[w - 1]$. In other words, *in* is rotated by one bit, inverted, and delayed by one clock cycle. The component contains w latches, of course.

Let *pipe* denote the process consisting of d component processes (d stands for depth) such that inputs of component i are driven by outputs of component $i - 1$. In data flow notation, the pipe can be specified as

$$out = \underbrace{comp(comp(\ldots comp(in)\ldots))}_{d \text{ times}}$$

The pipe contains $d * w$ latches, of course.

Let f be some boolean function on a word of bits. In our example f is simply the w-wide "or", and the property, or rather its commitment part, is

$$f(out) \wedge \neg f(out^{-1})$$

where

$$out^{-1} = \underbrace{comp(comp(\ldots comp(in)\ldots))}_{d-1 \text{ times}}$$

The example is used to illustrate how the incremental simplification can automatically discover that the property which syntactically depends on $w * d$ latches, apparently (i.e., semantically) depends only on d latches.

The weakest observer of β w.r.t. *pipe* was constructed incrementally, going backwards through the components of the pipe, as described in Section 5. During this process, successive pre-observers were optimized using the retiming procedure from the SIS package [19]. The final weakest observer had only d latches.

We conducted several experiments on SPARCstation 5 with 64MB memory, using SIS version 1.2, with retime script `retime -nm -c 10000.0`. Each experiment consisted in executing a Tcl script which for a given pair (w, d) constructed the circuits for *pipe* and the initial observer (as BLIF files), and then invoked

$w\backslash d$	4		8		16	
4	6	2	9	3	19	17
8	6	3	10	18	21	266
16	7	17	13	261	30	>3600
	incr	mono	incr	mono	incr	mono

Table 1. Optimization by retiming

SIS (1 time for monolithic optimization, and d times for incremental optimization). The results are summarized in Table 1 which gives the time, in seconds, of running one experiment (rows correspond to w and columns correspond to d).

As expected, for small $w * d$, the incremental optimization is slower than the monolithic one, due to the overhead caused by many invocations of SIS, and construction of weakest observers. However, for bigger $w * d$ the incremental retiming was much faster than monolithic retiming. In fact, we were not patient enough to succeed in performing the monolithic retiming for $w = 16$ and $d = 16$.

8   Possible Extensions

Local signals can simply be treated as global ones (with the obvious restriction that they cannot be used in the assert-commit specification). This does not pose problems since the existential quantifier which models signal hiding can always be "factored out" as a universal quantifier, in the following way. The assert-commit formula $\alpha(P||Q)\beta$ is formalized as $\alpha \wedge \mathcal{P} \wedge \mathcal{Q} \rightarrow \beta$ while $\alpha(\text{\textbf{local }} x \text{ \textbf{in} } P||Q)\beta$ should be formalized as $\alpha \wedge (\exists x. \mathcal{P} \wedge \mathcal{Q}) \rightarrow \beta$. Although the existential quantifier does not, in general, distribute over conjunction, it does distribute in this case (no free x outside $\mathcal{P} \wedge \mathcal{Q}$), and thus the two formulae are equivalent.

In principle, one may also consider liveness properties, although of quite limited form. The logical framework is also sound for observers with special output signals interpreted with $\Diamond$ instead of $\Box$. Unfortunately, this encoding does not handle nested temporal modalities, and we are not aware of any hardware optimizer which could simplify circuits under such "eventual don't cares".

In principle, both the simple logical framework and the incremental verification method via successive simplifications of the weakest pre-conditions can be lifted to asynchronous networks, provided one works with the semantics in which $[\![P||Q]\!] = [\![P]\!] \cap [\![Q]\!]$, as in TLA [13]. Unfortunately, the known problem remains how to simplify the weakest pre-condition $P \rightarrow \beta$. The methods proposed, such as [4], are quite involved.

It is not clear to us under what assumptions our simple calculus is sound w.r.t. the constructive semantics of synchronous networks [21]. We do not know any simple syntactical characterization of the set of processes for which $[\![P||Q]\!] = [\![P]\!] \cap [\![Q]\!]$, under this semantics.

9   Conclusions

We have presented a simple logical framework for analyzing compositional verification of reactive networks. In this framework, the common forward/backward strategies for incremental verification, via the strongest post-conditions and weakest pre-conditions, can be derived formally, using just one propositional tautology (1).

Many ideas that we have presented are well known, when considered separately, and we do not claim any originality in this respect. In particular, we were influenced by [20] (the simple inference rule for $P\|Q$), [11] (the data flow semantics of synchronous networks) and [12] (synchronous observers).

However, we would like to emphasize the following novel treatment of the old ideas. First, our approach is much simpler compared with [1,2,3], for example.

Second, the explicit distinction between the strong and weak observer allows to simplify our calculus considerably, and may suggest that this distinction plays an important role. We derived the strong and weak observer purely syntactically, only later realizing that analogous concepts already appear, although somewhat hidden, in [12].

Third, the simple construction of the weakest precondition (i.e., $P \to \beta$) as parallel composition of circuits is in contrast with the usual, and quite involved, construction on the level of automata (by mimicking $\neg P \vee \beta$) [12,5] or logical formulae [4]. This may suggest that the very compact representation of reactive systems as circuits, largely neglected in favor of automata, temporal logic formulae and BDDs, may be actually quite useful in verification.

We have analyzed one example only, just to substantiate our claim that incremental hardware optimization can actually lead to substantial simplification of the verification process. To show any practical usefulness of the presented approach, much serious verification experiments must be conducted, and we consider this as a possible future work.

Acknowledgments

This research was supported by the SACRES project [18]). We are also grateful to Jorge Cuéllar and Klaus Winkelmann (Siemens AG, Munich) for fruitful discussions.

References

1. M. Abadi, L. Lamport, Composing specifications, *ACM Transactions on Programming Languages and Systems*, 15(1):73–132, Jan. 1993.
2. M. Abadi, L. Lamport, Conjoining specifications, *ACM Transactions on Programming Languages and Systems*, 17(3):507–534, May 1995.
3. M. Abadi, G.D. Plotkin, A logical view of composition. *Theoretical Computer Science*, 114(1):3–30, 1993.
4. H.R. Andersen, Partial Model Checking, Proceedings of LICS'95, IEEE Computer Society Press, 398–407, June 1995.

5. A. Aziz, F. Balarin, R. Brayton and A. Sangiovanni-Vincentelli, Sequential synthesis using S1S, *Int. Conf. on Computer-Aided Design ICCAD'95*, 1995.
6. G. Benveniste and P. Le Guernic, Synchronous programming with events and relations: the Signal language and its semantics, *Science of Computer Programming*, 16:103–149, 1991.
7. G. Berry and G. Gonthier, The synchronous programming language Esterel: design, semantics, implementation, *Science of Computer Programming*, 19:87–152, 1992.
8. G. Berry, A hardware implementation of pure Esterel, *Sadhana, Academy Proceedings in Engineering Sciencies, Indian Academy of Sciences*, 17:95–130, 1992.
9. N. Halbwachs, *Synchronous Programming of Reactive Systems*, Kluwer Academic Publishers, Dordrecht, 1993.
10. N. Halbwachs, P. Caspi, P. Raymond, and D. Pilaud, The synchronous data flow programming language Lustre, *Proceedings of the IEEE*, 79(9):1305–1321, Sep. 1991.
11. N. Halbwachs, J.-C. Fernandez and A. Bouajjanni, An executable temporal logic to express safety properties and its connection with the language Lustre, *Sixth Int. Symp. on Lucid and Intensional Programming, ISLIP'93*, Quebec, April 1993.
12. N. Halbwachs, F. Lagnier and P. Raymond, Synchronous observers and the verification of reactive systems, *Third Int. Conf. on Algebraic Methodology and Software Technology, AMAST'93*, Workshops in Computing, Springer, Twente, June 1993.
13. L. Lamport, The temporal logic of actions, *ACM Transactions on Programming Languages and Systems*, 16(3):872–923, May 1994.
14. F. Maraninchi, Operational and compositional semantics of synchronous automaton compositions, *CONCUR'92*, LNCS 630, Springer-Verlag, 550–564, Aug. 1992.
15. A. Poigné and L. Holenderski, On the Combination of Synchronous Languages, *Int. Symp. on Compositionality, COMPOS'97*, LNCS 1536, State-of-the-Art Survey, Springer, 490–514, Sep. 1997.
16. E. Sentovich, H. Toma, and G. Berry, Efficient Latch Optimization Using Incompatible Sets, *Int. Digital Automation Conf. DAC'97*, Anaheim, 1997.
17. H. Toma, E. Sentovich, and G. Berry, Latch Optimization in Circuits Generated from High-Level Descriptions, *Int. Conf. on Computer-Aided Design ICCAD'96*, 1996.
18. SACRES (Safety Critical Real-Time Embedded Systems), Esprit Project 20897, http://www.tni.fr/sacres.
19. SIS: a system for sequential circuit synthesis, *Tech. Rep. UCB/ERL M92/41*, 1–45, May 1992, ftp://ic.eecs.berkeley.edu/pub/Sis.
20. C. Stirling, A complete compositional modal proof system for a subset of CCS, LNCS 194, Springer-Verlag, 475–486, 1985.
21. T. Shiple, G. Berry, H. Touati, Constructive analysis of cyclic circuits, *Int. Design and Testing Conf. IDTC'96*, Paris, France, 1996.

Modelling Coordinated Atomic Actions in Timed CSP

Simeon Veloudis[1] and Nimal Nissanke[2]

[1] Department of Computer Science, The University of Reading, Whiteknights, P.O. Box 225, Reading RG6 6AY, UK,
`s.veloudis@reading.ac.uk`
[2] School of Computing, Information Systems and Mathematics, South Bank University, 103 Borough Road, London SE1 0AA, UK,
`nissanke@sbu.ac.uk`

Abstract. This paper proposes a formal framework for modelling the interaction of concurrent items of equipment in real–time safety–critical systems and reasoning about their behaviour abstractly. The framework is based on the concept of Coordinated Atomic (CA) actions, an approach widely used for structuring complex activities in fault–tolerant computer systems. It advocates a hierarchical approach and begins with the construction of a mathematical model of the behaviour of an individual item of equipment. Later on, the model is extended to incorporate the concept of a CA action. In the final stage, a formal representation of the ideal behaviour of an abstract CA action is provided. The framework uses Timed CSP – a well–established formalism used for representation and reasoning in real–time systems.

Keywords: CA actions, Timed CSP, safety–critical systems, real–time systems

1   Introduction

This paper proposes a mathematical framework for modelling the interaction of items of equipment in safety–critical systems. The framework is based on an approach originally presented in [5] using CSP and extended later in [11] to real–time systems using Timed CSP. The latter work proposes a hierarchy of abstractions of individual items of equipment, embodying their ideal and failure–prone behaviours both with and without sensors at equipment sites. Sensors have similar abstractions to the items of equipment. This paper summarises the work presented in [10] which further extends [11] through the incorporation of the concept of Coordinated Atomic (CA) actions. CA actions [7,14] constitute a unified approach to both structuring complex concurrent activities and supporting fault tolerance in a system of interacting processes. CA actions provide a conceptual framework for dealing with different kinds of concurrency (e.g. cooperative, competitive) and achieving fault–tolerance by extending and integrating two complementary concepts: conversations [6] and transactions [2]. They are

M. Joseph (Ed.): FTRTFT 2000, LNCS 1926, pp. 228–239, 2000.
© Springer-Verlag Berlin Heidelberg 2000

thus well–equipped for managing the complexity inherent in safety–critical systems [16,17]. Although CA actions are aimed at supporting fault–tolerance, our concern in this paper is with the construction of a mathematical framework for the representation of CA actions that comprise *ideally* behaving participants. This is undertaken with two objectives in mind. Firstly, such a framework allows a better understanding of a fundamental and highly complex software engineering concept, namely, that of a CA action. Secondly, although not sufficient for dealing with failures fully by itself, the work reported here forms the basis of a more general model [12] incorporating mechanisms for supporting *safety*.

The paper is structured as follows. Section 2 outlines the structure of CA actions. Section 3 presents a behavioural model of an item of equipment. Section 4 shows how CA actions can be incorporated into the model described in Section 3. In Section 5, a formal model for the representation of CA actions is constructed. Finally, Section 6 concludes the paper. The paper assumes the reader's familiarity with Timed CSP [1,9].

2   An Outline of CA Actions

This section outlines certain characteristics of CA actions essential for this paper. A CA action consists of a number of concurrently operating processes, referred to here as *participants*, grouped together in order to perform some coordinated activity. Within the scope of the action, the participants may freely interact with one another but must proceed independently of any other components in the system. With respect to other processes in the system, the sequence of actions performed within a given CA action is considered atomic. A CA action commences its operation when all its participants have been 'activated' (*entry synchronisation*), and commits (ends) when each and every participant has completed its operation (*exit synchronisation*). The CA action concept is intended to be recursive. That is, a complex CA action may consist of a number of nested CA actions enabling a better understanding of its structure. Once a nested action commits, all its participants continue their operations within the enclosing CA action. An action may commit only if all of its nested actions have already committed.

We consider a safety–critical system to consist of a *controlling system*, a *controlled system*, and an operator who interacts with the latter via the former. Each request made by the operator to the controlling system for a certain service is represented as a *top–level* CA action involving all *items of equipment* of the controlled system relevant to the delivery of the requested service. This top–level action persists *statically* throughout the system's operation but develops (decomposes) into nested actions *dynamically* as it progresses. As a result, each item of equipment always operates within a CA action context changing over time.

3   Items of Equipment

In modelling items of equipment, let Id denote a deterministic Timed CSP term that describes the ideal behaviour of an arbitrary item. Let it be specified as

$$Id \ \mathbf{sat}_\rho \ Spec(s, \aleph) \tag{1}$$

$Spec$ being a predicate describing all executions of an item that are deemed to be ideal. A detailed specification of $Spec$ is unnecessary at this level of abstraction. However, the behaviour of an item can in general be *failure–prone*. This can be modelled with reference to a set $\mathcal{B}$ of special events called *failure events*, which are essentially synchronisations between an item and its *fault environment* [4], modelled by a term $\mathcal{R}$. Such an environment is not the result of a deliberate act of design but of our inability to eliminate faults. Hence, a detailed specification of the behaviour of $\mathcal{R}$ is a difficult, if not an impossible, task. As one would expect, failure events are outside the events that an ideal item would normally engage in. Thus, $\sigma(Id) \cap \mathcal{B} = \emptyset$. As shown in (2), at any point during its operation a failure–prone item P may fail *non–deterministically* by engaging in an event $f \in \mathcal{B}$, with its subsequent behaviour being described by the term $F(f)$.

$$P = Id \ \bigtriangledown_{f \in \mathcal{B}} \ F(f) \tag{2}$$

From its semantic definition, P never refuses a failure event at least up until the first occurrence of such an event. The behaviour of a failure–prone item *Item* can be modelled as shown in the definition below.

Definition 1. $Item = ((Id \ \bigtriangledown_{f \in \mathcal{B}} \ F(f)) \ \|_{\mathcal{B}} \ \mathcal{R}) \backslash \mathcal{B}$

The failure events are concealed as they are not externally visible and, hence, do not require the environment's cooperation. Furthermore, an item of equipment operates ideally exactly when $Item = Id$.

4   Incorporation of CA Actions

This section extends the model outlined in Section 3 to incorporate CA actions; full details can be found in [10].

Systemic Events. The dynamically changing CA action context of operation of an item is captured through a special set E_{sys} of events called *systemic* events. These events are synchronisations between an item and the controlling system and are intended purely for altering the CA action context of an item. E_{sys} is partitioned into two sets of events: E (events that initiate CA actions) and $\widehat{E}$ (events that terminate CA actions). In addition, the following two functions are introduced: $sma : E_{sys} \twoheadrightarrow Act$ – total surjection which associates each systemic event with the unique action it either initiates or terminates (Act being the set of all action identifiers); and $bme : E \rightarrowtail\mkern-14mu\twoheadrightarrow \widehat{E}$ – total bijection which associates each $e \in E$ with the corresponding $\widehat{e} \in \widehat{E}$. Formally, $bme(e) = \widehat{e} \Leftrightarrow sma(e) = sma(\widehat{e})$.

We define the *nesting structure* of an item as a temporally ordered set of pairs of the form $(t, m) \in (\mathbb{R}^+ \times Act)$, where m identifies an action which has been initiated at time t but is yet to end. In order to determine the operation of an item subsequent to the observation of a systemic event, along with the identifier of the newly entered action, the duration of the action may also be required. This duration may be determined from the nesting structure of the action. The function sco given below is intended for this purpose and determines the 'subsequent context of operation' of an item.

Definition 2. $sco : seq(\mathbb{R}^+ \times Act) \nrightarrow (\mathbb{R}^+ \times E_{sys}) \nrightarrow seq(\mathbb{R}^+ \times Act)$

$$\text{dom } sco = \{u \in seq(\mathbb{R}^+ \times Act) \mid \forall k, j \in \text{dom } u \bullet$$
$$k < j \Leftrightarrow tstrip(u)[k] < tstrip(u)[j]\} \quad (3)$$
$$\text{dom } sco(u) \subseteq \{(t, e) \in (\mathbb{R}^+ \times E_{sys}) \mid t \geq end(u)\}$$

$$
\begin{aligned}
sco(u)(t, e) &= \langle (t, sma(e)) \rangle & &\text{if } u = \langle \rangle \wedge e \in E \\
sco(u)(t, e) &= u \mathbin{\frown} \langle (t, sma(e)) \rangle & &\text{if } e \in E \wedge sma(e) \notin \text{ran } u \\
&\quad u' & &\text{if } u = u' \mathbin{\frown} \langle (t', m) \rangle \wedge e \in \widehat{E} \wedge \\
& & &\quad sma(e) = m \quad \text{for some } u', t' \text{ and } m
\end{aligned}
\quad (4)
$$

The first argument of sco represents the item's nesting structure up until the time of occurrence of the (timed) systemic event specified in the function's second argument. The definition of sco preserves the requirement on CA actions according to which an action may terminate only if all its nested actions have already terminated. [Note that some of the mathematical notation follows [13]. Thus, for any sequence s and $k \in \text{dom } s$, $s[k]$ denotes the kth element of s. Symbol $\nrightarrow$ denotes a partial function and $tstrip(u)$ (see [1,9]) is a function application retaining only the timing information of a timed trace u.]

The Operational Environment. Occurrences of systemic events may be attributed to the interaction between an item of equipment and a term $\mathcal{O}$ representing the *operational environment*; the former engages in a systemic event exactly when the latter engages in the same event.

Definition 3. The interaction of an item of equipment and the operational environment is given by the term $Item \parallel_{E_{sys}} \mathcal{O}$

$\mathcal{O}$ models the *operational* part of the item's environment and is thus an abstraction of the controlling system. The purpose of $\mathcal{O}$ is solely to organise the items of equipment into CA actions. In other words, it does not engage in any event which directly affects the state of any item of equipment. The main focus of this work is on the behaviour of the controlled system and its equipment. Therefore, we assume that $\mathcal{O}$ never fails.

The executions of $\mathcal{O}$ are subject to a number of constraints, some of which are formulated below and others can be found in [10]. The first constraint requires that initially, at time 0, some systemic event is offered. Such an event, if accepted, initiates a top–level action within which the item operates.

$$\mathcal{O} \; \mathbf{sat}_\rho \; \exists\, e \in E \bullet e \in \sigma(s \uparrow 0) \vee (0, e) \notin \aleph \tag{5}$$

The second constraint places an upper bound of Δ units of time, Δ being a strictly positive constant, on the rate at which systemic events may be observed.

$$\mathcal{O} \; \mathbf{sat}_\rho \; \forall\, t \in \mathbb{R}^+, e \in E_{sys} \bullet \; e \in \sigma(s \uparrow t) \Rightarrow$$
$$\forall\, t' \in (t, t + \Delta], e' \in E_{sys} \bullet e' \notin \sigma(s \uparrow t') \tag{6}$$

It is an assumption in our framework that an ideally behaving item must be prepared to participate in any systemic event offered by $\mathcal{O}$. In other words, each and every systemic event observed depends solely on the particular behaviour shown by $\mathcal{O}$ in response to a unique service request made by the underlying application. By restricting the timed trace s of $\mathcal{O}$'s behaviour to E_{sys}, we obtain a temporally ordered set of systemic events that occur during the *ideal* operation of an item. This set of events may be determined a priori to match the requirements of the requested task. In addition, there is an one–to–one correspondence between a task request and the top–level action within which an item operates. The function $\mathcal{T}$ below and constraint (8) summarise this discussion.

Definition 4. $\mathcal{T} : E_{sys} \rightarrowtail TT$ *where* $\operatorname{dom} \mathcal{T} \subseteq E$ *and*

$$\operatorname{ran} \mathcal{T} = \{ s \in TT \mid \sigma(s) \subseteq E_{sys} \wedge begin(s) > 0 \wedge$$
$$\forall\, t > 0 \bullet s \uparrow t = \langle\rangle \vee \#(s \uparrow t) = \#s \uparrow [t, t + \Delta) = 1 \} \tag{7}$$

where TT denotes the set of timed traces. Given the observation of a systemic event that initiates a top–level action, the function $\mathcal{T}$ returns a temporally ordered sequence of systemic events. These events are observed in the ideal behaviour of the item concerned within the given top–level action as it performs the required task. The sequence $tstrip(\mathcal{T}_{e_0})$ contains all such observation times.

$$\mathcal{O} \; \mathbf{sat}_\rho \; Asm \Rightarrow (\forall\, e \in E_{sys} \bullet e \in \sigma(s \uparrow 0) \Rightarrow \mathcal{T}(e) = (s{\upharpoonright}0){\downharpoonleft}E_{sys}) \tag{8}$$

where

$$Asm \equiv \forall\, t \in \mathbb{R}^+, e \in E_{sys} \bullet$$
$$e \in \sigma(s \uparrow t) \Rightarrow ([t + \xi, \infty) \cap [0, begin(s{\downharpoonleft}E_{sys} \uparrow [t + \xi, \infty)))) \times E_{sys}) \subseteq \aleph$$

The predicate Asm above requires that, for any initially observed $e \in E_{sys}$, $\mathcal{O}$ may perform the systemic events determined by $\mathcal{T}(e)$, if its environment offers to participate in each such event at least up until the time of occurrence of the event. As it will be seen, this amounts to an ideally behaving underlying item. Symbol ξ denotes a strictly positive constant such that $\xi < \Delta$. Its significance will become apparent once Definition 5 is introduced.

CA Action–Dependent Operation. Operation of an item following the observation of a systemic event depends both on the newly entered action and the duration of the action up until the observation time of the event. In specifying the item's behaviour, it is therefore important that both these two factors are taken into account, thus requiring a redefinition of (1). For this, consider the observation of a systemic event at time t and let m and $t_0 \leq t$ be respectively the identifier and initiation time of the action entered at t. Then

$$Id^{act}(m, t - t_0) \; \mathbf{sat}_\rho \; Spec_{m, t-t_0}(s, \aleph) \tag{9}$$

where $Id^{act}(m, t - t_0)$ denotes the Timed CSP term that describes the ideal operation of the item from t onwards, while the predicate $Spec_{m,t-t_0}$ describes all possible ideal behaviours of the item within the action m but after $(t-t_0)$ time units into m's duration. A detailed specification of $Spec_{m,t-t_0}$ is unnecessary at the current level of abstraction.

The following mutually recursive definition describes the (ideal) operation of a given item within the context of an evolving CA action.

Definition 5. $Id = e_0 : S_{sys} \to R_{e_0}$ where,

$$R_{e_0} = \langle X_k(u_k, e_0) = Q_k(u_k, e_0) \rangle_0 \qquad k \in (\mathrm{dom}\, \mathcal{T}_{e_0}) \cup \{0\} \tag{10}$$

such that $u_0 = \langle (0, e_0) \rangle$, $u_k \in \mathrm{dom}\, sco$ and, for $k \in \mathrm{dom}\, \mathcal{T}_{e_0} \cup \{0\}$,

$$Q_k(u_k, e_0) = WAIT(\xi); (Id^{act}(last(u_k), tstrip(\mathcal{T}_{e_0})[k] - end(u_k))$$
$$\triangledown$$
$$\underset{e \in E_{sys}}{}$$
$$X_{k+1}(sco(u_k)(tstrip(\mathcal{T}_{e_0})[k+1], e), e_0) \tag{11}$$
$$\langle\!\langle e \neq bme(e_0) \rangle\!\rangle \; SKIP)$$

where $\mathcal{T}_{e_0}$ is an abbreviation for $\mathcal{T}(e_0)$.

Initially, the item engages in a systemic event e_0 that commences a top–level action. Symbol S_{sys} denotes the set of all such events; trivially, $S_{sys} \subseteq E$. Subsequently, the item continues its operation within this top–level action as described by term R_{e_0}. As in Definition 2, for any k, the sequence u_k gives the nesting structure of the item at time $tstrip(\mathcal{T}_{e_0})[k]$. Upon the observation of a systemic event, as long as this does not terminate the top–level action, as seen in its externally visible behaviour the item pauses for a (small) strictly positive length of time ξ and then resumes operation within the newly emerged CA action. The ξ–long pause is intended for the item to adjust to operating according to the requirements of the new action. In addition, the ξ–long delay has a semantic significance since it makes each recursive call *time–guarded* and, hence, guarantees a well–defined semantics for Id. Upon the observation of a systemic event which ends the operation of the top–level action, the item terminates successfully (by behaving like $SKIP$). This reflects an assumption in our model (stated in Section 2) according to which an item may only operate within the context of only one CA action.

5   Ideal CA Actions

This section develops a formal framework for the representation of CA actions which comprise ideally behaving participants.

Reconfiguration Events. Reconfiguration events are a special set of events E_r intended for capturing the dynamically evolving nesting structure of a given CA action. They too have no direct effect on the state of any item. The observation of a reconfiguration event triggers the initiation and/or the termination of one or more CA actions. However, as explained earlier, a given CA action $m \in Act$ starts/ends its operation only when at least two items (its participants) synchronise with $\mathcal{O}$ on the same systemic event e such that $sma(e) = m$. Note that E_r (reconfiguration events) and E_{sys} (systemic events) are mutually exclusive, because the former is intended for altering the nesting structure of CA actions, while the latter for changing the CA action context of items of equipment. Clearly, there exists a correspondence between these two sets of events; this is captured by the injective function $rms : E_r \rightarrowtail \mathbb{P}E_{sys}$. For any $e_r \in E_r$, $rms(e_r)$ returns a non–empty set of systemic events, each one of which is to be performed collectively by a number of items in order to implement the reconfiguration intended by e_r. As indicated by the function type of rms, each event from E_r corresponds to a unique reconfiguration of the nesting structure of an action. As will be seen in the constraint (19), the observation of an $e_r \in E_r$ coincides temporally with the offer of each of the systemic events in $rms(e_r)$. The need of both systemic and reconfiguration events is justified in [10].

5.1   Structural Information About CA Actions

Formalisation of the operation of an action requires several mathematical structures for recording information concerning its participants and the nesting structure of the action.

Action Participants. Any action comprises at least two participants, each ith one of which must contain in its interface with $\mathcal{O}$ the systemic events E_{sys}^i which initiate/terminate the action[1].

Definition 6. $part : Act \rightarrow \mathbb{P}Eq$ such that, for $m \in Act$,

(i) $sma^{-1}(m) \subseteq \bigcap_{i \in part(m)} E_{sys}^i$ and   (ii) $\#part(m) \geq 2$

Eq being an index set.

---

[1] Since this section considers the operation of several concurrently operating items of equipment, in order to distinguish between different items the sets E, $\widehat{E}$, E_{sys} and Δ are indexed by the elements of an index set Eq. Obviously, E^i's partitions E; the same applies to other sets.

Nesting Structure. The nesting structure of an action at a given time t can be determined from the set of reconfiguration events in which the action has engaged up to t. Let u denote a temporally ordered set of such timed reconfiguration events. The set of nested actions active at t may be derived by considering elements (t', e_r) in u such that: a) e_r gives rise to at least one CA action start systemic event e_s, and b) there is no element (t'', e_r') in u such that $t'' \geq t$ and e_r' gives rise to the event $bme(e_s)$. In other words, our interest is in reconfiguration events which have initiated at least one nested action which is yet to terminate.

Definition 7. For $m \in Act$, $\theta^m \;:\; seq(\mathbb{R}^+ \times E_r) \twoheadrightarrow \mathbb{P}(\mathbb{R}^+ \times Act)$, where

$$\text{dom } \theta^m = \{u \in seq(\mathbb{R}^+ \times E_r) \mid$$
$$\forall\, i,j \in \text{dom } u \bullet i < j \Leftrightarrow tstrip(u)[i] < tstrip(u)[j]\} \tag{12}$$
$$\theta^m(u) = \{(t, m) \in (\mathbb{R}^+ \times Act) \mid$$
$$\exists\, e_r \in E_r, e_s \in E \bullet \langle(t, e_r)\rangle \text{ in } u \wedge e_s \in rms(e_r) \wedge m = sma(e_s) \wedge$$
$$\forall(t', e_r') \in (\mathbb{R}^+ \times E_r) \bullet \langle(t', e_r')\rangle \text{ in } u \wedge t' \geq t \Rightarrow$$
$$bme(e_s) \notin rms(e_r')\} \tag{13}$$

Note that in between any two consecutive reconfiguration event occurrences, m undergoes no change in its nesting structure. Furthermore, let κ^m denote the following function:

Definition 8. For $m \in Act$, $\kappa^m \;:\; seq(\mathbb{R}^+ \times E_r) \twoheadrightarrow \mathbb{P}Eq$, where $\text{dom } \kappa^m = \text{dom } \theta^m$ and

$$\kappa^m(u) = \{i \in Eq \mid i \notin \bigcup_{a \in \theta^m(u)} part(\sigma(\langle a\rangle))\} \tag{14}$$

The set $\kappa^m(u)$ comprises participants of m which are not engaged in any nested action.

Interrupting Reconfiguration Events. Not all reconfiguration events may interrupt the operation of a given action. For any $m \in Act$, m is affected by the occurrence of a reconfiguration event e_r at time t if and only if $rms(e_r)$ contains at least one systemic event e_s such that: a) if $e_s \in E$ then e_s must belong to the alphabets of <u>at least two</u> of the participants of m operating at time t within m but not within any of m's nested actions, and b) if $e_s \in \widehat{E}$ then e_s must belong to the alphabet of <u>each and every</u> participant of an action m' nested <u>immediately below</u> m but not below any of m's nested actions. Formally,

Definition 9. For $m \in Act$, $S^m \;:\; seq(\mathbb{R}^+ \times E_r) \twoheadrightarrow \mathbb{P}E_r$, where $\text{dom } S^m = \text{dom } \theta^m$ and

$$S^m(u) = \{e_r \in E_r \mid \exists\, e_s \in rms(e_r) \bullet e_s \in E \Rightarrow part(sma(e_s)) \subseteq \kappa^m(u) \wedge$$
$$e_s \in \widehat{E} \Rightarrow sma(e_s) \in \sigma(\theta^m(u))\} \tag{15}$$

As will be seen in Definition 12, each sequence u in the domain of S^m consists of observed timed reconfiguration events that affect the operation of m.

5.2   The Operational Environment Revisited

Occurrences of reconfiguration events may be attributed to the interaction between a CA action and the term $\mathcal{O}$; the former engages in a reconfiguration event exactly when the latter engages in the same event.

Definition 10. For an arbitrary[2] $e \in E_r, m \in Act, t_m \in \mathbb{R}^+$, the interaction of a CA action with $\mathcal{O}$ takes the form $CA_{e,m}(t_m) \underset{E_{sys} \cup E_r}{\Big\|} \mathcal{O}$

Analogous to the case of ideally behaving items of equipment under systemic events (Section 4), it is an assumption in our framework that a CA action which comprises ideally behaving items must be prepared to participate in any reconfiguration event offered by $\mathcal{O}$. In other words, the occurrence of every reconfiguration event in the behaviour of such an action depends only on the particular behaviour exhibited by $\mathcal{O}$. Analogous to the account given in Section 4 in relation to systemic events, for each top–level CA action the occurrences of reconfiguration events may be determined a priori. Similarly to function $\mathcal{T}$ of Definition 4 and constraint (8), let us introduce below function $\mathcal{T}^r$ and constraint (18).

Definition 11. $\mathcal{T}^r : E_r \rightarrowtail TT$

$$\text{dom}\,\mathcal{T}^r = \{e_r \in E_r \mid \#rms(e_r) = 1 \wedge rms(e_r) \subseteq \bigcap_{i \in Eq} E^i\} \tag{16}$$

$$\text{ran}\,\mathcal{T}^r = \{s \in TT \mid \sigma(s) \subseteq E_r \wedge begin(s) > 0 \wedge$$
$$\forall\, t > 0 \bullet s \uparrow t = \langle\rangle \vee \#(s \uparrow t) = \#(s \uparrow [t, t + \Delta') = 1\} \tag{17}$$

where Δ' is a strictly positive constant such that $\Delta' > \max\{\Delta_i \mid i \in Eq\}$.

It is to be noted that a reconfiguration event initiates a top–level action only if it gives rise to a unique systemic event which may be performed by all items of equipment; this justifies the definition (16) of the domain of $\mathcal{T}^r$.

$$\mathcal{O}\,\mathbf{sat}_\rho\,\mathbb{R}^+ \times E_r \subseteq \aleph \Rightarrow (\forall\, e_r \in E_r \bullet e_r \in \sigma(s \uparrow 0) \Rightarrow \mathcal{T}^r(e_r) = s{\upharpoonright}0){\downharpoonright}E_r) \tag{18}$$

The antecedent $\mathbb{R}^+ \times E_r \subseteq \aleph$ of the implication above corresponds to the assumption that $\mathcal{O}$'s environment is always prepared to engage in any offer of a reconfiguration event. Furthermore, the constraint below states that any observation of $e_r \in E_r$ temporally coincides with the offer of each and every event from $rms(e_r)$.

$$\mathcal{O}\,\mathbf{sat}_\rho\,\forall\, e_r \in E_r, t \in \mathbb{R}^+ \bullet e_r \in \sigma(s \uparrow t) \Leftrightarrow \forall\, e_s \in rms(e_r) \bullet$$
$$e_s \in \sigma(s \uparrow t) \vee e_s \notin (\aleph \uparrow t) \tag{19}$$

A number of additional constraints on $\mathcal{O}$'s operation may be found in [10].

---

[2] As will be seen shortly, e is not really arbitrary, but must be within the domain of $\mathcal{T}^r$.

5.3   A Representation of CA Actions

Let us now define the Timed CSP term that describes the operation of a CA action under an arbitrary execution of the term $\mathcal{O}$.

Definition 12. Let CA_{TL} denote a top–level action. Let us define it as

$$CA_{TL} = e_r : \operatorname{dom} \mathcal{T}^r \to CA_{e_r, sma(e_0)}(0) \tag{20}$$

where event e_0 is the element in the singleton $rms(e_r)$. For arbitrary $m \in Act$, $t_m \in \mathbb{R}^+$ such that t_m is the initiation time of m,

$$CA_{e_r, m}(t_m) = \langle X_k^m(e_r, t_m, u_k) = P_k^m(e_r, t_m, u_k) \rangle_0 \quad k \in (\operatorname{dom} \mathcal{T}_{e_r}^r \! \upharpoonright t_m) \cup \{0\}$$

where $u_0 = \langle \rangle$ and for $k \in \operatorname{dom} \mathcal{T}_{e_r}^r \! \upharpoonright t_m \cup \{0\}$,

$$P_k^m(e_r, t_m, u_k) \; =$$

$$\left(\underset{(t,w) \in \theta^m(u_k)}{\vertbar\vertbar\vertbar} CA_{e_r, w}(t) \! \upharpoonright (end(u_k) - t) \right) \vertbar\vertbar\vertbar \left(\overset{j \leq n}{\underset{\mathcal{A}_j}{\Vert}} Item_{\alpha(j)} \! \upharpoonright (end(u_k)) \right) \setminus \mathcal{A}_j$$

$$\bigtriangledown \tag{21}$$

$$\underset{e \in S^m(u_k) \cup \{(\widehat{E} \lhd sma)^{-1}(m)\}}{}$$

$$(X_{k+1}(e_r, t_m, u_k \frown \langle (time(e_r)(e)(t_m)(u_k), e) \rangle) \nleq (\widehat{E} \lhd sma)^{-1}(m) \notin rms(e) \nrightarrow SKIP)$$

where $\alpha \in (1..n \rightarrowtail \kappa^m(u_k))$, $n = \#(\kappa^m(u_k))$.

Note that each execution of $\mathcal{O}$ corresponds to a unique top–level action designed to deliver the service requested by the operator of the underlying application. The function *time* in the definition above returns the time of occurrence of a reconfiguration event which actually affects the operation of the action. Its definition is given in [10]. Symbol α denotes an arbitrary sequence of elements from $\kappa^m(u_k)$. This is required simply for the application of the indexed interface parallel operator (see [10]). We note that both $E \lhd sma$ and $\widehat{E} \lhd sma$ are bijections (symbol $\lhd$ denotes domain restriction; see [13] for the notation). The use of the event interrupt operator in each mutually recursive equation ensures that a CA action always accepts any offers of reconfiguration events from the term $\mathcal{O}$ and, hence, constitutes a suitable environment for that term. The concealment of events from $\mathcal{A}_j$ indicates that such events require only the cooperation of the participants of the action, thus maintaining the atomicity of the action. Finally, it is to be noted that the mutual recursion of Definition 12 does not have a well–defined semantics as none of its recursive calls are time–guarded. However, by placing $CA_{e,m}(t_m)$ in its intended environment, namely with $\mathcal{O}$, we end up in a well–timed term[3].

---

[3] This is ensured by the constraint (18).

6   Related Work and Conclusions

This paper presents a novel mathematical framework for the representation of CA actions for use in real–time safety–critical systems. As evident from [8,15, 16,17], it is not the first time that the concept of CA action has been used in the development of safety–critical systems. However, with the exception of formalisation of properties of CA actions in the form of preconditions and postconditions using temporal logic, formal studies on behavioural aspects of CA actions are limited. Consequently, rigorous reasoning about the adherence by a given action to these properties has not been possible. In [3], a CSP–based formalism, namely the ERT model of behaviour, is employed to model CA actions. However, such an abstraction is inherently untimed and hence inadequate for real–time systems.

Despite the omission of failure–handling mechanisms due to limitations of space, the framework proposed in this paper constitutes one of the first steps towards understanding the complex issues encountered in the formalisation of CA actions within a context relevant to real–time safety–critical systems. In addition, such a framework serves as the necessary basis for a more general model, as the one outlined in [12], embodying failure–handling mechanisms and capabilities for formal reasoning about safety. At the *equipment level*, our approach advocates two levels of abstraction. At the higher level, a formal model of the failure–prone behaviour of an item is presented. At the lower level, the item is considered within an environment which allows for the dynamic evolution of its CA action context. The CA action model provided is structured on the basis of: a) the behaviours of the action's participants, b) the behaviour of the operational environment $\mathcal{O}$, and c) a number of functions which capture the dynamic evolution of the nesting structure of the action. Constraints are imposed to ensure that the requirements of the CA action concept are not violated. Finally, the choice of Timed CSP and, in particular, of the Timed Failures Model TM_F, can be justified on the basis that such a formalism is especially suitable for modelling and reasoning abstractly of externally visible behavioural characteristics of concurrently executing processes. In addition, it is well equipped to deal with the complex timing constraints encountered in the design of real–time systems.

Acknowledgements

The authors wish to thank Dr Manoranjan Satpathy for his encouragement and the anonymous reviewers for their comments and suggestions.

References

1. J. Davies. *Specification and Proof in Real-Time CSP*. Distinguished Dissertations in Computer Science. Cambridge University Press, 1993.
2. J. Gray and A. Reuter. *Transaction Processing: Concepts and Techniques*. Morgan Kaufmann, 1993.

3. M. Koutney and G. Pappalardo. The ERT model of fault-tolerant computing and its application to a formalisation of coordinated atomic actions. Technical Report 636, Department of Computing Science, University of Newcastle upon Tyne, 1998.
4. Z. Liu and M. Joseph. Transformation of programs for fault-tolerance. *Formal Aspects of Computing*, 4(5):442–469, 1992.
5. N. Nissanke, J. Pascoe, and A. E. Abdallah. Csp in safety critical systems design. Technical report, University of Reading Department of Computer Science, 1999.
6. B. Randell. System structure for software fault tolerance. *IEEE Trans. on Software Engineering*, 1(2):220–232, June 1975.
7. B. Randell, A. Romanovsky, R.J. Stroud, J. Xu, A.F. Zorzo, Schwier D., and F. von Henke. Coordinated atomic actions: Formal model, case study and system implementation. Technical Report 628, Department of Computing Science, University of Newcastle upon Tyne, 1998.
8. A. Romanovsky, J. Xu, and B. Randell. Exception handling in object-oriented real-time distributed systems. Technical Report 624, Department of Computing Science, University of Newcastle upon Tyne, 1998.
9. S. Schneider. *Concurrent and Real-time Systems, The CSP Approach.* Worldwide Series in Computer Science by David Barron and Peter Wegner. John Wiley & Sons, 2000.
10. S. Veloudis and N. Nissanke. A formal framework for modelling interactions within a safety–critical system. Technical Report RUCS/2000/TR/002/B, University of Reading Department of Computer Science, 2000.
11. S. Veloudis and N. Nissanke. Modelling abstract items of equipment – a formal framework. Technical Report RUCS/2000/TR/001/A (submitted for publication), University of Reading Department of Computer Science, 2000.
12. S. Veloudis and N. Nissanke. Reasoning about safety in critical systems. Technical Report (to appear), University of Reading Department of Computer Science, 2000.
13. J. Woodcock and J. Davies. *Using Z – Specification, Refinement and Proof.* Prentice Hall Series in Computer Science by Tony Hoare and Richard Bird. Prentice Hall, 1996.
14. J. Xu, B. Randell, A. Romanovsky, C.M.F. Rubira, R.J. Stroud, and Z. Wu. Fault tolerance in concurrent object-oriented software through coordinated error recovery. Technical Report 507, Department of Computing Science, University of Newcastle upon Tyne, 1995.
15. J. Xu, A. Romanovsky, R.J. Stroud, and A.F. Zorzo. Rigorous development of a safety-critical system based on coordinated atomic actions. Technical Report 662, Department of Computing Science, University of Newcastle upon Tyne, 1999.
16. A.F. Zorzo. A production cell controlled by dependable multiparty interactions. Technical Report 667, Department of Computing Science, University of Newcastle upon Tyne, 1999.
17. A.F. Zorzo, A. Romanovsky, J. Xu, B. Randell, R.J. Stroud, and I.S. Welch. Using coordinated atomic actions to design dependable distributed object systems. Technical Report 619, Department of Computing Science, University of Newcastle upon Tyne, 1998.

A Logical Characterisation of Event Recording Automata

Deepak D'Souza

Chennai Mathematical Institute,
92 G. N. Chetty Road, Chennai, India.
deepak@smi.ernet.in,

Abstract. We show that the class of Event Recording Automata [2] admit a logical characterisation via an *unrestricted* monadic second order logic interpreted over timed words. We point out the closure properties corresponding to existential quantification in the logic. A timed temporal logic considered earlier in the literature is shown to be expressively complete with respect to our monadic logic.
The results in this paper extend smoothly to the class of event clock automata (also introduced in [2]).

1 Introduction

The timed automata of Alur and Dill [1] are a standard model for describing timed behaviours. They augment classical automata with clocks which can be read and reset while taking transitions. These automata are very powerful in language theoretic terms: while their languages are closed under union and intersection and their emptiness problem is decidable, their languages are not closed under complementation and their language inclusion problem is undecidable. Consequently, the verification problem—which is often phrased as whether $L(\mathcal{A}_{Pr}) \subseteq L(\mathcal{A}_{spec})$—cannot be solved for these automata in general. One must then either work with deterministic specifications or with a restricted class of timed automata which has the required closure properties.

The *event recording automata* of Alur, Fix, and Henzinger [2] are a subclass of timed automata which are both determinisable and closed under the boolean operations of union, intersection and complementation. The key feature of these automata is that they have an *implicit* clock associated with each action. This clock is reset with every occurrence of the associated action. This permits the modeller to record the time elapsed since the last occurrence of each action. As a result common real-time requirements like "consecutive requests are separated by a distance of at least 5 time units" can be naturally modelled using these automata.

In this paper we argue in favour of these automata from a logical viewpoint. In the classical setting, the existence of a monadic second order logical characterisation for a class of languages is a strong endorsement of its regularity. Such a characterisation can also help in identifying natural temporal logics which can

M. Joseph (Ed.): FTRTFT 2000, LNCS 1926, pp. 240–251, 2000.
© Springer-Verlag Berlin Heidelberg 2000

be expected to have advantages in terms of relatively efficient algorithms for solving their verification problem. As is well-known, Linear Time Temporal Logic (LTL) is expressively equivalent to the first-order fragment of S1S, Büchi's monadic second-order logic which characterises untimed regular languages. LTL is natural to use, and has an exponential time algorithm for deciding its satisfiability problem as against the non-elementary decision procedure for the first-order fragment of S1S. The aim of this paper is to show that event recording automata admit a similar logical framework.

We characterise event recording automata via a monadic second order logic interpreted over timed words. This logic, called MSO_{er}, has a timed modality of the form $\Delta_a(x) \in I$ which asserts that w.r.t. the position x in the timed word, the time elapsed since the last a action lies in the interval I. The logic is unrestricted and in particular it allows full existential quantification over set variables (or monadic predicates).

We further show that a timed temporal logic proposed earlier in the literature is expressively complete with respect to our logic in that it corresponds to the first-order fragment of our monadic logic. The logic, called here LTL_{er}, has a timed modality of the form $\lhd_a \in I$ which asserts that the time elapsed since the last a action lies in the interval I. This logic has been studied earlier by Raskin in [10] and its satisfiability and model-checking problems are solved there. The issue of its expressive completeness was however not addressed.

There have been several logical characterisations of timed automata and its subclasses proposed in the literature [13,9,10]. Unfortunately these logics are all restricted in their syntax, typically in their use of existential quantification. One of the first such characterisations was given by Wilke in [13], where he characterises the class of timed automata via the logic $\overleftrightarrow{\mathcal{L}d}$, the monadic second order logic of relative distance. $\overleftrightarrow{\mathcal{L}d}$ has a restricted syntax due to the fact that timed automata are not closed under complementation. In particular, set variables used in a distance predicate must be existentially quantified only at the beginning of the formula.

In [9] Raskin, Schobbens, and Henzinger propose the class of *recursive event clock automata* and a corresponding monadic logic called MinMaxML. Once again the second-order quantification is restricted as one cannot quantify over set variables which are in the scope of a distance operator. The authors also propose a timed temporal logic called EventCLockTL that is expressively complete w.r.t. to MinMaxML. These results are shown in the setting of the so-called "continuous" time semantics [10], which turn out to be distinguishable from the more classical interpretation used in both [13] and this paper.

In [6] a subclass of event recording automata called *product interval automata* is studied. These automata admit a logical characterisation which comprises boolean combinations of "local" monadic second order logic assertions. A corresponding timed temporal logic called $\mathrm{TLTL}^{\otimes}$ is identified which is expressively complete w.r.t. this characterisation. The study of these automata and its extensions lead us in a natural way to the class of event recording automata. The techniques used in this paper essentially build on the ones used in [6].

There is an interesting aspect of our characterisation of event recording automata (which we elaborate on towards the end of Section 3). Existential quantification in a monadic logic usually corresponds to the associated class of languages being closed under the operation of projection, or renaming. Event recording automata are however *not* closed under renaming, despite the fact that they admit an unrestricted logical characterisation. We explain this phenomenon by showing that existential quantification in our logic actually corresponds to closure under renaming of a weaker class of event recording automata which we call *quasi* event recording automata.

Finally, we would like to point out that the results presented in this paper extend easily to the class of *event clock automata*. These automata were also introduced in [2] and extend event recording automata with "event-predicting" clocks. Some further details on the extension of our results to this class can be found in [5].

2   Event Recording Automata

Let $\mathbb{N}$ denote the set of natural numbers $\{0, 1, \ldots\}$. We will use $\mathbb{R}^{>0}$ and $\mathbb{R}^{\geq 0}$ to denote the set of positive and non-negative reals respectively, and $\mathbb{Q}^{\geq 0}$ to denote the non-negative rationals. As usual the set of finite and infinite words over an alphabet A will be denoted by A^* and A^ω respectively.

A Büchi automaton over an alphabet A is a structure $\mathcal{A} = (Q, \longrightarrow, Q_{in}, F)$ where Q is a finite set of states, $\longrightarrow \subseteq Q \times A \times Q$ is the transition relation, $Q_{in} \subseteq Q$ is a set of initial states, and $F \subseteq Q$ is a set of accepting states.

Let $\alpha \in A^\omega$. A run of $\mathcal{A}$ over α is a map $\rho : \mathbb{N} \to Q$ which satisfies: $\rho(0) \in Q_{in}$ and $\rho(i) \xrightarrow{\alpha(i)} \rho(i+1)$ for every $i \in \mathbb{N}$. We say ρ is an *accepting* run of $\mathcal{A}$ on α if $\rho(i) \in F$ for infinitely many $i \in \mathbb{N}$. The set of words accepted by $\mathcal{A}$, denoted here (for reasons which will soon be clear) as $L_{sym}(\mathcal{A})$, is defined to be the set of words in A^ω on which $\mathcal{A}$ has an accepting run. We term a subset L of A^ω ω-*regular* if $L = L_{sym}(\mathcal{A})$ for some Büchi automaton $\mathcal{A}$ over A.

In what follows, we will concentrate on infinite timed behaviours. The results can be easily extended to cover finite timed behaviours as well.

An infinite *timed word* over Σ is a member σ of $(\Sigma \times \mathbb{R}^{>0})^\omega$ which satisfies the following conditions. Let $\sigma = (a_0, t_0)(a_1, t_1) \cdots$. Then:

1. For each $i \in \mathbb{N}$, $t_i < t_{i+1}$ (strict monotonicity).
2. For each $t \in \mathbb{R}^{>0}$ there exists $i \in \mathbb{N}$ such that $t_i > t$ (progressiveness).

We use $T\Sigma^\omega$ to denote the set of infinite timed words over Σ.

For an infinite timed word σ we will also use the representation of σ as (α, η) where $\alpha \in \Sigma^\omega$ and $\eta : \mathbb{N} \to \mathbb{R}^{>0}$.

In what follows, we will use intervals with rational bounds to specify timing constraints (and use ∞ as the upper bound to capture unbounded intervals). These intervals will be of the form (l, r), $[l, r)$, $(l, r]$, or $[l, r]$, where $l, r \in \mathbb{Q}^{\geq 0} \cup \{\infty\}$ with $l \leq r$. For an interval of the form $(l, r]$ or $[l, r]$ we require $r \neq \infty$, and for intervals of the form $[l, r)$ or $[l, r]$ we require $l \neq 0$. Further, to avoid empty intervals, unless an interval is of the form $[l, r]$, we require $l < r$. An interval will denote a non-empty, convex subset of reals in the obvious way. For example the interval $[1, \infty)$ denotes the set $\{t \in \mathbb{R} \mid 1 \leq t\}$. The set of all intervals will be denoted by $\mathcal{IR}$.

An event recording automaton over an alphabet Σ is a timed automaton over Σ which has a clock x_a for each action a in Σ. With each transition—labelled by say a—the set of clocks to be reset is fixed: it is the singleton $\{x_a\}$. Thus if the transitions of a timed automaton in general are of the form $q \xrightarrow[X]{a, g} q'$ where q and q' are states of the automaton, a is an action from Σ, g is a guard (a boolean combination of atomic guards of the form $(x \in I)$), and X is a set of clocks to be reset; then the transitions of an event recording automaton are of the form $q \xrightarrow{a, g} q'$, since the set of clocks to be reset is understood to be $\{x_a\}$.

It will be convenient for us to define event recording automata in a slightly different manner, as it will help to make our arguments more transparent. The definition which follows can be seen to be equivalent to the one above. We first note that the guards can be canonicalised in the form $\bigwedge_{a \in \Sigma}(x_a \in I)$. This does not involve any loss of generality since a transition labelled by an arbitrary guard can be replaced by a collection of transitions, each of which is labelled by a guard of the above form. We can make use of the guards $x_a \in (0, \infty)$ to model the fact that x_a does not play a role in the guard. With this in mind we introduce the notion of an interval alphabet.

An *(event recording) interval alphabet* based on Σ is a finite non-empty subset of $\Sigma \times \mathcal{IR}^{\Sigma}$. Thus, elements of an interval alphabet are of the form (a, J) with $a \in \Sigma$ and $J : \Sigma \to \mathcal{IR}$.

Let $\sigma \in T\Sigma^{\omega}$ with $\sigma(i) = (a_i, t_i)$ for each $i \in \mathbb{N}$. We will use $time_a^i(\sigma)$ to denote the time of occurrence of the last a action w.r.t. the position i in σ. We will use the position -1 to denote the point at which we begin to count time. We define inductively

- $time_a^{-1}(\sigma) = 0$ for all $a \in \Sigma$
- $time_a^i(\sigma) = \begin{cases} t_i & \text{if } a_i = a, \\ time_a^{i-1}(\sigma) & \text{otherwise.} \end{cases}$

Let Γ be an interval alphabet based on Σ. Let $\widehat{\sigma} \in \Gamma^{\omega}$ with $\widehat{\sigma}(i) = (a_i, J_i)$ for each $i \in \mathbb{N}$. Then $\widehat{\sigma}$ induces in a natural way a set of timed words—denoted $tw(\widehat{\sigma})$—as follows. Let $\sigma \in T\Sigma^{\omega}$ with $\sigma(i) = (b_i, t_i)$ for each $i \in \mathbb{N}$. Then $\sigma \in tw(\widehat{\sigma})$ iff for each $i \in \mathbb{N}$: $b_i = a_i$ and for each $a \in \Sigma$ $(t_i - time_a^{i-1}(\sigma)) \in J_i(a)$.

We extend the map tw to work on subsets of Γ^{ω} in the natural way. Thus, for $\widehat{L} \subseteq \Gamma^{\omega}$, we define $tw(\widehat{L}) = \bigcup_{\widehat{\sigma} \in \widehat{L}} tw(\widehat{\sigma})$.

We are now in a position to define an event recording automaton and the timed language accepted by it. An *event recording automaton* over an alphabet Σ is simply a Büchi automaton over an interval alphabet based on Σ. Viewed as a Büchi automaton over an interval alphabet Γ, an event recording automaton $\mathcal{A}$ accepts the language $L_{sym}(\mathcal{A}) \subseteq \Gamma^{\omega}$ which we will call the "symbolic" language accepted by $\mathcal{A}$. However, we will be more interested in the timed language accepted by $\mathcal{A}$: this is denoted $L(\mathcal{A})$ and is defined to be $tw(L_{sym}(\mathcal{A}))$. We say that $L \subseteq T\Sigma^\omega$ is a *ω-regular event recording language* over Σ if $L = L(\mathcal{A})$ for some event recording automaton $\mathcal{A}$ over Σ. Thus, event recording languages over Σ are precisely those of the form $tw(\widehat{L})$, where $\widehat{L}$ is an ω-regular language over an interval alphabet based on Σ.

3   Logical Characterisation

The aim of this section is to characterise the class of ω-regular event recording languages via a monadic second order logic interpreted over timed words. We call the logic $\mathrm{MSO}_{er}(\Sigma)$ and it is parameterised by the alphabet Σ.

Here and in the logics to follow, we assume a supply of individual variables $x, y, \ldots$, and set variables $X, Y, \ldots$. These variables will range over positions (respectively sets of positions) of a given timed word. We will make use of the predicates $Q_a(x)$ (one for each $a \in \Sigma$) and $\Delta_a(x) \in I$, where x is an individual variable, $a \in \Sigma$ and I is an element of $\mathcal{IR}$. The syntax of $\mathrm{MSO}_{er}(\Sigma)$ is given by:

$$\varphi ::= (x \in X) \mid (x < y) \mid Q_a(x) \mid (\Delta_a(x) \in I) \mid \neg\varphi \mid (\varphi \vee \varphi) \mid \exists x\varphi \mid \exists X\varphi.$$

A structure for a formula of the logic will be a pair $(\sigma, \mathbb{I})$ where $\sigma \in T\Sigma^\omega$ and $\mathbb{I}$ is an interpretation which assigns to each individual variable a position of σ (i.e. an element of $\mathbb{N}$), and to each set variable a set of positions of σ. The predicate '$<$' is interpreted as the usual ordering on $\mathbb{N}$.

The satisfaction relation $\sigma \models_{\mathbb{I}} \varphi$ for atomic formulas φ is given below. Let $\sigma = (\alpha, \eta)$. Then

$$\begin{aligned}
\sigma &\models_{\mathbb{I}} (x \in X) &&\text{iff } \mathbb{I}(x) \in \mathbb{I}(X) \\
\sigma &\models_{\mathbb{I}} (x < y) &&\text{iff } \mathbb{I}(x) < \mathbb{I}(y) \\
\sigma &\models_{\mathbb{I}} Q_a(x) &&\text{iff } \alpha(\mathbb{I}(x)) = a \\
\sigma &\models_{\mathbb{I}} (\Delta_a(x) \in I) &&\text{iff } (\eta(\mathbb{I}(x)) - time_a^{\mathbb{I}(x)-1}(\sigma)) \in I.
\end{aligned}$$

The operator $\Delta_a(x)$ measures the time elapsed since the last a action w.r.t. the position x, and the predicate $\Delta_a(x) \in I$ asserts that this value lies in the interval I.

The operators $\neg$, $\vee$, and the existential quantifiers $\exists x$ and $\exists X$ are interpreted in the usual manner. In particular the quantifier $\exists X$ is interpreted as follows. Let $\mathbb{I}$ be an interpretation for variables with respect to σ. Let $i \in \mathbb{N}$. We will use the notation $\mathbb{I}[i/x]$ to denote the interpretation which maps x to i and agrees with $\mathbb{I}$ on all other individual and set variables. Similarly, for a subset S of $\mathbb{N}$, the notation $\mathbb{I}[S/X]$ will denote the interpretation which sends X to S, and agrees with $\mathbb{I}$ on all other variables.

$$\sigma \models_{\mathbb{I}} \exists X\varphi \text{ iff there exists } S \subseteq \mathbb{N} \text{ such that } \sigma \models_{\mathbb{I}[S/X]} \varphi.$$

Given a sentence φ in $\mathrm{MSO}_{er}(\Sigma)$ we define $L(\varphi) = \{\sigma \in T\Sigma^\omega \mid \sigma \models \varphi\}$.

As an example, let $\Sigma' = \{a, r\}$. Then the following sentence ϕ in $\mathrm{MSO}_{er}(\Sigma)$ asserts that consecutive requests (r's) are separated by at least 5 time units: $\forall x(Q_r(x) \Rightarrow (\Delta_r(x) \in [5, \infty)))$.

Theorem 1. *Let $L \subseteq T\Sigma^\omega$. Then L is an ω-regular event recording language over Σ iff $L = L(\varphi)$ for some sentence φ in $\mathrm{MSO}_{er}(\Sigma)$.*

We will devote the rest of this section to the proof of this theorem. The proof will factor through the well-known logical characterisation of ω-regular languages due to Büchi [4] (see also [12]). Recall that for an alphabet A, Büchi's monadic second order logic (denoted here by $\mathrm{MSO}(A)$) is given as follows:

$$\varphi ::= (x \in X) \mid (x < y) \mid Q_a(x) \mid \neg\varphi \mid (\varphi \vee \varphi) \mid \exists x\varphi \mid \exists X\varphi.$$

A structure for this logic is a pair of the form $(\alpha, \mathbb{I})$ where $\alpha \in A^\omega$ and $\mathbb{I}$ assigns elements of $\mathbb{N}$ to individual variables, and subsets of $\mathbb{N}$ to set variables. The semantics of the logic is given in a similar manner to that of MSO_{er}. In particular, the atomic formula $Q_a(x)$—here a is required to be in A—is interpreted as follows: $\alpha \models_{\mathbb{I}} Q_a(x)$ iff $\alpha(\mathbb{I}(x)) = a$. For a sentence φ in $\mathrm{MSO}(A)$ we set $L(\varphi) = \{\sigma \in A^\omega \mid \sigma \models \varphi\}$. Büchi's result then states that a language $L \subseteq A^\omega$ is an ω-regular language over A iff $L = L(\varphi)$ for some sentence φ in $\mathrm{MSO}(A)$.

Next, we introduce the notion of a *proper* interval alphabet which will play an important role in this paper. We say a finite set of intervals $\mathcal{I} \subseteq \mathbb{IR}$ is *proper* if it forms a finite partition of $\mathbb{R}^{>0}$. Thus, if $\mathcal{I}$ is a proper interval set, then for each $t \in \mathbb{R}^{>0}$ there exists an $I \in \mathcal{I}$ such that $t \in I$, and for each $I, I' \in \mathcal{I}, I \neq I'$ implies $I \cap I' = \emptyset$. An interval alphabet Γ based on Σ will be termed proper if for each $a \in \Sigma$ the set $\Gamma_a = \{I \mid \exists(b, J) \in \Gamma \text{ with } J(a) = I\}$ is a proper interval set. We say an interval set $\mathcal{I}$ *covers* an interval set $\mathcal{I}'$ if every interval in $\mathcal{I}'$ is the union of some collection of intervals in $\mathcal{I}$. Finally, an interval alphabet Γ covers an interval alphabet Γ' (both based on Σ) if Γ_a covers Γ'_a for each $a \in \Sigma$.

Each interval alphabet Γ induces in a canonical way a proper interval alphabet, denoted $prop(\Gamma)$, with the property that it covers Γ. It is given by

$$prop(\Gamma) = \{(a, J) \mid a \in \Sigma \text{ and } \forall b \in \Sigma, \ J(b) \in prop(\Gamma_b)\}$$

where for each b, the set $prop(\Gamma_b)$ is obtained from Γ_b by the procedure outlined below.

Let $\mathcal{I}$ be a non-empty finite set of intervals (if it is empty, we simply set $prop(\mathcal{I}) = \{(0, \infty)\}$). Let $V = \{0, v_1, v_2, \ldots, v_n, \infty\}$ where for $1 \leq i \leq n, \ v_i \in V$ iff there exists $I \in \mathcal{I}$ with v_i as the left or right end of I. Without loss of generality, we assume that $n \geq 1$ and $0 < v_1 < v_2 < \cdots < v_n \neq \infty$. Now define $prop(\mathcal{I})$ via:

$$prop(\mathcal{I}) = \{(0, v_1)\} \cup \{[v_j, v_j], \ (v_j, v_{j+1}) \mid 1 \leq j \leq n\}$$

where we set $v_{n+1} = \infty$. It is easy to verify that $prop(\mathcal{I})$ is a proper interval set which covers $\mathcal{I}$.

The following is an important property of proper interval alphabets.

Proposition 2 *Let Γ be a proper interval alphabet based on Σ. Then for each $\sigma \in T\Sigma^\omega$ there exists a unique word $\widehat{\sigma} \in \Gamma^\omega$ such that $\sigma \in tw(\widehat{\sigma})$.*

Proof. The proposition is easy to verify once we note that for each $t \in \mathbb{R}^{>0}$ and $a \in \Sigma$, there exists a unique $I \in \Gamma_a$ such that $t \in I$. $\qquad \blacksquare$ $\qquad \square$

Now, given a formula $\varphi \in \mathrm{MSO}_{er}(\Sigma)$ we show how to translate it to a formula $t\text{-}s(\varphi) \in \mathrm{MSO}(\Gamma)$, for a suitably defined interval alphabet Γ. The translation will preserve—in a sense to be made precise—the timed models of φ. (The name $t\text{-}s$ is a mnemonic for "timed-to-symbolic".) Let Γ be any proper interval alphabet over Σ such that for each $a \in \Sigma$, Γ_a covers

$$voc_a(\varphi) = \{I \mid \varphi \text{ has a subformula of the form } (\Delta_a(x) \in I)\}.$$

Note that $\{(a, J) \mid a \in \Sigma, \text{ and } \forall b \in \Sigma, J(b) \in prop(voc_b(\varphi))\}$ is at least one such Γ. Then $t\text{-}s(\varphi)$ (w.r.t. Γ) is obtained from φ by replacing sub-formulas of the form $Q_a(x)$ by the formula $\bigvee_{(b,J) \in \Gamma, \ b=a} Q_{(b,J)}(x)$, and sub-formulas of the form $\Delta_a(x) \in I$ by the formula $\bigvee_{(b,J) \in \Gamma, \ J(a) \subseteq I} Q_{(b,J)}(x)$.

Lemma 1. *Let $\varphi \in \mathrm{MSO}_{er}(\Sigma)$ and let Γ be a proper interval alphabet based on Σ such that Γ_a covers $voc_a(\varphi)$ for each $a \in \Sigma$. Let $\widehat{\sigma} \in \Gamma^\omega$ and $\sigma \in T\Sigma^\omega$ be such that $\sigma \in tw(\widehat{\sigma})$. Suppose further that $\mathbb{I}$ is an interpretation for variables. Then*

1. $\sigma \models_{\mathbb{I}} \varphi$ iff $\widehat{\sigma} \models_{\mathbb{I}} t\text{-}s(\varphi)$.
2. If φ is a sentence, then $L(\varphi) = tw(L(t\text{-}s(\varphi))$.

Proof. (1) We prove the statement by induction on the structure of φ. The interesting cases are $\varphi = Q_a(x)$ and $\varphi = (\Delta_a(x) \in I)$. Let $\sigma = (\alpha, \eta)$, and $\widehat{\sigma} = (a_0, J_0)(a_1, J_1) \cdots$.

Case $\varphi = Q_a(x)$: We know $\sigma \models_{\mathbb{I}} Q_a(x)$ iff $\alpha(\mathbb{I}(x)) = a$. But since $\sigma \in tw(\widehat{\sigma})$, we know that this holds iff $\widehat{\sigma}(\mathbb{I}(x)) = (a, J)$ for some J such that $(a, J) \in \Gamma$. This in turn holds iff $\widehat{\sigma} \models_{\mathbb{I}} \bigvee_{(b,J') \in \Gamma, \ b=a} Q_{(b,J')}(x)$. Thus, $\sigma \models_{\mathbb{I}} \varphi$ iff $\widehat{\sigma} \models_{\mathbb{I}} t\text{-}s(\varphi)$.

Case $\varphi = (\Delta_a(x) \in I)$: Let $\sigma \models_{\mathbb{I}} (\Delta_a(x) \in I)$. Then we know that $(\eta(\mathbb{I}(x)) - time_a^{\mathbb{I}(x)-1}(\sigma)) \in I$. Further, since $\sigma \in tw(\widehat{\sigma})$, we know that

$$(\eta(\mathbb{I}(x)) - time_a^{\mathbb{I}(x)-1}(\sigma)) \in J_{\mathbb{I}(x)}(a).$$

Using the fact that Γ is proper and covers $voc_a(\varphi)$, it must be the case that $J_{\mathbb{I}(x)}(a) \subseteq I$. Hence $\widehat{\sigma} \models_{\mathbb{I}} \bigvee_{(b,J) \in \Gamma, J(a) \subseteq I} Q_{(b,J)}(x)$.

Conversely, let $\widehat{\sigma} \models_{\mathbb{I}} \bigvee_{(b,J) \in \Gamma, \ J(a) \subseteq I} Q_{(b,J)}(x)$. Then $\widehat{\sigma}(\mathbb{I}(x)) = (b, J)$ for some $(b, J) \in \Gamma$ such that $J(a) \subseteq I$. Since $\sigma \in tw(\widehat{\sigma})$ we have $(\eta(\mathbb{I}(x)) - time_a^{\mathbb{I}(x)-1}(\sigma)) \in J(a)$. Since $J(a) \subseteq I$, we have $(\eta(\mathbb{I}(x)) - time_a^{\mathbb{I}(x)-1}(\sigma)) \in I$, and hence $\sigma \models_{\mathbb{I}} (\Delta_a(x) \in I)$.

(2) This is easy to see once we have (1) above. Let $\sigma \models \varphi$. Then, again using properties of proper alphabets (Proposition 2), there exists a $\widehat{\sigma} \in \Gamma^\omega$ such that $\sigma \in tw(\widehat{\sigma})$. Using (1) above, we have $\widehat{\sigma} \in L(t\text{-}s(\varphi))$ and hence $\sigma \in tw(L(t\text{-}s(\varphi)))$. Conversely, if $\sigma \in tw(\widehat{\sigma})$ and $\widehat{\sigma} \models t\text{-}s(\varphi)$, then by (1) again we have that $\sigma \models \varphi$, and hence $\sigma \in L(\varphi)$. $\qquad \square$

Let Γ be an interval alphabet based on Σ. We now show how we can associate a formula $s\text{-}t(\widehat{\varphi}) \in \mathrm{MSO}_{er}(\Sigma)$ with a formula $\widehat{\varphi} \in \mathrm{MSO}(\Gamma)$, such that, once again, the translated formula preserves timed models. The formula $s\text{-}t(\widehat{\varphi})$ is obtained by replacing atomic sub-formulas in $\widehat{\varphi}$ of the form $Q_{(a,J)}(x)$ by the formula $Q_a(x) \wedge \bigwedge_{b \in \Sigma}(\Delta_b(x) \in J(b))$.

The following lemma is easy to show along the lines of Lemma 1:

Lemma 2. *Let Γ be a proper interval alphabet based on Σ and let $\widehat{\varphi} \in \mathrm{MSO}(\Gamma)$. Let $\widehat{\sigma} \in \Gamma^{\omega}$ and $\sigma \in T\Sigma^{\omega}$ such that $\sigma \in tw(\widehat{\sigma})$. Suppose further that $\mathbb{I}$ is an interpretation for variables. Then*

1. *$\sigma \models_{\mathbb{I}} s\text{-}t(\widehat{\varphi})$ iff $\widehat{\sigma} \models_{\mathbb{I}} \widehat{\varphi}$.*
2. *If φ is a sentence, then we have $L(s\text{-}t(\widehat{\varphi})) = tw(L(\widehat{\varphi}))$.*   □

We are now in a position to provide a proof of Theorem 1. Let L be an ω-regular event recording language over Σ. It is not difficult to see that there must be a *proper* interval alphabet Γ based on Σ, and an ω-regular subset $\widehat{L}$ of Γ^{ω} such that $L = tw(\widehat{L})$. Büchi's theorem tells us that there exists an $\mathrm{MSO}(\Gamma)$-sentence $\widehat{\varphi}$ such that $L(\widehat{\varphi}) = \widehat{L}$. Hence $L = tw(L(\widehat{\varphi}))$. By Lemma 2, we have a $\mathrm{MSO}_{er}(\Sigma)$-sentence, namely $\varphi = s\text{-}t(\widehat{\varphi})$, such that $L = L(\varphi)$.

Conversely, let φ be a $\mathrm{MSO}_{er}(\Sigma)$-sentence. Let Γ be a proper interval alphabet based on Σ such that Γ_a covers $voc_a(\varphi)$ for each $a \in \Sigma$. Then, by Lemma 1, we know that there exists a formula $\widehat{\varphi} = t\text{-}s(\varphi)$ in $\mathrm{MSO}(\Gamma)$, such that $L(\varphi) = tw(L(\widehat{\varphi}))$. Using Büchi's theorem once more, we know that $L(\widehat{\varphi})$ is an ω-regular language over Γ. Thus $L(\varphi)$ is an ω-regular event recording language over Σ. This completes the proof of Theorem 1.   □

To conclude this section we point out the nature of the projection (or renaming) operation associated with existential quantification in our logic. In classical monadic logics (as in S1S) it is usually the case that both open formulas and sentences correspond to languages in the same class under consideration. In the case of MSO_{er} however, while sentences correspond to event recording languages, the open formulas correspond more naturally to a class of languages we call *quasi* event recording languages. The associated closure under projection is thus with respect to these languages, and not event recording languages which are *not* closed under projection. We will formalise these ideas below.

Let U be a (possibly infinite) universe of letters (from which our alphabets will be drawn). Consider a finite partition of this universe, given by a function f from the universe U to a finite indexing set X.

Let us fix such a triple (U, f, X). Let $A \subseteq U$ be an alphabet of actions. Then a *quasi* event recording automaton (qERA) over A (w.r.t. the triple (U, f, X)) is a timed automaton over A with a set of clocks X and the restriction that for every action $a \in A$, the set of clocks reset along a transition labelled a is exactly $\{f(a)\}$. A qERA is thus a weaker form of event recording automata (it is not difficult to see that an event recording automaton over A can simulate a qERA over A). We will say $L \subseteq TU^{\omega}$ is an (ω-regular) *quasi event recording language* (qERL) w.r.t (U, f, X) if $L = L(\mathcal{A})$ for some alphabet $A \subseteq U$, and qERA $\mathcal{A}$ over A.

Let A, A' be alphabets, with $A, A' \subseteq U$. A renaming from A to A' is a map from A to A'. We say $\varsigma : A \to A'$ is a *valid* renaming w.r.t. (U, f, X) iff for each $a \in A : f(a) = f(\varsigma(a))$ (i.e. both $\varsigma(a)$ and a belong to the same block of the partition). For a timed word $\sigma \in TA^\omega$ the timed word $\varsigma(\sigma) \in TA'^\omega$ is defined in the expected manner. The following proposition is then easily verified:

Proposition 3 *The class of quasi event recording languages over (U, f, X) is closed under renaming operations which are valid w.r.t. (U, f, X).*   □

If we now consider a direct proof of Theorem 1 along the lines of the one for MSO (see [12]), it will be clear that existential quantification in MSO_{er} corresponds to the class qERL being closed under the restricted renaming defined above. We will concentrate on one direction of the proof where we show that every $\text{MSO}_{er}(\Sigma)$ sentence can be captured by an event recording automaton over Σ. This is done by associating, inductively, a qERA with each formula in $\text{MSO}_{er}(\Sigma)$. Let $\varphi(m, n)$ denote a formula whose free variables are among $\{x_1, \ldots, x_m, X_1, \ldots, X_n\}$. A structure $(\sigma, \mathbb{I})$ for a formula $\varphi(m, n)$ in $\text{MSO}_{er}(\Sigma)$ is encoded as a timed word over Σ_{m+n} where for $i \geq 0$, Σ_i is defined to be

$$\Sigma \times \overbrace{\{0, 1\} \times \cdots \times \{0, 1\}}^{i}.$$

Let $\sigma = (\alpha, \eta)$. Then $(\sigma, \mathbb{I})$ is represented as $\sigma' \in T(\Sigma_{m+n})^\omega$ with $\sigma' = (\alpha', \eta)$ where α' is given as follows: for each $i \in \mathbb{N}$, $\alpha'(i) = (a, b_1, \ldots b_m, c_1, \ldots, c_n)$ where $a = \alpha(i)$, $b_j = 1$ iff $\mathbb{I}(x_j) = i$ and $c_j = 1$ iff $i \in \mathbb{I}(X_j)$. The satisfaction relation $\sigma' \models \varphi(m, n)$, is defined in the expected manner based on the semantics given earlier. Each formula $\varphi(m, n)$ in $\text{MSO}_{er}(\Sigma)$ thus defines a subset of $T(\Sigma_{m+n})^\omega$, denoted $L(\varphi(m, n))$, which is the set of models of φ.

In the induction step for the "$\exists X$" case, we assume that the formula $\varphi(m, n+1)$ is such that $L(\varphi(m, n+1)) \subseteq T\Sigma_{m+n+1}^\omega$ is accepted by a qERA over Σ_{m+n+1}, with respect to the triple (U, g, Σ) where g (restricted to $\bigcup_{i \geq 0} \Sigma_i$) is given by $g((a, d_1, \ldots, d_l)) = a$. Then the set of models of the formula $(\exists X_{n+1} \varphi)(m, n)$ is simply obtained from $L(\varphi(m, n+1))$ by projecting each letter of Σ_{m+n+1} to the dimensions 1 to $m + n$. This projection is clearly a valid renaming w.r.t. (U, g, Σ) and by Proposition 3 the language $L((\exists X_{n+1}\varphi)(m, n))$ is also a qERL over Σ_{m+n}. Note that in this way, for a sentence φ, the language $L(\varphi)$ is accepted by a qERA over Σ (w.r.t. (U, g, Σ)), which is nothing but an event recording automaton over Σ.

4   Expressive Completeness of LTL$_{er}$

In this section we formulate a version of the timed temporal logic nrEventClockTL introduced in [10] and called here LTL$_{er}$. The satisfiability and model-checking problems for LTL$_{er}$ are solved in [10] and shown to be PSPACE-complete. Here we concentrate on proving the expressive completeness of LTL$_{er}$.

Let Σ be an alphabet of actions. Then the formulas of $\mathrm{LTL}_{er}(\Sigma)$ (parameterised by the alphabet Σ) are given by:

$$\varphi ::= \top \mid \triangleleft_a \in I \mid \langle a \rangle \varphi \mid O\varphi \mid \neg\varphi \mid (\varphi \vee \varphi) \mid (\varphi U \varphi).$$

Here we require $a \in \Sigma$.

The models for $\mathrm{LTL}_{er}(\Sigma)$ formulas are timed words over Σ. Let $\sigma \in T\Sigma^\omega$, with $\sigma = (\alpha, \eta)$, and let $i \in \{-1\} \cup \mathbb{N}$. Then the satisfaction relation $\sigma, i \models \varphi$ is given by

$$
\begin{aligned}
&\sigma, i \models \top \\
&\sigma, i \models \triangleleft_a \in I \text{ iff } i \geq 0 \text{ and } (\eta(i) - time_a^{i-1}(\sigma)) \in I \\
&\sigma, i \models \langle a \rangle \varphi \text{ iff } \alpha(i+1) = a \text{ and } \sigma, i+1 \models \varphi \\
&\sigma, i \models O\varphi \text{ iff } \sigma, i+1 \models \varphi \\
&\sigma, i \models \neg\varphi \text{ iff } \sigma, i \not\models \varphi \\
&\sigma, i \models \varphi \vee \varphi' \text{ iff } \sigma, i \models \varphi \text{ or } \sigma, i \models \varphi' \\
&\sigma, i \models \varphi U \varphi' \text{ iff } \exists k \geq i : \sigma, k \models \varphi' \text{ and } \forall j : i \leq j < k, \ \sigma, j \models \varphi.
\end{aligned}
$$

We say $\sigma \models \varphi$ iff $\sigma, -1 \models \varphi$. Define $L(\varphi) = \{\sigma \in T\Sigma^\omega \mid \sigma \models \varphi\}$.
As an example, the $\mathrm{LTL}_{er}(\Sigma')$ formula

$$\Box(\langle r \rangle \top \Rightarrow O(\triangleleft_r \in [5, \infty))),$$

where $\Box\alpha$ is an abbreviation for $\neg(\top U \neg \alpha)$, rephrases the property ϕ of Section 3.

It will be convenient for us to combine the two modalities $\langle a \rangle \varphi$ and $\triangleleft_a \in I$ into a single modality of the form $\langle (a, J) \rangle \varphi$ where $a \in \Sigma$ and $J \in \mathcal{IR}^\Sigma$. The semantics of the new modality is given by

$$
\begin{aligned}
\sigma, i \models \langle (a, J) \rangle \varphi \text{ iff } &\alpha(i+1) = a, \ \forall b \in \Sigma \ (\eta(i+1) - time_b^i(\sigma)) \in J(b), \\
&\text{and } \sigma, i+1 \models \varphi.
\end{aligned}
$$

The expressiveness of the logic can be seen to remain the same despite this change.

Let $\mathrm{FO}_{er}(\Sigma)$ denote the first-order fragment of the logic $\mathrm{MSO}_{er}(\Sigma)$. Thus $\mathrm{FO}_{er}(\Sigma)$ is obtained from $\mathrm{MSO}_{er}(\Sigma)$ by disallowing the use of quantification over set variables. The aim of the rest of this section is to prove the following result.

Theorem 4. $\mathrm{LTL}_{er}(\Sigma)$ *is expressively equivalent to* $\mathrm{FO}_{er}(\Sigma)$.

The method of proof will be to translate LTL_{er} formulas into classical LTL over an appropriate interval alphabet. The method is similar to the proof of Theorem 1 and we will also make use of the translation used there.

It will be useful to first recall the definition of LTL and the result concerning its expressive completeness. Let A be an alphabet of actions. Then the formulas of the so-called "action-based" LTL, denoted $\mathrm{LTL}(A)$, are given by the syntax:

$$\varphi ::= \top \mid \langle a \rangle \varphi \mid O\varphi \mid \neg\varphi \mid (\varphi \vee \varphi) \mid (\varphi U \varphi).$$

In the formula $\langle a \rangle \varphi$ we require $a \in A$. The semantics of $\mathrm{LTL}(A)$ is given similarly to $\mathrm{LTL}_{er}(\Sigma)$ above, with models being infinite words over A. In particular, for a word $\alpha \in A^\omega$ we have

$$\alpha, i \models \langle a \rangle \varphi \text{ iff } \alpha(i+1) = a \text{ and } \alpha, i+1 \models \varphi.$$

We will say that $\sigma \models \varphi$ iff $\sigma, -1 \models \varphi$. We set $L_{sym}(\varphi) = \{\sigma \in A^\omega \mid \sigma \models \varphi\}$.

Let $\mathrm{FO}(A)$ denote the first-order fragment of the logic $\mathrm{MSO}(A)$. As before, $\mathrm{FO}(A)$ is obtained from the logic $\mathrm{MSO}(A)$ defined in Section 3, by disallowing the use of set variables. Then a well known result due to the work of Kamp, and Gabbay et. al, is:

Theorem 5 ([7,8]). $\mathrm{LTL}(A)$ *is expressively equivalent to* $\mathrm{FO}(A)$. □

Looking back at the syntax of $\mathrm{LTL}_{er}(\Sigma)$ formulas, we see that they are simply $\mathrm{LTL}(\Gamma)$ formulas for some interval alphabet Γ based on Σ. Of course, we must bear in mind that $\mathrm{LTL}_{er}(\Sigma)$ formulas are interpreted over *timed* words over Σ. Thus, a formula $\varphi \in \mathrm{LTL}(\Gamma)$ defines a language $L_{sym}(\varphi) \subseteq \Gamma^\omega$ when interpreted as an $\mathrm{LTL}(\Gamma)$ formula, and it defines a timed language $L(\varphi) \subseteq T\Sigma^\omega$ when interpreted as an $\mathrm{LTL}_{er}(\Sigma)$ formula.

The following lemma describes the relationship between these two languages:

Lemma 3. *Let Γ be a proper interval alphabet based on Σ. Let φ be a formula in $\mathrm{LTL}(\Gamma)$. Then $L(\varphi) = tw(L_{sym}(\varphi))$.*

Proof. The proof of this is very similar to our earlier arguments which make use of the properties of proper interval sets. □

Returning now to the proof of Theorem 4, let $\varphi_0 \in \mathrm{LTL}_{er}(\Sigma)$. Then it is not difficult to see that we can construct a proper interval alphabet Γ based on Σ such that Γ_a covers $voc_a(\varphi)$ for each $a \in \Sigma$, and a formula $\varphi_1 \in \mathrm{LTL}(\Gamma)$ such that $L(\varphi_0) = L(\varphi_1)$. From Lemma 3, we know that $L(\varphi_1) = tw(L_{sym}(\varphi_1))$. Now, by Theorem 5, we know that there exists a sentence φ_2 in $\mathrm{FO}(\Gamma)$ such that $L(\varphi_2) = L_{sym}(\varphi_1)$. Now consider the sentence $\varphi_3 = s\text{-}t(\varphi_2)$ w.r.t. the proper interval alphabet Γ (cf. Section 3). The translations $s\text{-}t$ and $t\text{-}s$ are such that if the given formula is first-order, then so is the translated formula. Thus φ_3 is a $\mathrm{FO}_{er}(\Sigma)$ sentence. Further, since Γ is proper, by Lemma 2 we know that $L(\varphi_3) = tw(L(\varphi_2))$. Thus φ_3 is the required $\mathrm{FO}_{er}(\Sigma)$ sentence with $L(\varphi_0) = L(\varphi_3)$.

Conversely, let φ_0 be a sentence in $\mathrm{FO}_{er}(\Sigma)$. Then, once again, there exists a proper interval alphabet Γ based on A such that Γ_a covers $voc_a(\varphi_0)$ for each $a \in \Sigma$. Consider the $\mathrm{MSO}(\Gamma)$ sentence $\varphi_1 = t\text{-}s(\varphi_0)$ with respect to the interval alphabet Γ (cf. Section 3). By Lemma 1, $L(\varphi_0) = tw(L(\varphi_1))$. Further, φ_1 is a sentence in $\mathrm{FO}(\Gamma)$. Now, again appealing to Theorem 5, we know that there exists an $\mathrm{LTL}(\Gamma)$ formula φ_2 such that $L_{sym}(\varphi_2) = L(\varphi_1)$. By Lemma 3, we know that $L(\varphi_2) = tw(L_{sym}(\varphi_2))$. Thus φ_2 is the required formula in $\mathrm{LTL}_{er}(\Sigma)$ such that $L(\varphi_2) = L(\varphi_0)$. □

In conclusion we would like to point out that the results here (including Theorems 1 and 4) can be readily extended to the class of event clock automata. For this we will need to extend MSO_{er} with a "predicting" modality $\Delta_a^+(x)$ which measures the time to the next occurrence of action a with respect to the position x. Correspondingly the logic LTL_{er} can be extended with the operator $\triangleright_a$ as originally formulated in [10].

Acknowledgments: I am grateful to P. S. Thiagarajan for several useful inputs, and to Ramesh Vishwanathan for his comments on a draft of this paper.

References

1. R. Alur, D. L. Dill: A theory of timed automata, *Theoretical Computer Science* 126: 183–235 (1994).
2. R. Alur, L. Fix, T. A. Henzinger: Event-clock automata: a determinizable class of timed automata, *Proc. 6th International Conference on Computer-aided Verification, LNCS 818*, 1–13, Springer-Verlag (1994).
3. R. Alur, T. A. Henzinger: Real-time logics: complexity and expressiveness, *Information and Computation 104*, 35–77 (1993).
4. J. R. Büchi: Weak second-order arithmetic and finite automata, *Zeitschrift für Math. Logik und Grundlagen der Mathematik, 6*, 66–92 (1960).
5. D. D'Souza, T. Hune: An on-the-fly Construction for an Event Clock Logic, Manuscript (1999).
6. D. D'Souza, P. S. Thiagarajan: Product Interval Automata: A Subclass of Timed Automata, *Proc. 19th Foundations of Software Technology and Theoretical Computer Science (FSTTCS), LNCS 1732* (1999).
7. A. W. H. Kamp: Tense Logic and the Theory of Linear Order, PhD Thesis, University of California (1968).
8. D. Gabbay, A. Pnueli, S. Shelah, J. Stavi: The Temporal Analysis of Fairness, *Seventh ACM Symposium on Principles of Programming Languages*, 163–173, (1980).
9. T. A. Henzinger, J.-F. Raskin, and P.-Y. Schobbens: The regular real-time languages, *Proc. 25th International Colloquium on Automata, Languages, and Programming 1998, LNCS 1443*, 580–591 (1998).
10. J. -F. Raskin: Logics, Automata and Classical Theories for Deciding Real Time, Ph.D Thesis, FUNDP, Belgium.
11. J. -F. Raskin, P. -Y. Schobbens: State-clock Logic: A Decidable Real-Time Logic, *Proc. HART '97: Hybrid and Real-Time Systems, LNCS 1201*, 33–47 (1997).
12. W. Thomas: Automata on Infinite Objects, in J. V. Leeuwen (Ed.), *Handbook of Theoretical Computer Science*, Vol. B, 133–191, Elsevier Science Publ., Amsterdam (1990).
13. Th. Wilke: Specifying Timed State Sequences in Powerful Decidable Logics and Timed Automata, in *Formal Techniques in Real-Time and Fault-Tolerant Systems, LNCS 863*, 694–715 (1994).

Using Cylindrical Algebraic Decomposition for the Analysis of Slope Parametric Hybrid Automata

Michaël Adélaïde* and Olivier Roux *

Institut de Recherche en Communication et Cybernétique de Nantes

Abstract. We address the ambitious problem of synthesizing the parameters which stand for the execution speeds in time constrained executions of a real-time system. The core of the paper is a new method based on the *Gröbner bases* and the so-called *Cylindrical Algebraic Decomposition* in order to design a simplification algorithm and a test inclusion upon sets of inequalities. The method is illustrated throughout the paper with a small example.

1 Introduction

Objective and Framework. The *parametric analysis* of a real-time system consists in computing some parameters of the system to ensure its correct behaviour. More precisely, the purpose of our work presented in this paper is to attempt to achieve paramatric analysis of evolution laws in a hybrid automaton [ACD90,MMP92,AH94,AD94,AMP95,ACH+95] which are intended to model the possible executions of a dynamical system. It means that, given a hybrid automaton for which the evolution speeds of one of its variables is unknown, we try to determine the set of speeds of the aforementioned variable which make it possible to meet some temporal requirements. Unknowns are usually referred to as parameters in the literature, hence the name of *Parametric analysis*. The evolution speeds are indeed the slopes of the variables which are not constant but affine expressions on a set of parameters.

---

* IRCCyN/CNRS UMR 6597 (1 rue de la Noë, BP 92101, 44321 Nantes cedex 03, France) e-mail: {Michael.Adelaide | Olivier.Roux}@ircyn.ec-nantes.fr

M. Joseph (Ed.): FTRTFT 2000, LNCS 1926, pp. 252–263, 2000.

Related works. This paper follows [BBRR97,BR97] and it goes further in the way we now deal with parametric polyhedra which are symbolic representations of the set of states of the system. We elaborated a simplification algorithm and an inclusion test for the systems of inequalities. This algorithm and this test are based on the *Gröbner bases* [BW93] and the *Cylindrical Algebraic Decomposition* [Jir95].

Other works have already contributed to "parametric reasoning about real-time" [AHV93,HH95,Wan96], but the difference with our work is that they are mostly concerned with delays as parameters, while we study speeds as parameters.

Outline of the Paper. The definitions are recalled and our method is illustrated throughout the paper owing to the small example of the control of a water-tank level. We first introduce, in section 2, the definitions of Slope Parametric Linear Hybrid Automata. Then, section 3 gives a quick overview of the key concepts of reachability analysis that will be used in section 4. This section is the core of the paper: we give an algorithm for simplifying systems of parametric inequations and an inclusion test. Section 5 provides with some results achieved from the example that illustrates the method. Eventually, in section 6, we conclude and give some directions for future work.

2   Slope Parametric Linear Hybrid Automata

2.1   Definitions

The Slope Parametric Linear Hybrid Automaton (SPLHA) model is an extension of the Linear Hybrid Automaton (LHA) [Hen96] model. In SPLHA, a set of parameters $K = \{k_1, ..., k_q\}$ is added to formulate the slopes of the variables. When the parameters are set to specific values, one obtains again LHA. We must focus the attention on the definition of the states for SPLHA. For LHA, a state is given by a node and values of the clocks in this node. For SPLHA, one must also consider the conditions C on the parameters. In the genaral case, the values of the clocks (given by the set $X = \{x_1, ..., x_n\}$) are set by parametric polyhedra. It is a set Π of inequalities $f_j(k, x) \geq 0$ which are linear over the set X of clocks, but not linear when considering the parameters ($f_j(k, x) = a_{j,0}(k) + \sum_{i=1}^{n} a_{j,i} x_i$).

2.2   An Example

In order to have a better understanding of *Parametric Slopes* , let us take an example. We want to model a water tank (see Figure 1) the behaviour

of which is a succession of filling and emptying operations. The water level
x_2 is controlled by the clock x_1. The clock rate is 1, and the parameter k
is used to define the filling speed of the tank.

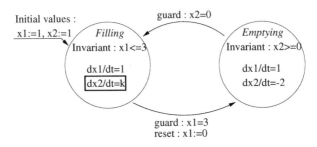

Fig. 1. Example

All along the paper, we are going to show how the conditions that
enable a correct behaviour appear, studing the states of the automaton.
For instance, entering the 'emptying' node, the states are given by the
condition $k \geq -\frac{1}{2}$, and the clocks by the polyhedron $x_1 = 0 \wedge x_2 = 1+2.k$.

3   Outline of the Reachability Analysis

We are interested in finding the conditions on the parameters that ensure a correct behaviour of the automaton. Frequently, the problem is
turned into a reachability one. It consists in finding the conditions on the
parameters for which a state is reachable. This analysis has been first
developed in [BBRR97,BR97,Bur98]. It is based upon both an analysis
of the evolution of the automaton and a fix-point computation according
to the following formulas:

$$Reach(A) = Least\,Fix\,Point(Crossing(Start)) \qquad (1)$$
$$Crossing(Q) = \{d | \exists s \in Q, s \rightarrow_\delta^t \rightarrow_0^L d\} \qquad (2)$$

All the operations are quantifier eliminations (QE) in real algebra. In
the next paragraphs, we are going to define the operations done in the
elementary step and the fix-point computation.

3.1   The Elementary Step : Crossing an Edge

For a given set of states Q, the elementary step computes all states d
(destination) reachable from any sates s (source) which belongs to Q after

one edge crossing. Showing the different steps of the analysis, we are going to underline the intermadiate conditions C_i and polyhedra Π_i found from the start condition $C_0 \Leftrightarrow true$ and polyhedron $\Pi_0 \Leftrightarrow (x_1 = x_2 = 1)$.

The Extension Operation. The first operation is the extension one. It represents the time elapsing in the source node. It is expressed as the existence of a δ predecessor. In other words, one can say : "Both the node-invariant and the entering condition polyhedron were satisfied δ time units ago, and the node-invariant is true now". This is equivalent to the following formula:

$$\Pi_1 \Leftrightarrow \exists \delta.((\delta \geq 0) \wedge Inv_s(x - v_s * \delta) \wedge \Pi_0(k, x - v_s * \delta)) \wedge Inv_s(x)$$

Since Π_1 is the set of inequalities which stands for time-elapsing in the 'filling' node:

$$\Pi_1 \Leftrightarrow (\exists \delta.(x_1 - \delta = 1 \wedge x_2 - k.\delta = 1)) \wedge (x_1 \leq 3)) \tag{3}$$

$$\Pi_1 \Leftrightarrow (1 \leq x_1 \leq 3 \wedge x_2 = k.(x_1 - 1) + 1) \tag{4}$$

The Restriction Operation. The elimination of all linear variables is called restriction. This method is used twice in the analysis.

First, when crossing an edge, the guard of the discrete transition has to be verified. It is solved by finding the conditions on the parameters than enable it. Then C_2 being the conditions to verify the guard :

$$C_2 \Leftrightarrow (\exists x.\Pi_1(k, x) \wedge Guard_{s \to d}(x))$$

Thus, the condition C_2 and the polyhedron $\Pi_2 \Leftrightarrow (\Pi_1 \wedge Guard_{s \to d}(x))$ give the new definition of the state at this stage. For instance, when the clock reaches 3 time-units:

$$\exists x_1.\exists x_2.(x_1 = 3 \wedge \Pi_1(k, x)) \Leftrightarrow true$$

Secondly [1], when entering the destination node, its invariant has to be verified. Assume that after the reset of the needed clocks, the current polyhedron is Π_3. Then one must find the parameters values that allow entering the destination node. They are given by the following quantifier elimination:

$$C_4 \Leftrightarrow \exists x_1...\exists x_n.(\Pi_3(k, x) \wedge Inv_d(x))$$

In the example:

$$C_4 \Leftrightarrow (\exists x_1.\exists x_2.(x_1 = 0 \wedge x_2 = 2 * k + 1 \wedge x_2 \geq 0)) \Leftrightarrow (k \geq -\frac{1}{2})$$

---

[1] chronologically the variables are reset before going in the node, which leads to the polyhedron Π_3.

The Projection Operation. The projection operation is used to reset clocks $x_{i_1}...x_{i_p}$ when an edge is crossed. Reset clocks means first, be sure that the system has solutions in the clocks to reset, and secondly set to zero those variables:

$$\Pi_3 \Leftrightarrow (\exists x_{i_1}...\exists x_{i_p}.\Pi_2(k, x)) \wedge \bigwedge_{k=1}^{p} (x_{i_p} = 0)$$

Before entering the 'emptying' node:

$$\Pi_3 \Leftrightarrow (\exists x_1.\Pi_2(k, x)) \wedge (x_1 = 0) \Leftrightarrow (x_1 = 0 \wedge x_2 = 2.k + 1)$$

3.2   The Fix-Point Computation

We have shown that the "*Edge Crossing*" parametric analysis is quantifier eliminations for parametric linear formulas. In this part, we depict the global algorithm.

It is a fix-point computation. At each step, a new region R_n (a region is a set of states) is computed using the "*Edge Crossing*" analysis to find all the states reachable after no more than n edges crossing. It completes when an integer n such that $R_{n+1} = R_n$ is found. One can note that the reachability for S.P.L.H.A. is undecidable [Bur98], since nothing guarantees the termination of the algorithm.

Consequently, semi-algorithms have been implemented to realize this function which computes the reachable region $R_{\mathcal{I}}$. Up to now, the test of equality of regions and the systems solving over parameters (more precisely, finding the existential conditions on the parameters) had been implemented in using an approximate analysis [Bur98]. [Adé99] presents an approach to solve the equality of regions. This approach can be used to find the existential conditions on parameters and to simplify the polyhedra. In the next section, the two algorithms designed for this purpose will be described.

4   The Simplification Algorithm and the Inclusion Test

When entering a visited node, one must check if the new states have not been already found by a former analysis. This is the purpose of the inclusion test. Also, there is another goal to achieve. It consists in shortening the writing of the polyhedra because the QE methods increase the size of the formulas (in terms of inequalities) when they eliminate variables. We are going to show the simplification algorithm first. As a matter of fact, it gives an easy way to answer the inclusion problem.

4.1 The Simplification Algorithm   .

Given a parametric polyhedron, the simplification algorithm follows two goals:

- Find the condition on the parameters such that the polyhedron is not empty
- For each found condition, shorten the writing of the polyhedron.

   The main idea is to answer the two questions by solving non parametric inequalities. It means that we must find a partition E_K of the space of the parameters and work on each cell of the partition taking any representative of the cell. To this end, the expected properties must be invariant on each cell.

Introduction of the Distances. We first turn the original problem upon clocks and parameters into a new one introducing the *"distances"* [2] to the hyperplanes. We write :

$$(f_j(k, x) \succ 0) \Leftrightarrow \exists p_j.(h_j(k, p, x) = 0 \land p_j \succ 0)$$

with $h_j(k, p, x) = f_j(k, x) - p_j$ and p is the vector $(p_1, ..., p_m)$.

   Therefore, using all polynomials f_j, $F(k, x) \succ 0$ is equivalent to $\exists p.(H(k, p, x) = 0 \land p \succ 0)$. To obtain a new system, equivalent to the first one, in the unknowns p and k, we compute $Gb(k, p, x)$ the Gröbner basis of $H(k, p, x)$ with a lexicographic order that satisfies the following property : any parameter is lower than any distance, and, any distance is lower than any variable, which is noted $K \prec P \prec X$ (P be the list of p_j).

   Gröbner bases have been invented by Bruno Buchberger in 1965 [Buc]. A Gröbner basis [DCO92,BW93,Coh96] of a set of polynomials is another representation of the original one. Both systems have the same zeroes. They are the generalisation of the Gaussian transformation of a system into an upper triangular form for the linear case (when lexicographic orderings are used). A good introduction to Gröbner bases is given in [Coh96].

   Using the extension theorem [DCO92] and the linearity of the original system $H(k, p, x) = 0$, the polynomials in k and p are extracted from

---

[2] the term *"distance"* is quoted because what matters is not the exact value of the Euclidean distance but whether it is null or not.

$Gb(k, p, x)$. They make a system $Gb_1(k, p)$. And the equivalence [3] :

$$(\exists x \in \mathbb{R}^n.(F(k, x) \succ 0)) \Leftrightarrow (\exists p \in \mathbb{R}^m.(Gb_1(k, p) = 0 \land p \succ 0))$$

turns the original problem upon parameters and variables into a new one upon parameters and distances.

For instance, when entering the 'emptying' node for the second time, the variables values are given by:

$$x_2 = k.(3 - \frac{1 + 2.k}{2}) \land x_1 = 3 \land x_2 \geq 0$$

Let $h_1 = x_2 - k.(3 - \frac{1+2.k}{2}) - p_1, h_2 = x_1 - 3 - p_2, h_3 = x_2 - p_3$. Then,

$$Gb(k, p, x) = [-5.k + 2.k^2 - 2.p_1 + 2.p_3, -3 + x_1 + p_2, 2.x_2 - 5.k - 2.k^2 - 2.p_1]$$

Only the first polynomial of Gb has no coefficient in x, then has to be considered in the rest of the analysis (according to the extension theorem).

Partition of the Space of the Parameters using the CAD Algorithm. In the latter part, the problem upon variables and parameters has been turned into one upon "distances" and parameters :

$$Gb_1(k, p) = 0 \land p \succ 0$$

(For the example, we consider: $-5.k + 2.k^2 - 2.p_1 + 2.p_3 = 0 \land p_1 = p_2 = 0 \land p_3 \geq 0$). In order to obtain both the conditions on the parameters and the useless inequalities, a partition of $E_K{}^4$, the real space of parameters, is computed using the Cylindrical Algebraic Decomposition (C.A.D.).

The C.A.D. has been introduced by Collins in 1975 [Col75]. Given a set of multivariate polynomials in $\mathbb{R}[x_1, ..., x_n]$, it computes a partition of $\mathbb{R}^n$ such that the polynomials have a constant sign (strictly negative, null, or strictly positive) over each cell [Jir95], [Rod96]. The built partition has a tree-structure, each level of the tree corresponding to the partition of $\mathbb{R}$ for one variable. Taking into account an ordering on the variables

---

[3] The extension theorem requires to work in algebraic closed fields. Our study belongs to ordered real fields theory. Using extension theorem, one obtains a complex vector which the real parts of its coordinates verify the original system $H(k, p, x) = 0$ (this system is linear upon x and p)

[4] In order to deal with the values of the the parameters $\{k_1, ..., k_q\}$, a vector $(k_1, ..., k_q)$ of parameters is used. It belongs to $\mathbb{R}^q$. E_K stands for $\mathbb{R}^q$ to make easier the distinction between the parameters-space, the variables-space and the distances-space.

$(x_1 < x_2 < ... < x_n$ for example), the algorithm proceeds in 3 steps. The first one is called the Projection-Phase. It consists in finding recursively systems of polynomials which permit to determine a partition of $\mathbb{R}^i$ given polynomials of $\mathbb{R}[x_1, .., x_i, x_{i+1}]$. The second one, the Base-Phase builds the first partition (partition of $\mathbb{R}$). The last one called Extension-Phase builds a partition of $\mathbb{R}^{i+1}$ given a partition of $\mathbb{R}^i$. The complete algorithm is given in [Jir95]. We only explain the main ideas of the C.A.D. algorithm by analysing our example.

We have to consider the polynomial $g = -5.k + 2.k^2 - 2.p_1 + 2.p_3$, for the ordered unknowns $k < p1 < p2 < p3$.

First, we "eliminate" p_3 [5]. We make the following analysis. The sign of g seen as a polynomial in p_3 depends on the polynomials $proj_1 = \{-5.k+2.k^2-2.p_1, 2\}$. Thus, suppose we have a partition of $\mathbb{R}^3$ (unknowns $[k, p_1, p_2]$) for the polynomials of $proj_1$. The cells C_{4_k} of the partition of $\mathbb{R}^4$ are obtained from each cell C_{3_k} as follows [6] :

- $C_{4_{3.k}} \Leftrightarrow (C_{3_k} \wedge (2.p_3 < -5.k + 2.k^2 - 2.p_1))$
- $C_{4_{3.k+1}} \Leftrightarrow (C_{3_k} \wedge (2.p_3 = -5.k + 2 * k^2 - 2.p_1))$
- $C_{4_{3.k+2}} \Leftrightarrow (C_{3_k} \wedge (2.p_3 > -5.k + 2 * k^2 - 2.p_1))$

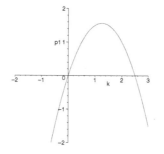

Fig. 2. plane k, p_1

Finally, having eliminated p_2 and p_1, and considering $proj_3 = \{-5.k + 2.k^2, 2\}$, the C.A.D. computes the roots of the first polynomial 2 and then the following partition of $\mathbb{R}$:

$$] - \infty, 0[\cup \{0\} \cup]0, \frac{5}{2}[\cup \{\frac{5}{2}\} \cup]\frac{5}{2}, +\infty[$$

---

[5] The meaning "eliminate" is different here. We are looking for a CAD of $\mathbb{R}^3$ for the variables $[k, p_1, p_2]$ which can be extended to $\mathbb{R}^4$ (taking into account p_3)

[6] Such operations are done in the Extension Phase which is the third step of the C.A.D. Computation.

Return to linear systems. On each cell of $partition_K$, the system $(Gb_1(k,p) = 0 \wedge p \succ 0)$ has to be solved, where k is any representative of the cell [7]. [Adé99] shows that this system in P is equivalent to a linear one given by adding the sign conditions $p \succ 0$ to the Gröbner basis computation of $Gb_1(k,p)$, for any lexicographic order on P [8]. Therefore, this system is built and solved.

In our example, the polynomials are still linear in the variables. Then, no more computation has to be done. One must solve $-5.k + 2 * k^2 - 2.p_1 + 2.p_3 = 0 \wedge p_1 = p_2 = 0 \wedge p_3 \geq 0$ replacing k by a representative of each cell.

Simplification in the non-parametric case. Then, non parametric linear systems have to be solved. We only give the main idea to eliminate useless inequalities for the shortening problem; the existence of solution is solved by eliminating all variables.

The argument to eliminate useless inequalities is to look if the border of the polyhedron intersects the hyperplans $f_j = 0$ (cf. [Adé99], proofs can be obtained from the authors). If it does not, the inequality can be removed (in Figure 3, the line δ is useless).

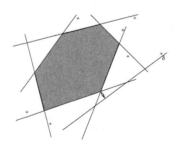

Fig. 3. General case

---

[7] We assume here that the exact values of the polynomial roots can be computed, which is not always possible. However, there are also techniques based on Sign Determination Scheme [GVRRT95] to solve the problem we are dealing with, when the exact values cannot be computed.

[8] in a earlier footnote, we have noticed that Gröbner basis computation of linear parametric systems does not lead to linear parametric system. What is claimed here is giving values to the parameters, and recalculating a Gröbner basis leads to a linear system.

For the example, there are solutions only for $0 \leq k \leq \frac{5}{2}$ and no relations have to be eliminated.

4.2   Inclusion Algorithm

In this section, the problem $A \subset B$ where A and B are both parametric polyhedra is tackled using the previous simplification algorithm, and the following equivalence, for a given polyhedron Π:

$$\text{simplification}(\Pi) = \emptyset \quad \Leftrightarrow \quad (\Pi = \emptyset)$$

It means that the inclusion test has to be transformed into emptiness tests. It is done according to the equivalence:

$$(A \subset B) \Leftrightarrow (A \bigcap \overline{B} = \emptyset)$$

Then, writing $B = \bigcap (g_i \succ 0)$, one must check :

$$\forall i, \text{simplification}(A \bigcap (g_i \overline{\succ} 0)) = \emptyset$$

to obtain the inclusion algorithm.

5   Results

In our example, the algoritm never completes because for most of the values of the parameter, the behaviour is asymptotic. Nevertheless, if we look at the values of k that allow entering 'filling node', they are in an infinite sequence of intervals $[0, M_n]$, where $lim_{n \to \infty} M_n = 2$, what can be mathematically proved. In conclusion, even if the semi-algorithm does not terminate, it gives us indications on the behaviour of the water-tank level control. These indications can then be used to complete the proof. Of course, in many examples, the algorithm completes but such examples are less appropriate to be used for explaining and illustrating.

6   Conclusion

We have shown a method to find out the set of fair dynamics of a hybrid system, i.e. the evolution rates that make the behaviour of the system is correct. It consists in using Slope Parametric Linear Hybrid Automata (S.P.L.H.A) which are hybrid automata the variable speeds of which are parametric functions. For those systems, we have outlined the analysis, which is an analysis on parametric polyhedra, and we have depicted two main algorithms. The simplification algorithm finds the conditions on parameters that guarantee non emptiness of parametric polyhedra and it shortens the description of these polyhedra. It uses the Gröbner bases and the Cylindrical Algebraic Decomposition which are two significant issues in algebraic geometry. Moreover, we have written an algorithm, based on the previous simplification procedure, in order to decide the inclusion of parametric polyhedra.

The next important work we are involved in now is to try to improve the quantifier elimination algorithm for the particular systems we deal with. We expect that such improvements will give results useful to handle such parametric analyses for large systems. As a matter of fact, we plan to process the problem of dealing with several parameters, as we are up to now limited to only one parameter. As a study example, we are on the way to be able to synthesize the maximal drift in the Philips communication protocol.

Acknowledgments

The authors wish to thank Augusto Burgueño who had first the idea of using Gröbner bases for our problem, and Frederic Boniol and Vlad Rusu who contributed to this parametric analysis work, at the beginning.

References

[ACD90]   R. Alur, C. Courcoubetis, and D. Dill. Model-checking for real-time systems. In *Proc. of the 5th. Annual Symposium on Logic in Computer Science, LICS'90*, pages 41–425. IEEE Computer Society Press, 1990.

[ACH+95]   R. Alur, C. Courcoubetis, N. Halbwachs, T. A. Henzinger, P-H. Ho, X. Nicollin, A. Olivero, J. Sifakis, and S. Yovine. The algorithmic analysis of hybrid systems. *Theoretical Computer Science*, 138:3–34, 1995.

[AD94]   R. Alur and D. Dill. A theory of timed automata. *Theoretical Computer Science*, 126:183–235, 1994.

[Adé99]   M. Adélaïde. Application des bases de gröbner à l'analyse paramétrique des systèmes hybrides. Master's thesis, Ecole Centrale de Nantes, august 1999.

[AH94]   R. Alur and T. A. Henzinger. Real-time system = discrete system + clock variables. In T. Rus and C. Rattray, editors, *Theories and Experiences for Real-Time System Development - Papers presented at First AMAST Workshop on Real-Time System Development*, pages 1–29, Iowa City, Iowa, 1994. World Scientific Publishing. Also available as Cornell University technical report CSD-TR-94-1403.

[AHV93]   R. Alur, T. A. Henzinger, and M. Y. Vardi. Parametric real-time reasoning. In *Proc. of the 25th Annual ACM Symposium on Theory of Computing, STOC'93*, pages 592–601, 1993.

[AMP95]   E. Asarin, O. Maler, and A. Pnueli. Reachability analysis of dynamical systems having piecewise-constant derivatives. *Theoretical Computer Science*, 138:35–65, 1995.

[Bur98]   A. Burgueño Arajona. *Vérification des Systèmes Temporisés par des Méthodes d'Observation et d'Analyse Paramétrique*. PhD thesis, Ecole Nationale Supérieure de l'Aéronautique et de l'Espace, june 1998.

[BBRR97]   F. Boniol, A. Burgueño, O. Roux, and V. Rusu. Analysis of slope-parametric hybrid automata. In O. Maler, editor, *Proc. of the International Workshop on Real time and Hybrid Systems, HART 97*, pages 75–80. Springer-Verlag, March 26-28 1997.

[BR97]   A. Burgueño and V. Rusu. Task-system analysis using slope-parametric hybrid automata. In *Proc. of the Euro-Par'97 Workshop on Real-Time Systems and Constraints*, Passau, Germany, August 26–29 1997. Springer-Verlag's Lecture Notes in Computer Science series N^o1300.

[Buc]   B. Buchberger. *Gröbner Bases : an Algorithmic Method in Polynomial Ideal Theory*, pages 184–232. Reidel.

[BW93]   T. Becker and V. Weispfenning. *Gröbner Bases : A Computationnal Approach to Commutative Algebra*. Springer Verlag, 1993.

[Coh96]   A.M. Cohen. Gröbner base : a primer. Technical report, Computer Algebra Information Network, Europe, 1996.

[Col75]   George E. Collins. Quantifier Elimination for Real Closed Fields by Cylindrical Algebraic Decomposition. In *Proceedings of the 2nd GI Conference*, volume 33 of *Lecture Notes in Computer Science*, pages 134–183, Kaiserslautern, 1975. Springer, Berlin.

[DCO92]   J. Little D. Cox and D. O'Shea. *Ideals, Varieties and Algorithms*. Springer Verlag, 1992.

[GVRRT95]   Laureano Gonzales-Vega, Fabrice Rouillier, Marie-Françoise Roy, and Guadalupe Trujillo. *Some Tapas of Computer Algebra*. Eindoven University of Technology, a.m. cohen and h. cuypers and h. sterk edition, 1995.

[Hen96]   T. Henziger. The theroie of hybrid auromata. In *IEEE Symposium on Logic In Computer Science*, pages 278–282, 1996.

[HH95]   T.A. Henzinger and P.-H. Ho. HyTech: The Cornell Hybrid Technology Tool. In P. Antsaklis, A. Nerode, W. Kohn, and S. Sastry, editors, *Hybrid Systems II*, Lecture Notes in Computer Science 999, pages 265–293. Springer-Verlag, 1995.

[MMP92]   O. Maler, Z. Manna, and A. Pnueli. From timed to hybrid systems. In J. W. de Bakker, K. Huizing, W.-P. de Roever, and G. Rozenberg, editors, *Proc. of the REX workshop 'Real-Time: theory in practice'*, volume 600 of *Lecture Notes in Computer Science*, pages 447–484, Berlin, New York, 1992. Springer-Verlag.

[Jir95]   M. Jirstrand. Cylindrical algebraic decomposition - an introduction. Technical report, Computer Algebra Information Network, Europe, Departement of Electrical Engineering, Linköping university, S-581 83 Linköping. Sweden, October 1995.

[Rod96]   G. Roda. Quantifier elimination - lecture notes based on a course by g.e. collins, risc- summer semester 96. Technical report, Computer Algebra Information Network, Europe, July 1996.

[Wan96]   Farn Wang. Parametric timing analysis for real-time systems. 130(2):131–150, 1 November 1996.

Probabilistic Neighbourhood Logic

Dimitar P. Guelev

International Institute for Software Technology
of the United Nations University
(UNU/IIST), Macau, P.O.Box 3058.
E-mail: dg@iist.unu.edu

Abstract. This paper presents a probabilistic extension of Neighbourhood Logic (NL,[14,1]). The study of such an extension is motivated by
the need to supply the Probabilistic Duration Calculus (PDC, [10,4])
with a proof system. The relation between the new logic and PDC is
similar to that between DC [15] and ITL [12,3]. We present a complete
proof system for the new logic.

Introduction

The Probabilistic Duration Calculus (PDC) was introduced in [10] as an extension of Duration Calculus[15]. The approach to introducing PDC is as follows:
Consider some finite probabilistic timed automaton **A**. The behaviours of **A** can
be represented as a set **M** of DC models. The probabilistic laws that govern the
working of **A** are used to introduce probability on the subsets of **M**. Given a
DC formula D, the term $\mu(D)(t)$ denotes the probability of those models from
M that satisfy D at the interval $[0, t]$. Terms of this sort are the component of
PDC language that is new in PDC, relative to DC. In [10] the authors focused
on the case of discrete time for the sake of simplicity. In a later work, [4], PDC
was introduced for the case of real time too.

Both papers present examples of specification by PDC and a number of valid
PDC formulas, that represent basic properties of the probabilistic operator μ. A
section on specification by PDC can be found in [11] too. However, no complete
proof system for PDC has been proposed so far.

DC is an extension of Interval Temporal Logic (ITL), and so is its proof
system. ITL has a complete proof system with respect to an abstract class of
frames[3]. In this paper, we introduce Probabilistic Neighbourhood Logic (PNL)
by generalising the semantics of PDC. PNL is designed to take the role that
ITL has for DC, yet for PDC. PNL is based on Neighbourhood Logic (NL,
[14]), which is another interval-based temporal logic, closely related to ITL.
Unlike ITL, NL has modal operators which allow reference to intervals outside
the current one. This feature has proved useful for the axiomatisation of the
probabilistic operator of PNL. NL has a proof system, that is complete with
respect to an abstract semantics, which is similar to that of ITL[1].

In this paper we extend the proof system of NL to obtain a complete one
for PNL for a similarly abstract semantics. Earlier versions of PNL have been
studied by the author in [6,7] and by Vladimir Trifonov in [13].

M. Joseph (Ed.): FTRTFT 2000, LNCS 1926, pp. 264–275, 2000.
© Springer-Verlag Berlin Heidelberg 2000

1   Preliminaries on Neighbourhood Logic

Neighbourhood logic is a classical first order predicate logic with equality and two unary normal modal operators.

1.1   Language

A language of NL is determined by a countable set of *individual variables* x, y, $\ldots$, and several other sets of symbols. These are *constant* symbols c, d, $\ldots$, *function* symbols f, g, $\ldots$ and *relation* symbols R, S, $\ldots$. Symbols of every kind can be either *rigid* or *flexible*, depending on the way they are interpreted.

Given the sets of symbols, the *terms* t and the *formulas* φ of the corresponding NL languages are defined by the BNFs:
$$t ::= c \,|\, x \,|\, f(t, \ldots, t)$$
$$\varphi ::= \bot \,|\, R(t, \ldots, t) \,|\, (\varphi \Rightarrow \varphi) \,|\, \exists x \varphi \,|\, \Diamond_l \varphi \,|\, \Diamond_r \varphi$$
Function symbols and relation symbols are assigned *arity* to denote the number of arguments they admit. Every NL language contains the rigid constant symbol 0, the rigid binary function symbol $+$, the rigid binary relation symbols $=$ and $\leq$ and the flexible constant ℓ.

Individual variables are regarded as rigid. Formulas and terms which contain no flexible symbols, are called *rigid* too. The set of individual variables that have *free occurrences* in a formula φ is denoted by $FV(\varphi)$.

1.2   Frames, Models and Satisfaction

Definition 1. *A NL* time domain *is a linearly ordered set. A NL* duration domain *is an algebraic system of the type* $\langle D, +^{(2)}, 0^{(0)}, \leq^{(2)} \rangle$ *which satisfies the axioms:*

(D1) $x + (y + z) = (x + y) + z$ (D6) $x \leq x$
(D2) $x + 0 = x$ (D7) $x \leq y \wedge y \leq x \Rightarrow x = y$
(D3) $x + y = x + z \Rightarrow y = z$ (D8) $x \leq y \wedge y \leq z \Rightarrow x \leq z$
(D4) $\exists z (x + z = y)$ (D9) $x \leq y \Leftrightarrow \exists z (x + z = y \wedge 0 \leq z)$
(D5) $x + y = y + x$

We use $\leq$ to denote both the ordering of time and duration domains.

Definition 2. *Given a time domain* $\langle T, \leq \rangle$, *the set of the closed* intervals $\{[\tau_1, \tau_2] : \tau_1, \tau_2 \in T, \tau_1 \leq \tau_2\}$ *in* T *is denoted by* $\mathbf{I}(T)$. *Given a time domain* $\langle T, \leq \rangle$ *and a* duration domain $\langle D, +, 0, \leq \rangle$, *a* measure function m *is a surjective function of type* $\mathbf{I}(T) \to D$, *which satisfies the axioms:*

(M1) $m(\sigma) = m(\sigma') \wedge \min \sigma = \min \sigma' \Rightarrow \max \sigma = \max \sigma'$
(M2) $\max \sigma_1 = \min \sigma_2 \Rightarrow m(\sigma_1) + m(\sigma_2) = m(\sigma_1 \cup \sigma_2)$
(M3) $m(\sigma) = x + y \Rightarrow \exists \sigma' (\min \sigma' = \min \sigma \wedge m(\sigma') = x)$.

Definition 3. *A tuple of the kind* $\langle \langle T, \leq \rangle, \langle D, +, 0, \leq \rangle, m \rangle$, *where* $\langle T, \leq \rangle$ *is a* time domain, $\langle D, +, 0, \leq \rangle$ *is a* duration domain, *and* m *is a measure from* $\mathbf{I}(T)$ *to* D, *is called NL* frame.

Clearly, if a measure function from a time domain $\langle T, \leq \rangle$ to a duration domain $\langle D, +, 0, \leq \rangle$ exists, $\langle D, \leq \rangle$ is isomorphic to $\langle T, \leq \rangle$. For this reason NL is usually regarded as having just duration domains in its frames. We keep the two components of NL frames distinct for the sake of compatibility with ITL semantics, where they may differ more.

Let $\mathbf{L}$ be an NL language.

Definition 4. *Let $F = \langle \langle T, \leq \rangle, \langle D, +, 0, \leq \rangle, m \rangle$, where $\langle T, \leq \rangle$ be an NL frame. A function I which is defined on the set of symbols of $\mathbf{L}$ and satisfies the requirements:*

$I(x), I(c) \in D$ *for individual variables x and rigid constants c*
$I(f) \in (D^n \to D)$ *for n-place rigid function symbols f*
$I(R) \in (D^n \to \{0,1\})$ *for n-place rigid relation symbols R*
$I(c) \in (\mathbf{I}(T) \to D)$ *for flexible constants c*
$I(f) \in (\mathbf{I}(T) \times D^n \to D)$ *for n-place flexible function symbols f*
$I(R) \in (\mathbf{I}(T) \times D^n \to \{0,1\})$ *for n-place flexible relation symbols R*
$I(0) = 0$, $I(+) = +$, $I(\ell) = m$, $I(\leq)$ *is* $\leq$ *and* $I(=)$ *is* $=$
is called interpretation *of $\mathbf{L}$ into F.*

Definition 5. *A model for $\mathbf{L}$ is a tuple of the kind $\langle F, I \rangle$, where F is a frame, and I is an interpretation of $\mathbf{L}$ into F.*

Given a frame F, we denote its components by $\langle T_F, \leq_F \rangle$, $\langle D_F, +_F, 0_F, \leq_F \rangle$ and m_F, respectively. The same applies to models. We denote the frame and the interpretation of a model M by F_M and I_M, respectively.

Given a symbol s from $\mathbf{L}$, interpretations I and J of $\mathbf{L}$ into frame $\mathbf{F}$ are said to s-*agree*, if $I(s') = J(s')$ for $\mathbf{L}$ symbols s' other than s.

Definition 6. *Let M be a model for $\mathbf{L}$. Let $\sigma \in \mathbf{I}(T_M)$. The values $I_\sigma(t)$ of terms t from $\mathbf{L}$ are defined as follows:*

$I_\sigma(x) = I_M(x)$, $I_\sigma(c) = I_M(c)$ *for variables x and rigid constants c*
$I_\sigma(f(t_1, \ldots, t_n)) = I_M(f)(I_\sigma(t_1), \ldots, I_\sigma(t_n))$ *for rigid n-place function symbols f*
$I_\sigma(f(t_1, \ldots, t_n)) = I_M(f)(\sigma, I_\sigma(t_1), \ldots, I_\sigma(t_n))$ *for flexible n-place function symbols f*
The relation $M, \sigma \models \varphi$ for formulas φ from $\mathbf{L}$ is defined as follows:

$M, \sigma \not\models \bot$
$M, \sigma \models R(t_1, \ldots, t_n)$ *iff* $I_M(R)(I_\sigma(t_1), \ldots, I_\sigma(t_n)) = 1$ *for rigid relation symbols R*
$M, \sigma \models R(t_1, \ldots, t_n)$ *iff* $I_M(R)(\sigma, I_\sigma(t_1), \ldots, I_\sigma(t_n)) = 1$ *for flexible relation symbols R*
$M, \sigma \models (\varphi \Rightarrow \psi)$ *iff either* $M, \sigma \models \psi$, *or* $M, \sigma \not\models \varphi$
$M, \sigma \models \exists x \varphi$ *iff* $\langle F_M, J \rangle, \sigma \models \varphi$ *for some J that x-agrees with I_M*
$M, \sigma \models \Diamond_l \varphi$ *iff* $M, \sigma' \models \varphi$ *for some $\sigma' \in \mathbf{I}(T_M)$ such that* $\max \sigma' = \min \sigma$
$M, \sigma \models \Diamond_r \varphi$ *iff* $M, \sigma' \models \varphi$ *for some $\sigma' \in \mathbf{I}(T_M)$ such that* $\min \sigma' = \max \sigma$

1.3 Abbreviations

Along with ordinary classical first order predicate logic abbreviations and infix notation, the following NL-specific abbreviations are used:

$$\Diamond_d^c \varphi \rightleftharpoons \Diamond_d \Diamond_{\bar{d}} \varphi \quad \Box_d \varphi \rightleftharpoons \neg \Diamond_d \neg \varphi \quad \Box_d^c \varphi \rightleftharpoons \neg \Box_d^c \neg \varphi \qquad d \in \{l, r\}, \ \bar{l} = r \text{ and}$$
$\bar{r} = l$.

The modal operator $(.; .)$ of ITL is defined as an abbreviation in NL by putting:

$$(\varphi; \psi) \rightleftharpoons \exists x \exists y (x + y = \ell \wedge \Diamond_l^c(\varphi \wedge \ell = x) \wedge \Diamond_r^c(\psi \wedge \ell = y)), \; x, y \notin FV((\varphi; \psi)).$$

1.4 Proof System for NL

The proof system of NL consists of axioms for classical first order predicate logic with equality, the axioms $D1$-$D9$ and the following axioms and rules:

(A1) $\Diamond_d \varphi \Rightarrow \varphi$ if φ is rigid.   (A4') $\Diamond_d \exists x \varphi \Rightarrow \exists x \Diamond_d \varphi$

(A2) $0 \le l$ (A5) $\Diamond_d(\ell = x \wedge \varphi) \Rightarrow \Box_d(\ell = x \Rightarrow \varphi)$

(A3) $0 \le x \Rightarrow \Diamond_d(\ell = x)$ (A6) $\Diamond_d^c \varphi \Rightarrow \Box_d \Diamond_{\overline{d}} \varphi$

(A4) $\Diamond_d(\varphi \vee \psi) \Rightarrow \Diamond_d \varphi \vee \Diamond_d \psi$ (A7) $\ell = x \Rightarrow (\varphi \Leftrightarrow \Diamond_d^c(\ell = x \wedge \varphi))$

(A8) $0 \le x \Rightarrow 0 \le y \Rightarrow \Diamond_d(\ell = x \wedge \Diamond_d(\ell = y \wedge \Diamond_d \varphi)) \Rightarrow \Diamond_d(\ell = x + y \wedge \Diamond_d \varphi)$

$$(Mono) \; \frac{\varphi \Rightarrow \psi}{\Diamond_d \varphi \Rightarrow \Diamond_d \psi} \quad (Nec) \; \frac{\varphi}{\Box_d \varphi} \quad (MP) \; \frac{\varphi \quad \varphi \Rightarrow \psi}{\psi} \quad (G) \; \frac{\varphi}{\forall x \varphi}$$

Substitution $[t/x]\varphi$ of variable x by term t in formula φ is allowed in proofs only if either t is rigid, or x does not occur in the scope of modal operators in φ. This system is complete with respect to the above semantics[1].

2 Probabilistic Timed Automata: an Introductory Example to PNL

Here we slightly generalise the notion of finite probabilistic timed automaton from [4].

Definition 1. *A finite probabilistic timed automaton is a system of the kind*
$\mathbf{A} = \langle S, A, s_0, \langle D, +, 0, \le \rangle, \langle q_a, a \in A \rangle, \langle P_a : a \in A \rangle \rangle$, *where*

S is a finite set of states;

$A \subset \{\langle s, s' \rangle : s, s' \in S, s \ne s'\}$ is a set of transitions;

$s_0 \in S$ is called initial state;

$\langle D, +, 0, \le \rangle$ is a duration domain;

$q_a \in [0, 1]$ is the choice probability for transition $a \in A$;

$P_a \in (D \to [0, 1])$ is the duration distribution of transition a.

Given $\mathbf{A}$ with its components named as above, A_s, denotes $\{s' \in S : \langle s, s' \rangle \in A\}$. $\langle q_a : a \in A \rangle$ are required to satisfy $\sum_{a \in A_s} q_a = 1$ for $A_s \ne \emptyset$. $\langle P_a : a \in A \rangle$, are required to satisfy $P_a(0) \ge 0$, to be non-strictly monotonic and to converge towards 1.

An automaton $\mathbf{A}$ of the above kind works by going through a finite or infinite sequence of states $s_0, s_1, \ldots, s_n, \ldots$ such that $\langle s_i, s_{i+1} \rangle \in A$ for all i. Each transition has a duration, d_i. Thus, individual *behaviours* of $\mathbf{A}$ are recorded as sequences of the kind $\langle a_0, d_0 \rangle, \ldots \langle a_n, d_n \rangle, \ldots$, $a_i \in A$, $d_i \in D$, where the initial state of a_0 is s_0, and every transition arrives at the initial state of the next one. Having arrived at state s, $\mathbf{A}$ chooses transition $a \in A_s$ with probability q_a. The probability for its duration to be no bigger than d is $P_a(d)$.

Given a language $\mathbf{L}$ for NL with a 0-place temporal relation symbol a for every $a \in A$, a behaviour $\langle a_i, d_i \rangle$, $i = 0, 1, \ldots$ can be represented as a model $\langle F, I \rangle$ for this language, where $F = \langle \langle D, \leq \rangle, \langle D, +, 0, \leq \rangle, \lambda\sigma. \max\sigma - \min\sigma \rangle$ by putting $I(a)(\sigma) = 1$ iff $a = a_i$ and $\sigma = \left[\sum\limits_{j<i} d_i, \sum\limits_{j\leq i} d_i \right]$ for some i.

Some properties of $\mathbf{A}$ behaviours can be straightforwardly expressed under this convention. For example, if $a = \langle s, s' \rangle \in A$,

$$\Diamond_r^c a \Rightarrow \neg \left(\bigvee_{b \notin A_{s'}} \Diamond_r b \right)$$

means that a behaviour which ends at a can only continue with a transition whose initial state is the final state of a, and

$$a \Rightarrow \neg(a; \ell \neq 0)$$

means that no transition can begin at some time point and end in two distinct time points.

Now consider the set $\mathbf{M}$ of all the interpretations of $\mathbf{L}$ into F that represent behaviours of $\mathbf{A}$ in the above way. We need the following definition:

Definition 2. Let $\tau \in T_F$. We say that interpretations I and J of $\mathbf{L}$ into F τ-agree iff they coincide for rigid symbols from $\mathbf{L}$, and coincide for flexible symbols from $\mathbf{L}$ on intervals σ such that $\max\sigma \leq \tau$.

The probabilistic components $\langle q_a : a \in A \rangle$ and $\langle P_a : a \in A \rangle$ of $\mathbf{A}$ can be used to endow $\mathbf{M}$ with probabilistic structure as follows:

For every $\tau \in D$ and every $I \in \mathbf{M}$ a probability measure $P_{I,\tau}$ is introduced on the subsets of $\mathbf{M}_{I,\tau} = \{I' \in \mathbf{M} : I' \; \tau\text{-agrees with } I\}$. Given $\mathbf{N} \subset \mathbf{M}_{I,\tau}$, $P_{I,\tau}(\mathbf{N})$ denotes the probability for $\mathbf{A}$ to continue a behaviour that is described by I up to time τ by one from $\mathbf{N}$.

Assume that, in addition to the temporal relation symbols $a \in A$, $\mathbf{L}$ contains the rigid symbols q_a and P_a, $a \in A$, and they are interpreted by the corresponding components of $\mathbf{A}$ in all the interpretations from $\mathbf{M}$. Assume that we introduce an operator p to $\mathbf{L}$ in the following way

○ If φ is a formula, then $p(\varphi)$ is a term.

○ $I_\sigma(p(\varphi)) = P_{I,\max\sigma}(\{I' \in \mathbf{M}_{I,\max\sigma} : \exists \tau \geq \min\sigma \; \langle F, I' \rangle, [\min\sigma, \tau] \models \varphi\})$

In words, let $p(\varphi)$ evaluate under I to the probability of the set of those interpretations of $\mathbf{L}$ which are continuations of I from time $\max\sigma$ on and satisfy φ at some interval starting at time $\min\sigma$.

Using p, the probabilistic law about $\mathbf{A}$ behaviours can be expressed as follows:

$a \Rightarrow p((a; b \wedge \ell = x)) = q_b.P_b(x)$, if $a = \langle s, s' \rangle$ and $b = \langle s', s'' \rangle$ for some $s, s', s'' \in S$;

$a \Rightarrow p((a; b)) = 0$ otherwise.

To carry out this way of introducing p and its interpretation rigorously, we can consider models that consist of a NL frame F, a set of interpretations $\mathbf{M}$ of $\mathbf{L}$ into F, and a system of probability measures $P_{I,\tau}$, $I \in \mathbf{M}, \tau \in T_F$, as specified as above.

Having in mind that the values of p-terms are not necessarily similar to durations, F should contain a separate domain for probabilities too. Accordingly, languages that interpretations from $\mathbf{M}$ are defined on should have a sort for this domain. This is essentially what PNL models are.

3   A Formal Definition of PNL

3.1   Languages

A PNL language is built starting from the same kinds of symbols as a NL language. PNL languages are two-sorted. Together with the well-known sort of *durations*, they have a sort of *probabilities*. Along with the arity, each non-logical symbol of a PNL language has a description of the sorts of each of its arguments, and of its value, in case it is an individual variable, a constant or a function symbol. For example, the function symbols P_a from automata-related languages take an argument of the duration sort to make a term of the probability sort. A PNL language should contain countably many individual variables of both sorts. Together with the symbols 0, $+$, $=$, $\leq$ and ℓ of the sort of durations, PNL languages always contain the rigid constants 0 and 1, the rigid function symbol $+$, and the rigid relation symbols $\leq$ and $=$ of the new sort of probabilities. Using the same notation for both probability and duration 0, $+$ and $=$ does not cause confusion.

The BNF for formulas is as in NL. The BNF for terms in NL languages is extended to capture the terms that express probability in PNL languages as follows:

$t ::= x|c|f(t,\ldots,t)|p(\varphi,t,\ldots,t)$

Terms of the kind $f(t,\ldots,t)$ are well-formed only if the sorts of the subterms t match the requirements for f. A similar condition applies to atomic formulas. Terms of the kind $p(\varphi,t,\ldots,t)$ (p-terms) have the probability sort. They contain one formula-argument φ and as many term arguments, as are the free variables of φ. Let $x_1,\ldots,x_n$ be the free variables of φ, listed in the order of their first free occurrences in φ. Then $p(\varphi,t_1,\ldots,t_n)$ is well-formed, iff t_i has the sort of x_i, $i=1,\ldots,n$. Besides $p(\varphi,x_1,\ldots,x_n)$ is abbreviated to $p(\varphi)$. This looks the same as for closed φ, but is no source of confusion. We put

$$FV(p(\varphi,t_1,\ldots,t_n)) = \bigcup_{i=1}^{n} FV(t_i)$$

and

$$[t/x]p(\varphi,t_1,\ldots,t_n) \rightleftharpoons p(\varphi,[t/x]t_1,\ldots,[t/x]t_n).$$

The symbol p is not a non-logical symbol in PNL languages. Its role is rather like that of modal operators, yet it is used to construct terms, not formulas.

3.2   Frames, Models and Satisfaction

In order to enable a finite complete first order proof system for PNL, we introduce probability domains in PNL abstractly, like the other NL domains:

Definition 1. *A system of the kind* $\langle U, +^{(2)}, 0^{(0)}, 1^{(0)} \rangle$ *is a probability domain, if it satisfies the axioms:*

$(U1)$ $x + (y + z) = (x + y) + z$ $(U5)$ $x + y = 0 \Rightarrow x = 0$
$(U2)$ $x + 0 = x$ $(U6)$ $\exists z (x + z = y \vee y + z = x)$
$(U3)$ $x + y = y + x$ $(U7)$ $0 \neq 1$
$(U4)$ $x + y = x + z \Rightarrow y = z$

The classical probability domain is $\langle \mathbf{R}_+, +, 0, 1 \rangle$. Another example is $\langle \{ \frac{i}{n} : i < \omega \}, +, 0, 1 \rangle$, where n is a fixed positive integer.

We assume that the linear ordering $\leq$ which is defined by the equivalence $x \leq y \leftrightarrow \exists z (x + z = y)$ is available for probability domains.

Definition 2. *A tuple of the kind* $\langle \langle T, \leq \rangle, \langle D, +, 0 \rangle, \langle U, +, 0, 1 \rangle, m \rangle$ *is a PNL frame, if* $\langle \langle T, \leq \rangle, \langle D, +, 0 \rangle, m \rangle$ *is an (ordinary, one-sorted) NL frame, and* $\langle U, +, 0, 1 \rangle$ *is a probability domain.*

Interpretations of symbols from PNL languages into PNL frames are defined like in (one-sorted) NL languages. Of course, the types of the functions and relations that symbols evaluate to should match the types of the symbols. Besides, the obligatory symbols 0, 1, $+$, and $\leq$ of the probability sort should be interpreted by the corresponding components of the frame's probability domain.

The setting given in the previous section makes it clear that the values of the probability measures $P_{I,\tau}$ are relevant to the interpretation of p-terms only for some, *formula-definable* subsets of the set of interpretations that is part of every PNL model. These subsets are difficult to describe prior to defining the relation $\models$ in corresponding model. On the other hand, requesting $P_{I,\tau}$ to be defined on the entire powersets of interpretations would render the forthcoming completeness theorem unreasonably difficult to prove.

That is why, before defining PNL models, we introduce an auxiliary notion of *partial PNL* models:

Definition 3. *Let* **L** *be a language for PNL. A triple* $\langle F, \mathbf{M}, P \rangle$ *is a partial PNL model for* **L** *if* F *is a PNL frame,* $\mathbf{M}$ *is a set of interpretations of the non-logical symbols of* **L** *into* F*, and* $P = \langle P_{I,\tau} : I \in \mathbf{M}, \tau \in T_F \rangle$ *is a system of partial functions* $P_{I,\tau} \in (2^{\mathbf{M}_{I,\tau}} \to U_F)$*, where* $\mathbf{M}_{I,\tau} = \{ I' \in \mathbf{M} : I' \ \tau\text{-agrees with } I \}$*, which satisfy the equalities*

$$P_{I,\tau}(\emptyset) = 0, \_, \tau(\mathbf{M}_{I,\tau}) = 1, \ P_{I,\tau}(\mathbf{N}_1) + P_{I,\tau}(\mathbf{N}_2) = P_{I,\tau}(\mathbf{N}_1 \cup \mathbf{N}_2) + P_{I,\tau}(\mathbf{N}_1 \cap \mathbf{N}_2).$$

for whichever $\mathbf{N}_1, \mathbf{N}_2 \subseteq \mathbf{M}_{I,\tau}$ $P_{I,\tau}$ *is defined.*

In the above definition $P_{I,\tau}$ are partial probability functions on the sets of interpretations $\mathbf{M}_{I,\tau}$. They take the abstract kind of probabilities we introduced as their values.

We proceed to define the satisfaction relation $\models$ on partial PNL models. In order to define $\models$ for formulas of the kind $\exists x\varphi$, we need a technical definition:

Definition 4. *Given an interpretation I of language $\mathbf{L}$ into frame F and a nonlogical symbol s from $\mathbf{L}$, I_s^a stands for the interpretation of $\mathbf{L}$ into F that s-agrees with I and interprets s as a. Given a set of interpretations $\mathbf{N}$ of $\mathbf{L}$ into F, $\mathbf{N}_s^a$ is $\{I_s^a : I \in \mathbf{N}\}$. Given a partial function $f : 2^{\mathbf{A}} \to U_F$, the partial function $f_s^a : 2^{\mathbf{A}_s^a} \to U_F$ is defined by putting $f_s^a(\mathbf{N}_s^a) = f(\mathbf{N})$, if $f(\mathbf{N})$ is defined. If $f(\mathbf{N})$ is undefined, then $f_s^a(\mathbf{N})$ is undefined too. Given a partial PNL model $M = \langle F, \mathbf{M}, P \rangle$, M_s^a is $\langle F, \mathbf{M}_s^a, \langle (P_{I,\tau})_s^a : I \in \mathbf{M}, \tau \in T_F \rangle \rangle$.*

Obviously M_s^a is a partial PNL model, if M is one. We abbreviate $(\ldots I_{s_1}^{a_1} \ldots)_{s_n}^{a_n}$ to $I_{s_1,\ldots,s_n}^{a_1,\ldots,a_n}$. The same applies to models M.

Values $I_\sigma(t)$ of terms t and the modelling relation $\models$ are partially defined in PNL models by simultaneous induction on the length of terms and formulas. The clauses about the kinds of terms and formulas that are known from NL are as in NL: Given a PNL model $M = \langle F, \mathbf{M}, P \rangle$ and $I \in \mathbf{M}$, the clause for $M, I, \sigma \models \varphi$ is the same as that for $\langle F, I \rangle, \sigma \models \varphi$. Each clause applies only if the entities on its right side are defined. The only clause which is subjected to a somewhat greater change is the one about existential formulas:

$M, I, \sigma \models \exists x\varphi$ iff there exists an a such that $a \in D_F$, in case x is a duration variable,
and $a \in U_f$, in case x is a probability variable, and $M_x^a, I_x^a, \sigma \models \varphi$

The new, PNL-specific clause is about p-terms. Given a well-formed p-term $p(\varphi, t_1, \ldots, t_n)$, $I_\sigma(p(\varphi, t_1, \ldots, t_n))$ is

$$P_{I,\max\sigma}(\{I' \in \mathbf{M}_{I,\max\sigma} : \exists\tau \geq \min\sigma \ M_{x_1,\ \ldots\ ,x_n}^{I_\sigma(t_1),\ldots,I_\sigma(t_n)}, (I')_{x_1,\ \ldots\ ,x_n}^{I_\sigma(t_1),\ldots,I_\sigma(t_n)}, [\min\sigma, \tau] \models \varphi\}),$$

only if $P_{I,\max\sigma}$ is defined for the given set. In case φ is closed, this definition simplifies to

$$I_\sigma(p(\varphi)) = P_{I,\max\sigma}(\{I' \in \mathbf{M}_{I,\max\sigma} : \exists\tau \geq \min\sigma \ M, I', [\min\sigma, \tau] \models \varphi\}).$$

In words, given an interpretation $I \in \mathbf{M}$ and an interval σ, $I_\sigma(p(\varphi))$ represents the probability of the set of those interpretations $I' \in \mathbf{M}$ which are like I up to the end of the interval σ and satisfy φ at some interval which has the same beginning as σ. For a modelled system's behaviour which is represented by I for the time until $\max\sigma$, this term can represent the probability for this behaviour to continue so that φ eventually gets satisfied in the specified kind of interval.

In the general case the operator p evaluates the above probability under the assumption that the free variables of φ evaluate to the values which $t_1, \ldots, t_n$ have in the current interval σ.

Note that interpretations I' which $\max\sigma$-agree with the selected one I may happen to satisfy φ at intervals $[\min\sigma, \tau]$ where $\tau \leq \max\sigma$. In this case satisfaction of φ may happen to be a simple consequence of $\max\sigma$-agreeing with I, and no substantial probability evaluation is involved. For example

$(\varphi; \top) \Rightarrow p(\varphi) = 1$

is a valid PNL formula, if φ is retrospective (see definition 1), that is, if φ does not specify properties of interpretations beyond the end of the current interval.

Having defined (partial) $\models$ on partial PNL models, we are ready to define PNL total models:

Definition 5. *A partial PNL model M is a (total) PNL model, if values of terms and satisfaction of formulas from the corresponding language are everywhere defined in M.*

For the rest of the paper only total PNL models are considered.

4   A Complete Proof System for PNL

We need to specify a special class of PNL formulas, in order to introduce our proof system.

4.1   Retrospective Formulas and Interpretations Which τ-agree

Definition 1. *We call NL formulas that can be defined by the BNF*
$$\varphi ::= \bot \mid R(t, \ldots, t) \mid \neg\varphi \mid (\varphi \wedge \varphi) \mid (\varphi; \varphi) \mid \Diamond_l \varphi \mid \exists x \varphi$$
retrospective.

There is a close connection between retrospective formulas and interpretations that τ-agree:

Proposition 1. *Let F be a frame and $\tau \in T_F$. Let I and J be interpretations of $\mathbf{L}$ into F that τ-agree. Let $\sigma \in \mathbf{I}(T_F)$ and $\max \sigma \leq \tau$. Then $\langle F, I \rangle, \sigma \models \varphi$ iff $\langle F, J \rangle, \sigma \models \varphi$ for all retrospective φ from $\mathbf{L}$.*

Since occurrences of modal operators can be removed from rigid formulas due to $A1$, rigid formulas share the properties of retrospective formulas.

4.2   The System

The proof system for PNL that we propose is an extension of that for NL with the axioms $U1$-$U7$ about probabilities, and the following axioms and rules:
$(P_\bot)$ $p(\bot) = 0$ (P_+) $p(\varphi) + p(\psi) = p(\varphi \vee \psi) + p((\varphi; \top) \wedge (\psi; \top))$
$(P_\top)$ $p(\top) = 1$ $(P_=)$ $x_1 = y_1 \wedge \ldots \wedge x_n = y_n \Rightarrow p(\varphi, x_1, \ldots, x_n) = p(\varphi, y_1, \ldots, y_n)$

$$(P_\Diamond) \ \frac{\varphi \Rightarrow (\Diamond_i^c \psi \Rightarrow \Diamond_i^c \chi)}{\varphi \Rightarrow p(\psi) \leq p(\chi)} \ \text{if } \varphi \text{ is retrospective,} \quad (P_;) \ \frac{\varphi \Rightarrow \neg(\varphi; \ell \neq 0)}{(\varphi; p(\psi) = x) \Rightarrow p((\varphi; \psi)) = x}$$

Note that in the above axioms and rules terms like $p(\varphi)$ should be understood as abbreviations of the kind $p(\varphi, x_1, \ldots, x_n)$, as stated in Subsection 3.1. This means that these axioms and rules have instanced with formulas that have free variables. $P_\Diamond$ and $P_;$ can be applied only to theorems of PNL. Substitution in p-terms is allowed in proofs only if the substitute term is rigid.

The soundness of the above system is established in the ordinary way. Given a PNL language $\mathbf{L}$, we denote the set of all PNL theorems in $\mathbf{L}$ by $PNL_\mathbf{L}$.

Consistency and maximal consistency are defined for sets of formulas in a PNL language with respect to the above proof system in the ordinary way. We have the following completeness result about our proof system:

Theorem 1. *Let Γ be a set of formulas from a PNL language* **L**. *Then Γ is consistent iff there exists a model $M = \langle F, \mathbf{M}, P \rangle$ for* **L**, *an interpretation $I \in \mathbf{M}$ and an interval $\sigma \in \mathbf{I}(T_F)$ such that $M, I, \sigma \models \Gamma$.*

A proof of this theorem can be found in [7,9].

5   Chapman-Kolmogorov's Equality for Composition in *PNL*

The means to express sequential composition of (probabilistic) processes in *PNL* is the defined operator $(.;.)$. In this section we extend the semantics of *PNL* and its proof system so that probabilities of formulas with $(.;.)$ satisfy Chapman-Kolmogorov's equality about sequential composition under reasonable assumptions.

Since this equality involves integration, probability domains are extended with multiplication, which is needed to define integration. Multiplication of probabilities is required to satisfy the axioms:

$(U8)$ $x.1 = x$ $\qquad\qquad$ $(U11)$ $x.(y + z) = x.y + x.z$

$(U9)$ $x.(y.z) = (x.y).z$ $\quad$ $(U12)$ $x.y = x.z \wedge x \neq 0 \Rightarrow y = z$

$(U10)$ $x.y = y.x$ $\qquad\qquad$ $(U13)$ $x \neq 0 \Rightarrow \exists y(x.y = z)$

We extend the proof system of *PNL* by the rules:

$$(\overline{P})\ \frac{\varphi \Rightarrow \neg(\varphi; \ell \neq 0)}{\ell = 0 \wedge p(\varphi \wedge \theta \Rightarrow p((\varphi; \psi)) \leq x) = 1 \Rightarrow p((\varphi \wedge \theta; \psi)) \leq x.p(\varphi \wedge \theta)}$$

$$(\underline{P})\ \frac{\varphi \Rightarrow \neg(\varphi; \ell \neq 0)}{\ell = 0 \wedge p(\varphi \wedge \theta \Rightarrow p((\varphi; \psi)) \geq x) = 1 \Rightarrow p((\varphi \wedge \theta; \psi)) \geq x.p(\varphi \wedge \theta)}$$

For a formula φ to specify a step in some process, it is natural to expect that $\vdash_{PNL} \varphi \Rightarrow \neg(\varphi; \ell \neq 0)$. That is why the latter formula is used as a premiss for $\overline{P}$ and $\underline{P}$. Let φ be a formula from some *PNL* language **L**. Let $M = \langle F, \mathbf{M}, P \rangle$ be a model for **L**. Let $\sigma_0 \in \mathbf{I}(T_F)$ be a 0-length interval and $I_0 \in \mathbf{M}$. Let $f = \lambda I. P_{I,\tau'}(\mathbf{M}_{I',[\tau,\tau'],(\varphi;\psi)})$. Then the equality of Chapman-Kolmogorov can be expressed as:

$$P_{I_0,\tau}(\mathbf{M}_{I_0,\sigma,(\varphi;\psi)}) = \int_{I \in \mathbf{M}_{I_0,\sigma,\varphi}} f(I) dP_{I_0,\tau}.$$

The integral which occurs above is defined as the least upper bound of the sums of the kind $\sum_{i=1}^{n} \inf_{I \in A_i} f(I) P_{I_0,\tau}(A_i)$, in case it is equal to the greatest lower bound of the sums of the kind $\sum_{i=1}^{n} \sup_{I \in A_i} f(I) P_{I_0,\tau}(A_i)$, where $\{A_1, \ldots, A_n\}$ ranges over the finite partititions of $\mathbf{M}_{I_0,\sigma,\varphi}$ for which $P_{I_0,\tau}(A_i)$, $i = 1, \ldots, n$ is defined.

In order to enable this definition, we need to require that the linear ordering of U_F is complete. Unfortunately, this cannot be enforced by first-order means. In the general case we can show that the above rules entail the following approximation of Chapman-Kolmogorov's equality for models $M = \langle F, \mathbf{M}, P \rangle$ which validate them:

Let $I_0 \in \mathbf{M}$, and $\sigma \in \mathbf{I}(T_F)$ be a 0-length interval. Let φ and ψ be formulas, and φ satisfy the premiss of our rules. Let $n < \omega$. Then there exists a partitition $\{A_i : i \leq n\}$ of $\mathbf{M}_{I_0,\sigma,\varphi}$ such that $(i-1) < n.f(I) \leq i$ for $I \in A_i$, $i = 0, \ldots, n$, and moreover $\sum_{i=1}^{n} (i-1).P_{I_0,\tau}(A_i) \leq n.P_{I_0,\tau}(\mathbf{M}_{I_0,\sigma,(\varphi;\psi)}) \leq \sum_{i=0}^{n} i.P_{I_0,\tau}(A_i)$.

Clearly, in the case $U = \mathbf{R}_+$, this is equivalent to the precise equality.

Conclusions

We believe that, by introducing PNL and finding a complete proof system for it, we have made the task of obtaining a similar system for PDC a lot simpler. In fact, PNL has the expressive power of PDC, except for state expressions and their durations. However they can be introduced to PNL using the constructions presented in, e.g. [5]. This makes it reasonable to believe that PNL is an appropriate tool for the specification and verification of probabilistic behaviour of real-time systems.

Acknowledgements

Thanks are due to Dang Van Hung for his remarks and suggestions on draft versions of this paper.

References

[1]   BARUA, R. S. ROY AND ZHOU CHAOCHEN. Completeness of Neighbourhood Logic. *Proceedings of STACS'99*, Trier, Germany, LNCD 1563, Springer Verlag, 1999.

[2]   CHANG, C. C. AND H. J. KEISLER. *Model Theory*. North Holland, Amsterdam, 1973.

[3]   DUTERTRE, B. *On First Order Interval Temporal Logic* Report no. CSD-TR-94-3 Department of Computer Science, Royal Holloway, University of London, Egham, Surrey TW20 0EX, England, 1995.

[4]   DANG VAN HUNG AND ZHOU CHAOCHEN. Probabilistic Duration Calculus for Continuous Time. *Formal Aspects of Computing*, 11, pp. 21-44, 1999.

[5]   GUELEV, D. P. *A Calculus of Durations on Abstract Domains: Completeness and Extensions*. Technical Report 139, UNU/IIST, P.O.Box 3058, Macau, May 1998.

[6]   GUELEV, D. P. *Probabilistic Interval Temporal Logic*, Technical Report 144, UNU/IIST, P.O.Box 3058, Macau, August 1998, Draft.

[7]   GUELEV, D. P. *Probabilistic and Temporal Modal Logics*, Ph.D. thesis, submitted.

[8]   GUELEV, D. P. *Interval-related Interpolation in Interval Temporal Logics*, submitted, 1999.

[9]   GUELEV, D. P. *Probabilistic Neighbourhood Logic*. Technical Report 196, UNU/IIST, P.O.Box 3058, Macau, April 2000.

[10]   LIU ZHIMING, A. P. RAVN, E. V. SØRENSEN AND ZHOU CHAOCHEN. A Probabilistic Duration Calculus. In: *Proceedings of the Second International Workshop on Responsive Computer Systems*. KDD Research and Development Laboratories, Saitama, Japan, 1992.

[11]   MATHAI, J. *Real-Time Systems*. Prentice Hall, 1995.

[12]   MOSZKOWSKI, B. Temporal Logic For Multilevel Reasoning About Hardware. *IEEE Computer*, 18(2):10-19, February 1985.

[13]   TRIFONOV, V. T. *A completeness theorem for the probabilistic interval temporal logic with respect to its standard semantics*, M.Sc. thesis, Sofia University, July 1999. (In Bulgarian)

[14]   ZHOU CHAOCHEN, AND M. R. HANSEN. An Adequate First Order Interval Logic. *International Symposium, Compositionality - The Significant Difference*, H. Langmaack, A. Pnueli and W.-P. de Roever (eds.), Springer, 1998.

[15]   ZHOU CHAOCHEN, C. A. R. HOARE AND A. P. RAVN. A Calculus of Durations. *Information Processing Letters*, 40(5), pp. 269-276, 1991.

Remark: UNU/IIST technical reports are available from URL
http://www.iist.unu.edu/newrh/III/1/page.html

An On-the-Fly Tableau Construction
for a Real-Time Temporal Logic

Marc Geilen and Dennis Dams

Faculty of Electrical Engineering, Eindhoven University of Technology
P.O.Box 513, 5600 MB Eindhoven, The Netherlands
E-mail: {m.c.w.geilen,d.dams}@tue.nl

Abstract. Temporal logic is a useful tool for specifying correctness properties of reactive programs. In particular, real-time temporal logics have been developed for expressing quantitative timing aspects of systems. A tableau construction is an algorithm that translates a temporal logic formula into a finite-state automaton that accepts precisely all the models of the formula. It is a key ingredient to checking satisfiability of a formula as well as to the automata-theoretic approach to model checking. An improvement to the efficiency of tableau constructions has been the development of on-the-fly versions. In the real-time domain, tableau constructions have been developed for various logics and their complexities have been studied. However, there has been considerably less work aimed at improving and implementing them. In this paper, we present an on-the-fly tableau construction for a linear temporal logic with dense time, a fragment of Metric Interval Temporal Logic that is decidable in PSPACE. We have implemented a prototype of the algorithm and give experimental results. Being on-the-fly, our algorithm is expected to use less memory and to give smaller tableaux in many cases in practice than existing constructions.

1 Introduction

Temporal logic has enjoyed an increased interest ever since it was suggested, in [12], as a formalism for specifying correctness properties of reactive programs. Using this approach, several questions about a program's specification can be phrased in formal terms. When the (abstraction of the) program is finite-state, model checking procedures can be used to verify correctness automatically. Today, a rich variety of temporal logics exist in which properties of various kinds can be expressed. In particular, *real-time* temporal logics have been developed for expressing timing aspects of systems.

A *tableau construction* is an algorithm that translates a temporal logic formula into a finite-state automaton (possibly on infinite words) that accepts precisely all the models of the formula. Tableau constructions play a role in several places in the area of specification and verification. For example, it is the key to deciding satisfiability of formulas. Furthermore, the *automata-theoretic* approach to model checking ([11,14]) relies on tableau algorithms to turn a temporal formula into an observer of a program's behaviours. Driven by practical needs,

M. Joseph (Ed.): FTRTFT 2000, LNCS 1926, pp. 276–290, 2000.

tableau constructions are being continuously improved and reimplemented (e.g. [8,5,6]). One such improvement has been the development of *on-the-fly* versions of tableau constructions. In general, this means that the tableau automaton is constructed in a lazy way, generating states and transitions as they are needed. At the heart of such on-the-fly tableau constructions is a normal form for temporal formulas in which the constraints on the current state are separated from the constraints on the future states. Another research topic is the search for fragments of temporal logics that reduce the complexity of tableau constructions, which is PSPACE or worse for many common logics. Furthermore, the limits of expressiveness of logics within certain complexity classes are explored ([4,13]).

In the real-time domain, tableau constructions have been developed for various logics and their complexities have been studied ([1,9,13]). The key observation behind the tableau constructions in the case of a real-valued time domain is the observation that, under certain restrictions on the logic, the continuous time axis can be discretised. More precisely, given a real-time temporal logic formula φ, time can be sliced into countably many intervals in such a way that along each interval, the truth value of any subformula of φ is invariant. There has been considerably less work aimed at improving and implementing tableau constructions for real-time temporal logics.

In this paper, we present an on-the-fly tableau construction for a linear temporal logic with dense time. The logic that we consider is based on a fragment of *Metric Interval Temporal Logic* (MITL, see [4]) that is decidable in PSPACE. To the best of our knowledge, our tableau construction is the first on-the-fly construction for this logic. Compared to the tableau construction for MITL presented in [1], our work is distinguished by the following points. Our tableau algorithm is on-the-fly. The technical underpinning of this construction is a generalisation to the real-time case of the normal form procedure for formulas, that separates constraints on the current time interval from those on the rest of the time axis. In order to define this normal form, the logic is extended with timers that can be explicitly set and tested, and with a *Next* operator referring to the beginning of the next time interval. As expected, the correctness of the normal form procedure hinges on the discretisation result mentioned above.

A technical complication of the tableau construction of [1] is caused by the two different forms that interval bounds may have: open or closed. As a result, the transition from an interval of time into the next, adjacent, interval can happen in two ways. In order to distinguish these, an additional clock in the timed tableau automaton is needed and furthermore, the type of transition must be remembered. We impose restrictions on the form of the models of formulas and restrict the timer constraints expressible in the logic, in such a way that it suffices to consider intervals that are left-closed and right open. Apart from saving a timer in the tableau automaton, this simplifies the presentation. We have implemented a prototype of the algorithm and give experimental results.

Section 2 introduces the versions of logic and timed automata we use. Section 3 presents the normal form for formulas. The tableau algorithm, its correctness, and the implementation are the topic of Section 4. Section 5 concludes.

2   Preliminaries

An $(\omega\text{-})word$ $\bar{w} = \sigma_0\sigma_1\sigma_2\ldots$ over an alphabet Σ is an infinite sequence of symbols from Σ; $\bar{w}(k)$ denotes σ_k and $\bar{w}^k$ refers to the *tail* $\sigma_k\sigma_{k+1}\sigma_{k+2}\ldots$. Indeed, we use the latter notations for other kinds of sequences as well. An *interval* $I = [a, b)$ is a convex, left-closed, and right-open subset of $\mathbb{R}^{\geq 0}$; $l(I)$ $(r(I))$ denotes the lower (upper) bound a (b) and $|I|$ the length of I. We use $I - t$ to denote the interval $\{t' - t \mid t' \in I\}$. An *interval sequence* $\bar{I} = I_0I_1I_2\ldots$ is an infinite sequence of intervals that are *adjacent*, meaning $r(I_i) = l(I_{i+1})$ for every i, for which $l(I_0) = 0$, and which is *diverging*, i.e. any $t \in \mathbb{R}^{\geq 0}$ belongs to some interval I_i. A *timed word* $\bar{u}$ over Σ is a pair $(\bar{w}, \bar{I})$ consisting of an ω-word $\bar{w}$ over Σ and an interval sequence $\bar{I}$. For $t \in \mathbb{R}^{\geq 0}$, $\bar{u}(t)$ denotes the symbol present at time t, this is $\bar{w}(k)$ if $t \in \bar{I}(k)$. For such a t and k, $\bar{u}^t$ is the tail of the timed word, consisting of the word $\bar{w}^k$ and of the interval sequence $[0, r(\bar{I}(k)) - t)$, $\bar{I}(k+1) - t, \ldots$. Timed words $\bar{u}_1$ and $\bar{u}_2$ are *equivalent* (denoted $\bar{u}_1 \equiv \bar{u}_2$) if for all $t \geq 0$, $\bar{u}_1(t) = \bar{u}_2(t)$. A *timed state sequence* over a set $Prop$ of propositions is a timed word over the alphabet 2^{Prop}.

2.1   Real-time Temporal Togic

We consider a restricted version of the real-time temporal logic MITL of [4], MITL$_\leq$, with formulas of the following form ($d \in \mathbb{N}$).

$$\varphi ::= \text{true} \mid p \mid \neg\varphi \mid \varphi_1 \vee \varphi_2 \mid \varphi_1 \mathsf{U}_{\leq d}\varphi_2$$

Formulas of this form are called *basic*, in order to distinguish them from formulas using an extended syntax that is to be defined in Section 3.1. A formula is interpreted over a timed state sequence $\bar{\rho}$ as follows.

- $\bar{\rho} \models \text{true}$ for every timed state sequence $\bar{\rho}$;
- $\bar{\rho} \models p$ iff $p \in \bar{\rho}(0)$;
- $\bar{\rho} \models \neg\varphi$ iff not $\bar{\rho} \models \varphi$;
- $\bar{\rho} \models \varphi_1 \vee \varphi_2$ iff $\bar{\rho} \models \varphi_1$ or $\bar{\rho} \models \varphi_2$;
- $\bar{\rho} \models \varphi_1 \mathsf{U}_{\leq d}\varphi_2$ iff there is some $0 \leq t \leq d$, such that $\bar{\rho}^t \models \varphi_2$ and for all $0 \leq t' < t$, $\bar{\rho}^{t'} \models \varphi_1$.

Note that no basic MITL$_\leq$ formula can discriminate between equivalent timed state sequences. The restriction of the bound d to finite naturals simplifies the presentation as it yields a logic in which only safety properties can be expressed, thus avoiding the need to handle acceptance conditions. It is straightforward to extend our results to a logic which also includes an unbounded Until operator.

2.2 φ-fine Interval Sequences

In the on-the-fly tableau constructions of [5,8] for untimed logics, a formula is rewritten so that the constraints on the current state are separated from those on the remainder of the state sequence. This is possible because of the discrete nature of the sequence. In the dense time case, there is no such thing as a next state. The discretisation suggested by the interval sequence $\bar{I}$ of a timed state sequence $\bar{\rho}$ is, in general, not fine enough for our purposes: when interpreted over tails of $\bar{\rho}$, the truth value of a formula may vary along a single interval of $\bar{I}$.

Definition 1. *Let $\varphi \in \text{MITL}_{\leq}$. An interval sequence $\bar{I}$ is called φ-fine for timed state sequence $\bar{\rho}$ if for every syntactic subformula ψ of φ, every $k \geq 0$, and every $t_1, t_2 \in \bar{I}(k)$, we have $\bar{\rho}^{t_1} \models \psi$ iff $\bar{\rho}^{t_2} \models \psi$. In case that $\bar{I}$ is φ-fine for a timed state sequence $(\bar{\sigma}, \bar{I})$, also $(\bar{\sigma}, \bar{I})$ will be called φ-fine.*

In [1] (Lemma 4.11) it was shown that the intervals of a timed state sequence can always be refined so that the value of a given MITL formula does not change within any interval. Although the timed state sequences have a slightly more restrictive definition in our case, a similar lemma can be proved for the restricted logic $\text{MITL}_{\leq}$.

Lemma 1. *Let φ be a basic $\text{MITL}_{\leq}$ formula and $\bar{\rho}$ a timed state sequence. Then there exists a φ-fine timed state sequence that is equivalent with $\bar{\rho}$.*

Note that this lemma also implies that, when confining to φ-fine timed state sequences, it suffices to consider intervals, which are left-closed and right-open by our definition. In particular, there is no need to introduce a more general notion of interval, as in [1].

2.3 Timed Automata

The target of our tableau construction are timed automata in the style of Alur and Dill ([3]). We use a variation that is adapted to our needs. The automata use *timers* that decrease as time advances, possibly taking negative values in $\mathbb{R}$. They may be set to nonnegative integer values and may be compared to zero in a restricted way. Given a set T of timers, a *timer valuation* $\nu \in TVal(T)$ is a mapping $T \to \mathbb{R}$. For $t \in \mathbb{R}^{\geq 0}$, $\nu - t$ denotes the timer valuation that assigns $\nu(x) - t$ to any timer x in the domain of ν. A *timer setting* $TS \in TSet(T)$ is a partial mapping $T \to \mathbb{N}$. We use $TS[x := d]$ (where $x \in T$ and $d \in \mathbb{N}$) to denote the timer setting that maps x to d and other timers to the same value as TS. $[x := d]$ is short for $\varnothing[x := d]$. For a timer valuation ν and a timer setting TS, $TS(\nu)$ is the timer valuation that maps any timer x in the domain of ν to $TS(x)$ if defined, and to $\nu(x)$ otherwise. The set $TCond(T)$ of *timer conditions* over T is $\{x > 0, x \leq 0 \mid x \in T\}$. As suggested by Lemma 1 above, our timed automata may be restricted in such a way that the period of time during which control resides in a location is always a (left-closed, right-open) interval.

Definition 2. *Let Σ be an alphabet. A timed automaton $A = \langle L, T, L_0, Q, TC, E \rangle$ over Σ consists of*

- *a finite set L of locations;*
- *a set T of timers;*
- *a finite set L_0 of initial extended locations $(\ell_0, \nu_0) \in L \times TVal(T)$, where ν_0 assigns integer values to the timers;*

- a mapping $Q : L \to 2^{\Sigma}$ labelling every location with a set of symbols from the alphabet;
- a mapping $TC : L \to 2^{TCond(T)}$ labelling every location with a set of timer conditions over T;
- a set $E \subseteq L \times TSet(T) \times L$ of edges labelled by timer settings.

An *extended location* λ is a pair (ℓ, ν) consisting of a location ℓ and a timer valuation ν. In the context of an automaton with the set T of timers, we use $\bar{0}$ to denote the timer valuation that maps every timer in T to 0.

A *timed run* describes the path taken by the timed automaton when accepting a timed word. It gives the location of the automaton and the values of its timers at any moment, by recording the sequence of locations, the intervals during which the automaton resides in those locations, and the timer values at the beginning of each such interval.

Definition 3. *A timed run $\bar{r}$ of a timed automaton $A = \langle L, T, L_0, Q, TC, E \rangle$ is a triple $(\bar{\ell}, \bar{I}, \bar{\nu})$ consisting of a sequence of locations, an interval sequence, and a sequence of timer valuations, such that:*

- *[Consecution] for all $k \geq 0$, there is an edge $(\bar{\ell}(k), TS_k, \bar{\ell}(k+1)) \in E$ such that $\bar{\nu}(k+1) = TS_k(\bar{\nu}(k) - |\bar{I}(k)|)$;*
- *[Timing] for all $k \geq 0$ and $t \in \bar{I}(k)$, the timer valuation at time t, $\bar{\nu}(k) - (t - l(\bar{I}(k)))$, satisfies all timer conditions in $TC(\bar{\ell}(k))$.*

In this case we also say that $\bar{r}$ is a run from extended location $(\bar{\ell}(0), \bar{\nu}(0))$, or an $(\bar{\ell}(0), \bar{\nu}(0))$-run (or simply an $\bar{\ell}(0)$-run). We write $\bar{r}(t)$ to denote the location of $\bar{r}$ at time t, i.e. $\bar{\ell}(k)$ if $t \in \bar{I}(k)$. Given a timed word $\bar{u}$, $\bar{r}$ is a run for $\bar{u}$ if[1]

- *[Symbol match] for all $t \geq 0$, $\bar{u}(t) \in Q(\bar{r}(t))$.*

A *accepts* $\bar{u}$ if it has a run for $\bar{u}$ from an initial extended location. The timed language $\mathcal{L}(A)$ of A is the set of all timed words that it accepts.

It follows from Definition 3 that the language of a timed automaton is closed under equivalence. Together with Lemma 1, this will allow us to restrict our attention to φ-fine sequences when arguing the correctness of the tableau construction for a basic MITL$_{\leq}$ formula φ.

3   Disjunctive Temporal Normal Form

Central to tableau constructions for temporal logics is the observation that every formula can be rewritten into a normal form in which the constraints on the current state are (syntactically) separated from the constraints on the future states. For example, in the case of Propositional Linear-time Temporal Logic (LTL), any formula can be written as a disjunction of terms of the form $\pi \wedge \bigcirc \varphi$,

---

[1] As locations are labelled with *sets* of symbols, a single run corresponds in general to a set of timed words.

where π is a conjunction of propositions dictating the constraints on the current state and the LTL formula φ is "guarded" by the *Next* operator $\bigcirc$, meaning that it must hold in the future starting from the next state. In order to define a similar normal form for $\text{MITL}_\leq$, the logic needs to be extended by adding a Next operator and by introducing timers and timer settings into the syntax of the logic.

3.1   Extending the Logic

In order to define the normal form, the logic is extended with timers that can be bound by timer setting operators or which can be free. A formula is interpreted in a timer environment which provides a value for every free timer. Moreover we assume that formulas are in positive normal form (negations only occur in front of propositions) using the dual operators (false, $\wedge$, $\vee$). The timer set operator can set timers to integer values, and timers can be compared to 0 only by checking the condition $x > 0$ or $x \leq 0$. Compared to other timed logics that use freeze/reset quantifiers (see e.g. [2,10]), the syntax of our logic is restricted: The arguments of an Until or Release operator must be basic $\text{MITL}_\leq$ formulas.

Definition 4. $\text{MITL}_\leq$ *is redefined. Besides the basic formulas defined in Section 2.1 we add formulas of the following form, where φ, φ_1, and φ_2 are basic formulas, $d \in \mathbb{N}$, TS is a timer setting, and x is a timer.*

$$\psi ::= \varphi \mid \psi_1 \vee \psi_2 \mid \psi_1 \wedge \psi_2 \mid TS.\psi \mid x > 0 \mid x \leq 0 \mid \varphi_1 \mathsf{V}_{<d} \varphi_2 \mid \varphi_1 \mathsf{U}_{\leq x} \varphi_2 \mid$$
$$\varphi_1 \mathsf{V}_{<x} \varphi_2 \mid \bigcirc \psi.$$

The semantics is extended as follows. We write $\bar{\rho} \models_\nu \psi$ to denote that the timed state sequence $\bar{\rho}$ satisfies ψ in the context of the timer valuation ν.

$$\bar{\rho} \models_\nu \varphi \qquad \textit{iff } \bar{\rho} \models \varphi;$$
$$\bar{\rho} \models_\nu \psi_1 \vee \psi_2 \quad \textit{iff } \bar{\rho} \models_\nu \psi_1 \textit{ or } \bar{\rho} \models_\nu \psi_2;$$
$$\bar{\rho} \models_\nu \psi_1 \wedge \psi_2 \quad \textit{iff } \bar{\rho} \models_\nu \psi_1 \textit{ and } \bar{\rho} \models_\nu \psi_2;$$
$$\bar{\rho} \models_\nu \varphi_1 \mathsf{V}_{<d} \varphi_2 \quad \textit{iff for all } 0 \leq t < d,\ \bar{\rho}^t \models_{\nu-t} \varphi_2 \textit{ or there is some } 0 \leq t' < t,$$
$$\textit{such that } \bar{\rho}^{t'} \models_{\nu-t'} \varphi_1;$$
$$\bar{\rho} \models_\nu TS.\psi \quad \textit{iff } \bar{\rho} \models_{TS(\nu)} \psi;$$
$$\bar{\rho} \models_\nu \varphi_1 \mathsf{U}_{\leq x} \varphi_2 \quad \textit{iff there is some } 0 \leq t \leq \nu(x),\ \textit{such that } \bar{\rho}^t \models_{\nu-t} \varphi_2 \textit{ and for}$$
$$\textit{all } 0 \leq t' < t,\ \bar{\rho}^{t'} \models_{\nu-t'} \varphi_1;$$
$$\bar{\rho} \models_\nu \varphi_1 \mathsf{V}_{<x} \varphi_2 \quad \textit{iff for all } 0 \leq t < \nu(x),\ \bar{\rho}^t \models_{\nu-t} \varphi_2 \textit{ or there is some } 0 \leq t' <$$
$$t,\ \textit{such that } \bar{\rho}^{t'} \models_{\nu-t'} \varphi_1;$$
$$\bar{\rho} \models_\nu x > 0 \quad \textit{iff } \nu(x) > 0;$$
$$\bar{\rho} \models_\nu x \leq 0 \quad \textit{iff } \nu(x) \leq 0;$$
$$\bar{\rho} \models_\nu \bigcirc \psi \quad \textit{iff } (\bar{\sigma}^1, \bar{I}^1) \models_{\nu-|\bar{I}(0)|} \psi \textit{ where } \bar{\rho} = (\bar{\sigma}, \bar{I}).$$

Note that with the $\bigcirc$ operator it is now possible to discriminate between equivalent timed state sequences. In our tableau construction for the timed case, formulas will also be rewritten to separate "now" from "next". More precisely, the "now" part will refer to the current *interval* of time, and so it will be thought of as being true during a non-zero *period*. In contrast, the "next" part of a formula in normal form will refer to the *first point* of the next interval. In addition, in rewriting a formula, we will also separate the setting of the timers to be effected when entering the current interval. The rewrite rules achieving this will be presented in the next subsection. Of the equivalences on which they are based, the most important ones are displayed below. Here, $\psi \equiv \psi'$ abbreviates $\bar{\rho} \models_\nu \psi$ iff $\bar{\rho} \models_\nu \psi'$, where $\bar{\rho}$ is a timed state sequence and ν a timer valuation, that are both implicitly universally quantified. For some equivalences, conditions on $\bar{\rho}$ and ν are required which are then explicitly listed. φ_1 and φ_2 are basic $\mathrm{MITL}_\leq$ formulas, $d \in \mathbb{N}$, and x and y are timers.

$$\varphi_1 \mathsf{U}_{\leq d}\varphi_2 \equiv [y := d].(\varphi_1 \mathsf{U}_{\leq y}\varphi_2) \tag{1}$$

$$\varphi_1 \mathsf{V}_{<d}\varphi_2 \equiv [y := d].(\varphi_1 \mathsf{V}_{<y}\varphi_2) \tag{2}$$

$$\varphi_1 \mathsf{U}_{\leq x}\varphi_2 \equiv \varphi_2 \vee (x > 0 \wedge \varphi_1 \wedge \bigcirc(\varphi_1 \mathsf{U}_{\leq x}\varphi_2)) \tag{3}$$
$$\text{if } \bar{\rho} \text{ is both } \varphi_1\text{-fine and } \varphi_2\text{-fine, and } \nu(x) \geq 0$$

$$\varphi_1 \mathsf{V}_{\leq d}\varphi_2 \equiv \varphi_2 \wedge (\varphi_1 \vee \bigcirc(\varphi_1 \mathsf{V}_{<d}\varphi_2)) \tag{4}$$
$$\text{if } \bar{\rho} \text{ is } \varphi_1\mathsf{V}_{\leq d}\varphi_2\text{-fine}$$

$$\varphi_1 \mathsf{V}_{<x}\varphi_2 \equiv x \leq 0 \vee (\varphi_2 \wedge (\varphi_1 \vee \bigcirc(\varphi_1 \mathsf{V}_{<x}\varphi_2))) \tag{5}$$
$$\text{if } \bar{\rho} \text{ is both } \varphi_1\text{-fine and } \varphi_2\text{-fine}$$

Lemma 2. *The equivalences between* $\mathrm{MITL}_\leq$ *formulas presented above hold.*

Proof. We will only prove the equivalence 4. Let $\bar{\rho}$ be a timed state sequence that is fine for $\varphi_1\mathsf{V}_{\leq d}\varphi_2$ and ν a timer valuation then $\bar{\rho} \models_\nu \varphi_1\mathsf{V}_{\leq d}\varphi_2$ iff $\bar{\rho} \models_\nu \varphi_2 \wedge (\varphi_1 \vee \bigcirc(\varphi_1\mathsf{V}_{<d}\varphi_2))$ ($\Rightarrow$) Let $\bar{\rho} \models_\nu \varphi_1\mathsf{V}_{\leq d}\varphi_2$. Obviously, $\bar{\rho}$ satisfies φ_2. Assume $\bar{\rho} \not\models_\nu \varphi_1$, then we need to show that $\bar{\rho} \models_\nu \bigcirc(\varphi_1\mathsf{V}_{<d}\varphi_2)$. Since $\bar{\rho}$ is $\varphi_1\mathsf{V}_{\leq d}\varphi_2$-fine, if $\varphi_1\mathsf{V}_{\leq d}\varphi_2$ does not hold at the first moment of the second interval, then this is the first moment where it does not hold. Thus at the first moment of the second interval $\varphi_1\mathsf{V}_{<d}\varphi_2$ holds. ($\Leftarrow$) obvious.

One may wonder why the timer condition $\nu(x) \geq 0$ in rule 3 is listed external to the formula, instead of making it part of the right-hand side: $(x \geq 0 \wedge \varphi_2) \vee (x > 0 \wedge \varphi_1 \wedge \bigcirc(\varphi_1\mathsf{U}_{\leq x}\varphi_2))$. The reason is that the truth value of a condition of the form $x \geq 0$ may change in a "left-open fashion": it may be true in the first (singular) point of an interval, but false in the remainder. By syntactically restricting the timer conditions to the forms $x > 0$ and $x \leq 0$ only, it is clearer that the "now" parts of a formula in normal form can indeed be made true during a full interval. Indeed, the condition $\nu(x) \geq 0$ will turn out to be always fulfilled when equivalence 3 is used as a rewrite rule in the tableau construction. This is also the reason for the introduction of the formula $\varphi_1\mathsf{V}_{<d}\varphi_2$: Unfolding the formula $\varphi_1\mathsf{V}_{\leq x}\varphi_2$ would lead to a timer condition $x < 0$.

3.2   Rewrite Rules

Definition 5. *An* $\mathrm{MITL}_\leq$ *formula is said to be in disjunctive temporal form if it is of the form* $\bigvee_{i=1}^{k} TS_i.(\Pi_i \wedge \bigcirc\Phi_i)$ *where* $k \geq 0$ *(for* $k = 0$ *the formula equals* false *represented as the empty disjunction), the* Π_i *are conjunctions of*

atomic propositions, negated atomic propositions and timer conditions, and the
Φ_i *conjunctions of* MITL$_\leq$ *formulas.*

For presentational purposes we introduce some notation. We will identify a set
Ψ of formulas with the conjunction $\bigwedge \Psi$, the empty conjunction being equivalent
to true. A *term* is a triple $\langle TS, Now, Next \rangle$, where TS is a timer setting and
Now and $Next$ are sets of MITL$_\leq$ formulas. Such a term is identified with the
MITL$_\leq$ formula $TS.(Now \wedge \bigcirc Next)$. A set of terms will be identified with the
disjunction of the formulas represented by the individual terms. Note that an
arbitrary MITL$_\leq$ formula ψ is represented by the set $\{\langle \varnothing, \{\psi\}, \varnothing \rangle\}$ of terms. We
now introduce a number of rewrite rules on sets of terms, that transform any such
set into disjunctive temporal form. These rules are presented in Figure 1, which
is interpreted as follows. Consider a set $\Phi \cup \{\langle TS, Now \cup \{\psi\}, Next \rangle\}$ of terms.
The row in the table in which the CASE field coincides with the shape of the
MITL$_\leq$ formula ψ determines how the set is rewritten. For a timer setting TS,
the function $rename_{TS}$ renames the timers occurring in any syntactical object
apart from the timers in TS. The following lemma states that the disjunctive

CASE	$\Phi \cup \{\langle TS, Now \cup \{\psi\}, Next \rangle\}$ REDUCES TO:
$\psi = \text{true}$	$\Phi \cup \{\langle TS, Now, Next \rangle\}$
$\psi = \text{false}$	Φ
$\psi = \psi_1 \vee \psi_2$	$\Phi \cup \{\langle TS, Now \cup \{\psi_1\}, Next \rangle, \langle TS, Now \cup \{\psi_2\}, Next \rangle\}$
$\psi = \psi_1 \wedge \psi_2$	$\Phi \cup \{\langle TS, Now \cup \{\psi_1, \psi_2\}, Next \rangle\}$
$\psi = \varphi_1 \mathsf{U}_{\leq d} \varphi_2$	$\Phi \cup \{\langle TS, Now \cup \{[x := d].(\varphi_1 \mathsf{U}_{\leq x} \varphi_2)\}, Next \rangle\}$
$\psi = \varphi_1 \mathsf{U}_{\leq x} \varphi_2$	$\Phi \cup \{\langle TS, Now \cup \{\varphi_2 \vee (x > 0 \wedge \varphi_1 \wedge \bigcirc(\varphi_1 \mathsf{U}_{\leq x} \varphi_2))\}, Next \rangle\}$
$\psi = \varphi_1 \mathsf{V}_{\leq d} \varphi_2$	$\Phi \cup \{\langle TS, Now \cup \{\varphi_2 \wedge (\varphi_1 \vee \bigcirc(\varphi_1 \mathsf{V}_{<d} \varphi_2))\}, Next \rangle\}$
$\psi = \varphi_1 \mathsf{V}_{<d} \varphi_2$	$\Phi \cup \{\langle TS, Now \cup \{[x := d].(\varphi_1 \mathsf{V}_{<x} \varphi_2)\}, Next \rangle\}$
$\psi = \varphi_1 \mathsf{V}_{<x} \varphi_2$	$\Phi \cup \{\langle TS, Now \cup \{x \leq 0 \vee (\varphi_2 \wedge (\varphi_1 \vee \bigcirc(\varphi_1 \mathsf{V}_{<x} \varphi_2)))\}, Next \rangle\}$
$\psi = TS'.\psi'$	$\Phi \cup \{\langle TS \cup TS', Now \cup \{\psi''\}, Next \rangle\}$ where $TS''.\psi'' = rename_{TS}(TS'.\psi')$
$\psi = \bigcirc \psi'$	$\Phi \cup \{\langle TS, Now, Next \cup \{\psi'\}\rangle\}$

Fig. 1. Rewrite rules for MITL$_\leq$.

temporal form is a normal form under these rules.

Lemma 3. *Let ψ be an* MITL$_\leq$ *formula and ψ' be obtained from ψ by repeated
application of rules from Figure 1 until no more rule applies. This process terminates, and ψ' is in disjunctive temporal form. Furthermore, for every timed
state sequence $\bar\rho$ and every timer valuation ν such that*

- *$\bar\rho$ is fine for every basic syntactic subformula of ψ;*
- *$\nu(x) \geq 0$ for every timer x that is free in ψ and that occurs in a subformula
of the form $\psi_1 \mathsf{U}_{\leq x} \psi_2$,*

we have $\bar\rho \models_\nu \psi$ iff $\bar\rho \models_\nu \psi'$.

Proof. Termination and the fact that ψ' is in disjunctive temporal form are easily seen. The equivalence of ψ and ψ' under the stated conditions follows from Lemma 2 and a few distributivity rules for the $\bigcirc$ and timer set operators.

Depending on the order in which terms from Φ and formulas from *Now* are selected, different normal forms may be obtained. In the sequel, we assume the existence of a deterministic procedure *NF* that computes a particular normal form for any given formula. The following lemma states that the timer setting *TS* and *Now* and *Next* parts of a term in a normal form have the properties we set out for. It will be used in the correctness proof in Section 4.3.

Lemma 4. *Let $\psi \in \mathrm{MITL}_{\leq}$, ν be a timer valuation, and $\bar{\rho}$ a timed state sequence with interval sequence $\bar{I}$ that is fine for all basic subformulas of ψ. If $\bar{\rho} \models_{\nu} \psi$, then there is some term $\langle TS, Now, Next \rangle \in NF(\psi)$ such that for all $0 \leq t < l(\bar{I}(1))$, $\bar{\rho}^t \models_{TS(\nu)-t} Now$, and furthermore $\bar{\rho}^{l(\bar{I}(1))} \models_{TS(\nu)-l(\bar{I}(1))} Next$.*

Proof. Follows by induction on the number of rewrite steps in the normal form procedure.

Example The (basic) $\mathrm{MITL}_{\leq}$ formula $\Diamond_{\leq 2}p = \mathrm{true}\mathsf{U}_{\leq 2}p$ has an equivalent formula in disjunctive temporal form:

$$\mathrm{true}\mathsf{U}_{\leq 2}p \equiv ([x := 2].p) \vee ([x := 2].\,(x > 0 \wedge \bigcirc (\mathrm{true}\mathsf{U}_{\leq x}p)))$$

Here, the equivalence holds for any timer valuation ν and any timed state sequence $\bar{\rho}$ that is fine for p. In terms of the normal form procedure, the rewriting process of $\mathrm{true}\mathsf{U}_{\leq 2}p$ proceeds as follows (we write $\Phi_1 \Rightarrow \Phi_2$ to express that Φ_2 is obtained from Φ_1 by one or more steps in the procedure).

$$\{\langle \varnothing, \{\mathrm{true}\mathsf{U}_{\leq 2}p\}, \varnothing \rangle\} \Rightarrow \{\langle [x := 2], \{\mathrm{true}\mathsf{U}_{\leq x}p\}, \varnothing \rangle\} \Rightarrow$$
$$\{\langle [x := 2], \{p \vee (x > 0 \wedge \mathrm{true} \wedge \bigcirc (\mathrm{true}\mathsf{U}_{\leq x}p))\}, \varnothing \rangle\} \Rightarrow$$
$$\{\langle [x := 2], \{p\}, \varnothing \rangle, \langle [x := 2], \{x > 0, \mathrm{true}, \bigcirc (\mathrm{true}\mathsf{U}_{\leq x}p)\}, \varnothing \rangle\} \Rightarrow$$
$$\{\langle [x := 2], \{p\}, \varnothing \rangle, \langle [x := 2], \{x > 0\}, \{\mathrm{true}\mathsf{U}_{\leq x}p\} \rangle\}$$

4   Tableau Construction

4.1   The Tableau Algorithm

The construction of a tableau automaton for a basic $\mathrm{MITL}_{\leq}$ formula φ, is based upon the normal form introduced in the previous section. The number of formulas that may occur in the *Now* and *Next* sets of the normal form terms is limited to syntactic subformulas of φ and a number of formulas derived from them such as timer conditions and Until or Release formulas indexed by a timer. However, the procedure introduces new timers when applying the reduction for $\psi = TS'.\psi'$. If not applied carefully, this could lead to an unbounded number of timers and locations of the tableau automaton. To prevent this, we use a unique timer x_ψ for every Until or release formula ψ occurring in φ. It follows from the normal form procedure that the only use of the timer of an Until (Release) will be in the $\varphi_1 U_{\leq x}\varphi_2$ ($\varphi_1 V_{<x}\varphi_2$) variant of its corresponding formula. Then we can apply the following equivalences to limit the number of timers.

$$(\varphi_1 U_{\leq x}\varphi_2) \wedge ([y := d].(\varphi_1 U_{\leq y}\varphi_2)) \equiv \varphi_1 U_{\leq x}\varphi_2 \qquad \text{if } \nu(x) \leq d \quad (6)$$

$$(\varphi_1 V_{<x}\varphi_2) \wedge ([y := d].(\varphi_1 V_{<y}\varphi_2)) \equiv [y := d].(\varphi_1 V_{<y}\varphi_2) \qquad \text{if } \nu(x) \leq d \quad (7)$$

The validity of these rules follows straightforwardly from the semantics. The use of the case $\psi = TS'.\psi'$ can be circumvented by replacing the corresponding rules in the normal form procedure with the following new rules for the cases $\varphi_1 U_{\leq d}\varphi_2$ and $\varphi_1 V_{<d}\varphi_2$, based on the equivalences presented above. In the remainder, $NF(\psi)$ refers to the updated version of the normal form procedure.

CASE	$\Phi \cup \{\langle TS, Now \cup \{\psi\}, Next\rangle\}$ REDUCES TO:
$\psi = \varphi_1 U_{\leq d}\varphi_2$	$\Phi \cup \{\langle TS[x_\psi := d], Now \cup \{\varphi_1 U_{\leq x_\psi}\varphi_2\}, Next\rangle\}$
	if $\{x_\psi > 0, \varphi_1 U_{\leq x_\psi}\varphi_2\} \cap Now = \varnothing$
$\psi = \varphi_1 U_{\leq d}\varphi_2$	$\Phi \cup \{\langle TS, Now \cup \{\varphi_1 U_{\leq x_\psi}\varphi_2\}, Next\rangle\}$
	if $\{x_\psi > 0, \varphi_1 U_{\leq x_\psi}\varphi_2\} \cap Now \neq \varnothing$
$\psi = \varphi_1 V_{<d}\varphi_2$	$\Phi \cup \{\langle TS[x_\psi := d], Now \cup \{\varphi_1 V_{<x_\psi}\varphi_2\}, Next\rangle\}$

The tableau automaton of an $\text{MITL}_{\leq}$ formula φ is computed in the following way.

Definition 6. *Let φ be a basic $\text{MITL}_{\leq}$ formula and Prop be the set of atomic propositions that occur in φ. Then the tableau automaton A_φ of φ is the automaton $\langle L, T, L_0, Q, TC, E\rangle$ over the alphabet 2^{Prop}, where*

- *T is the set of all timers x_ψ for every Until or Release formula ψ that occurs as a syntactic subformula of φ.*
- *The locations (L), initial extended locations (L_0) and transitions (E) are computed by the procedure depicted in Figure 2. The locations $\ell \in L$ are pairs (Now, Next) of sets. The first item of the location ℓ is denoted by $Now(\ell)$ and the last by $Next(\ell)$.*
- *$Q(\ell) = \{\sigma \in 2^{Prop} \mid \forall_{p \in Prop} p \in Now(\ell) \Rightarrow p \in \sigma, \neg p \in Now(\ell) \Rightarrow p \notin \sigma\}$. That is, a location ℓ is labelled with all sets of propositions that are consistent with the atomic propositions and the negated atomic propositions in $Now(\ell)$.*
- *$TC(\ell) = \{\xi \in TCond(T) \mid \xi \in Now(\ell)\}$, the location is labelled with all timer conditions in $Now(\ell)$.*

4.2 Example

If we take the formula $\square_{\leq 100}\diamond_{\leq 5} p = false V_{\leq 100} (true U_{\leq 5} p)$ and apply the tableau algorithm, we arrive at the automaton represented in Figure 3. Only the formulas in the *Now* set of the locations have been depicted. Initial extended locations are represented by a small arrow not originating from any location leading to the initial location and labelled with a timer setting that yields the initial timer valuation when applied to the timer valuation that assigns 0 to every timer. There is a timer associated with the formula $\diamond_{\leq 5} p$ named x and a timer associated with the formula $\square_{\leq 100}\diamond_{\leq 5} p$ named y.

```
L₀ := {((Now, Next), TS(0̄)) | ⟨TS, Now, Next⟩ ∈ NF(φ)}
LNew := {(Now, Next) | ((Now, Next), TS) ∈ L₀ }
L := ∅, E := ∅
while LNew ≠ ∅ do
  Let (Now, Next) ∈ LNew
  LNew := LNew\{(Now, Next)}
  L := L ∪ {(Now, Next)}
  for every (TS', Now', Next') ∈ NF(Next) do
    E := E ∪ {((Now, Next), TS', (Now', Next'))}
    if (Now', Next') ∉ L then LNew := LNew ∪ {(Now', Next')}
    od
od
```

Fig. 2. Algorithm for constructing the locations and edges of the on-the-fly tableau automaton.

4.3   Correctness

In this section we will give a sketch of the proof that the tableau construction is correct, i.e. that for any basic MITL$_\leq$ formula φ, the tableau automaton of φ accepts precisely those timed state sequences that satisfy φ, as expressed by the following theorem.

Theorem 1. *Let φ be a basic MITL$_\leq$ formula, A_φ the corresponding tableau automaton. Then for every timed state sequence $\bar\rho$, A_φ accepts $\bar\rho$ iff $\bar\rho \models \varphi$.*

This theorem follows from soundness (every state sequence accepted by A_φ satisfies φ) and completeness (every state sequence satisfying φ is accepted by A_φ) of the construction as expressed by Lemmas 7 and 10 below. The structure of the proof is similar to the correctness proof of the untimed on-the-fly tableau of [8]. In this section, we assume that φ is a basic MITL$_\leq$ formula and $A_\varphi = \langle L, T, L_0, Q, TC, E \rangle$ its tableau automaton.

Soundness In this paragraph it is demonstrated that the automaton accepts only timed state sequences that satisfy φ. It is shown that whenever a formula ψ leads to the normal form term that corresponds to a particular location ℓ, then any state sequence for which there is an ℓ-run satisfies the formula ψ. To do this, we associate with a location $\ell = (Now, Next)$, reached after performing the timer setting TS, the set $Old(TS, \ell)$ as the set of all formulas for which $\langle TS, Now, Next \rangle$ is a term of the normal form. Note that in [8], a similar Old set is computed during the construction of the tableau and is part of a location.

Definition 7. *Let TS be a timer setting and $\ell = (Now, Next)$.*

$$Old(TS, \ell) = \bigcup \{ Now' \mid \langle TS, Now, Next \rangle \in NF(\langle TS', Now', Next' \rangle) \\ \text{for some } TS', Next' \}$$

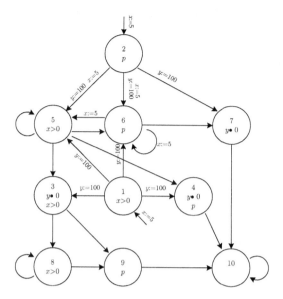

Fig. 3. Example tableau automaton of the formula $\Box_{\leq 100}\Diamond_{\leq 5}p$

The main lemma is the following, claiming that any formula in the *Old* set of a particular location is dealt with correctly.

Lemma 5. *Let $\bar{\rho}$ be a timed state sequence and $\bar{r} = (\bar{\ell}, \bar{I}, \bar{\nu})$ be a run of A_φ for $\bar{\rho}$, taking the edges $(\bar{\ell}(k), TS_{k+1}, \bar{\ell}(k+1))$. Furthermore, let TS be a timer setting such that $\bar{\nu}(0) = TS(\nu)$ for some timer valuation ν and $\psi \in Old(TS, \bar{\ell}(0))$. Then $\bar{\rho} \models_{\bar{\nu}(0)} \psi$.*

Proof. By induction on the structure of ψ. We only show the cases related to the Until formula.

- If $\varphi_1 U_{\leq d}\varphi_2 \in Old(TS, \bar{\ell}(0))$, then it can be shown by the reduction of $\varphi_1 U_{\leq d}\varphi_2$ in the disjunctive temporal form procedure that $\varphi_1 U_{\leq x}\varphi_2 \in Old(TS, \bar{\ell}(0))$. By induction it follows that $\bar{\rho} \models_{\bar{\nu}(0)} \varphi_1 U_{\leq x}\varphi_2$. Since x cannot be larger than d in $\bar{\nu}(0)$, it follows that $\bar{\rho} \models_{\bar{\nu}(0)} \varphi_1 U_{\leq d}\varphi_2$.
- If $\varphi_1 U_{\leq x}\varphi_2 \in Old(TS, \bar{\ell}(0))$, then by the construction of the automaton and the reduction of $\varphi_1 U_{\leq x}\varphi_2$ in the normal form procedure, there is some k, such that $\varphi_2 \in Old(TS_k, \bar{\ell}(k))$ and for every $0 \leq t < l(\bar{I}(k))$, $\varphi_1 \in Old(\varnothing, \bar{\ell}(t))$ and $x > 0 \in Old(\varnothing, \bar{\ell}(t))$. Moreover it can be shown that the timer x is never set to d in any TS_i, $0 < i \leq k$, and thus $l(\bar{I}(k)) \leq \bar{\nu}(0)(x)$. By induction it follows that $\bar{\rho} \models_{\bar{\nu}(0)} \varphi_1 U_{\leq x}\varphi_2$. □

One can furthermore show that the *Old* set of every initial location contains the original formula φ.

Lemma 6. *For every initial extended location (ℓ, ν) of A_φ, there exists some timer setting TS such that $\varphi \in Old(TS, \ell)$ and $\nu = TS(\bar{0})$.*

Proof. Follows straightforwardly from the definitions of the automaton and the disjunctive temporal form procedure.

From the Lemmas 5 and 6, it follows immediately that every state sequence accepted by the tableau automaton A_φ satisfies φ.

Lemma 7. *Let $\bar{\rho}$ be a timed state sequence. If A_φ accepts $\bar{\rho}$, then $\bar{\rho} \models \varphi$.*

Completeness In this paragraph it is demonstrated that every timed state sequence that satisfies φ is accepted by the tableau automaton. The normal form procedure guarantees that if a timed state sequence $\bar{\rho}$ satisfies a formula ψ, then there is a term in the normal form of ψ, that is satisfied by $\bar{\rho}$. Moreover, it has been shown in Lemma 4 that the formulas in the *Now* set of the term hold during the entire first interval of $\bar{\rho}$. Since the remainder of the state sequence satisfies the formulas in the *Next* set, there is a transition that can be taken by the automaton. This argument can be repeated to construct a run of the automaton for $\bar{\rho}$.

The following lemma states that if a timed state sequence is φ-fine and satisfies all formulas in the *Next* set of a location, then there is an edge in the automaton to a new location where the first interval satisfies all *Now* formulas and the tail of the state sequence satisfies all *Next* formulas again.

Lemma 8. *Let $\ell \in L$, $\bar{\rho} = (\bar{\sigma}, \bar{I})$ a φ-fine timed state sequence, and ν a timer valuation, such that $\bar{\rho} \models_\nu Next(\ell)$. Then there exists an edge $(\ell, TS, \ell') \in E$ such that for all $0 \le t < l(\bar{I}(1))$, we have that $\bar{\rho}^t \models_{TS(\nu)-t} Now(\ell')$ and $\bar{\rho}^{l(\bar{I}(1))} \models_{TS(\nu)-l(\bar{I}(1))} Next(\ell')$.*

Proof. Follows from Lemma 4 and the construction of the tableau automaton.

Similarly we can use Lemma 4 to show that if a timed state sequence $\bar{\rho}$ satisfies φ, then there is an appropriate initial extended location to start a run for $\bar{\rho}$.

Lemma 9. *Let $\bar{\rho} = (\bar{\sigma}, \bar{I})$ be a φ-fine timed state sequence such that $\bar{\rho} \models \varphi$. Then there is some $(\ell, \nu) \in L_0$ such that for all $0 \le t < l(\bar{I}(1))$, $\bar{\rho}^t \models_{\nu-t} Now(\ell)$ and $\bar{\rho}^{l(\bar{I}(1))} \models_{\nu-l(\bar{I}(1))} Next(\ell)$.*

From Lemma 9 and repeatedly applying Lemma 8 to construct a run, it follows that A_φ accepts all timed state sequences that satisfy φ.

Lemma 10. *Let $\bar{\rho}$ be a timed state sequence. If $\bar{\rho} \models \varphi$, then A_φ accepts $\bar{\rho}$.*

4.4   Implementation

In order to validate the tableau construction described in this section, a prototype implementation of the algorithm has been made. Table 1 shows a few of the formulas that have been tested and the numbers of locations, edges and timers of the corresponding tableau automata. The size of the automata grows relatively mildly with the size of the formula. As we know of no other implementations, we have been unable to collect comparative results.

Table 1. Numbers of states, transitions and timers of the tableaux of different formulas

Formula	Numb. of states	Numb. of transitions	Numb. of timers
$\neg \Diamond_{\leq 5} p$	4	6	1
$\Box_{\leq 100} \Diamond_{\leq 5} p$	10	22	2
$\Diamond_{\leq 5} (\Box_{\leq 1} p \vee \Box_{\leq 1} q)$	11	21	3
$p \mathsf{U}_{\leq 1} (q \mathsf{U}_{\leq 1} (r \mathsf{U}_{\leq 1} s))$	14	30	3
$p \Rightarrow (\Box_{\leq 5} (q \Rightarrow \Box_{\leq 1} r))$	15	48	2
$(p \Rightarrow \Diamond_{\leq 5} q) \mathsf{U}_{\leq 100} \Box_{\leq 5} \neg p$	21	64	3
$(((p \mathsf{U}_{\leq 4} q) \mathsf{U}_{\leq 3} r) \mathsf{U}_{\leq 2} s) \mathsf{U}_{\leq 1} t$	60	271	4

5   Conclusions and Future Work

We have presented an on-the-fly tableau construction for the fragment $\mathrm{MITL}_{\leq}$ of MITL. Technically, this required the introduction of explicit timers and timer set operators into the logic, as well as a Next operator. Within this extended syntax, we could then define equivalence-preserving rewrite rules that syntactically separate any given formula into three parts: the timer settings, the constraints on the current time interval, and the constraints on the future intervals. The resulting normal form procedure is the first ingredient to the tableau construction. The second ingredient is given by two more equivalences that are used to restrict the number of timers introduced in the tableau automaton to one timer per Until and per Release formula.

In [4] it has been shown that the construction of tableaux for $\mathrm{MITL}_{0,\infty}$, a slightly different fragment of MITL, is PSPACE-complete, and this result can be adapted to the case of $\mathrm{MITL}_{\leq}$. Thus, the theoretical worst-case complexity of our construction is the same as that of the construction in [4]. Being on-the-fly, we expect our algorithm to use less memory and to give smaller tableaux in many cases in practice. However, as we know of no other implementations, we have been unable to collect comparative results.

By restricting the interval sequences of models to be left-closed and right-open, and subscripts of (basic) Until formulas to be of the form $\leq d$, we could confine ourselves to timed automata of a restricted form, so that in the tableaux no extra clocks are needed to distinguish between transitions from a right-open into a left-closed interval and transitions from a right-closed into a left-open interval. To demonstrate the construction, we have implemented the algorithm and shown experimental results for several formulas. We are currently extending the results of this paper to also include Until formulas without time bounds, leading to timed automata with acceptance conditions. We also consider an implementation of the presented algorithm in the context of the SHESim platform for specification and simulation ([7]). Another direction for future work is the generalisation of optimisations that have been developed for (on-the-fly) tableau constructions in the untimed case (see e.g. [5,6,8]).

References

1. R. Alur. *Techniques for automatic verification of real-time systems.* PhD thesis, Stanford University, 1991.
2. R. Alur, C. Courcoubetis, and D. Dill. Model-checking in dense real-time. *Information and Computation*, 104:2–34, 1993.
3. R. Alur and D.L. Dill. A theory of timed automata. *Theoretical Computer Science*, 126:183–235, 1994.
4. R. Alur, T. Feder, and T. Henzinger. The benefits of relaxing punctuality. *Journal of the ACM*, 43(1):116–146, January 1996.
5. M. Daniele, F. Giunchiglia, and M. Y. Vardi. Improved automata generation for linear temporal logic. In N. Halbwachs and D. Peled, editors, *Computer Aided Verification: 11th International Conference Proceedings, CAV'99, Trento, Italy, July 6-10, 1999 (LNCS 1633)*, pages 249–260. Springer, 1999.
6. K. Etessami and G. Holzmann. Optimizing Büchi automata. To appear in Proceedings of CONCUR'2000, 2000.
7. M.C.W. Geilen and J.P.M. Voeten. Object-oriented modelling and specification using SHE. In R.C. Backhouse and J.C.M. Baeten, editors, *Proceedings of the First International Symposium on Visual Formal Methods VFM'99*, pages 16–24. Computing Science Reports 99/08 Department of Mathematics and Computer Science, Eindhoven University of Technology, 1999.
8. R. Gerth, D. Peled, M.Y. Vardi, and P. Wolper. Simple on-the-fly automatic verification of linear temporal logic. In *Proc. IFIP/WG6.1 Symp. Protocol Specification Testing and Verification (PSTV95), Warsaw Poland*, pages 3–18. Chapman & Hall, June 1995.
9. T. Henzinger. It's about time: real-time logics reviewed. In D. Sangiorgi and R. de Simone, editors, *Proceedings of the 9th International Conference on Concurrency Theory (CONCUR 1998)*, pages 439–454, Berlin, 1998. Springer.
10. T. Henzinger, X. Nicollin, J. Sifakis, and S. Yovine. Symbolic model checking for real-time systems. *Information and Computation*, 111(1):193–244, June 1994.
11. O. Lichtenstein and A. Pnueli. Checking that finite state concurrent programs satisfy their linear specification. In *Twelfth Annual ACM Symposium on Principles of Programming Languages*, pages 97–107. ACM SIGACT/SIGPLAN, 1985.
12. A. Pnueli. The temporal logic of programs. In *Proc. of the 18th Annual Symposium on Foundations of Computer Science*, pages 46–57. IEEE Computer Society Press, 1977.
13. J.-F. Raskin. *Logics, automata and classical theories for deciding real time.* PhD thesis, Facultés Universitaires Notre-Dame de la Paix, Namur (Belgium), June 1999.
14. M. Y. Vardi and P. Wolper. An automata-theoretic approach to automatic program verification (preliminary report). In *Logic in Computer Science*, pages 332–344. IEEE TC-MFC, IEEE Computer Society Press, 1986.

Verifying Universal Properties of Parameterized Networks [*]

Kai Baukus[1], Yassine Lakhnech[2], and Karsten Stahl[1]

[1] Institute of Computer Science and Applied Mathematics
CAU Kiel, Preusserstr. 1–9, D-24105 Kiel, Germany.
{kba, kst}@informatik.uni-kiel.de
[2] VERIMAG[***], Centre Equation, 2 Av. de Vignate,
38610 Gières, France. lakhnech@imag.fr

Abstract. We present a method for verifying *universal* properties of fair parameterized networks of finite processes, that is, properties of the form $\forall p_1 \ldots p_n : \psi$, where ψ is a quantifier-free LTL formula. The starting point of our verification method is an encoding of the infinite family of networks by a single fair transition system whose variables are set (2nd-order) variables and transitions are described in WS1S, such a system is called a WS1S transition system. We abstract the WS1S system into a finite state system that can be model-checked. We present a generic abstraction relation for verifying universal properties as well as an algorithm for computing an abstract system. Since, the abstract system may contain infinite computations that have no corresponding fair computations at the concrete level, the verification of progress property often fails. Therefore, we present methods that allow to synthesize fairness conditions from the parameterized network and discuss under which conditions and how to lift fairness conditions of this network to fairness conditions on the abstract system. We implemented our methods in a tool, called PAX, and applied it to several examples.

1 Introduction

Problem statement and contributions We present a method for verifying *universal* properties of fair parameterized networks of finite processes. In other words, we present a method for tackling the following problem: *Given a parameterized network $P_1 \parallel \cdots \parallel P_n$, fairness conditions, and a quantifier-free linear-time temporal property $\psi(p_1, \ldots, p_k)$, we want to prove $P_1 \parallel \cdots \parallel P_n \models \forall p_1, \ldots, p_k \leq n : \psi(p_1, \ldots, p_k)$, for every $n \in \omega$, i.e., every fair computation of $P_1 \parallel \cdots \parallel P_n$ satisfies $\forall p_1, \ldots, p_k \leq n : \psi(p_1, \ldots, p_k)$.*

[*] This work has been partially supported by the Esprit-LTR project Vires.
[***] Verimag is a joint research laboratory of the University Joseph Fourier (Grenoble I), National Polytechnical Institute of Grenoble (INPG) and the National Center of Scientific Research (CNRS).

M. Joseph (Ed.): FTRTFT 2000, LNCS 1926, pp. 291–303, 2000.

Our approach is verification by abstraction [CC77,CGL94,DGG94] and consists of the following steps:

1. Representing the infinite family of fair networks $P_1 \| \cdots \| P_n$ as a single fair transition system $\mathcal{S}$ whose variables range over finite sub-sets of ω and whose transitions are expressed in WS1S, the weak second-order logic of one-successor [Büc60]. We call such systems fair WS1S transition systems.

2. Constructing an abstraction relation that maps the states of the WS1S transition system $\mathcal{S}$ to abstract states which are valuations of boolean variables. We present a generic abstraction relation for verifying universal properties.

3. Automatically constructing a finite abstract system $\mathcal{S}_A$ that is an abstraction of $\mathcal{S}$ which implies that every computation of $\mathcal{S}$ can be mapped to a computation of $\mathcal{S}_A$. Moreover, we construct an abstract formula ψ_A such that if $\mathcal{S}_A$ satisfies ψ_A, then we can deduce $P_1 \| \cdots \| P_n \models \forall p_1, \ldots, p_k \leq n : \psi(p_1, \ldots, p_k)$, for every $n \in \omega$.

4. Since the abstract system is finite, we can use model-checking to verify that it satisfies ψ_A. However, verifying progress properties using abstractions often fails because of infinite computations in the abstract system that do not correspond to fair infinite ones in the concrete one. To mitigate this problem, we augment the abstract system with *safe* fairness conditions, that is, conditions that only remove infinite computations that do not correspond to concrete ones. We present two techniques for synthesizing fairness conditions from the concrete system that can be safely added to the abstract one:

   a) An algorithm that given a WS1S formula characterizing a ranking function computes pairs of sets of transitions expressing strong fairness conditions that are *guaranteed* to hold for the parameterized network, and hence, abstractions of them can be safely added at the abstract level.

   b) A method that allows to generate fairness conditions at the abstract level from the fairness conditions of the parameterized network. In particular, we discuss which kind of weak/strong fairness can be lifted from the concrete to the abstract level.

We implemented our method in a tool, we call PAX [1], that uses the decision procedures of MONA [HJJ+96] to check the satisfiability of WS1S formulae. We then applied our tool and method to several examples including Dijkstra's and Szymanski's mutual exclusion algorithms.

---

[1] http://www.informatik.uni-kiel.de/~kba/pax

Relevance and related work There has been recently much interest in the automatic and semi-automatic verification of parameterized networks. The methods presented in [GS92,EN96] show that for restricted classes of ring networks of arbitrary size, there exists k such that the verification of the parameterized network can be reduced to the verification of networks of size up to k. Alternative methods presented in [KM89,WL89,BCG89] are based on induction on the number of processes. These methods require finding a network invariant that abstracts any arbitrary number of processes with respect to a pre-order that preserves the property to be verified. While this method has been originally presented for linear networks, it has been generalized in [CGJ95] to networks generated by context-free grammars. In [CGJ95], abstract transition systems were used to specify the invariant. An abstract transition system consists of abstract states specified by regular expressions and transitions between abstract states. The idea of representing sets of states of parameterized networks by regular languages is applied in [KMM+97], where additionally finite-state transducers are used to compute predecessors. These ideas are applied to linear networks as well as to processes arranged in a tree architecture and semi-automatic symbolic backward analysis methods for solving the reachability problem are given. The work in [ABJN99,JN00] extends the ideas in [KMM+97] by considering the effect of applying infinitely often a transition that satisfies certain restrictions. In [BBLS00], we presented a method based on abstraction for verifying invariance and a restricted class of liveness properties of parameterized networks. The method we present here allows us to deal with a larger class of progress properties.

2   Preliminaries

In this section we briefly recall the definition of weak second order theory of one successor (WS1S for short) [Büc60,Tho90].

Terms of WS1S are built up from the constant 0 and 1st-order variables by applying the successor function $\text{suc}(t)$ ("$t+1$"). *Atomic formulae* are of the form b, $t = t'$, $t < t'$, $t \in X$, where b is a boolean variable, t and t' are terms, and X is a set variable (2nd-order variable). WS1S-formulae are built up from atomic formulae by applying the boolean connectives as well as quantification over both 1st-order and 2nd-order variables.

WS1S-formulae are interpreted in models that assign finite sub-sets of ω to 2nd-order variables and elements of ω to 1st-order variables. The interpretation is defined in the usual way.

Given a WS1S formula f, we denote by $[\![f]\!]$ the set of models of f. The set of free variables in f is denoted by $free(f)$.

In addition to the usual abbreviations, given a 2nd-order variable P, we write $\forall_P i : f$ instead of $\forall i : i \in P \Rightarrow f$ and $\exists_P i : f$ instead of $\exists i : i \in P \wedge f$.

Finally, we recall that by Büchi [Büc60] and Elgot [Elg61] the satisfiability problem for WS1S is decidable. Indeed, the set of all models of a WS1S-formula is representable by a finite automaton (see, e.g., [Tho90]).

3 Parameterized Networks as WS1S Transition Systems

We introduce WS1S transition systems which are transition systems with variables ranging over finite sub-sets of ω and show how they can be used to represent parameterized networks. In order to simulate the behavior of parameterized networks with fairness conditions we also need the notion of fairness for WS1S transition systems.

Definition 1 (Fair WS1S Transition Systems).
A fair WS1S transition system $\mathcal{S} = (\mathcal{V}, \Theta, \mathcal{T}, \mathcal{J}, \mathcal{C})$ is given by the following components:

- $\mathcal{V} = \{X_1, \ldots, X_k\}$: A finite set of second order variables X_i ranging over finite sets of natural numbers.
- Θ: A WS1S formula with $free(\Theta) \subseteq \mathcal{V}$ describing the initial condition of the system.
- $\mathcal{T}$: A finite set of transitions where each $\tau \in \mathcal{T}$ is represented as a WS1S formula $\rho_\tau(\mathcal{V}, \mathcal{V}')$, i.e., $free(\rho_\tau) \subseteq \mathcal{V} \cup \mathcal{V}'$.
- $\mathcal{J}$: A set of pairs of second order variables expressing a weak fairness condition. Each pair $(X_m, X_{m'})$ requires, for each $i \in \omega$, the weak fairness condition that i cannot be continuously in X_m without being eventually in $X_{m'}$, that is, $\forall i \in \omega : (\Diamond \Box (i \in X_m) \rightarrow \Box \Diamond (i \in X_{m'}))$.
- $\mathcal{C}$: A set of pairs $(X_m, X_{m'})$ of second order variables expressing the strong fairness condition $\forall i \in \omega : (\Box \Diamond (i \in X_m) \rightarrow \Box \Diamond (i \in X_{m'}))$. □

A state s of $\mathcal{S}$ is a mapping from the variables in $\mathcal{V}$ into finite subsets of ω. A *computation* of $\mathcal{S}$ is a sequence $(s_i)_{i \in \omega}$ of states such that $\Theta[s_0(\mathcal{V})/\mathcal{V}]$ and $\bigvee_{\tau \in \mathcal{T}} \tau[s_i(\mathcal{V}), s_{i+1}(\mathcal{V})/\mathcal{V}, \mathcal{V}']$ are valid formulae. A computation $(s_i)_{i \in \omega}$ satisfies a weak fairness condition $(X_m, X_{m'}) \in \mathcal{J}$ iff the following condition holds for every $x \in \omega$:

if $\exists i \in \omega. \forall j \geq i : x \in s_j(X_m)$, then there exist infinitely many i's such that $x \in s_i(X_{m'})$.

The computation satisfies the strong fairness condition $(X_m, X_{m'}) \in \mathcal{C}$ iff the following condition holds for every $x \in \omega$:

if there exist infinitely many i's such that $x \in s_i(X_m)$, then there exist infinitely many i's such that $x \in s_i(X_{m'})$.

Then, a *fair computation* of $\mathcal{S}$ is a computation that satisfies all fairness conditions in $\mathcal{J}$ and $\mathcal{C}$. Henceforth, we denote the set of fair computations of $\mathcal{S}$ by $[\![\mathcal{S}]\!]$.

As a running example we use a simple mutual exclusion algorithm to illustrate how to represent a parameterized network as a WS1S system and how to analyze it.

Example 1. The parameterized network consists of processes where each process is described as follows:

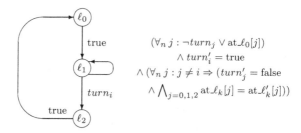

The transition from ℓ_0 to ℓ_1 is weak fair whereas the loop from ℓ_1 to ℓ_1 is strong fair. Initially, all processes are at ℓ_0. Location ℓ_2 represents the critical section.

It is easy to see how each process P_i can be described using a boolean variable at$\_\ell_m[i]$ for each control point $\ell_m[i]$.

We will verify that the algorithm satisfies the mutual exclusion property as well as the universal property that each process p reaches its critical section infinitely often, i.e., $\forall_n p : \square\lozenge$at$\_\ell_2[p]$.

To represent this network as a WS1S system we introduce three set variables At$\_\ell_0$, At$\_\ell_1$, At$\_\ell_2$ corresponding to the control locations, the set variable $Turn$ corresponding to $turn$, and a set variable P representing the set of processes part of the network. Moreover, we need two additional set variables E_τ and T_τ for each transition to express the fairness conditions, a process index will be member of these sets whenever the corresponding transition is enabled (resp. just taken) for this process. Let $\tilde{V}$ denote this set of variables. If we denote by τ_0 the self-loop in ℓ_1, then $\tilde{\mathcal{C}} = \{(E_{\tau_0}, T_{\tau_0})\}$. The liveness property we will check later can then be expressed by $\forall_P p : \square\lozenge(p \in$ At$\_\ell_2)$. For the sake of illustration, we show the representation of τ_0:

$$\exists_P i : i \in \text{At}\_\ell_1 \wedge (\forall_P j : j \notin Turn \vee j \in \text{At}\_\ell_0) \wedge i \in \text{At}\_\ell'_1 \wedge i \in Turn'$$
$$\wedge (\forall_P j : j \neq i \Rightarrow (j \notin Turn' \wedge \bigwedge_{j=0,1,2}(j \in \text{At}\_\ell_k \Leftrightarrow j \in \text{At}\_\ell'_k)))$$
$$\wedge P = P' \wedge \bigcup_{B \in \widetilde{V}} B' \subseteq P' \wedge \bigcup_{\tau_0 \neq \tau'} T'_{\tau'} = \emptyset \wedge T'_{\tau_0} = \{i\}$$
$$\wedge \bigwedge_{\tau \in T} E'_\tau = \{i \in P \mid \exists V'' : \rho_\tau(V', V'')\} \ .$$

The existential quantification corresponds to an interleaving semantics where only one process proceeds in one step. Of course, it is also possible to model synchronous systems by using universal quantification.   □

Note that the class of systems we can model as WS1S systems is restricted such that each process has to be finite state and the transitions can be characterized in WS1S. The definition of a class that can be modeled as WS1S system and the translation can be found in the full paper [BLS00].

4   Abstracting WS1S Systems

In Section 3, we have shown how we model parameterized networks as fair WS1S systems. An infinite family of systems is represented by a single, though infinite-state, transition system. In the following, we present a method to construct a finite abstraction of a given WS1S systems. Then, we show in Section 5 how the obtained abstract system can be enriched with fairness conditions such that interesting progress properties of the WS1S system can be verified. Let us first define what we mean by universal temporal properties.

Let Π be a countable set of process indices p that range over natural numbers and let Ξ be a countable set of variables X that range over finite sets of natural numbers. We do not write the universal quantifier as free variables are understood as universally quantified. The set LTL of linear-time temporal properties over Π and Ξ is defined as follows:

$$\varphi ::= i \in \omega \mid p \in X \mid \neg\varphi \mid \varphi \wedge \varphi \mid \bigcirc\varphi \mid \varphi\mathcal{U}\varphi, \text{ where } i \text{ is a constant in } \omega.$$

As usual, we use that temporal modalities □ (always) and ◇ (eventually) which can be introduced as abbreviations.

Formulae in LTL are interpreted over infinite sequences of structures of the form $(\mathcal{I}, \mathcal{I}')$, where $\mathcal{I}$ maps each variable $X \in \Xi$ to a finite sub-set of ω and $\mathcal{I}'$ maps each variable in Π to an element of ω. The definition of the interpretation of LTL is not given here as it is standard.

Let φ be an LTL formula with $\{X_1, \ldots, X_k\}$ as free set-variables and $\{p_1, \ldots, p_n\}$ as free 1st-order variables. Moreover, let S be a WS1S transition system with $\{X_1, \ldots, X_k\}$ as variables. A computation $(s_i)_{i \in \omega}$ satisfies φ iff for every injective mapping $\mathcal{I}'$ from $\{p_1, \ldots, p_n\}$ into ω, the sequence $(s_i, \mathcal{I}')_{i \in \omega}$ satisfies φ. In other words, the computation $(s_i)_{i \in \omega}$ satisfies φ, if it satisfies all the temporal formulae obtained by instantiating the variables $p_1, \ldots, p_n$. We say that S satisfies φ, denoted by $S \models \varphi$, if every fair computation of S satisfies φ.

A temporal property is called *universal*, if it can be described by a formula in LTL. For instance, mutual-exclusion of Szymanski's algorithm can be described by the formula $\Box \neg (p_1 \in \text{At\_}\ell_7 \wedge p_2 \in \text{At\_}\ell_7)$, which is an universal temporal property. However, the communal liveness property stating whenever some process is in $\text{At\_}\ell_2$, eventually some process (not necessarily the same) reaches $\text{At\_}\ell_7$ is not an universal temporal property. On the other hand, the stronger liveness property stating that every process in $\text{At\_}\ell_2$ eventually reaches $\text{At\_}\ell_7$ is an universal property as it can be described by the property $\Box (p \in \text{At\_}\ell_2 \Rightarrow \Diamond p \in \text{At\_}\ell_7)$.

The problem we are interested in is given a WS1S system S and given an universal temporal formula φ to show $S \models \varphi$.

Abstractions and fair abstractions Given a deadlock-free[2] transition system $S = (\mathcal{V}, \Theta, \mathcal{T})$ and a total abstraction relation $\alpha \subseteq \Sigma \times \Sigma_A$, we say that $S_A = (\mathcal{V}_A, \Theta_A, \mathcal{T}_A)$ is an *abstraction* of S w.r.t. α, denoted by $S \sqsubseteq_\alpha S_A$, if the following conditions are satisfied: (1) $s_0 \models \Theta$ implies $\alpha(s_0) \models \Theta_A$ and (2) $\tau \circ \alpha^{-1} \subseteq \alpha^{-1} \circ \tau_A$.

In case Σ_A is finite, we call α finite abstraction relation. Let φ, φ_A be LTL formulae and let $[\![\varphi]\!]$ (resp. $[\![\varphi_A]\!]$) denote the set of models of φ (resp. φ_A). Then, from $S \sqsubseteq_\alpha S_A$, $\alpha^{-1}([\![\varphi_A]\!]) \subseteq [\![\varphi]\!]$, and $S_A \models \varphi_A$ we can conclude $S \models \varphi$ (here we identify α^{-1} and its point-wise lifting to sequences). In case S is a fair TS with $\mathcal{F}$ as fairness formula and if $\mathcal{F}_A$ is the fairness formula of S_A, then by requiring $\alpha^{-1}([\![\neg \mathcal{F}_A]\!]) \subseteq [\![\neg \mathcal{F}]\!]$, we have the same preservation result as above. We indicate this type of abstraction by $S \sqsubseteq_\alpha^F S_A$.

Next, we explain the main steps of our approach for verifying universal temporal properties before presenting each step in more detail.

Approach Let $S = (\mathcal{V}, \Theta, \mathcal{T}, \mathcal{J}, \mathcal{C})$ be a fair WS1S system modeling a parameterized network and let ψ be an universal temporal formula with

---

[2] Throughout this paper we only consider deadlock free transition systems which can be achieved by adding an idle transition.

$\{X_1, \ldots, X_k\} \cup \{p_1, \ldots, p_m\}$ as free variables. To simplify the presentation assume that $m = 1$ and write p instead of p_1. Moreover, we denote by $\psi(i)$ the formula obtained from ψ by replacing p by the constant $i \in \omega$.

For each $i \in \omega$, we construct a finite abstraction relation α_i which maps states of $\mathcal{S}$ to abstract states. The abstract state space defined by α_i is such that it contains for each sub-formula $i \in X$ of $\psi(i)$ a boolean variable b_X^i and for each X_j an abstract variable b_j. Then, α_i relates a concrete state s to an abstract state s^A iff $s^A(b_X^i) \Leftrightarrow i \in s(X)$ and $s^A(b_j) \Leftrightarrow s(X_j) \neq \emptyset$. Henceforth, let $\widehat{\alpha_i}$ be a predicate defining α_i. Clearly, the abstract state spaces defined by α_i and α_j are the same modulo renaming of the variables b_X^i.

Then, for each $i \in \omega$, one can *effectively* construct a finite abstract system S_A^i and an LTL-formula ψ_A^i such that $S_A^i \models \psi_A^i$ implies $\mathcal{S} \models \psi(i)$. One can even effectively construct the set $\{S_A^i \mid i \in \omega\}$ of abstract systems. However, although this set is finite, it is computationally costly to construct. Therefore, we present an algorithm for constructing a *single* finite abstract system S_A which is itself an abstraction of each S_A^i and, as we show, is an abstraction of $\mathcal{S}$. Moreover, we show how to construct an LTL-formula ψ_A such that $S_A \models \psi_A$ implies $\mathcal{S} \models \psi$.

Abstraction relation α_i The set $\mathcal{V}_A^i$ of abstract variables consists of boolean variables. For each set X in the WS1S system $\mathcal{S}$ we have an abstract boolean variable $b_X^i \in \mathcal{V}_A^i$ corresponding to $i \in X$. Thus, in particular we have the variable $b_{E_\tau}^i$ and $b_{T_\tau}^i$, for each $\tau \in \mathcal{T}$. Additionally, for each strong fairness condition $(E_\tau, T_\tau) \in \mathcal{C}$ we introduce boolean variables e_τ, t_τ such that α_i implies:

$$e_\tau \equiv \exists_P j : j \in E_\tau$$
$$t_\tau \equiv \exists_P j : j \in T_\tau \; .$$

For all other global state properties φ that may influence the progress of a certain process p another variable is added for which the abstraction is given by φ. This includes an adequate abstraction of the used natural numbers to express their influence on the behavior of the system.

Henceforth, we also use $\widehat{\alpha_i}(\mathcal{V}', \mathcal{V}_A^{i})$ to denote the predicate obtained from $\widehat{\alpha_i}$ by substituting the unprimed variables with their primed versions.

Construction of S_A As mentioned it is costly to compute $\{S_A^i \mid i \in \omega\}$ explicitly. Therefore, we show how one can construct a system that abstracts each of the elements of this set, and hence, by transitivity of

$\sqsubseteq$ abstracts $\mathcal{S}$. The set $\mathcal{V}_A$ of abstract variables of $\mathcal{S}_A$ contains for each abstract variable $b_X^i \in \mathcal{V}_A^i$ a variable b_X.

We define the transitions of $\mathcal{S}_A$ by the following WS1S formula:

$$\exists_P \, p : \exists \mathcal{V}, \mathcal{V}' : \widehat{\alpha}_p(\mathcal{V}, \mathcal{V}_A) \wedge \rho_\tau(\mathcal{V}, \mathcal{V}') \wedge \widehat{\alpha}_p(\mathcal{V}', \mathcal{V}_A') \ .$$

Thus, we make sure that the choice of p in the concretizations of the source and target states of an abstract transition is the same. We can then show the following:

Proposition 1. $\mathcal{S}_A$ is an abstraction of $\mathcal{S}$, i.e., $\mathcal{S} \sqsubseteq_\alpha \mathcal{S}_A$ with $\widehat{\alpha} \equiv \exists i \in \omega.\widehat{\alpha}_i[b_X/b_X^i]$.

Notice that the formulae above are WS1S formulae, and hence, by Büchi and Elgot's result, the sets of numbers satisfying these formulae can be characterized by finite automata. We use MONA [HJJ$^+$96] to construct these automata.

5 Fair Abstractions

It is well known that an obstacle to the verification of liveness properties using abstraction, is that often the abstract system contains cycles that do not correspond to fair computations of the concrete system. A way to overcome this difficulty is to enrich the abstract system with fairness conditions or more generally ranking functions over well-founded sets that eliminate undesirable computations. We present a marking algorithm that given a reachability state graph of an abstraction of a WS1S system enriches the graph with strong fairness conditions while preserving the property that to each concrete computation corresponds an abstract *fair* one. The enriched graph is used to prove liveness properties of the WS1S systems, and consequently, of the parameterized network. Moreover, we discuss under which requirements the fairness conditions of the parameterized system can be lifted to the finite abstract one. In particular, we show that by requiring some conditions on the abstraction relation, it is sound to lift strong fairness. Weak fairness can only be lifted for a distinguished process.

Throughout this section, we fix a WS1S system $\mathcal{S} = (\mathcal{V}, \Theta, \mathcal{T}, \mathcal{J}, \mathcal{C})$ modeling a parameterized network and an abstraction relation α constructed as explained in Section 4. Then, let $\mathcal{S}_A = (\mathcal{V}_A, \Theta_A, \mathcal{T}_A)$ be the finite abstract system (without fairness) obtained by the method introduced in Section 4. We show how to add fairness conditions to $\mathcal{S}_A$ leading to a fair abstract system $\mathcal{S}_A^F = (\mathcal{V}_A, \Theta_A, \mathcal{T}_A, \mathcal{J}_A, \mathcal{C}_A)$ such that $\mathcal{S} \sqsubseteq_\alpha^F \mathcal{S}_A^F$.

Marking algorithm We use WS1S formulae to express ranking functions. Let $\chi(i, X_1, \cdots, X_k)$ be a predicate with i as free 1st-order variable and $X_1, \cdots, X_k \in \mathcal{V}$ as free 2nd-order variables. Given a state s of $\mathcal{S}$, i.e., a valuation of the variables in $\mathcal{V}$, the ranking value $\zeta(s)$ associated to s by ζ is the cardinality of $\{i \in \omega \mid \chi(i, s(X_1), \ldots, s(X_k))\}$. The marking algorithm we present labels each abstract transition of the abstract system with one of the symbols $\{+_\chi, -_\chi, =_\chi\}$. Intuitively, an abstract transition τ_A is labeled by $-_\chi$, if it is guaranteed that the concrete transition τ associated with τ_A decreases the ranking value, i.e., $(s, s') \in \tau$ implies $\zeta(s) > \zeta(s')$. The label $+_\chi$ denotes that τ increases the value for some concrete state. In the other cases we label τ_A with $=_\chi$.

Input: WS1S system $\mathcal{S} = (\mathcal{V}, \Theta, \mathcal{T})$, abstraction $\mathcal{S}_A = (\mathcal{V}_A, \Theta_A, \mathcal{T}_A)$, set of predicates $\chi(i, X_1, \cdots, X_k)$

Output: Labeling of $\mathcal{T}_A$

Description: For each $\chi(i, X_1, \cdots, X_k)$, for each edge $\tau_A \in \mathcal{T}_A$, let τ be the concrete transition in $\mathcal{T}$ corresponding to τ_A.
Mark τ_A with $-_\chi$ if the following formula is valid:

$$\forall \mathcal{V}, \mathcal{V}' : \widehat{\alpha}(\mathcal{V}, \mathcal{V}_A) \wedge \widehat{\alpha}(\mathcal{V}', \mathcal{V}'_A) \wedge \rho_\tau(\mathcal{V}, \mathcal{V}') \Rightarrow \{i \mid \chi'(i)\} \subset \{i \mid \chi(i)\} \ .$$

Mark τ_A with $+_\chi$ if

$$\exists \mathcal{V}, \mathcal{V}' : \widehat{\alpha}(\mathcal{V}, \mathcal{V}_A) \wedge \widehat{\alpha}(\mathcal{V}', \mathcal{V}'_A) \wedge \rho_\tau(\mathcal{V}, \mathcal{V}') \Rightarrow \{i \mid \chi'(i)\} \supset \{i \mid \chi(i)\}$$

is valid. Otherwise, label the transition with $=_\chi$.

Now, for a set formula χ we denote with $\mathcal{T}_\chi^+$ the set of edges labeled with $+_\chi$. Then, we add for each such χ and each transition τ_A labeled with $-_\chi$ the fairness condition $(\tau_A, \mathcal{T}_\chi^+)$ which states that τ_A can only be taken infinitely often when one of the transitions in $\mathcal{T}_\chi^+$ are taken infinitely often.

Lifting fairness Recall that by definition of α (see Section 4), we introduce the abstract variables $e_\tau \equiv \exists_P i : i \in E_\tau$ and $t_\tau \equiv \exists_P i : i \in T_\tau$. We now argue that it is safe to augment $\mathcal{S}_A$ with the strong fairness $\mathcal{C}_A = \{(e_\tau, t_\tau) \mid (E_\tau, T_\tau) \in \mathcal{C}\}$, i.e., if e_τ is infinitely often true, then also t_τ is infinitely often true. Consider a computation where e_τ is infinitely often true, that is, $\exists_P i : i \in E_\tau$ is infinitely often true. Now, each instance of the parameterized system only contains a bounded number of processes, hence, by König's lemma, there must exists some i such that $i \in E_\tau$ infinitely often in this computation. Therefore, by the strong fairness condition of the concrete system, we must have $i \in T_\tau$ infinitely often, and hence, the computation satisfies $\Box \Diamond (\exists_P i : i \in T_\tau)$. Consequently:

Lemma 1. *Under the assumptions above we have* $\mathcal{S} \sqsubseteq_\alpha^F \mathcal{S}_A$. $\qquad\Box$

The reasoning above does not hold for weak fairness. Indeed, $\Diamond\Box e_\tau$ may hold for a computation without the existence of an i with $\Diamond\Box(i \in E_\tau)$.

Recall also that as explained in Section 4, we introduce for each transition of the distinguished process p abstract variables b_{E_τ} and b_{T_τ} expressing whether the transition is enabled, respectively, taken. We can show that it is safe to augment the abstract system with strong and weak fairness conditions on the transitions of p.

Lemma 2. *For the concrete WS1S system* $\mathcal{S}$ *and the abstract system* $\mathcal{S}_A$ *we have:*

$$\mathcal{S} \sqsubseteq_{\widehat{\alpha}}^F \mathcal{S}_A^F \ ,$$

where $\widehat{\alpha} \equiv \exists i \in \omega . \widehat{\alpha_i}[b_X/b_X^i]$ *for a generic abstraction function* α_i *and* $\mathcal{S}_A^F$ *with strong fairness requirements* $\mathcal{C}_A = \{(b_{E_\tau}, b_{T_\tau}) \mid (E_\tau, T_\tau) \in \mathcal{C}\}$ *and weak fairness requirements* $\mathcal{J}_A = \{(b_{E_\tau}, b_{T_\tau}) \mid (E_\tau, T_\tau) \in \mathcal{J}\}$. $\qquad\Box$

Example 2. Recall that we want to verify that our algorithm satisfies the mutual exclusion property as well as the universal property that each process p reaches its critical section infinitely often, i.e., $\forall_n p : \Box\Diamond \text{at\_}\ell_2[p]$.

According to the method presented in Section 4 we construct the abstract system $\mathcal{S}_A$ from the WS1S translation. For the mutual exclusion property we take as abstract variable $inv \equiv \text{At\_}\ell_2 \subseteq Turn \wedge \forall_P i, j : (i \in Turn \wedge j \in Turn) \Rightarrow i = j$. Our tool PAX constructs the abstract system and provides translations to several input languages for model-checkers, e.g., Spin and SMV. Also, the abstract state space can be explored to prove that inv is indeed an invariant of the abstract system and, hence, mutual exclusion holds for the original system.

Next, using the marking algorithm, we augment $\mathcal{S}_A$ with the strong fairness requirements $\{(t_{01}, \{t_{20}\}), (t_{12}, \{t_{01}\}), (t_{20}, \{t_{12}\})\}$ to obtain a fair abstract system $\mathcal{S}_A^F$. Moreover, with Lemma 1 we can lift the strong fairness (e_{11}, t_{11}). Lemma 2 allows us to augment $\mathcal{S}_A^F$ with another strong fairness condition $(b_{E_{11}}, b_{T_{11}})$ for the distinguished process as well as with the weak fairness $(b_{E_{01}}, b_{T_{01}})$.

All the fairness conditions can be expressed as LTL formulae. We used Spin to prove that $\Box\Diamond b_{\text{At\_}\ell_2}$ holds in $\mathcal{S}_A^F$ which means that, in the original system, each process reaches its critical section infinitely often.

6   Conclusion

We presented a method for the verification of universal properties of parameterized networks. Our method is based on the transformation of an infinite family of systems into a single WS1S transition system and applying abstraction techniques on this system. To be able to prove liveness properties we presented a method to add fairness requirements to the abstract system. We have successfully applied this method, which has been implemented in our tool PAX, to a number of parameterized protocols, including Dijkstra's and Szymanski's mutual exclusion protocol.

References

[ABJN99] P.A. Abdulla, A. Bouajjani, B. Jonsson, and M. Nilsson. Handling Global Conditions in Parameterized System Verification. In N. Halbwachs and D. Peled, editors, *CAV '99*, volume 1633 of *LNCS*, pages 134–145. Springer, 1999.

[BBLS00] K. Baukus, S. Bensalem, Y. Lakhnech, and K. Stahl. Abstracting WS1S Systems to Verify Parameterized Networks. In S. Graf and M. Schwartzbach, editors, *TACAS'00*, volume 1785. Springer, 2000.

[BCG89] M.C. Browne, E.M. Clarke, and O. Grumberg. Reasoning about networks with many identical finite state processes. *Information and Computation*, 1989.

[BLS00] K. Baukus, Y. Lakhnech, and K. Stahl. Verifying Universal Properties of Parameterized Networks. Technical Report TR-ST-00-4, CAU Kiel, 2000.

[Büc60] J.R. Büchi. Weak Second-Order Arithmetic and Finite Automata. *Z. Math. Logik Grundl. Math.*, 6:66–92, 1960.

[CC77] P. Cousot and R. Cousot. Abstract interpretation: A unified lattice model for static analysis of programs by construction or approximation of fixpoints. In *4th ACM symp. of Prog. Lang.*, pages 238–252. ACM Press, 1977.

[CGJ95] E. Clarke, O. Grumberg, and S. Jha. Verifying Parameterized Networks using Abstraction and Regular Languages. In I. Lee and S. Smolka, editors, *CONCUR '95: Concurrency Theory*, LNCS. Springer, 1995.

[CGL94] E. M. Clarke, O. Grumberg, and D. E. Long. Model checking and abstraction. *ACM Transactions on Programming Languages and Systems*, 16(5), 1994.

[DGG94] D. Dams, R. Gerth, and O. Grumberg. Abstract interpretation of reactive systems: Abstractions preserving ACTL*, ECTL* and CTL*. In E.-R. Olderog, editor, *Proceedings of PROCOMET '94*. North-Holland, 1994.

[Elg61] C.C. Elgot. Decision problems of finite automata design and related arithmetics. *Trans. Amer. Math. Soc.*, 98:21–52, 1961.

[EN96] E. A. Emerson and K. S. Namjoshi. Automatic verification of parameterized synchronous systems. In *8th Conference on Computer Aided Verification*, LNCS 1102, pages 87–98, 1996.

[GS92]   S.M. German and A.P. Sistla. Reasoning about systems with many
             processes. *Journal of the ACM*, 39(3):675–735, 1992.
[HJJ⁺96]   J.G. Henriksen, J. Jensen, M. Jørgensen, N. Klarlund, B. Paige,
             T. Rauhe, and A. Sandholm. Mona: Monadic Second-Order Logic in
             Practice. In *TACAS '95*, volume 1019 of *LNCS*. Springer, 1996.
[JN00]   B. Jonsson and M. Nilsson. Transitive closures of regular relations for
             verifying infinite-state systems. In S. Graf and M. Schwartzbach, editors,
             TACAS'00, volume 1785. Lecture Notes in Computer Science, 2000.
[KM89]   R.P. Kurshan and K. McMillan. A structural induction theorem for pro-
             cesses. In *ACM Symp. on Principles of Distributed Computing, Canada*,
             pages 239–247, Edmonton, Alberta, 1989.
[KMM⁺97]   Y. Kesten, O. Maler, M. Marcus, A. Pnueli, and E. Shahar. Symbolic
             Model Checking with Rich Assertional Languages. In O. Grumberg,
             editor, *Proceedings of CAV '97*, volume 1256 of *LNCS*, pages 424–435.
             Springer, 1997.
[Tho90]   W. Thomas. Automata on infinite objects. In *Handbook of Theoretical
             Computer Science, Volume B: Formal Methods and Semantics*, pages
             134–191. Elsevier Science Publishers B. V., 1990.
[WL89]   P. Wolper and V. Lovinfosse. Verifying properties of large sets of pro-
             cesses with network invariants (extended abstract). In Sifakis, editor,
             Workshop on Computer Aided Verification, LNCS 407, pages 68–80,
             1989.

Author Index

Lecture Notes in Computer Science

For information about Vols. 1–1835
please contact your bookseller or Springer-Verlag

Vol. 1875: K. Bauknecht, S.K. Madria, G. Pernul (Eds.), Electronic Commerce and Web Technologies. Proceedings, 2000. XII, 488 pages. 2000.

Vol. 1876: F. J. Ferri, J.M. Iñesta, A. Amin, P. Pudil (Eds.), Advances in Pattern Recognition. Proceedings, 2000. XVIII, 901 pages. 2000.

Vol. 1877: C. Palamidessi (Ed.), CONCUR 2000 – Concurrency Theory. Proceedings, 2000. XI, 612 pages. 2000.

Vol. 1878: J.P. Bowen, S. Dunne, A. Galloway, S. King (Eds.), ZB 2000: Formal Specification and Development in Z and B. Proceedings, 2000. XIV, 511 pages. 2000.

Vol. 1879: M. Paterson (Ed.), Algorithms – ESA 2000. Proceedings, 2000. IX, 450 pages. 2000.

Vol. 1880: M. Bellare (Ed.), Advances in Cryptology – CRYPTO 2000. Proceedings, 2000. XI, 545 pages. 2000.

Vol. 1881: C. Zhang, V.-W. Soo (Eds.), Design and Applications of Intelligent Agents. Proceedings, 2000. X, 183 pages. 2000. (Subseries LNAI).

Vol. 1882: D. Kotz, F. Mattern (Eds.), Agent Systems, Mobile Agents, and Applications. Proceedings, 2000. XII, 275 pages. 2000.

Vol. 1883: B. Triggs, A. Zisserman, R. Szeliski (Eds.), Vision Algorithms: Theory and Practice. Proceedings, 1999. X, 383 pages. 2000.

Vol. 1884: J. Štuller, J. Pokorný, B. Thalheim, Y. Masunaga (Eds.), Current Issues in Databases and Information Systems. Proceedings, 2000. XIII, 396 pages. 2000.

Vol. 1885: K. Havelund, J. Penix, W. Visser (Eds.), SPIN Model Checking and Software Verification. Proceedings, 2000. X, 343 pages. 2000.

Vol. 1886: R. Mizoguchi, J. Slaney /Eds.), PRICAI 2000: Topics in Artificial Intelligence. Proceedings, 2000. XX, 835 pages. 2000. (Subseries LNAI).

Vol. 1888: G. Sommer, Y.Y. Zeevi (Eds.), Algebraic Frames for the Perception-Action Cycle. Proceedings, 2000. X, 349 pages. 2000.

Vol. 1889: M. Anderson, P. Cheng, V. Haarslev (Eds.), Theory and Application of Diagrams. Proceedings, 2000. XII, 504 pages. 2000. (Subseries LNAI).

Vol. 1890: C. Linnhoff-Popien, H.-G. Hegering (Eds.), Trends in Distributed Systems: Towards a Universal Service Market. Proceedings, 2000. XI, 341 pages. 2000.

Vol. 1891: A.L. Oliveira (Ed.), Grammatical Inference: Algorithms and Applications. Proceedings, 2000. VIII, 313 pages. 2000. (Subseries LNAI).

Vol. 1892: P. Brusilovsky, O. Stock, C. Strapparava (Eds.), Adaptive Hypermedia and Adaptive Web-Based Systems. Proceedings, 2000. XIII, 422 pages. 2000.

Vol. 1893: M. Nielsen, B. Rovan (Eds.), Mathematical Foundations of Computer Science 2000. Proceedings, 2000. XIII, 710 pages. 2000.

Vol. 1894: R. Dechter (Ed.), Principles and Practice of Constraint Programming – CP 2000. Proceedings, 2000. XII, 556 pages. 2000.

Vol. 1895: F. Cuppens, Y. Deswarte, D. Gollmann, M. Waidner (Eds.), Computer Security – ESORICS 2000. Proceedings, 2000. X, 325 pages. 2000.

Vol. 1896: R. W. Hartenstein, H. Grünbacher (Eds.), Field-Programmable Logic and Applications. Proceedings, 2000. XVII, 856 pages. 2000.

Vol. 1897: J. Gutknecht, W. Weck (Eds.), Modular Programming Languages. Proceedings, 2000. XII, 299 pages. 2000.

Vol. 1898: E. Blanzieri, L. Portinale (Eds.), Advances in Case-Based Reasoning. Proceedings, 2000. XII, 530 pages. 2000. (Subseries LNAI).

Vol. 1899: H.-H. Nagel, F.J. Perales López (Eds.), Articulated Motion and Deformable Objects. Proceedings, 2000. X, 183 pages. 2000.

Vol. 1900: A. Bode, T. Ludwig, W. Karl, R. Wismüller (Eds.), Euro-Par 2000 Parallel Processing. Proceedings, 2000. XXXV, 1368 pages. 2000.

Vol. 1901: O. Etzion, P. Scheuermann (Eds.), Cooperative Information Systems. Proceedings, 2000. XI, 336 pages. 2000.

Vol. 1902: P. Sojka, I. Kopeček, K. Pala (Eds.), Text, Speech and Dialogue. Proceedings, 2000. XIII, 463 pages. 2000. (Subseries LNAI).

Vol. 1904: S.A. Cerri, D. Dochev (Eds.), Artificial Intelligence: Methodology, Systems, and Applications. Proceedings, 2000. XII, 366 pages. 2000. (Subseries LNAI).

Vol. 1906: A. Porto, G.-C. Roman (Eds.), Coordination Languages and Models. Proceedings, 2000. IX, 353 pages. 2000.

Vol. 1908: J. Dongarra, P. Kacsuk, N. Podhorszki (Eds.), Recent Advances in Parallel Virtual Machine and Message Passing Interface. Proceedings, 2000. XV, 364 pages. 2000.

Vol. 1910: D.A. Zighed, J. Komorowski, J. Żytkow (Eds.), Principles of Data Mining and Knowledge Discovery. Proceedings, 2000. XV, 701 pages. 2000. (Subseries LNAI).

Vol. 1912: Y. Gurevich, P.W. Kutter, M. Odersky, L. Thiele (Eds.), Abstract State Machines. Proceedings, 2000. X, 381 pages. 2000.

Vol. 1913: K. Jansen, S. Khuller (Eds.), Approximation Algorithms for Combinatorial Optimization. Proceedings, 2000. IX, 275 pages. 2000.

Vol. 1917: M. Schoenauer, K. Deb, G. Rudolph, X. Yao, E. Lutton, J.J. Merelo, H.-P. Schwefel (Eds.), Parallel Problem Solving from Nature – PPSN VI. Proceedings, 2000. XXI, 914 pages. 2000.

Vol. 1918: D. Soudris, P. Pirsch, E. Barke (Eds.), Integrated Circuit Design. Proceedings, 2000. XII, 338 pages. 2000.

Vol. 1923: J. Borbinha, T. Baker (Eds.), Research and Advanced Technology for Digital Libraries. Proceedings, 2000. XVII, 513 pages. 2000.

Vol. 1924: W. Taha (Ed.), Semantics, Applications, and Implementation of Program Generation. Proceedings, 2000. VIII, 231 pages. 2000.

Vol. 1926: M. Joseph (Ed.), Formal Techniques in Real-Time and Fault-Tolerant Systems. Proceedings, 2000. X, 305 pages. 2000.

Vol. 1931: E. Horlait (Ed.), Mobile Agents for Telecommunication Applications. Proceedings, 2000. IX, 271 pages. 2000.